Lecture Notes
in Business Information P

[

Joaquim Filipe
José Cordeiro
Vitor Pedrosa (Eds.)

Web Information Systems and Technologies

International Conferences,
WEBIST 2005 and WEBIST 2006
Revised Selected Papers

 Springer

Volume Editors

Joaquim Filipe
José Cordeiro
Polytechnic Institute of Setúbal
School of Technology, Dept. of Informatics and Systems
Rua do Vale de Chaves - Estefanilha, 2910-761 Setúbal, Portugal
E-mail: {j.filipe,jcordeiro}@est.ips.pt

Vitor Pedrosa
INSTICC
Rua D. Manuel I, 27A 2° Esq., 2910-595 Setúbal, Portugal
vitor@insticc.org

Library of Congress Control Number: 2007932801

ACM Computing Classification (1998): J.1, H.4, H.3

ISSN   1865-1348
ISBN-10   3-540-74062-7 Springer Berlin Heidelberg New York
ISBN-13   978-3-540-74062-9 Springer Berlin Heidelberg New York

Springer is a part of Springer Science+Business Media

springer.com

© Springer-Verlag Berlin Heidelberg 2007
Printed in Germany

Typesetting: Camera-ready by author, data conversion by Scientific Publishing Services, Chennai, India
Printed on acid-free paper   SPIN: 12103317   45/3180   5 4 3 2 1 0

Preface

This book contains the best papers from the first two instances of the International Conference on Web Information Systems and Technologies (WEBIST 2005 and 2006), organized by the Institute for Systems and Technologies of Information, Control and Communication (INSTICC) in collaboration with the OMG (Object Management Group), held in Miami (USA) and Setúbal (Portugal) respectively.

The purpose of WEBIST is to bring together researchers, engineers and practitioners interested in the technological advances and business applications of web-based information systems. It has four main topic areas, covering different aspects of Web Information Systems, including Internet Technology, Web Interfaces and Applications, Society, e-Business, e-Government and e-Learning.

WEBIST received submissions from more than 40 countries in all continents. We are happy to note that from 110 submissions in 2005 WEBIST grew to 218 paper submissions in 2006, an increase of practically 100%. After a double-blind review process, with the help of more than 120 experts from the international program committee, and also after presentation at the conference, 25 papers were finally selected to be published and presented in this book.

The organization of these conferences required the dedicated effort of many people. Firstly, we must thank the authors, whose research and development efforts are recorded here. Secondly, we thank the members of the program committee and the additional reviewers for their diligence and expert reviewing. Thirdly, we congratulate the INSTICC organizing team for their excellent work. Last but not least, we thank the invited speakers for their invaluable contribution and for taking the time to synthesize and prepare their talks.

We are certain that a new book will present the successful results of next year's conference: the 3rd WEBIST, to be held in Barcelona (Spain), in March 2007.

June 2006

Joaquim Filipe
José Cordeiro
Vitor Pedrosa

Conference Committee

Conference Chair

Joaquim Filipe, Polytechnic Institute of Setúbal / INSTICC, Portugal

Program Chair

José Cordeiro, Polytechnic Institute of Setúbal / INSTICC, Portugal

Organizing Committee

Marina Carvalho, INSTICC, Portugal
Hélder Coelhas, INSTICC, Portugal
Bruno Encarnação, INSTICC, Portugal
Vitor Pedrosa, INSTICC, Portugal
Mónica Saramago, INSTICC, Portugal

Program Committee

Adel Abunawass, U.S.A.
K. Al-Begain, U.K.
Margherita Antona, Greece
Valeria de Antonellis, Italy
Liliana Ardissono, Italy
Azita Bahrami, U.S.A.
Cristina Baroglio, Italy
Zohra Bellahsene, France
Orlando Belo, Portugal
Bettina Berendt, Germany
Sonia Bergamaschi, Italy
Bharat Bhargava, U.S.A.
Christos Bouras, Greece
Amy Bruckman, U.S.A.
Sonja Buchegger, Switzerland
Maria Claudia Buzzi, Italy
Sergio de Cesare, U.K.
Ku-Ming Chao, U.K.
Weiqin Chen, Norway
Christophe Claramunt, France
Mark Claypool, U.S.A.
Andrea Clematis, Italy
Nigel Collier, Japan

Bin Cong, U.S.A.
Michel Crampes, France
Alexandra Cristea, The Netherlands
Daniel Cunliffe, U.K.
John Philip Cuthell, U.K.
Alfredo Cuzzocrea, Italy
Tom Daniels, U.S.A.
Alessandro D'Atri, Italy
Danco Davcev, Macedonia
Steven Demurjian, U.S.A.
Vladan Devedzic, Serbia and Montenegro
Darina Dicheva, U.S.A.
Ying Ding, Austria
Josep Domingo-Ferrer, Spain
Chyi-Ren Dow, Taiwan
Schahram Dustdar, Austria
Barry Eaglestone, U.K.
Max J. Egenhofer, U.S.A.
Filomena Ferrucci, Italy
Joseph Fong, Hong Kong, China
Akira Fukuda, Japan
Giovanni Fulantelli, Italy
Martin Gaedke, Germany

Invited Speakers

Mark M. Davydov, U.S.A.
Bebo White, U.S.A.
Carmel McNaught, Hong Kong, China
Piet Kommers, The Netherlands
Hermann Maurer, Austria

Table of Contents

Invited Papers

Part I: Internet Technology

Part II: Web Interfaces and Applications

Part III: Society, e-Business and e-Government

Part IV: e-Learning

Invited Papers

The Implications of Web 2.0 on Web Information Systems

Bebo White

Stanford Linear Accelerator Center, 2575 Sand Hill Road, Menlo Park, CA 94025, USA
bebo@slac.stanford.edu

Abstract. "Web 2.0" is rapidly becoming a buzzword in the Web design and development communities. Despite this attention, a definition of the term and its scope are still evolving. To many observers "Web 2.0" appears to be a loose collection of recently developed concepts and technologies including Weblogs, Wikis, podcasts, Web feeds and other forms of collaborative publishing. Added to this mix are social software, Web APIs, Web standards, online Web services, AJAX, and more. There are common unifying goals in Web 2.0 which suggest that rather than being based on new technologies it instead represents a natural evolution of World Wide Web applications and services. As a result, the concepts incorporated in "Web 2.0" should be strongly considered in the development of Web Information Systems.

Keywords: Web 2.0, Web information systems.

1 Introduction

A recent (July 2006) search of Google News (news.google.com) for the term "Web 2.0" yielded over 1,300 references from the 4,500 news sources the service indexes. There is hardly an issue of any recent Internet-related publication that does not contain some reference to the term either with respect to some technology or in describing a new start-up effort. It rapidly becomes clear to the reader that a definition for "Web 2.0" is still evolving and that the use of the term borders on the hype so often associated with so-called "cutting edge," or "bleeding edge" technologies.

The term, coined by O'Reilly and Associates to publicize a series of conferences, does not suggest a new version of the Web, but simply a marketing phrase for the well-known Sebastopol, California book publisher.[1] O'Reilly has, in fact, threatened legal action against other conference organizers choosing to use a "Web 2.0" reference.[2]

However, whether it is referred to as "Web 2.0" or not, there is a new direction for Web applications and services occurring that promises to affect Web design and development in the future. The results of this direction (I hesitate to say revolution) has been described as "the Living Web and "putting the 'We' in the 'Web.'" [3]

J. Filipe, J. Cordeiro, and V. Pedrosa (Eds.): WEBIST 2005/2006, LNBIP 1, pp. 3–7, 2007.
© Springer-Verlag Berlin Heidelberg 2007

2   A Definition of Web 2.0

Before attempting to define "Web 2.0," it is probably more useful to describe what it is not.

- "Web 2.0" is <u>not</u> the same as the Semantic Web, a model of the future Web described by the World Wide Web Consortium (W3C). There are, however, some shared technological concepts and goals.
- "Web 2.0" is <u>not</u> a collection of new Web technologies. Instead "Web 2.0" applications are more likely innovative applications of existing technologies and techniques.
- "Web 2.0" is <u>not</u> simply blogs, wikis, and RSS (Really Simple Syndication). It is true, however, that these applications have contributed a great deal to the overall perception of "Web 2.0."

More accurately, "Web 2.0" can be described as a change in "<u>Web attitude</u>" that shifts the focus of Web-based information from the creator/author of that information to the user of that information. In order to affect this 'attitude shift'

- Information moves 'beyond' Web sites;
- Information has properties and these properties follow each other and find/establish/define relationships;
- Information comes to users as they move between Web-enabled devices and applications;
- To accomplish these ends, information is defined into units of 'microcontent' capable to being distributed over multiple application domains.

In order to take advantage of this new information model, users must be able to more closely control how Web-based information is categorized and manipulated. This requires the definition of new tools for the aggregation and remixing of "microcontent" in new and creative ways. Such tools should be concentrated in the user agent resulting in a "fat" rather than "thin" client model. The presence of such tools in the client suggests a far "richer" user experience and interaction capabilities than are typically available with (X)HTML. Implementations of such "rich user interfaces" in current "Web 2.0" applications are accomplished using technologies such as Flash and AJAX.

It could be argued that this "user-centric" model of the Web is just as consistent with the evolution of the technology as the "data-centric" model represented by the Semantic Web (Figure 1.)

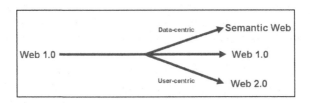

Fig. 1. Evolution of "Data-centric" and "User- centric" Webs

3 The Evolution of Web 2.0

The emergence of "Web 2.0 attitudes" can be traced to the time period following the "dot.com crash" in approximately 1999-2000. It has been suggested that these attitudes resulted from a philosophical examination of the overall usefulness of Web technology given the failures experienced at that time. The volume of information and data sources on the Web had reached a "critical mass" and search engine technologies were grappling with the problem of making the Web searchable. At the same time, Web users had developed an expectation of fulfilment and trust. Simple mechanisms such as Google's "I'm Feeling Lucky," Amazon's personalization features, and eBay's ratings systems addressed some of their user's basic needs and expectations at the time. Many of the most successful Web companies at that time (e.g., Google, Amazon, eBay, etc.) could be described as embodying a convergence of 'individual traits and social and technological forces.' The introduction of blog and wiki technologies during that time period served to further support strong user involvement in the future direction of the Web.

Tim O'Reilly cites the basic paradigm shifts that he observed during this time frame from the existing application of Web technology (unfortunately referred to as "Web 1.0") to the new user-centric "Web 2.0." (Table 1.)[1]

Table 1. "Web 1.0" to "Web 2.0" Paradigm Shift

	Web 1.0	Web 2.0
Governance	Top down	Bottom Up
Communications	People to Machine	Machine to Machine and People to People
Information Discovery	Search and Browse	Publish and Subscribe
Information Retrieval	Transactional	Relationships
Information Aggregation	Portals, Commercial Aggregators	Micro-Aggregation
Marketing, Selling	Push, Contextual	Conversational, Personal
Content Control	Publishers, Aggregators	Content Authors
Content Structure	Documents, Pages	Tagged Objects
Applications	Closed, Proprietary	Open, Standards-based
Technology	HTML, Solaris, Oracle	XML, AJAX, RSS, PHP, MySQL, XQuery

The technology shifts shown in Table 1. help to define the fundamental characteristics of a "Web 2.0" infrastructure.

1. "The Web as a Platform" – the familiar model of the Web as a client server application limits its functionality. The Web instead needs to become a distributed system of services and applications integrated as a software platform.
2. "The Web as a Point of Presence" – "Web 1.0" perpetuates the model of "visiting Web sites." "Web 2.0" emphasizes the popular notion of a user navigating through and becoming immersed within 'cyberspace.'
3. "A Web composed of Microcontent" – information defined in terms of microcontent supports an open, decentralized, bottom-up, and self-organizing infrastructure.
4. "A Web of MetaContent" – the content of Web sites, services, etc. should be meaningful 'out of context,' and viewed as 're-usable objects' for applications not intended by the content authors/creators.
5. "A Semantic Web" – a Web of objects connected by rich and meaningful semantic relationships.

4 The Key Elements of Web 2.0

"Web 2.0" adds three new data elements not previously emphasized in the Web information model:

- The "Long Tail,"[4]
- Collective Intelligence[1], and
- Data Re-use.

The "long tail" refers to the belief that the majority of truly relevant and important information available on the Web resides not on the large, prominent, well-known Web servers, but on many smaller servers and in smaller database systems. The ability to "tap into" this lesser-known source of data can add great value to a Web information system.

"Collective intelligence" refers to the value that users add to existing data on the Web supported by an 'architecture of participation.' What began philosophically with user ratings on sites such as Amazon.com and eBay has evolved into sophisticated *folksonomies*[5] – user alternatives to the rigid formalisms of taxonomies. Such collaborative categorization of Web sites using freely chosen keywords (tags) supports rich retrieval methods generated by user activity.

Such "user tagging" is best demonstrated by the impact it has had on Web-based social networking. Popular services such as del.icio.us[6], Flickr[7], and LinkedIn[8] are but a few "Web 2.0" instances based upon "user tagging" and linking.

"Data re-use" has lead to some of the most exciting and provocative applications of "Web 2.0." By providing APIs (application programming interfaces) to their databases, organizations such as Google and Yahoo have enabled some of the most creative Web applications in recent times. "Mash-ups" are examples of "programming on the Web" where the data streams come from rich sources such as Google maps or Yahoo databases. The result has been applications of the data that the creators could have never anticipated.

5   Web 2.0 and WIS

The scope of Web Information Systems (WIS) can be described as:

- Web information modeling;
- Web information representation, storage, and access;
- Web information extraction;
- Web information mining.

The basic presumption in WIS is that Web technology can be used as a 'front-end' to an online information system (e.g., application is available on the Web via a client/browser, or on the 'back-end' by means of a Web server or service and/or by using a Web protocol (e.g., HTTP, SOAP, etc.). As a result, most WIS implementations are database driven, require rich, expressive user interfaces, and typically support volatile and dynamic data.

Some of the techniques that have evolved in the definition of "Web 2.0" such as rich interfaces, "user tagging," and database APIs for "data re-use" have great potential in advanced WIS applications. WIS developers and designers should explore the innovations being implemented by the so-called "Web 2.0" applications.

References

What is Web 2.0, http://www.oreillynet.com/pub/a/oreilly/tim/news/2005/09/30/what-is-web-20.html

Please Cease-and-Desist From Using 'Web 2.0', http://arstechnica.com/news.ars/post/20060526-6922.html

Putting the 'We' in 'Web', – Newsweek (April 3, 2006)

The Long Tail, http://www.thelongtail.com/the_long_tail/2005/10/web_20_and_the_.html

http://en.wikipedia.org/wiki/Folksonomy

http://del.icio.us/

http://www.flickr.com/

http://www.linkedin.com/

Developing Criteria for Successful
Learning Repositories

Carmel McNaught

Centre for Learning Enhancement And Research, The Chinese University of Hong Kong
Shatin, New Territories, Hong Kong
carmel.mcnaught@cuhk.edu.hk
http://www.cuhk.edu.hk/clear/staff/staff7.htm

Abstract. There are now a number of learning repositories available for teachers to use to source content material (learning objects) to use in their teaching. How have these learning repositories come into being? How are they organized? Just what is a learning object? There are several factors which must work together to make a learning repository sustainable. In this paper these cultural, social and technical factors will be explored. Two cases will be contrasted – a struggling repository in Hong Kong and a successful digital library in the US. From this comparison, a number of key success factors emerge.

Keywords: Learning objects, Learning repositories, Community digital libraries.

1 Information-Rich Learning Environments

Online environments facilitate access to and retrieval of information. They can also facilitate learners' communication with teachers and other learners that can be useful in evaluating the usefulness of any resource. The two aspects of the wealth of information, and the possibility of an online community which can explore and work with that information to construct knowledge, have led to the rosy promises for the future of eLearning that have been predicted for some time (e.g. Siemens, 2003).

With the importance of eLearning growing every year, producing and locating quality resources is a major focus of educational institutions and communities; but what is the most effective and cost-efficient way of answering this need? The expense of producing resources has led many educational communities to the idea of sharable Learning Objects (LOs), which not only reduce the economic burden on individual institutions but also provide a competitive edge over those institutions which do not share their resources (Downes, 2001; Littlejohn, 2003). Over recent years a number of eLearning and LO digital repositories have been created to help educators catalogue and find available resources in their field. A few examples are in Table 1. Well-known examples are MERLOT in the US (http://www.merlot.org/), the eduSourceCanada network in Canada (http://www.edusource.ca/), and the Ariadne Foundation in Europe (http://www.ariadne-eu.org/). The well-publicized move of the Massachusetts Institute of Technology to make its online courses available as learning objects for others to use (MITOpenCourseWare; http://ocw.mit.edu/) has made the link between discrete learning objects and whole course units much more real.

J. Filipe, J. Cordeiro, and V. Pedrosa (Eds.): WEBIST 2005/2006, LNBIP 1, pp. 8–18, 2007.
© Springer-Verlag Berlin Heidelberg 2007

Table 1. A Selection of eLearning and Learning Object Repositories

Title of Repository	URLs (accessed 7 February 2006)	Number of resources & accessibility (7 Feb. 2006)
Apple Learning Interchange	http://ali.apple.com/ali/resources.shtml	147; open
Ariadne Foundation	http://www.ariadne-eu.org/	Broad European involvement; closed (though now linked into MERLOT's federated searching)
CLOE (The Co-operative Learning Object Exchange)	http://cloe.on.ca/	Peer-reviewed; closed
Canada's SchoolNet	http://www.schoolnet.ca/home/e/	> 7,000; open
IDEAS (Interactive Dialogue with Educators from Across the State)	http://ideas.wisconsin.edu/	3,618; open
MIT OpenCourseware	http://ocw.mit.edu/OcwWeb/	1,250 courses (Dec 2005); open
Wisconsin Online Resource Center	http://www.wisc-online.com/index.htm	2,017; open
CAREO (Campus Alberta Repository of Educational Objects)	http://careo.ucalgary.ca	*4,137; open*
MERLOT (Multimedia Educational Resource for Learning and Online Teaching)	http://www.merlot.org	*14,376; open*
EdNA (Education Network Australia)	http://www.edna.edu.au/	*28,471; open*
LRC (The Learning Resource Catalogue/ Community). Has federated searching to CAREO, MERLOT and EdNA	http://www.learnet.hku.hk:8052/	**1,056; 365of them from LEARNet project in Hong Kong; closed**
DLESE (Digital Library for Earth System Education)	http://www.dlese.org/	**11,864; open**

2 Overview of This Paper

In Hong Kong, the LEARNet project (http://learnet.hku.hk/) was set up to encourage both the development and sharing of quality LOs among Hong Kong's eight higher education institutions. These LOs, catalogued within the Learning Resource Catalogue/ Community (LRC), were to serve as exemplars within the Hong Kong context – ideally, seeding further development and sharing of resources among Hong Kong universities. In this paper, after a brief discussion of what learning objects and learning object repositories are, I will present the story of LEARNet and the LRC. It is a sad and wasteful story, and highlights the problems that can occur. This dismal saga will be contrasted with a community digital library in the field of earth systems education, DLESE (Digital Library for Earth System Education). Note that in most comparative papers, the less successful example is usually 'someone else's' and the better example is the one the author has been associated with. In this paper the reverse is true. I was associated with the Hong Kong LEARNet project (member of the Advisory Committee) and admit the lack of engagement of the Hong Kong academic community with this repository. I have only observed the 'good' example for many years and can take no credit for it.

3 Learning Objects

Learning objects are of interest for both education and training because they are flexible and have been designed to answer an educational need for tailored, adaptable online learning (Gibbons, Nelson & Richards, 2000). As pointed out by Friesen "governments around the world are spending large sums of money on initiatives that promise the development of learning objects, learning object metadata and learning object repositories to store both this data and these objects" (Friesen, 2004, p. 59). This is true in Hong Kong, as will be described later. LOs are defined in the literature in numerous ways. IEEE's definition of an LO as "any entity, digital or non-digital, that may be used for learning, education or training" (2002, p. 6) lacks the specificity that many educators are looking for. An alternate definition, which states that LOs are "educational materials designed and created in small chunks for the purpose of maximizing the number of learning situations in which the resource can be utilized" (Wiley, 2002, p. 2), brings in the ideas of reusability and adaptability. LEARNet's description followed this more specific line and described LOs as units of learning that are reusable, updateable, aggregatable and tagged with metadata. In several repositories, there is a growing number of LOs which can be described as teaching strategies or learning designs; for example, 'lesson plan' is a resource type in IDEAS. Some LOs combine content with a learning design; for example in interactive tutorials. However, most learning objects are specific, relatively fixed learning assets that are developed for a particular content domain with a particular educational intent (Boyle, 2003).

Recent discussions (Agostinho, Bennett, Lockyer & Harper, 2004; Boyle, Bradley, Chalk, Jones, Haynes & Pickard, 2003) have noted that the initial focus of LO literature was overwhelmingly on delineating the concept of LOs, their technical specifications and their metadata. This imbalance has led to a call for greater consideration of pedagogical purpose (Agostinho et al., 2004; Jonassen & Churchill, 2004; Wiley, 2003), reflective practice and evaluation (Laurillard & McAndrew, 2003). The major function of any learning object should be to provide teachers with the opportunity to match desired educational outcomes with student activities which have the greatest potential to achieve those outcomes (Kennedy, McNaught & Fritze, 2004). The challenge for any LO project is to develop a reflective and evaluative culture that will not only help developers improve their products but also gives users confidence that a specific object is worthy of further investigation and potential reuse.

The packaged modular approach to the provision of learning resources is not plain sailing. The crux of the matter is the tension between producing something which is generic enough to fit many educational contexts (including subject matter, and teacher and student preferences), and yet adaptable/ customizable to fit each context in an educationally satisfying way. Parrish (2004) is a recent authoritative review of this tension. Also, as Boyle (2003) pointed out, eLearning does not have a good track record in designing learning materials; why should the somewhat more complex job of designing reusable learning objects be carried out in a better fashion?

4   The Saga of Learnet in Hong Kong

The LEARNet project was set up with a government grant of HKD5,000,000 (~Euro538,200). The project used an existing database called the Learning Resource Catalogue/ Community (LRC) which had been developed by staff at the University of New South Wales in Australia for the Universitas21 consortium of universities (http://www.universitas21.com/). The LRC is described in Koppi and Hodgson (2001) and Koppi, Bogle and Lavitt (2004). A LEARNet production fund provided small grants to local developers to develop new LOs or repurpose existing legacy materials.

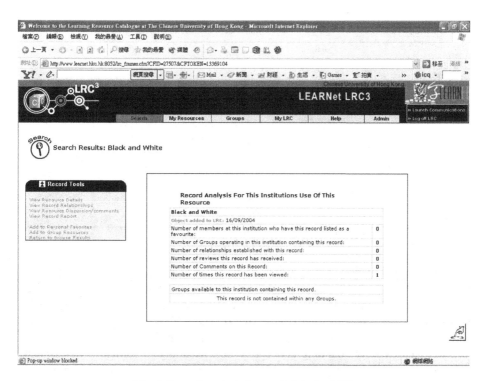

Fig. 1. Record analysis for one LO in the LRC

In total 120 LOs were finally produced by this process. In addition, another 245 LOs were entered into the LRC; these LOs were mostly repurposed materials from previous projects at the host institution (University of Hong Kong). Only one LO has been voluntarily added from any other university in Hong Kong. At the end of 2005 the LEARNet project ended and there are no plans to continue 'renting' the LRC software after the current licence expires.

Figure 1 shows a record analysis for one LO produced with a grant from the production fund. While the record states 'This Institutions Use' (sic.), in reality this is the full Hong Kong access record. This record is for a game which is part of a suite of mathematics games that have now been available free for well over a year and have not been used. It is not an unusual record.

Of course, if no-one looks at a record, it is immaterial whether the LO is good or bad. However, we have evidence that this LO is perceived to be a useful one. An evaluation scheme was established for the LOs in the LRC and 16 sets of LOs were formally peer-reviewed (Jones & McNaught, 2005). The process of getting Hong Kong developers and their colleagues to engage in evaluative reflection was very challenging; however, evaluation reports were produced and published for all 16 sets of LOs (http://learnet.hku.hk/production/evaluation/reports.htm). The report for the Mathematical Garden is at http://learnet.hku.hk/production/evaluation/Mathematical%20-%20Display.pdf and it has a four-star rating on a five-point scale.

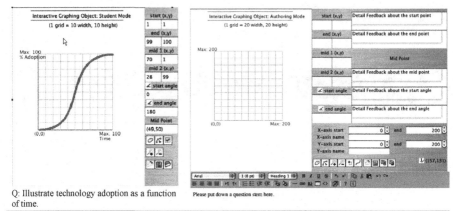

Q: Illustrate technology adoption as a function of time.

a) Student has graphed the answer to the question.

b) Author mode

Fig. 2. Operation of the Interactive Graphing Object

Some of the LOs in the LRC are very innovative in design. One with a rating of 4¾ stars is the Interactive Graphing Object (IGO). The IGO is a generic, customizable learning object that can be used in a variety of content domains, for a variety of purposes (for example, building conceptual understanding or formative assessment and feedback). In the IGO's student mode, there is an interactive space for learners to answer questions of a graphical nature and, in its author mode, a space for content experts and/or students to create graphical questions. In the student mode, the learner is presented with a question; they then use a mouse to draw the graphical answer. The student can then 'fine tune' their curve by changing the numbers in the column or adjusting curve 'handles' (Figure 2a). As the student works through the question, they may click on the checkmark icon to receive feedback or clues to help them complete the problem. Feedback on five aspects of the curve – start point, end point, mid point, start angle and end angle – can be built into the question by developers when they create the questions (Figure 2b). The IGO can be viewed at http://home. ied.edu.hk/~kennedy/igo/index.html. The IGO makes no assumptions about the content, but instead has been developed to 'recognize' seven key parameters of a large number of curves. Initial development of the IGO was in Director (Kennedy & Fritze, 1998). The LRC version (Kennedy, 2004) is in Java in order to enhance cross-platform deployment, improve reliability and stability, improve and simplify the ongoing maintenance of the tool, and increase the range of curves that can be recognized and displayed so as to support a wider range of graph types. It also runs in mobile format using Windows Mobile for Pocket PCs with the objects written in Java and Microsoft.Net programming languages (Kennedy, Vogel & Xu, 2005).

So, we have good LOs and a system by which they can be accessed. In my own University I advertised the LRC widely, through leaflets and emails and I offered several information and training sessions. In the most recent workshop with 20 participants the response to the item 'In the LRC I found information about learning resources that will be useful to me' was 2.69 on a five-point scale, whereas the response to 'I have found useful information about learning resources in repositories other than the LRC' was 3.71. Some comments are:

- *I am yet to be convinced that HK teachers will use such a system. Why do I have to log in when I just want to browse? This does not occur with Merlot.*
- *The resources range widely in terms of quality.*
- *Password protection makes it even less user friendly and I am not convinced about how useful it will be for me to upload information onto this site. I enjoyed the presentation.*
- *The idea is good but LRC is not user-friendly enough. This will lower my incentive to make use of it in the future.*

The LRC is not being used and, at this point, its future seems uncertain. Before analyzing this very unfortunate waste of time, effort and money further, I will present a description of a more successful resource collection.

5   Realistic Repositories

I began this paper by noting that online environments facilitate access to and retrieval of information, and can also facilitate communication. A recent analysis (McNaught, 2006) of the possibilities and problems of web-assisted learning is summarized in Table 2.

In the final column under 'implications', there are references to material in subject domains, to actions involving that material, and to groups of people working together to maintain and support the collections of material. ***Material, activities and people*** – these three elements are all needed. Wegner (1998) coined the phrase 'community of practice'. He proposed that there are three fundamental elements in a community of practice; a knowledge domain, practices based on the knowledge, and a community of learning practitioners. This implies that future effective information-rich learning environments might be, to some extent, communities of practice. What might one of these communities of practice look like?

Several of the functions listed under 'implications' are currently performed by university (and other) libraries, digital repositories and professional subject organizations. The potential of a combination of all three together could be a way forward. Examples of organizations that have these characteristics can be found in a relatively recent move towards the creation of 'community digital libraries'. Digital libraries have existed for some time, with the focus being on how to best gather relevant and accessible digital collections. Cole (2002) described the three primary constructs of digitization projects as digital collections, digital objects and metadata. His checklists of principles for these constructs are recommended for those embarking or refining a digital library.

However, the 'people' aspect also needs attention. As Wright, Marlino and Sumner (2002) commented, "a community digital library is distinct through having a community of potential users define and guide the development of the library". They were writing about a community digital library dealing with the broad subject domain of earth system education. The Digital Library for Earth System Education (DLESE)

Table 2. Implications of the challenges of using technology (after McNaught, 2006, p. 39)

Access to information and tasks		
Positive contribution	*Challenges*	***Implications: Need for:***
More information available to more people	Chaotic and fragmented nature of the web	Guidelines to facilitate searching
Cross-referencing through hyperlinking	Poor navigation; being 'lost in the web'	Good navigation models
Large number of perspectives because there are multiple publishers	Difficult to find evidence of the authority of much material	Models of how to display information with adequate authentication
Finding appropriate information in a given area	Often only low level information is found, or information is out-of-date	Dedicated subject repositories with staff who keep them up-to-date
Being able to self-assess	Often only low-level multiple choice questions are available	Tasks that are demanding and can have customized, possibly real-time, feedback from others
Enabling communication		
Positive contribution	*Challenges*	***Implications: Need for:***
Multiple perspectives on the value of a resource	'Dead' forums where queries or ideas are not answered	Skilled online facilitators
Potential access to others working in the same field	Finding others with similar learning needs	Online communities that have defined goals
Building links between 'experts' and novice learners	Without support, few novice learners will make this type of outreach	Organizations which have an active educational outreach

website (http://www.dlese.org/) has this description which clear shows the three elements of material, activities and people:

"The Digital Library for Earth System Education (DLESE) is a distributed community effort involving educators, students, and scientists working together to improve the quality, quantity, and efficiency of teaching and learning about the Earth system at all levels. DLESE supports Earth system science education by providing:

- access to high-quality collections of educational resources;
- access to Earth data sets and imagery, including the tools and interfaces that enable their effective use in educational settings;
- support services to help educators and learners effectively create, use, and share educational resources; and
- communication networks to facilitate interactions and collaborations across all dimensions of Earth system education."

Retrieved February 7, 2006, from http://www.dlese.org/about/index.html

DLESE is a partnership between the National Science Foundation (NSF); the DLESE community that is open to all interested in earth system education; the Steering Committee; and the DLESE Program Center, a group of core staff. The concept of the library took shape in 1998, and is now governed by an elected Steering Committee that is broadly representative of the diverse interests in Earth system science education. Its future growth and development is guided by the DLESE Strategic Plan, which outlines the broad functionalities of the library to be developed over the next five years (2002 - 2006). Its goals cover six core functions: 1) collection-building; 2) community-building; 3) library services to support creation, discovery, assessment, and use of resources, as well as community networks; 4) accessibility and use; 5) catering for a diversity of user needs; and 6) research and evaluation on many aspects of community digital libraries (http://www.dlese.org/documents/plans/stratplanver12.html).

It is this final core function that was the reason this example has been chosen for this paper – there has been extensive evaluation research on the model. A search of the Association for Computing Machinery (ACM) digital library (http://portal.acm.org/dl.cfm) on 'dlese' yields 200 papers. Some of those of particular relevance to the educational potential of DLESE are Khoo (2001); Marlino and Sumner (2001); Wright, Marlino and Sumner (2002); Sumner, Khoo, Recker and Marlino (2003); and Sumner and Marlino (2004). These series of papers show a clear endeavour towards ensuring that the needs of the earth system education community are a strong driving force towards the development of policy for the library.

As Lynch (2002) so aptly commented: "…digital libraries are somehow the key construct in building community, making community happen and exploiting community. Indeed, much of what we have learned about designing successful digital libraries emphasizes the discipline of user-centered design. Effective digital libraries are designed both for purpose and audience, very much in contrast to digital collections."

6 A Successful Model

In Table 3 a comparison between the LRC, as viewed in Hong Kong, and DLESE is presented. It is clear by examining this table that learning repositories are more likely to be successful if they:

- are developed out of a genuine need within a community;
- have a core of committed promoters whose enthusiasm is sustained over a number of years;
- articulate a clear direction and focus. While this does not have be a discipline focus (as is the case with DLESE) there does need to a clearly defined community, or perhaps a constellation of communities;
- consult with their user community(ies) to ensure that the resource collection is wanted and valued;
- establish a good management process that ensures regular review and updating of resources;
- are open access;
- facilitate easy addition of resources; and
- have suitable granularity in the search mechanisms.

Well-managed community digital libraries seem to offer a model for learning repositories that higher education universities should examine carefully, not as something 'out there' but as an option for close integration with university education. *If* community digital libraries become more pervasive, while still retaining their fresh responsiveness to their user communities; *if* more discipline domains are served by such community digital libraries; and *if* university libraries take on the role of being liaison between these community digital libraries and university teachers, then we have a foundation for the design and development of effective university programmes. It may well be that the future of the global community depends on new models such as this.

Table 3. Comparison between LRC and DLESE

Factor	LRC & the LEARNet project	DLESE
Reason for establishment	An isolated opportunity for securing funding. There was no systematic consultation or consideration of the cultures within Hong Kong educational institutions before LEARNet was established.	From recognized needs of a community – in this case a discipline-focused community.
Planning basis	Advisory Committee with representation from all universities in Hong Kong. Members were selected mostly by direct contact from the first Principal Supervisor after the project was established. No plan for continuation after initial funding.	Full strategic plan http://www.dlese.org/documents/plans/stratplanver12.html
Ongoing management	Two changes in Principal Supervisor for the LEARNet project. Initial enthusiasm waned after the first year. Advisory Committee meetings ceased well before the LEARNet project finished.	Long-term committed Director. Sufficient core staff. Evolving Governance plan with annual updates; latest at http://www.dlese.org/documents/plans/GovernancePlan_ver4.0approved.html
Accessibility	Complicated system of 'bubbles'. Authorization needed for access.	Open
Quality control	Evaluation process formed but was difficult to implement (Jones & McNaught, 2005). No further uptake after evaluation project finished. No quality guidelines for continuing management of resources. Series of evaluation questions at http://www.learnet.hku.hk:8052/TopsiteInfo/project/Success.cfm but these are not monitored.	Clear quality guidelines. Regular collections management process – see http://www.dlese.org/Metadata/collections/management-process.htm
Ease of submitting resources	The barrier of establishing an account exists. As the process for registration is automated, there seems little point to it. There is no check on whether the registrant 'belongs to' a Hong Kong university. Once registered, the submission of resources is easy.	Submission of resources is easy and is more focused than in the LRC.
Ease of searching	For the federated catalogue only simple searching is possible. Advance searching is possible only within the quite small LRC collection.	The granularity of searching is much finer and allows users to see quite quickly if this library is likely to meet their needs. There are 32 subject categories, nine grade levels, and 60 resources types in eight groups. See http://www.dlese.org/dds/browse.htm

Acknowledgements

This is an extended version of a Keynote address presented at the 2nd International Conference on Web Information Systems and Technologies, Setubal, Portugal, 11-13 April 2006.

Jennifer Jones did much of the evaluation work on LOs in the LRC. Her perseverance in this challenging environment and her attention to detail are gratefully acknowledged. Also acknowledged are the academics who developed the LOs which reside in the Hong Kong LRC. The quality of these LOs is high and perhaps, in time, the quality of these colleagues' work will be more widely accessed and utilized.

References

Agostinho, S., Bennett, S., Lockyer, L., Harper, B.: Developing a learning object metadata application profile based on LOM suitable for the Australian higher education context. Australasian Journal of Educational Technology 20(2), 191–208 (2004)

Boyle, T.: Design principles for authoring dynamic, reusable learning objects. Australian Journal of Educational Technology 19(1), 46–58 (2003)

Boyle, T., Bradley, C., Chalk, P., Jones, R., Haynes, R., Pickard, P.: Can learning objects contribute to pedagogical improvement in higher education: Lessons from a case study? Paper based on presentation given at CAL (April 2003) (Retrieved February 7, 2006), from http://www.londonmet.ac.uk/ltri/learningobjects/papers_pres/CAL_Objects_paper.doc

Cole, T. W.: Creating a framework of guidance for building good digital collections. First Monday 7(5) (2002) Retrieved February 7, 2006, from http://firstmonday.org/issues/issue7_5/cole/index.html

Downes, S.: Learning objects. International Review of Research in Open and Distance Learning 2(1) (2001), Retrieved February 7, 2006, from http://www.irrodl.org/content/v2.1/downes.html

Friesen, N.: Three objections to learning objects and e-learning standards. In: McGreal, R. (ed.) Online education using learning objects, pp. 59–70.RoutledgeFalmer, London (2004)

Gibbons, A.S., Nelson, J., Richards, R.: The nature and origin of instructional objects. In: Wiley, D. A. (ed.) The instructional use of learning objects: Online version. (2000)Retrieved February 7, 2006, from http://reusability.org/read/chapters/gibbons.doc

IEEE. Draft standard for learning object metadata (proposed standard) (2002), Retrieved February 7, 2006, from http://ltsc.ieee.org/wg12/files/LOM_148_12_1_v_Final_Draft.pdf

Jonassen, D., Churchill, D.: Is there a learning orientation in learning objects? International Journal on E-Learning 3(2), 32–41 (2004)

Jones, J., McNaught, C.: Using learning object evaluation: Challenges and lessons learned in the Hong Kong context. In: Richards, G., Kommers, P. (eds.) ED-MEDIA 2005, Proceedings of the 17th annual World Conference on Educational Multimedia, Hypermedia & Telecommunications, Montreal, Canada, 27 June - 2 July. pp. 3580–3585. Association for the Advancement of Computers in Education, Norfolk, VA (2005)

Kennedy, D. M.: Continuous refinement of reusable learning objects: The case of the Interactive Graphing Object. In: Cantoni, L., McLoughlin, C. (eds.). ED-MEDIA 2004 Proceedings of the 16th World Conference on Educational Multimedia and Hypermedia & World Conference on Educational Telecommunications, Lugano, Switzerland, pp. 1398–1404. Association for the Advancement of Computing in Education, Norfolk, VA(2004)

Kennedy, D.M., Fritze, P.: An Interactive Graphing Tool for web-based courses. In: Ottmann, T., Tomek, I., (eds.) ED-MEDIA & ED-TELECOM 98, 10th World Conference on Educational Multimedia and Hypermedia and World Conference on Educational Telecommunications, Freiburg, Germany, 20-25 June, vol. 1, pp. 703–708. Association for the Advancement of Computers in Education (AACE) Charlottesville (1998)

Kennedy, D.M., McNaught, C., Fritze, P.: Conceptual tools for designing and learning. In: Kommers, P. (ed.) Cognitive support for learning: Imagining the unknown, pp. 141–154. IOS Press, Amsterdam (2004)

Kennedy, D.M., Vogel, D.R., Xu, T.: Increasing opportunities for learning: Mobile graphing. In: Atkinson, R., McBeath, C., Jonas-Dwyer, D., Phillips, R. (eds.) Beyond the comfort zone Proceedings of the 21st annual Australian Society for Computers in Learning in Tertiary Education, conference, University of Western Australia, 5-8 December. pp. 493–502. Retrieved February 7, 2006, from http://www.ascilite.org.au/conferences/perth04/procs/kennedy.html

Khoo, M.: Community design of DLESE's collections review policy: A technological frames analysis. In: Proceedings of the 1st ACM/IEEE-CS joint conference on digital libraries, pp. 157–164. ACM Press, New York, NY, USA (2001), http://portal.acm.org/dl.cfm

Koppi, T., Bogle, L., Lavitt, N.: Institutional use of learning objects: Lessons learned and future directions. Journal of Educational Multimedia and Hypermedia 13(4), 449–463 (2004)

Koppi, T., Hodgson, L.: Universitas 21 learning resource catalogue using IMS metadata and a new classification of learning objects. In: Montgomerie,C., Viteli,J. (eds.) ED-MEDIA 2001, Proceedings of the 13th Annual World Conference on Educational Multimedia, Hypermedia & Telecommunications, Tampere, Finland, 25-30 June. pp. 998–1001. Association for the Advancement of Computers in Education (AACE), Norfolk, VA (2001)

Laurillard, D., McAndrew, P.: Reuseable educational software: A basis for generic learning activities. In: A. Littlejohn (Ed.). Reusing online resources: A sustainable approach to e-learning (pp. 81–93). Kogan Page, London (2003)

Littlejohn, A(ed.): Reusing online resources: A sustainable approach to eLearning. Kogan Page, London (2003)

Lynch, C.: Digital collections, digital libraries and the digitization of cultural heritage information. First Monday, 7(5) (2002), Retrieved February 7, 2006, from http://firstmonday.org/issues/issue7_5/lynch/index.html

Marlino, M., Sumner, T.: The digital library for earth system education: Building community, building the library. In: Proceedings of the 3rd ACM/IEEE-CS joint conference on digital libraries, pp. 80–81. ACM Press, Houston, Texas. New York (2001), http://portal.acm.org/dl.cfm

McNaught, C.: The synergy between information literacy and eLearning. In: Ching, H.S., Poon, P.W.T., McNaught, C. (eds.) eLearning and digital publishing, pp. 29–43. Springer, Dordrecht (2006)

Parrish, P.E.: The trouble with learning objects. Educational Technology, Research and Development 52(1), 49–67 (2004)

Siemens, G,: The whole picture of eLearning.(2003) Retrieved February 7, 2006, from http://www.elearnspace.org/Articles/wholepicture.htm

Sumner, T., Khoo, M., Recker, M., Marlino, M.: Understanding educator perceptions of 'quality' in digital libraries. In: Proceedings of the 3rd ACM/IEEE-CS joint conference on digital librariesHouston, Texas, US, pp. 269–279. IEEE Computer Society, Washington, DC (2003), (Retrieved February 7, 2006), http://portal.acm.org/dl.cfm

Sumner, T., Marlino, M.: Digital libraries and educational practice: A case for new models. In: Proceedings of the 4th ACM/IEEE-CS joint conference on Digital libraries table of contents, Tuscon, AZ, pp. 170–178. ACM Press, New York (2004), (Retrieved February 7, 2006), http://portal.acm.org/dl.cfm

Wiley, D. A.: Learning objects. A definition. In: Kovalchick,A., Dawson, K. (eds.) Education and technology: An encyclopedia. Santa Barbara: ABC-CLIO (2002)

Wiley, D. A.: Learning objects: Difficulties and opportunities. Academic ADL Co-Lab News Report: No. 152-030406.(2003) (Retrieved February 7, 2006) , from http://wiley.ed.usu.edu/docs/lo_do.pdf

Wegner, E.: Communities of practice: Learning, meaning and identity. Cambridge University Press, Cambridge (1998)

Wright, M., Marlino, M., Sumner, T.: Meta-design of a community digital library. D-Lib Magazine, 8(5) (2002) (Retrieved February 7, 2006), from http://www.dlib.org/dlib/may02/wright/05wright.html

All in-text URLs accessed on (February 7 2006)

The Growing Importance of e-Communities
on the Web

Josef Kolbitsch[1] and Hermann Maurer[2]

[1] Graz University of Technology, Steyrergasse 30, 8010 Graz, Austria
`josef.kolbitsch@tugraz.at`
[2] Institute for Information Processing and Computer Media
Graz University of Technology, Inffeldgasse 16c, 8010 Graz, Austria
`hmaurer@iicm.edu`

Abstract. Until recently, one of the main aims of the World Wide Web has
been to offer users a wide range of information. This information was authored,
by and large, by professional information providers. Recent advancements on
the Internet, however, have changed this paradigm and the clear distinction
between information producers and consumers is becoming blurred. New
technologies such as weblogs, wikis, file sharing services, podcasting and social
networks allow users to become an active part on the Web and let them
participate in developing content.

In this chapter, an overview of several successful community-based concepts
and services is given. The fact that many of these concepts have existed before
is pointed out together with true novelties of their current implementations.
Moreover, a critical view of recent communities, their importance and impact is
presented. Especially the potential loss of individuality and the movement
towards an "integrated society" with a common shared memory is discussed.
We also venture to look at the future development of e-Communities in the light
of ubiquitous access to information with technologies such as "always-on"
wearable cameras and E-Ink.

Keywords: Communities, Collaborative Work, Web-Based Applications,
Information Systems, Wikis, Blogs, File Sharing, Podcasting, Social Networks.

1 Introduction

During the last decade, the World Wide Web has evolved into a truly worldwide
computer network. Traditionally, most information on the Web was published by
professional information providers such as news services, companies advertising their
products and offering support, or research institutions. Moreover, personal homepages
could be established by users.

Although millions of individuals make use of the Web every day, in the past only a
small percentage was capable of actually authoring content and *participating* in the
Web. Primarily technological obstacles including the lack of technical background
and complicated tools prevented users from producing web-pages and from
participating in other services on the Web (e.g., (Lindahl and Blount 2003)). The only
successful exceptions to this rule are discussion forums and communities for diseases
and disabilities, eLearning systems, and dating services.

J. Filipe, J. Cordeiro, and V. Pedrosa (Eds.): WEBIST 2005/2006, LNBIP 1, pp. 19–37, 2007.

Fig. 1. Blogger, one of the free and easy-to-use services for creating blogs

Recently, however, concepts and services that let users become a part of the content creation and distribution process have been introduced on the Web. "Novel" systems including blogs, wikis, file sharing services, and social networks have started a movement towards more user participation, and users are not only information consumers but are capable of authoring content, modifying existing content, and sharing it with other users on the Internet.

This chapter gives an overview of a number of popular, community-based services on the Internet, discusses their impact on our lives, and gives an outlook on future applications and their significance. Section 2 introduces blogs, wikis with Wikipedia being the most prominent example, file sharing services including podcasting, and social networks. The novelty and effects of these technologies are discussed in sections 3 and 4. Section 5 makes an attempt to forecast the role of these concepts in conjunction with forthcoming technical developments.

2 Community-Based Services on the Web

In recent years, a host of new, mainly community-based concepts and services was introduced on the Internet. By some, these new technologies were coined the "Web 2.0", emphasising both the evolutionary process the Web is undergoing and the innovation of the novel products (see (O'Reilly 2006; Kolbitsch and Maurer 2006)). The following sub-sections describe a selection of relevant community-based services on the Web.

2.1 Blogs

Blogs, short for weblogs, are a form of web pages that contain articles similar to newsgroup postings in a reverse chronological order. Blog entries are usually produced by a single author or by a small group of authors and cannot be edited by the public. Postings on blogs are regular, typically once a day (see (Blood 2002)).

Fig. 2. Slashdot—probably the best known and most popular filter-style blog currently available

Their content is similar to a combination of diaries, editorials in magazines, "hotlists", and the "breaking news" section on news channels. Contributions frequently refer to a current event such as a news story, a discussion in parliament, the release of a new record, etc.

In May 2006, Technorati, a service tracking blogs and the links between blogs[1], indexes almost 40 million blogs (source: (Technorati 2006)). About eleven percent of American Internet users have read blogs, and two percent have actually maintained blogs in 2004 (see (Lenhart et al. 2004)).

2.1.1 Blog Styles

Currently, two notable types of blogs are available: diaries or personal journals (accounting for about seventy percent of all blogs) and filters (about ten to fifteen percent, see (Herring et al. 2004)). In diaries and personal journals, authors make details of their personal lives and their views on various topics public. The first diary-style blog believed to have been published was started in January 1994 by Justin Hall, then a college student (e.g., (Pollock 2001)). Nowadays, personal journals are particularly well-liked among young people who want to tell friends (and absolute strangers) about their experiences. An example for a young woman's blog discussing taboo and provocative topics is "Miss Izzy", a rather popular web-site in Singapore (see Figure 3; (MissIzzy 2006)).

Filter-style blogs aggregate links to noteworthy resources on the Internet. Links are usually complemented with short summaries of the respective resources' content and comments added by the author. The scope of such blogs is often limited to a particular topic such as globalisation, music, or computers and technology. One of the best known filter-style blogs is Slashdot, a web-site with a very large user base focussing on technology (see Figure 2; (Slashdot 2006)).

---

[1] The links between blogs are used for determining the relevance and popularity of single blogs. This is approach is not unlike Google's ranking mechanism.

Fig. 3. MissIzzy with its sometimes controversial topics is one of the most popular diary-style blogs in Singapore

Due to their nature, blogs are intrinsically opinionated. They allow users to express themselves and present their views to a broad audience. However, weblogs are not only employed in personal environments but also in organisations and enterprises. They are utilised for keeping employees informed of the status of projects, of new policies or similar news (e.g., (Treese 2004)). Moreover, they can be used to encourage the communication and co-operation between various departments in large organisations.

2.1.2 Technical Aspects

A major part of the success of blogs is their ease-of-use—even for novices. Using blogs is about as difficult as writing e-mails and organising them in mailboxes. Moreover, free services like Blogger make it possible to start a new weblog within a few minutes (see Figure 1; (Blogger 2006)). Hence, they are often used as a replacement for traditional homepages.

Another aspect that makes blogs a popular means for communication is a set of technologies that greatly enhance community-building among users: permalinks, trackback and RSS (see (Efimova and de Moor 2004)). *Permalinks* are persistent URLs to single postings on a blog. When an author refers to another blogger's article, the permalink to this entry can be used. If the two blogs are *trackback*-enabled a link from the newer blog entry to the existing one is established automatically. Thus with trackback, blog entries can be linked practically bidirectionally, and blog authors are notified about being cited by someone else (cf., (Maurer and Tochtermann 2002)).

RSS ("RDF Site Syndication" or "Really Simple Syndication") is a technology that lets users retrieve a list of changes made to a blog, or a web-site in general. Users subscribing to an *RSS feed* are provided with the titles of new articles, short summaries, and the URLs to the full blog entries. When users read an interesting article on a blog they have subscribed to (using RSS) they can write a blog entry in their own blog and refer to the original posting using a permalink. The author of the initial posting is informed trough trackback.

Fig. 4. No other wiki has more pages or more authors than Wikipedia

This combination of technologies builds a network of more or less loosely connected blogs—the *blogosphere*. RSS feeds in particular foster community-building among bloggers. This relatively simple mechanism helps users stay up-to-date on blogs and people they are interested in, and transforms occasional visitors into frequent readers.

2.2 Wikis

The term "wiki" is derived from *wiki wiki*, which is Hawaiian for "quick". This word is an appropriate description for Ward Cunningham's notion of a concept for the rapid development and organisation of web pages (see (Leuf and Cunningham 2001)). Wikis are collaborative, web-based authoring environments, where anyone on the Internet can edit existing content and add new pages any time they wish. In other words, every reader can instantly become a writer.

This concept is in stark contrast to authoring system previously widely available on the Web. Content management systems, the de-facto standard for large web-sites, for instance, make use of hierarchical rights management, and a publishing process similar to the one employed in newspaper publishing. Such a system usually incorporates administrators, editors, authors, and mere readers. A wiki, on the other hand, does not distinguish between readers, authors and editors; they have the same capabilities in the system.

This aspect is of particular interest because initial authors of articles allow other users to modify "their" content. Although this approach may seem utterly chaotic, there are several very large wiki sites offering quality content provided by the community (see below). One characteristic that makes wikis work is the aim to reach an agreement among all authors of an article. Hence, the content of single wiki articles is usually agreed upon, unbiased, and neutral.

Fig. 5. Flickr—a popular photo sharing service that makes use of tagging

2.2.1 Advantages and Drawbacks of Wikis

Their "open" nature makes wikis more flexible than conventional, editor-based web-sites. When new information becomes available it can be added to the wiki immediately, without an editor's approval. Similarly, when an error is found by a reader it can be corrected by the reader, without the need to contact the site's administrator or the author of the document. Moreover, wiki documents can be written using a relatively uncomplicated syntax, and features such as version control make wikis well-suited for collaborative environments.

At the same time, the openness of wikis poses a number of problems. Since quality control through editors is not in place errors might be inserted accidentally, or even deliberately. Readers, on the other hand, might mistake the information provided on a wiki site for reliable. Another problem is vandalism, where incorrect information, defamatory content, and advertisements are inserted, existing content is deleted or

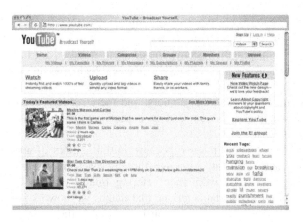

Fig. 6. YouTube is a service where users of the community can post the video clips they produced

overwritten, etc. In many cases, however, such acts of vandalism are repaired within minutes by reverting a page to its previous version (cf., (Viégas et al. 2004)).

2.2.2 Wikipedia

The largest wiki to date is Wikipedia, a free online encyclopaedia available in more than 200 languages (see Figure 4; (Wikipedia 2006)). Since it is based on the wiki concept, every reader is also an author and can add or modify information instantly—even anonymously. This is one of the reasons for the project's rapid and steady growth: from Wikipedia's founding in 2001, more than 1.1 million articles have been written in the English edition, and about 400.000 pages in the German edition. Wikipedia offers more material than many other, commercial encyclopaedias, and can deliver more supplementary content such as hyperlinks to information on the Web than many other works of reference. This makes people trust in Wikipedia more than in other resources.

However, as in any other wiki, any information provided might be erroneous because quality assurance mechanisms are not available. Research shows, though, that Wikipedia articles contain, on average, only about 25 percent more errors than renowned, for-profit encyclopaedias (see (Giles 2005)).

One of the most striking examples of incorrect data in Wikipedia is the case of journalist John Seigenthaler. A false biography published on Wikipedia associated him with the assassination of John F. Kennedy and alleged that he collaborated with the Soviet Union in the 1970s (see (Seigenthaler 2005)). As a consequence, the rights of anonymous authors have been restricted. In addition to this, a peer review mechanism for articles in Wikipedia has been discussed. (Although this feature was due for January 2006 (see (Wales 2005)), it has not been realised yet).

In some cases, incomplete content can be just as bad as wrong information. An article that lists a politician's successes while deliberately omitting the promises that were not implemented is obviously not balanced and leaves a wrong impression.

Fig. 7. YouTube does not only offer home-made videos on their web-site but also broadcasts a selection on a traditional TV channel

Similarly, due to systematic bias it is difficult to provide unified views in Wikipedia. Although one of aims of the encyclopaedia is to be unbiased, social and cultural differences as well as different national and lingual backgrounds might have an influence on the content. On May 14th, 2006, the English article on the Hungarian scientist John von Neumann, for instance, was about five times as long as the corresponding article in the German edition and included detailed accounts of his research and a comprehensive list of external references. Thus, even if both articles are written in an unbiased and objective way, an imbalance due to the background of the authors and the target group can be observed. In professional, editor-based encyclopaedias this kind of systematic bias is countered by authoring guidelines that set standards for the length of articles, etc.

2.3   File Sharing Services

File sharing is probably best known in conjunction with applications that allow users to share any kind of files over the Internet such as Napster or Kazaa. These services are primarily used for downloading music and movies illegally. Recently, however, also several legal file sharing services have been introduced. These systems are usually web-based, provide users with a private space for storing documents, help users organise content, and let them make documents publicly available.

A popular file sharing tool is Flickr, a service for sharing and organising photos (see Figure 5; (Flickr 2006)). With Flickr, users upload their photos to a server, can add comments and leave notes inside images. Additionally, users can attach tags to every photo uploaded. Tags resemble keywords that loosely describe the content of the corresponding image. A photo of a family can, for instance, be tagged "wedding", "May 2006", and "Vienna". Consequently, a query for "Vienna" would also list this photo as a result. Besides searching, users can also browse the vast archive using tags. Every photo shown in Flickr is supplemented with the tags assigned by the author. By selecting a tag, all images with the same tag are displayed.

Fig. 8. The podcast directory integrated in Apple's iTunes Music player

A service extending this concept to the domain of motion pictures is YouTube (see Figure 6; (YouTube 2006)). With YouTube, users can share video clips they produced and employ a tagging mechanism similar to the one in Flickr. CurrentTV takes video sharing a step further. Not only can viewers produce their own video clips and publish them on CurrentTV's web-site, but a selection of video clips is also broadcast on conventional television channels (see Figure 7; (YouTube 2006)). Thus, viewers may even become TV producers.

2.3.1 Podcasting

A slightly different approach to sharing content on the Internet is podcasting. Basically, podcasting means blogging audio content. Content producers regularly upload audio files in MP3 audio format to a server and insert references to these new files into an RSS feed. Listeners subscribing to a podcast (actually to the RSS feed) have access to the full list of audio files made available by the producer and are notified about newly published content. On the users' request, audio files are downloaded. Therefore, podcasting can be seen as a type of "audio on demand" service (see (Biever 2005)).

A directory integrated in Apple's iTunes music player software catalogues thousands of podcasts (see Figure 8). Podcasts are available on a wide range of topics ranging from self-made music to amateur talk and radio shows, from religious programmes and masses to professionally produced shows such as the Nature Podcast (see (Nature 2006)). Lately, podcasting has also been identified as a technology for enhancing existing e-Learning applications and distance learning initiatives. Lectures and discussions are recorded and provided free-of-charge as podcasts (e.g., (DukeCast 2006)). In a similar fashion, conference presentations are disseminated as podcasts on the Internet (e.g., (JISC-CETIS 2006)).

Fig. 9. MySpace, a social network with more than 78 mn registered users—the sixth most popular web-site worldwide

2.4   Social Networks

Social networks are structures that describe the social relations among individuals. Every node in the network is a person, and edges between nodes are the connections among individuals, where the weight of edges can be used to denote the degree of "amity". In recent developments, the concept of social networks, previously mainly used for describing existing social structures, was successfully applied to the online world.

On the Web, social networks are chiefly utilised for maintaining relations with friends and acquaintances and for making new friends. Such services offer basic functionality for chatting with members of the network, for sharing information, etc. Users joining a social network have to fill out a profile containing information such as the person's name, date of birth, and a photo. These data are made available to members of the network in order that they can find their friends. Moreover, most social networks do not only let users view their friends but also their friends' friends (second degree friends). This feature clearly facilitates creating new connections in the network.

Fig. 10. With about 25 mn members, Friendster is one of the most successful social networks

Well-known examples for general-purpose social networks are MySpace, the sixth most popular web-site worldwide (source: (Alexa 2006)) with more than 78 million registered users, and Friendster with about 27 million users (see Figures 9 and 10; (MySpace 2006; Friendster 2006)). In addition to this, specialised services for people with similar interests have been established. OpenBC, for instance, is a social network of professionals with the aim of creating a web of trusted business partners and experts (see Figure 11; (OpenBC 2006)).

2.5 Other Community-Based Applications

A new class of applications combines features of social networks and file sharing systems. del.icio.us, for example, is a social bookmarking service (see Figure 12;

(del.icio.us 2006)). Users can retain bookmarks of favourite pages in the del.icio.us database instead of storing them on their local computers. Like in Flickr, users can attach tags to bookmarks and use these tags for finding similar bookmarks in the system. Since users can see who else bookmarked the same web page, it is possible to find people with similar interests. Hence, del.icio.us is not only a platform for sharing information but also includes mechanisms from social networks.

Furl is a service similar to del.icio.us (see Figure 13; (Furl 2006)). In Furl, not only bookmarks but the actual resources from the Internet are stored in an internal database. This means that users can create a space only containing the web pages they want to store—their own "Private Web".

Further services driven entirely by the community are, for instance, Eventful and OhmyNews. Eventful is a web-site listing events for almost any region in the world (see Figure 14; (Eventful 2006)). The events offered by this service together with a short description, the exact location and additional information are submitted by members of the community. The second application, Ohmy News, is a blog-like news service in which articles are authored by "citizen reporters"—amateur journalists from the global community (OhmyNews 2006). Ohmy News is often faster than traditional news providers and can offer in-depth information written by locals and first-hand witnesses.

Fig. 11. OpenBC is a social network of professionals

3   What Is Really New? What Is Different?

On close inspection, it can be seen that the "novel" concepts and technologies introduced above are essentially nothing new (cf., (O'Reilly 2005)). Similar services have been in use earlier, for example, in hypermedia systems such as Xanadu, Microcosm or Hyperwave ((Nelson 1981; Fountain et al. 1990; Maurer 1996)).

However, there are certain aspects that distinguish these new applications from previous implementations. The novelty is not what these services do but how they achieve it. Moreover, all of the concepts and services introduced in this chapter have one aspect in common: they get better the more people use them (see (O'Reilly 2005)). The more people get involved in environments such as Wikipedia or Ohmy News, the more respectable the results get.

Fig. 12. Del.icio.us, one of the pioneers in social bookmarking services

3.1 Blogs

Newsgroups, letters to the editor, editorials, and "what's new" pages as parts of larger systems have existed before weblogs were conceived. Blogs, however, let users *only* write short articles and comments, while they are not offering functionality beyond these simple operations. Blogging software is usually a lightweight application that is not overloaded with functions users rarely make use of. Moreover, most blogging tools are free, easy to use, and hardly any special skills or technical background knowledge are required.

Most importantly, weblogs give users on the Web a chance to participate. Editorials, for example, are "passive" for most users. There is a small group of authors and a large mass of readers. Readers, however, do usually not have a way to comment on editorials on the same level; they could write a letter to the editor, but this letter might be shortened or not published at all. With blogs, however, every reader can start a new blog and discuss, or comment on, someone else's article. Additionally, a small set of technologies including trackback and RSS helps forming a blogging community.

3.2 Wikis

Although wikis put forward a new concept that was previously unknown on the Web, the basic idea is far from original. In one of the early designs of the World Wide Web, Tim Berners-Lee describes the system as the "read/write Web", where users are not only able to read documents but can also author documents (cf., (BBC 2005; Gillmor 2004)). Even earlier, Ted Nelson's concept for Xanadu, the genuine hypertext system, involved versioning and allowed any user of the system to produce new content and share it with other users. Software such as Hyperwave implemented these features.

Fig. 13. Furl is a social bookmarking service that lets users not only store references to pages but the actual resources

Further, Wikipedia is not the first attempt to establish a free encyclopaedia on the Internet. This notion dates back to October 1993 when the Interpedia Project was proposed on the Usenet (e.g., (Foust 1994)). While letting users participate in developing the content of the encyclopaedia, Interpedia offered an approach to quality assurance by providing seals of approval (SOAP). With this mechanism, various independent organisations could rate articles in the encyclopaedia and confirm the accuracy and quality of content. Displaying an article would also present the various seals of approval granted by organisations, making it easier for users to trust the information provided by the community.

3.3 File Sharing

Although the file sharing concept on a large scale is relatively new, the basic technologies for enabling file sharing have existed since the early days of the Internet. Anyone can set up an FTP or HTTP server on their computers, for example, and offer any kind of content to other users on the Internet. Software such as Napster employ proprietary protocols for the same purpose and add indexing and search functionality to the service. This makes the application purpose-built and easier to use. The same is true of podcasts: even years ago it was possible to make audio files publicly available on a web server. However, only with technologies such as RSS this became attractive and relatively consumer-friendly.

An innovative feature in recent web-based file sharing services is tagging. This functionality distinguishes Flickr from other approaches to organising large amounts of data (cf., (Mathes 2004)). In previous environments, strict taxonomies were employed, which usually limited the use of such systems to (domain) experts. Although annotations could have been employed for organising content in the same way as tags are used nowadays, a classification of data based on such loose metadata did not seem reasonable.

Fig. 14. A worldwide event directory, where users submit information on upcoming events

3.4 Social Networks

Social networks in the physical world have existed for a long time. Clubs, associations of people with shared interests, workgroups and similar societies were successful even before the Internet was developed. In the 1980s, characteristics of social networks were introduced in computer-mediated systems. Among other functionality, these "computer supported cooperative work" environments allow for collaboratively authoring content, sharing and organising information, maintaining relations among members of the systems, and direct communication (e.g., (Schmidt and Bannon 1992)).

Today's social networks include significantly less functionality. Most systems currently available only focus on their main purpose—communication—and do not incorporate diverse functionality such as collaborative authoring. This lowers the barrier to entry and makes social networks easier to handle even for novice users.

4   Impact of Recent Community-Based Developments

The driving factor behind the transformations the Web is undergoing is probably not a set of new technologies but a fundamental mind shift in users and organisations alike. Users wish to participate instead of using the Web only passively as readers. Furthermore, there is a willingness to share content, and even companies grant access to their content databases. One of the best examples is Google Earth, where satellite images and geographic information are made publicly available (Google 2006).

For private users, this new tendency "materialises" in a combination of blogs, file sharing services and social networks. Regular postings on weblogs provide a continuous stream of thoughts, experiences and emotions, while services such as Flickr or YouTube deliver complementing photos and videos. A social network offers the infrastructure for maintaining the ties with friends and acquaintances (cf., (Kolbitsch 2006)).

An immediate effect of these developments is that the world is getting yet "smaller". Teenagers in Europe, for example, can have friends in New Zealand and Singapore and can be a part of their lives as if they were next-door neighbours. Although, from a technical perspective, this was possible years ago it has become reality only recently with the services detailed above (and other technologies such as free Internet telephony). Especially the blend of social networks and blogging is intriguing: in social networks, it is possible to find new friends or rediscover "old" friends one has not been in touch with for a long time. Friends' blogs, on the other hand, are the means to stay informed on their daily activities—from minor events such as buying a new CD or doing a mountain bike tour to a three-month trip to South America.

From a less enthusiastic perspective, it can be argued that our society is heading in a direction where individual experiences become increasingly rare. Imagine holidays in Papua New Guinea. On the Internet, there are travel-related blogs written by people with first-hand experience, there is a wide range of photos and videos from the country, etc. Thus, even before actually going on holidays to a country we have not been before, we will have a very good impression of what to expect, what we will see and what it will be like.

5 Future Advancements

Looking back at the development of communication among human beings, we can see that written language started about 6,000 years ago. About 600 years ago, the invention of book printing increased the importance of written language, and some 200 years ago the introduction of compulsory education further spread reading and writing. About 150 years ago, photography and telephony were invented, and some 100 years ago moving pictures were introduced. About 80 years ago, radio broadcasting was started. 70 years ago, anyone interested and able to afford it, could buy a camera; forty years ago, the same was true of video cameras. Also about forty years ago, television was widely accepted. About twenty-five years ago, the Walkman was introduced. Twenty years ago, amateur video cameras became affordable and widely available. Fifteen years ago, computer networks were implemented in numerous organisations. Ten years ago, the Web (and the Internet in general) took off. About five to ten years ago, concepts such as wikis, weblogs, and social networks were introduced.

Considering that reading and writing became available to the public only about 200 years ago, that widespread technologies such as television have been accepted for only forty years or so, and that blogging came into being only ten years ago, it can be assumed that recent technologies permitting user participation will have a deep impact on almost anyone on the Internet in only a few years.

We believe that, in the future, most information will be accessed through a networked computer. Moreover, most people on the Web will be members of at least one social network or specialised community. Thus, it can be assumed that the technologies we see today and their usage are just the beginning of a movement towards an "integrated society". Already today we reveal more personal and intimate details on the Internet (even to absolute strangers) than most people would have expected a few years ago. (MissIzzy 2006), mentioned above, is a good example (see section 2.1.1). On the one hand, the young female author posts very personal experiences and intimacies on her weblog. On the other hand, readers can relate to the experiences and feelings, sometimes even to a degree where they have the perception that *they* had the experiences, although they only read about it.

To an increasing degree, individuals merge their own experiences with the experiences of other users on the Internet. This is an important side-effect of modern communication systems. Consequently, in the future people might find it hard to have any truly individual experiences.

5.1 Upcoming Technologies

We believe that the key to the further success of the recent community-based services, and the formation of an integrated society, is ubiquity. In order to be able to have a "live experience" of someone else's life, this other person has to provide a stream of data (text, images, video, sound, etc.) from virtually anywhere. At the same time, viewers need to have ubiquitous access to this information.

Both aspects will be possible in the future, as current technologies readily demonstrate. Hewlett-Packard, for instance, conducts research on an "always-on" wearable camera that captures what the user sees (see (HP 2004)). The data is recorded continuously and is to be stored in data centres. With such a camera, individuals could provide a continuous stream of their life, from their perspective, on the Internet.

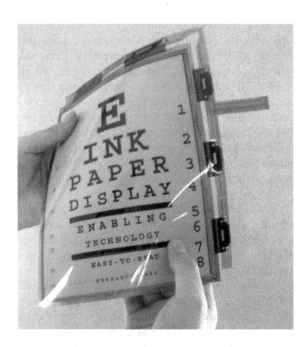

Fig. 15. Demonstration of e-Ink technology. e-Ink paper is thin, flexible, and content can be changed as if it were a regular display. Source: (eInk 2005).

E-Ink paper is another technology that has the potential to revolutionise the way we have access to information. E-Ink paper is a material that requires electricity to "load" an image into a matrix-based display but does not consume any energy while displaying the image. The content of a page can be changed as if it were a regular computer display. However, electronic paper is thin, flexible, can display both monochrome and colour images, and is low in power consumption (see Figure 15; (eInk 2006)).

With high resolution wearable cameras, foldable displays, and fast, wireless network connections, users can publish information anytime from anyplace and can have ubiquitous access to information on the Internet. Imagine, for example, your partner sitting at home, watching your first presentation at a conference—from your perspective. Or imagine being on holidays in Papua New Guinea. With the upcoming technologies, your friends can "tune in" to your holidays anytime they want to (when you make the video stream publicly available). After a few weeks or months, absolute strangers can watch part of the video stream on your video blog. For these users, your video blog can be a replacement for a conventional travel guidebook. Or, even more radically, your video stream can be a complete substitute for the actual trip!

6 Conclusion

In recent years, the Web has grown into a network for community-based systems and global collaboration. Concepts for creating and managing information such as weblogs and wikis, file sharing services and social networks attract millions of users on the Web. With these novel developments, users are both willing to participate and willing to share content, experiences, thoughts and emotions. Although these advances are able to offer users unprecedented opportunities and are generally viewed positively, we should be well aware of the risks that may be involved.

The new forms of communication are part of a transformation that goes almost unnoticed. In fact, we are about to develop an integrated society with a "shared memory" stored on the Internet. As a consequence, a reduction of unique individual experiences seems unavoidable. What is more, our society relies increasingly on network-based services, even to a degree where we become dependent on the Internet. This can be particularly problematic in such sensitive areas as interpersonal communication. Hence, it will be exciting, on the one hand, to see future developments in electronic communities on the Web. On the other hand, it remains to be seen which effects the growing influence of information technology will have on our society and everyday lives.

Acknowledgements

Research for this publication was supported by the Styria Professorship for Revolutionary Media Technologies.

References

Alexa Internet, Inc. Related Info for: myspace.com (2006) (Accessed May 17th, 2006), http://www.alexa.com/data/details/ traffic_details?q=&url=www.myspace.com

BBC News. Berners-Lee on the read/write web (2005) (Accessed May 10th, 2006), http://news.bbc.co.uk/1/hi/technology/ 4132752.stm

Biever, C.: 'Podcasters' deliver radio-on-demand, New Scientist, 185, 2486 (2005)

Blogger, http://www.blogger.com

Blood, R.: The Weblog Handbook: Practical Advice on Creating and Maintaining Your Blog. Perseus Publishing, Cambridge, MA (2002)

CurrentTV. http://www.currenttv.com/

del.icio.us. http://del.icio.us/

DukeCast. http://dukecast.oit.duke.edu/

Efimova, L., de Moor, A.: Beyond Personal Webpublishing: An Exploratory Study of Conversational Blogging Practices. In: Proceedings of the 37th Annual Hawaii Internation Conference on System Sciences (HICSS'04), Big Island (2004), See also http://doi.ieeecomputersociety.org/10.1109/HICSS.2005.118

LG.Philips LCD, E Ink Corporation, Tablet-Sized Felxible Display (2005) Accessed May 7th, 2006, http://www.eink.com/press/images/highres_downloads/LG.Philips_LCD_E_E_Ink_Flex_T ablet_Display.jpg

E Ink, http://www.eink.com/

Eventful. http://eventful.com/

Fountain, A.M., Hall, W., Heath, I., Davis, H.C.: MICROCOSM: An Open Model for Hypermedia with Dynamic Linking. In: Proceedings of Hypertext: Concepts, Systems and Applications, November, 1990, Paris, France, pp. 298–311 (1990)

Foust, J. A.: Welcome to the Interpedia!, Posting in the comp.infosystems.interpedia newsgroup, February 12th, 1994 (1994) Retrieved from http://groups.google.com/group/ comp. infosystems.interpedia/browse_thread/thread/6ec8bc1f8bece5a1/590f92a599e06589# 590f92a599e06589

Flickr. http://www.flickr.com/

Friendster. http://www.friendster.com/

LookSmart Furl. http://furl.net/

Giles, J.: Internet encyclopaedias go head to head, Nature, Issue 438, 900–901. (2005), See also http://www.nature.com/nature/journal/v438/n7070/full/438900a.html

Gillmor, D.: We the Media, O'Reilly Media, Sebastopol (2004)

Google Earth. http://earth.google.com/

Herring, S.C., Scheidt, L.A., Bonus, S., Wright, E.: Bridging the Gap: A Genre Analysis of Weblogs. In: Proceedings of the 37th Annual Hawaii Internation Conference on System Sciences (HICSS'04), Big Island, HI, U.S.A (2004), See also http://doi. ieeecomputersociety.org/10.1109/HICSS.2004.1265271

Firth, S.: Photographic memories: Always-on camera captures life's fleeting moments (2004) (Accessed May 21st 2006), http://www.hpl.hp.com/news/2004/jan-mar/casualcapture.html

JISC/CETIS Conference Podcast, http://www.e-framework.org/events/conference/conference_ audio.xml

Kolbitsch. J.: Körero: An Integrated, Community-Based Platform for Collaboration (to appear, 2006), See http://www.kolbitsch.org/research/papers/2006-Korero.pdf

Kolbitsch, J., Maurer, H.: The Transformation of the Web: How Emerging Communities Shape the Information We Consume. Journal of Universal Computer Science 12(2), 187–213 (2006)

Lenhart, A., Fallows, D., and Horrigan, J.: Content Creation Online: 44% of U.S. Internet users have contributed their thoughts and their files to the online world, Pew Internet & American Life Project (2004) (Accessed May 8th, 2006), http://www.pewinternet.org/pdfs/ PIP_Content_Creation_Report.pdf

Leuf, B., Cunningham, W.: The Wiki Way. Quick Collaboration on the Web, Addison-Wesley, London, UK (2001)

Lindahl, C., Blount, E.: Weblogs. Simplifying Web Publishing, Computer 36(11), 114–116 (2003)

Mathes, A.:Folksonomies Cooperative Classification and Communication Through Shared Metadata (2004) (Accessed January 25th, 2006), http://www.adammathes.com/academic/ computer-mediated-communication/ folksonomies. pdf

Maurer, H.: Hyperwave: The Next Generation Web Solution. Addison-Wesley, Harlow, U.K (1996)

Maurer, H., Tochtermann, K.: On a New Powerful Model for Knowledge Management and its Applications. Journal of Universal Computer Science 8(1), 85–96 (2002), See also http://www.jucs.org/jucs_8_1/on_a_new_powerful/

Miss Izzy. http://www.missizzy.org/

MySpace. http://www.myspace.com/

Nature Podcast. http://www.nature.com/nature/podcast/

Nelson, T.H.: Literary Machines, Mindful Press (1981)

Ohmy News. http://english.ohmynews.com/

OpenBC. http://www.openbc.com/

O'Reilly, T.: What Is Web 2.0. Design Patterns and Business Models for the Next Generation of Software (2005) (Accessed April 30th, 2006), http://www.oreillynet.com/pub/a/oreilly/ tim/news/2005/09/30/

Pollock, H.: Who Let the Blogs Out?, Yahoo Internet Life (2001), See also http://web.archive. org/web/20010813193029/http://yil.com/features/feature.asp?volume=07&issue=05&keyw ord=blogs

Schmidt, K., Bannon, L.: Taking CSCW Seriously: Supporting Articulation Work, Computer Supported Cooperative Work (CSCW). An International Journal 1(1), 7–40 (1992), See also http://www.it-c.dk/people/schmidt/papers/cscw_seriously.pdf

Seigenthaler, J.: A false Wikipedia 'biography', USA Today, November 29th, 2005 (2005) (Accessed January 12th, 2006), http://www.usatoday.com/news/opinion/editorials/2005-11-29-wikipedia-edit_x.htm

Slashdot. http://slashdot.org/

Technorati. http://www.technorati.com/

Treese, W.: Open Systems for Collaboration. netWorker 8(1), 13–16 (2004)

Viégas, F.B., Wattenberg, M., Kushal, D.: Studying cooperation and conflict between authors with history flow visualizations. In: Proceedings of the 2004 Conference on Human Factors in Computing Systems (CHI 2004), pp. 575–582. Vienna, Austria (2004)

Wales, J.: Re: [Wiki-research-l] Re: Comparison of Wikipedia with Brittannica, Posting on the Wiki-research-l mailing list (2005) (December 16th, 2005), See also http://mail.wikipedia. org/pipermail/wiki-research-l/2005-December/000105.html

Wikipedia. http://www.wikipedia.org/

YouTube. http://www.youtube.com/

All screenshots of web pages were taken on May 6th and 7th, from the URLs shown in the respective images (2006)

Part I

Internet Technology

Design, Implementation and Testing of Mobile Agent Protection Mechanism for Manets

Khaled E.A. Negm

ISS-ME, 59 Iran Street, Dokki, Giza 12311, Egypt
`knegm@iss.net`

Abstract. In the current research, we present an operation framework and protection mechanism to facilitate secure environment to protect mobile agents against tampering. The system depends on the presence of an authentication authority. The advantage of the proposed system is that security measures is an integral part of the design, thus common security retrofitting problems do not arise. This is due to the presence of AlGamal encryption mechanism to protect its confidential content and any collected data by the agent from the visited host. So that eavesdropping on information from the agent is no longer possible to reveal any confidential information. Also the inherent security constraints within the framework allow the system to operate as an intrusion detection system for any mobile agent environment. The mechanism is tested for most of the well known severe attacks against agents and networked systems. The scheme proved a promising performance that makes it very recommended for the types of transactions that needs highly secure environments, e. g., business to business, stock market updates, and any real time data synchronization.

Keywords: Secure Mobile Transactions, Mobile Agent Protection, Business to Business Secure Transaction.

1 Introduction

In a broad sense, a software agent is any program that acts on the behalf of a user, just as different types of agents (e.g., travel agent and insurance agents) that represent other people in day-to-day transactions in real world. Applications can inject mobile agents into a network, allowing them to roam the network on either a predetermined path, or agents themselves determine their paths based on dynamically gathered information. Having accomplished their goals, the agents return to their "hosts" in order to report their results to the user.

However; the mobile agent paradigm also adds significant problems in the area of security and robustness. Malicious agents are similar to viruses and trojans, they can expose hosts, they visit, to the risk of system penetration. While in transient, the agent's state becomes vulnerable to attacks in different ways. An agent is likely to carry-as part of its state-sensitive information about the user identity, e.g., credit

J. Filipe, J. Cordeiro, and V. Pedrosa (Eds.): WEBIST 2005/2006, LNBIP 1, pp. 41–52, 2007.

card information, personal confidential preferences, or any other form of electronic credentials. Such data must not be reveled to any unauthorized hosts or modified by unauthorized users. Unless some countermeasures are taken, such agents can potentially leak or destroy sensitive data and disrupt the normal functioning of the host.

In the current research we present a protection scheme for the mobile agents that incorporate standard cryptographic mechanisms into the agent transfer protocol functions. The use of the one-way-hashing and digital signatures is two fold; *first* detect active, passive and tampering attacks, and *second* to establish the identity of the servers participating in the anti-tampering program (ATP) (Vincenzetti 1993 and Sielken 1999). Also encryption is used to prevent passive attacks on the agent's state while it is in transient (Roth 2000 and Gary 1998).

2 Mobile Agent Security Analysis

Mobility allows an agent to move among hosts seeking computational environment in which an agent can operate. The host from which an agent originates is referred to as the home host that normally is the most trusted environment for an agent (Fuggetta 1998, FIPA 1998, and OMG-TC 1997).

In the mobile agent environment, security problem stems from the inability to effectively extend the trusted environment of an agent's home host to other hosts. The user may digitally sign an agent on its home host before it moves onto a second platform, but this resembles a limited protection. The next host receiving the agent can rely on this signature to verify the source and integrity of the agent's code, data, and state information provided that the private key of the user has not been compromised. For some applications, such minimal protection may be adequate through which agents do not accumulate state. For other applications, these simple schemes may prove inadequate. For example; the Jumping Beans agent system addresses some security issues by implementing a client- server architecture, whereby an agent always returns to a secure central host first before moving to any other platform (Ad Astra 1998, Negm 2003, and Negm 2004).

Some other category of attacks on the agent involves tampering by its executing visited hosts. As such, if that server is corrupted or becomes malicious, the agent's state is vulnerable to modification (Farmer 1996). Although a lot of research has been done in this area, one of the remaining problems is the presence of a nontrusted malicious host that attacks mobile agents, for example; a travel agency's agent system might modify the best offer the agent has collected, so that its own offer appears to be the cheapest one. Also, the travel agency might change the list of travel agencies that the agent is going to visit to increase its chances to propose a better offer and/or get the prices of other travel agencies before making its offer to the agent. All of these attacks involve eavesdropping and tampering and yet all the published schemes represent a simple mechanism of protection that can not guarantee secure transactions for the agents.

3   Protection Mechanism and Its Implementation

Several In the current research we implement a mechanism by which tampering of sensitive parts of the state can be detected, stopped, and reported to the Master Agent (MA). The framework is composed of different modules.

First the initialization module, this module includes two coordinating entities MA and Slave Agents (SAs). The user resides on its own platform and/or on a server to create the MA acquiring only that MA must exclusively reside on a secure trusted host. Then the MA creates SAs on another host (or the same MA host) in which being created on a secure host is not a must. Next MA defines tasks and subtasks to the SAs to achieve based on the user preferences. Then the SAs move from host to host to finish the tasks (and/or subtasks) given from the MA (that includes a central knowledge-base and a central management components.).

Table 1. MA pseudo code

```
Public class MA extends Agent {
   private ConstarintManager cm;
   private Vector Tasks;
private vector sentSAIds;
   protected void doTask() {
   do {
     getCurrentHost().transfer(this object)
     splitTasks();
     waitForResults();
     mergeResults();
     } while (!supertask.finished());
     sendResultsMAHome();
   }
   private void splitTask() {
     // 1. apply strategy to divide the task
     // 2. refine constraints for the subtasks
     for (int i=0; i < tasks.size();++){
     SA = new SA (subtask, constraints);
     sentWorkIds.add(w.getId());
     w.doTask();
     }
   }
}
```

The *second* module is the Constraints Module that contains conditions and rules for each agent to follow. This module presents the first line of defense in which the characteristic details and operational parameters of the visited host are listed. The *third* Module is the Encryption Module, presenting the second line of defense to afford the security for the agents' states. The encryption module contains two parts. The *startup* part, allows the user to declare which part of the agent as a read-only in which any tampering with the read-only objects can be detected. The *second* part is a secure storage container, that allows the agent to create an append-only container by which the agent can check in data (when executed) and store it in the container, so no one can delete or modify it without detection.

3.1   The Initialization Module

The concept of MA-SA was first introduced by Buschmann in 1996 to support fault tolerance, parallel computation and computational accuracy (Buschmann 1996). Also Lange demonstrated in 1997 that it is also applicable to support tasks at remote destinations and extended it to fit mobile agents (White 1997). The MA-SA concept is interacting as follows: the MA creates SAs, then the master delegates the subtasks to the SAs, and finally after the slaves have returned the results, the master combines the results. The master can assign more than one task at a time and the slaves can execute them concurrently. A major benefit of this abstraction is the exchangeability and the extensibility in which decoupling the SA from the MA and creating an abstract slave class allows to exchange the slaves' implementation without changes in the master's code.

Depending on the MA-SA concept, we built up a system to facilitate a solution to the mobile agent security problem. To achieve this, confidential data is contained in a secure place that is the MA host (or heavily protected if carried by the SAs). Then the SA must carry essential data to fulfill the task assigned by the MA (Tripathi 1999).

Tables 1 and 2 present the two listings of the pseudo code implementation of MA and SA. First, the doTask() method is called so the MA moves to the first host where it uses its strategies to split the tasks into subtasks. Then the MA assigns subtasks to the SAs. Afterwards it waits for the results which will be returned by the SAs.

Table 2. SA pseudo code

```
Public class SA extends Agent {
   private ConstarintManager;
   private Vector Tasks;
   SA (Task t){task=t; }
   protected void doTask() {
     do {
   task.execute();
   addResult(task.getResults());
   getCurrentHost().transfer(this object)
   } while (!task.finished());
 }

    private void addResult(Results=r){
       if (cm.checkConstarints(task,r))
         sendResulstToMA;
     }
 }
```

3.2 The Constraint Module

After starting the initialization module, the constraints module starts running in a supervisory parallel fashion during the transactions. The constraints module is composed of three parts:

a. *Routing Constraints*: which define variables for the agent's itinerary that lists hosts, operating systems' type and version number including hopes for travelling. This type has to be checked every time before an agent moves to another location.
b. *Execution Constraints*: which define requirements on the SA visited system's environment which contain a limitation list of hardware (the amount of memory storage) or software (for example a specific version of the database-access software or an LDAP-service) requirements.
c. *Merging Constraints*: which define the relations between subtasks that are generated by the strategies. In contrast to the other constraints, merging constraints are stored exclusively by the MA.

3.3 The Cryptography Module

The cryptography module provides a secure container for any credentials that the agent might carry and acts as an intrusion detection system to discover tampering. This protection mechanism contains two parts:

a. The read only-state: in which it function to assign part of the "agent's object" as read-only sub-object in which its credentials could not be modified by anyone, and thus are read-only during its travels. To protect such read-only state we have to declare the associated objects as constants and incorporate a cryptographic mechanism to protect these constants.

In Table 3 we list the pseudo code of this object. It contains a vector of objects of arbitrary type, along with the agent owner's digital signature on these objects. The digital signature is computed by first using a one-way hash function to digest the vector of objects down to a single 128-bit value, and then encrypt it using the private key of the agent's owner. The Digital Signature Algorithm (DSA) is used for this purpose (Bellare, M.1997).

$$sign = K_A^- \big(h(objs)\big)$$

The `verify` method of the `ReadOnlyContainer` object allows any host on the SA's path to check whether the read-only state has been tampered via contacting the certifying authority to honor the user's signature (while it needs an access to the agent's public key.) It uses the public key to decrypt the signature, and compares the result with a recomputed one-way hash of the vector of objects. If these values match, the visited host can assume that none of the objects has been modified since the signature was computed. Thus, the condition it checks are:

$$h(objs) = K_A^+ (sign)$$

The read-only container mechanism is limited in utility to those parts of the state that remain constant throughout the agent's travels. But in real life, SAs collect data from

Table 3. The ReadOnlyContainer pseudo code

```
class ReadOnlyContainer {
  Vector objs; // the read-only objects being carried along
  byte[] sign; // owner's signature on the above vector
  // Constructor
  ReadOnlyContainer(Vector o, PrivateKey k) {
    objs = o;
    sign = DSA-Signature (hash(objs), k);
  }
  public boolean verify(PublicKey k) {
    // Verify the agent owner's signature on the objects
    // using the owner's public key
  }
}
```

Table 4. The AppendOnlyContainer

```
class AppendOnlyContainer -{
  Vector objs; // the objects to be protected
  Vector signs; // corresponding signatures
  Vector signers; // corresponding signers' URNs
  byte[] checkSum; // a checksum to detect tampering
  // Constructor
  AppendOnlyContainer(PublicKey k, int nonce) {
    objs = new Vector(); // initially empty
    signs = new Vector(); // initially empty
    signers = new Vector(); // initially empty
    checkSum = encrypt (nonce); // with ElGamal key k
  }
  public void checkIn (Object X) {
    // Ask the current server to sign this object
    sig = host.sign (X);
    // Next, update the vectors
    objs.addElement (X);
    signs.addElement (sig);
    signers.addElement (current server);
    // Finally, update the checksum as follows
    checkSum = encrypt (checkSum + sig + current server);
  }
  public boolean verify (PrivateKey k, int nonce) {
    loop {
      checkSum = decrypt (checkSum); // using private key k
      // Now chop off the ''sig'' and server's URN at its end.
      // These should match the last elements of the signs and
      // signers vectors. Verify this signature.
    } until what ever is left is the initial nonce;
  }
}
```

the hosts it visits and need to prevent any subsequent modification of the data. This could be termed as write-once data.

b. Append-only logs: This object guarantees that the stored entries within it can not be deleted, modified or read by an unauthorized user. When data object needs to be nonmodifiable for the remainder of the agent's journey, it can be inserted into this append only log and to provide secrecy, the data is then encrypted with the MA's public key before it is stored in the log file. We used this module to preserve the results that the SA's had gathered. The pseudo code of this object is shown in Table 4.

The `AppendOnlyContainer` object contains vector of objects to be protect, along with their corresponding digital signatures and the identities of the signers (in case of MA only). It also contains a `checkSum` array to detect tampering. When an SA is created, its `AppendOnlyContainer` is empty. The checksum is initialized by encrypting a nonce with the agent's public key

$$checkSum = K_A^+(N_a)$$

This nonce N_a is not known to any host other than the MA's host, and must be kept secret. Therefore, it is not carried by the SA. The encryption is performed using the ElGamal cryptosystem (ElGamal 1984). At any stage during the SAs travel, the agent can use the `checkIn` method to insert an object X (of any type) into an `AppendOnlyContainer`. For example, after collecting a quotation from a travel agent, it can check the in-value, in order to protect it from any further modification. The `checkIn` procedure requests the current server "C" to sign the object using its own private key. The object, its signature and the identity of the signer are inserted into the corresponding vectors in the `AppendOnlyContainer`. Then, the checksum is updated as follows

$$checkSum = K_A^+(checkSum + Sig_C(X) + C)_.$$

First, the signature and the signer's identity is concatenated to the current value of the checksum. This byte array is then encrypted further using the MA's `ElGamal` public key, rendering it to be unreadable by anyone other than the agent's owner. Then, the encrypted version of the object would be carried along and protected from tampering. When the agent returns, the user can use the verify method to ensure that the `AppendOnlyContainer` has not been tampered. As shown in Table 4, the verify process works backwards, unrolling the nested encryptions of the checksum, and verifying the signature corresponding to each item in the protected state. In each iteration of this loop, the following decryption is performed

$$K_A^-(checkSum) \Rightarrow checkSum + Sig_S(X) + S_,$$

where S is the server in the current position of the `objs` vector. The verify procedure then ensures that

$$K_S^+(Sig_S(X)) == h(X)_.$$

If any mismatches are found, the agent's owner knows that the corresponding object has been tampered and then it can discard the value. The objects extracted up to this point can still be relied upon to be valid, but other objects whose signatures are nested deeper within the checksum can not be used. When the unrolling is complete, we are left with the random nonce that was used in the initialization of the checksum. This number is compared with the original random number N_a. If it does not match, a security exception can be thrown.

4 Testing

The basic goal of the testing is to monitor the system behavior against malicious attacks and measure the network utilization for different operational scenarios. We executed the most common well know attacks for agents, systems, and networks against the proposed system and collected the results to study the feasibility (CVE 2005). Five traffic generators are installed and distributed among its testing network to simulate the real world environment. Additional normal www traffic is generated while activating and running the system to introduce the normal competitive packet dynamics and latencies within the queuing buffers in each router (TG 2004), see Figure 1.

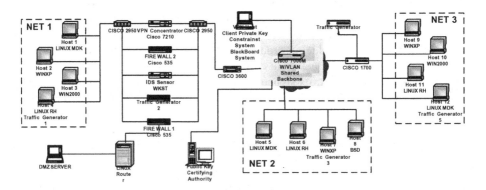

Fig. 1. The testing network

The major role of the utilization testing is to evaluate the network resources usage while implementing the framework. Also we performed functionality testing of the framework in which *"Parallelizing"* scheme enables concurrent task execution. In every testing scenario, there is a list of hosts for the SAs to visit according to their respective predefined strategy.

4.1 Validity and Parallelizing Test

In this scenario, the client operates from the VPN host at which he creates the MA Then the MA creates three ASs on the DMZ host from which they start travelling to their designated hosts according to the predefined constraints.

Each SA queries its target host via the dedicated port for such a process. Then each SA will activate a security query to the CVE host requesting security clearance to communicate to the dedicated target hosts. On receiving the clearance it will proceed to collect and/or communicate to the target host. In case of successful transaction, the collected information is returned to MA. Then the MA prepares the final report and pass it to the user. Note that this is not a fully guaranteed security check, but it helps in some ways to eliminate some security risks especially for home users.

Table 5. Testing Scenario Parameters

Scenario	Client	Master (I/O)	Slave Host: ports	Target Hosts
1	VPN host	VPN host: (4444/3333)	DMZ host: 3062 DMZ host: 3063 DMZ host: 3064	H1: 3155 H5: 3150 H10: 2774
2	VPN host	DMZ host (44444/60000)	H4: 3009 H11: 3010 H12: 3011	NET1 NET2 NET3

Table 6. Validity and Parallelizing Test Parameters

packets	Bytes	Source Ports	Destination Ports
20	3000	Any	3150
40	7050	Any	3155
14	2683	Any	2774
56	6388	Any	All the remaining
138	19121	All traffic	All traffic

In here two of the SAs are targeting hosts 5 and 10 will stop execution due to the fact that the dedicated ports of communication assigned by these host match malicious attacks (according to the CVEs) on the SA itself, namely the deep throat, the Foreplay and the Mini BackLash attacks on port 3150 and the subseven, and subseven 2.1 Gold on port 2774, see Tables 5 and 6. This is achieved through the confirmation channel between the SAs and the MA to approve communication via the designated port by the visited host. The MA confirms communication after checking the CVEs list.

4.2 DDoS Attack Test

In this scenario a malicious software is activated at Host 1 acting against the three networks in which host 6 and 9 are trojaned to be malicious to deny any execution to all arriving agents. In general the MA creates five the SAs at Host 5. Then each one moves to all hosts to collect the desired information. During this test, the MA enforces a new constraint that concerns retries in denial-of-service attacks as:

```
* if repeatedCreation() < 3 then begin true end
else alarm_user(); false end.
```

The method `repeatedCreation()` returns the number of already done retries to create a SA for a certain task. So for example if one of the SA failes and the MA creates another one, then the return value of this method would be one. The constrains for the SAs are the same as in the previous scenario:

```
* if placename == "Host 2→12" then begin true end.
* if ostype == "LINUX MDK or RH" then begin true end.
```

In here the system information is not collected from hosts in NET1 because it suffers from DDoS and host 11 because it does not have the correct name and the last one because it is not the desired Linux machine. But the encryption module will detect this behavior, file it, and report it back to the user via the blackboard system.

The DDoS will not propagate from NET1 to the other networks because of the network intrusion detection systems (NIDS) and host based intrusion detection systems (HIDS) installed to filter out any traffic back and forth. The SA that moves to host 1 do not return any status report or result within the given deadline so the MA retried to send it several time. After retrying it twice the MA's constraint number one returns false. Thus, the MA stops trying to send an agent to these hosts and returns a special report to the user.

This shows that a malicious host can not trap or stop the overall process by a denial of service attack. When the SA does not return within a given deadline the MA could start another one or redefine the subtasks and then start a new one.

5   Summary and Conclusion

Mobile agents differ from other techniques in regard to security issues and security mechanisms, whose requirements are not met by classical security systems. Concerning security in traditional operating systems, the system is always trusted. This is not true for mobile agents, here the visited operating system can be the untrusted one and the agent is the trusted one. The problem arising is that the users have no chance to check the functionality of the operating system.

To eliminate some of the security risks we incorporate a sophisticated mechanism to be built in within the mobile agent design by which none would be able to retrofit into the application. This aim is fully accomplished. The framework limits the risks of leakage and tampering as the data stored in the Master Agent will never be accessible to potential malicious hosts, since it will only reside on trusted hosts. In addition to implementing the MA-SA system in an enhanced way to facilitate full optimizad operation and protection to the agent system.

Besides the main intent to make mobile agent technology more secure the Master Agent-Slave Agent Framework provides additional benefits and boosts some of the mobile agent's advantages due to its design and structure (e.g. flexibility, simplicity, separation of concerns, etc.). Its separation of code focusing on coordination and code focusing on computation make the pattern an ideal basis for the framework. This design allows easy integration of this framework in applications and eases porting to other mobile agent systems.

The framework consists of a coordinating entity (the MA) and several independent entities (the SAs). The MA holds all the current knowledge found by the Slave Agents and uses this knowledge to accomplish its task. The key difference to the client-server paradigm is that the MA component is mobile as well. So it can move to a host near the area its SAs scenarios will operate in. The only prerequisite is that the MA must exclusively visit secure trusted places. In the worst case this is the host where it has been initialized. We have demonstrated that this framework solves special aspects of mobile agent security, in addition to that eavesdropping information and tampering the agent is no longer possible or does not reveal any confidential information.

Every time the agent departs a host, its server inserts a log entry into the AppendOnlyContainer. This entry includes the current server's name, the name of the server from which the agent arrived, and the name of its intended destination. This travel log can be used by the agent's owner when the agent returns, to verify that it followed the itinerary prescribed when it was dispatched.

If the agent's itinerary is known in advance of its dispatch, we can insert a copy of the itinerary into the agent's ReadOnlyContainer. Thus, each host visited by the agent has access to the original itinerary, as intended by the agent's creator. The receiving host can check the current itinerary to ensure that the agent is following the specified path, and that the method to be executed is as specified originally.

This ensures that any tampering with the method's parameters by any host on the agent's path can be detected, before the agent is allowed to execute. In addition, an audit trail of the agent's migration path can be maintained using an instance of the AppendOnlyContainer class. One limitation of AppendOnlyContainer scheme is that the verification process requires the agent's private key, and can thus only be done by the agent's host.

6 Future Work

Currently we are working on enhancing the IDS feature of the system by adding a backboard system to the encryption module. But in this case we have to implement a rigorous reporting mechanism from the slave agents to the master agent.

Acknowledgements

The author would like to thank Cisco systems in Dubai, UAE to support this research by the needed Cisco equipments. Also the author would like to acknowledge the Etisalat Academy in Dubai to facilitate the premises to run this research.

References

Bellare, M., et al.: Pseudo-Random Number Generation with Cryptographic Algorithms: the DSS Case. In: Kaliski Jr., B.S. (ed.) CRYPTO 1997. LNCS, vol. 1294, pp. 1–12. Springer, Heidelberg (1997)

Buschmann, F., et al.: Pattern-Oriented Software Architecture: A System of Patterns, John Wiley, UK (1996)

CVE: Common Vulnerability Exposure (2005), http://cve.mitre.org/

ElGamal, T.: A public Key Cryptosystem and a Signature Scheme Based on Discrete Logarithms, Proc. of Crypto '84, LNCS 196. In: Blakely, G.R., Chaum, D. (eds.) CRYPTO 1984. LNCS, vol. 196, pp. 10–18. Springer, Heidelberg (1985)

Farmer, W., et al.: Security for Mobile Agents: Issues and Requirements. In: Proc. of the 19th International Information Systems Security Conference, pp. 591–597 (1996)

FIPA (1998): Agent Management, Specification, part 1, ver. 2.0, Foundation for Intelligent Physical Agents (1998)

Fuggetta, G., Vigna, G.: Understanding Code Mobility. IEEE Transactions on Software Engineering 24, 342–361 (1998)

Gray, R.: D'Agents: Security in a Multiple Language, Mobile-Agent System, in Mobile Agents and Security. In: Vigna, G. (ed.) Mobile Agents and Security. LNCS, vol. 1419, pp. 154–187. Springer, Heidelberg (1998)

Negm, K.A.E.: Implementation of Secure Mobile Agent for Ad-Hoc Networks. WEAS Transactions on Communications 2, 519–526 (2003)

Negm, K.A.E., Adi, W.: Secure Mobile Code Computing in Distributed Remote Environment. In: Negm, K.A.E. (ed.) Proc. 2004 IEEE International Conference on Networking, Sensing and Control, pp. 270–275. IEEE Computer Society Press, Los Alamitos (2004)

OMG-TC: Mobile Agent System Interoperability Facilities Specification, OMG-TC-orbos/97 (1997)

Roth, V.: Scalable and Secure Global Name Services for Mobile Agents. In: Bertino, E. (ed.) ECOOP 2000. LNCS, vol. 1850, Springer, Heidelberg (2000)

Sielken, R.: Application Intrusion Detection, Univ. of Virginia Computer Science Technical Report CS-99-17 (1999)

TG: Traffic Generator (2004), http://www.postel.org/services.html

Tripathi, A., et al.: Mobile Agent Programming in Ajanta. In: Karnik, N., Vora, N., Ahmed, T., Singh, R. Proc. of 19th IEEE International Conference on Distributed Computing Systems, pp. 190–197. IEEE Computer Society Press, Los Alamitos (1999)

Vincenzetti, D., Cotrozzi, M.: ATP anti tampering program. In: DeHart, E. (ed.) Proc. of Security IV Conf.-USENIX Assoc, pp. 79–90 (1993)

White, J.: Mobile Agents. In: Bradshow, J. (ed.) Software Agents, pp. 437–472. MIT Press, Cambridge (1997)

An Automatic Generation Method of Differential XSLT Stylesheet from Two XML Documents

Takeshi Kato, Hidetoshi Ueno, and Norihiro Ishikawa

Network Management Development Department, NTT DoCoMo, Inc., 3-5 Hikarino-oka,
Yokosuka, Kanagawa, Japan
katoutke@nttdocomo.co.jp, uenohi@nttdocomo.co.jp,
ishikawanor@nttdocomo.co.jp

Abstract. We propose a differential XSLT stylesheet generation method for arbitrary pairs of XML contents. It is possible to obtain the revised XML document by supplying the XSLT stylesheet with the differential data to the original XML document. Comparing with sending whole revised XML document, the original XML document can be updated by sending less information, the differential data. This paper introduces a difference detection algorithm based on the DOM tree and a difference representation method that permits the expression of difference information. We also discuss a new XSLT function for the proposed method. We also introduce prototype software implemented based on proposed method and evaluation result that shows the effectiveness of our method. An experiment shows that the proposed method is suitable for updating XML contents, especially for web service in the costly mobile network.

Keywords: XML, DOM, XSLT, Differential Data.

1 Introduction

XML (eXtensible Markup Language)(Bray, 2000) is an extensible meta-language that is being widely applied in description languages such as XHTML (eXtensible HyperText Markup Language), SVG (Scalable Vector Graphic) and CC/PP (Composite Capability / Preference Profiles) as well as communication protocols such as SOAP (Simple Object Access Protocol). Unfortunately, XML content is generally large compared to CSV (Comma Separated Value) and TLV (Tag-Length-Value) content because XML uses element tags, attributes, and XML declarations. In mobile web services, XHTML(Baker, 2000) mobile profile has become the standard markup language for mobile phones. Retransmitting the whole content wastes bandwidth and time, especially in the wireless network. It is becoming more and more important to promote efficiency in the update process and version control of XML data. An effective idea is updating content locally by using difference data because the difference between the old content and the updated content tends to be small. Mogul et al (1997) confirmed the benefit of transmitting just the difference data, for example HTTP Delta-encoding(Mogul, 2002). If the differential data of two XML documents is generated and transmitted instead of the whole document, the amount of

J. Filipe, J. Cordeiro, and V. Pedrosa (Eds.): WEBIST 2005/2006, LNBIP 1, pp. 53–68, 2007.

transmitted data can be greatly reduced. When a client receives the differential data, it regenerates the new content, by applying the differential content to the original content.

To realize the above scenario, we propose a technique for the automatic generation method of a differential XSLT stylesheet from two arbitrary XML documents and show the availability of description of difference data using a differential XSLT stylesheet. This technique can also be provided to web services such as push information delivery service, weblog service and so on, in which content need to be frequently and partially updated. The proposed technique can promote efficiency in the update process and version control of them.

In this paper, section 2 describes overview of the proposed method. In section 3, the prototype software and the results of experiments are mentioned. Section 4 proposes some extensions to XSLT for the proposed method and related works are addressed in Section 5. We conclude this paper in Section 6.

2 Process of Differential XSLT Stylesheet Generation

The proposed method uses XSLT (eXtensible Stylesheet Language Transformations) (Clark, 2000) for updating XML document. XSLT is a language that provides the function of data structure transformation for XML documents. We adopted the Document Object Model (DOM) (Le Hors, 2000) to express the XML data structure. An original and updated XML documents are parsed and converted into two DOM trees. We generate differential XSLT stylesheets in three steps because it is difficult to perfectly extract differential data in one operation. The proposed method is shown in Fig. 1.

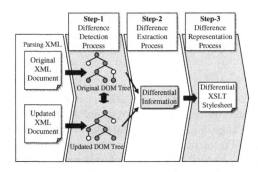

Fig. 1. Generation Process of Differential XSLT Stylesheet

Step-1. Difference Detection Process
The differences between the two DOM trees are detected. In this process, common parts and differential parts are identified.

Step-2. Difference Extraction Process
We define added nodes, deleted nodes and change nodes as differential data. In this process, added nodes, deleted nodes and change nodes are classified as described later.

Step-3. Difference Representation Process
Differential data is mapped to XSLT templates and a differential XSLT stylesheet is generated from them.

The following subsections describe these processes in detail.

2.1 Difference Detection Process

In the first step, accordant, appearing and disappearing nodes are detected. We propose a new detection algorithm that changes the DOM tree structures, maximizes the accordant tree and regards the remaining nodes as differential nodes. The assumptions of the algorithm are as follows.

i)   A virtual node is assumed at the head of an actual root node and regarded as a temporary root node. It is treated as a common node. (Fig. 2)
ii)   The goal is to maximize the number of common nodes.
iii)   The term "common" means that the nodes have the same element names, same attribute names, and same attribute values.

Fig. 2. Structure of XML Document

Note that it is not necessary to compare an element node, an attribute node and a text node if they are treated as DOM nodes. Nodes are compared type-by-type for efficiency.

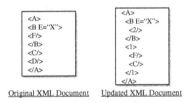

Original XML Document   Updated XML Document

Fig. 3. Example of original and updated XML Document

The proposed difference detection method is described below with reference to Fig. 4 using the XML document in Fig. 3.

(a)   Finding maximum number of common nodes (Fig. 4(a))
The method compares the components of the DOM trees to find the maximum number of common nodes.
(b)   Creating combination of nodes and comparing DOM tree structures (Fig. 4(b))
Combinations are compared in decreasing order of the number of nodes.
(c)   Detecting accordant nodes, appearing nodes and disappearing nodes (Fig. 4(c))

The node-set in the DOM tree that has the maximum number of accordant nodes, are regarded as determinate accordant node-set. Other nodes in the DOM trees than determinate accordant node-set are taken to be the determinate differential nodes, which are then classified into two types, appearing nodes and disappearing node. Appearing nodes are the determinate differential nodes in the original DOM tree. Disappearing nodes are the determinate differential nodes in the updated DOM tree. The information of each node is arranged into three tables. In the accordant node table, "Reference position" column indicates the position of each accordant node. "Original position" column means the position of the accordant node in the original DOM tree and "Updated position" column similarly indicates the position in the updated DOM tree. In the appearing node table, "appearance position" column indicates the position in the updated DOM tree. "Absolute position" column means the relative position of correspondent node in the accordant DOM tree. In the disappearing node table, "disappearance position" column indicates the position in the original DOM tree. "Absolute position" column similarly means the relative position of correspondent node in accordant DOM tree. In each table, other nodes than accordant nodes are represented using *node[n]* in which *n* is a position in the same siblings in the updated DOM tree. A leftmost node is expressed as *node[1]*. Attribute nodes are expressed as @ + *attribute name*.

The purpose of this process is to detect the maximum number of accordant nodes and the remaining differential nodes.

2.2 Difference Extraction Process

In this step, detailed differential data is extracted from the tables created in the previous step. The proposed method classifies appearing and disappearing nodes into three kinds of nodes.

i) Change node
Comparing an appearing node table and a disappearing node table, two nodes that have the same absolute position and the same type are regarded as change nodes. In Fig. 4, node "2" in the appearing node table and node "F" in the disappearing node table are change nodes.

ii) Added node
Other nodes than change nodes in an appearing node table are regarded as added nodes. In Fig. 4, node "1" and node "F" in the appearing node table are added nodes.

iii) Deleted node
Other nodes than change nodes in a disappearing node table are regarded as deleted nodes. In Fig. 4, node "D" in the disappearing node table is a deleted node.

Fig. 5 shows a table of differential nodes created from the XML documents in Fig. 3.

2.3 Difference Representation Process

In this step, differential data generated in the previous step are mapped to XSLT templates from which a differential XSLT stylesheet is generated. The proposed difference representation method consists of the following sequences.

(a) Determining a transformation position as a pattern of XSLT template rule

A XML data structure transformation is described specifying the following two items.

- Which position of XML data is transformed? (Determining a transformation position as a pattern of XSLT template rule)

- How is the corresponding part of XML data transformed? (Transformational description)

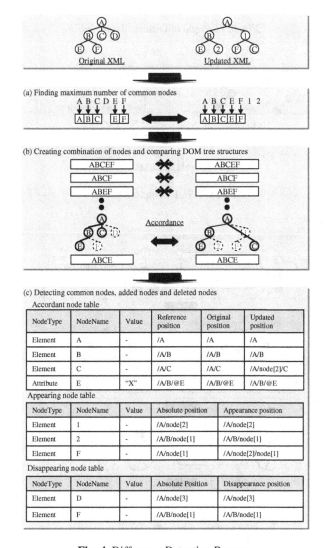

Fig. 4. Difference Detection Process

These items constitute a template rule and are represented as *xsl:temlate* element in the XSLT stylesheet. (Fig. 6) In a template rule, a pattern is an XPath(Clark, 1999) expression of the position of a node in an original DOM tree. We must specify

Reference Position	Node Type	Classification of difference	Additional Data		
			Node Type	Node Name	Node Value
/A/B/*[1]	Element	Change	Element	2	-
/A/*[2]	Element	Addition	Element	1	-
/A/*[2]/*[1]	Element	Addition	Element	F	-
/A/*[3]	Element	Deletion	-	-	-

Fig. 5. Example of Differential nodes

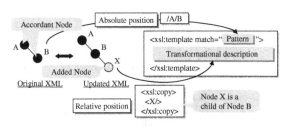

Fig. 6. XSLT Template rule

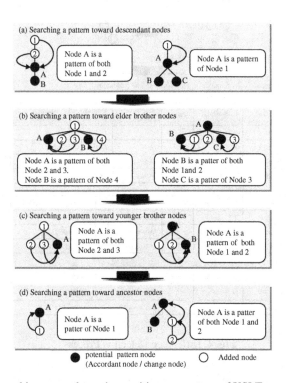

Fig. 7. Searching a transformation position as a pattern of XSLT template rule

transformation position as a pattern in a template rule. The position of an added node in an updated DOM tree is separated into a reference position and relative position and the reference position is specified as a pattern in a template rule.

In the proposed method, a pattern of a template rule is determined by tracing an updated DOM tree from top to bottom (from a parent to a child), and from left to right (from an elder brother to a younger brother) As a result, templates are generated in a tree structure that branch toward the descendant direction. Additionally, the positions of change and accordance nodes can be used as a pattern of a template rule because their own position can be specified in an original DOM tree. The method used to determine a pattern of a template rule is described with reference to Fig. 8. For change nodes and accordance nodes, their own positions are patterns. In case of added nodes, patterns are determined according to following sequences.

i)   Searching a pattern toward descendant nodes (Fig.7 (a))
A change node or an accordance node is searched for starting from the corresponding node and moving toward descendant nodes. The position of the nearest descendant appropriate node is regarded as a pattern. If there is no appropriate node, there are multiple appropriate nodes, or there is a branch in the tree, the next procedure is applied.

ii)   Searching a pattern toward elder brother nodes (Fig. 7(b)
A change node or an accordance node is searched starting from the corresponding node and moving toward elder brother nodes. The position of the nearest elder brother appropriate node is regarded as a pattern. If there is no appropriate node, the next procedure is applied.

iii)   Searching a pattern toward younger brother nodes (Fig. 7(c))
A change node or an accordance node is searched starting from the corresponding node toward younger brother nodes. The position of the nearest younger brother appropriate node is regarded as a pattern. If there is no appropriate node, the next procedure is applied.

iv)   Searching a pattern toward ancestor nodes (Fig. 7(d))
A change node or an accordance node is searched from the corresponding node toward ancestor nodes. The position of the nearest ancestor appropriate node is regarded as a pattern. If there is no appropriate node, the pattern of a parent node is taken as that of the corresponding node.

The reason why the search pattern direction begins with descendant nodes and leaves ancestor nodes to the last is that if a pattern search commences with ancestor nodes, a pattern is underspecified since XML has a tree structure.

The search process for deleted nodes starts with ancestor nodes. As shown in Fig. 8, if all descendant nodes are deleted nodes, the position of the top node is regarded as the pattern of these nodes and all deleted nodes can be deleted using the same template. Therefore, the position of the farthest ancestor node which has only deleted nodes is regarded as the pattern. If there is no appropriate node, the position of the corresponding node is regarded as the pattern.

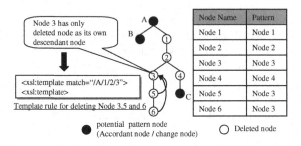

Fig. 8. Searching pattern of deletion node

The search for attribute nodes also starts toward ancestor nodes, because attribute nodes basically have only parent nodes.

(b) Generating mapping information

Differential data is organized according to the patterns identified in the previous step. The differential nodes are classified according to pattern because differential nodes that have the same pattern can be described using the same XSLT template. Fig. 9 shows the differential data for the XML documents in Fig. 3.

Pattern of template rule

Absolute position	Node Type	Difference	Transformation
/A	Element	Accordance	No
/A/B	Element	Accordance	Yes
/A/C	Element	Accordance	Yes
/A/D	Element	Deletion	Yes
/A/E	Attribute	Accordance	No
/A/B/F	Element	Change	Yes

Pattern node table

Node Name	Difference	Pattern
/A/1	Addition	/A/B
/A/B/2	Change	/A/B/F
/A/1/F	Addition	/A/C
/A/D	Deletion	/A/D

Transformational description of template rule

Absolute position	Relative position	Node Type	Difference	Addition Data		
				Node Type	Node Name	Node Value
/A/B	Parent	Element	Addition	Element	1	-
/A/C	Elder brother	Element	Addition	Element	F	-
/A/B/F	itself	Element	Change	Element	2	-
/A/D	itself	Element	Deletion	-	-	-

Fig. 9. Differential Information according to Patterns

(c) Mapping to XSLT template

Differential data is mapped to an XSLT template according to node type and classification of difference.

i) Mapping to XSLT template for accordant, changed and deleted nodes

Nodes that have the same pattern are collectively described by the same XSLT template. As shown in Appendix A at the end of this paper, each node is mapped to one XSLT template.

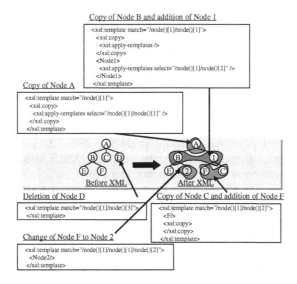

Fig. 10. Example of XSLT Templates

ii) Mapping to XSLT template for added nodes

Nodes that have the same pattern are collectively described by the same XSLT template. The added node is described as Appendix B. If a node regarded as a pattern has a descendant template, *xsl:apply-template* element is added in correspond template. If a node which share the same pattern are described by the same template. If there are multiple descendant templates of the correspond added node, multiple *xsl:apply-template* elements are used as shown in Appendix C.

Fig. 10 shows XSLT templates for the XML documents in Fig. 3.

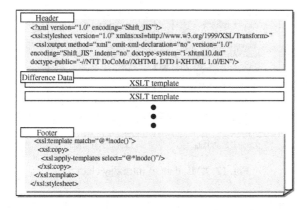

Fig. 11. Differential XSLT Stylesheet

(**d**) Generating a differential XSLT stylesheet

A Differential XSLT stylesheet is generated from XSLT templates as shown in Fig. 11. The header part includes a XML declaration and various XSLT parameters. The footer part includes a template to copy those accordance nodes that are not regarded as transformation position (pattern node).

3 Experiments

We have implemented prototype software in Java (J2SE 1.3.1).We used Apache Xalan-Java 2.4.0 (XSLT Engine) to verify the generated XSLT stylesheets and IBM XML Parser for Java to parse XML documents. Our prototype software has functions to generate differential XSLT stylesheets from arbitrary pairs of XML documents and verify them. Additionally, it provides a graphical viewer of the differential data of two XML documents and shows some values such as compression ratio, difference ratio and so on. We have examined the validity of our proposed method using this software.

3.1 Stock Price Information

We have investigated the relationship between compression ratio and difference ratio using the following stock price information. In Fig. 12, stock price is updated every minute; old price data are deleted and new price data are added. We changed XML data size and differential ratio and determined the resulting compression ratio.

The compression ratio is defined as the ratio of generated XSLT stylesheet to the before XML data. The difference ratio is defined rate of existence of unique nodes. (See formula (1) and (2)).

$$\text{Compression ratio} = \frac{\text{Size of Generated XSLT Stylesheet}}{\text{Size of updated XML data}} \times 100\,(\%) \qquad (1)$$

$$\text{Difference ratio} = \frac{\text{Number of discordance nodes}}{\text{Number of all nodes in updated XML document}} \times 100\,(\%) \qquad (2)$$

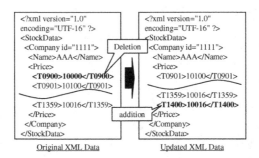

Fig. 12. XML data of intra-day chart

Fig. 13 shows the experimental result using stock price information. In our experiments, the size of a XML document was changed from 1Kbyte to 100Kbyte, the difference ratio was changed from about 4% to 50%. As shown in Fig. 13,

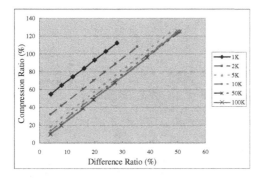

Fig. 13. Relationship between compression ratio and difference ratio using stock price information

compression ratio becomes high when the size of a XML document increases. This means that the overhead of the header and footer of the XSLT stylesheet can be decreased for a large XML document. Even a small XML document (i.e. 1Kbyte document) can be effectively compressed if the difference ratio is below 25%. Therefore, the proposed method is suitable even for a small XML document if it has only minor updates.

3.2 News Flash Content

Then we have investigated the relationship between actual compression ratio and difference ratio using the following news flash content. In Fig. 14, news flash is updated; an old item is deleted and a new item is added. We changed difference ratio and compared the compression ratio of a differential XSLT stylesheet (D-XSLT), a differential XSLT stylesheet compressed by gzip (D-XSLT+gzip), a Diff (GNU, 2002) file compressed by gzip (Diff+gzip) and an entirely updated content compressed using gzip (HTML+gzip).

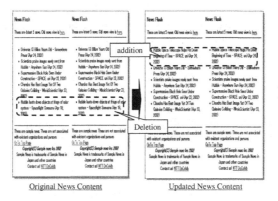

Fig. 14. News Flash Content

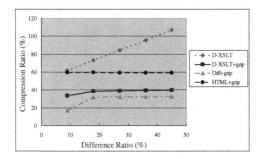

Fig. 15. Relationship between compression ratio and difference ratio using news flash content

Fig 15 shows the experimental result. The difference ratio is changed from about 10% to 45%. As shown in Fig. 15, a differential XSLT stylesheet complessed by gzip (D-XSLT+gzip) reduces about 63% of the size of entirely updated content compressed by gzip. Compared to Diff file compressed by gzip (Diff+gzip), the size of D-XSLT+gzip is about 38% larger. This result shows, although the proposed method is not optimised compared with Diff+gzip method, it realizes comparatively efficient compression.

4   Extension to XSLT Functions

XSLT is not optimized for generating differential XSLT stylesheets. We have considered new XSLT function for the proposed method as described below.

i)   Package copy of element and attribute nodes
In Fig. 16, node "e1" is entirely copied under the node "e3". However, XSLT can not copy any particular node. Thus the XSLT template repeats the same data of node "e1". The XSLT template must have the same data contained in the original XML document. This decreases the efficiency of compression.

ii)   Range copy
In Fig. 17, a sub-tree consists of the node "e1" and the node "e2", is copied under the node "e4". In XSLT, a sub-tree can be regarded as a node-set using *xsl:copy-of*

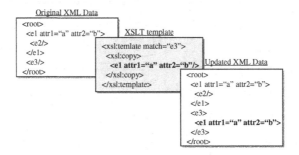

Fig. 16. Example 1 of XSLT Stylesheet

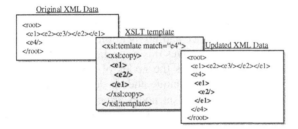

Fig. 17. Example 2 of XSLT Stylesheet

element. However a node-set must include all nodes under the root of a sub-tree. Thus a node-set cannot be used to designate some parts of a sub-tree. Some parts of a sub-tree can not be copied using *xsl:copy-of* element.

We propose a new XSLT function for *xsl:copy-of* element that designates nodes from the root of a sub-tree to the n-th generation descendants. If the proposed function is applied to above two examples, the resulting XSLT templates are generated as shown in Fig 18.

Introducing such a function can optimize the generation of a differential XSLT stylesheet.

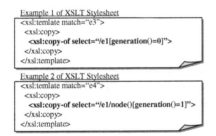

Fig. 18. Example of XSLT template using proposed function

5 Related Work

Compared to existing methods of differential data generation (La Fontaine, 2001)(Curbera, 1999), the proposed method has the advantage of easily adapting to expanded data as XML tree, and using existing XSLT engines. But there is a problem that mobile terminals have to deal with heavy process to expand XML navigation tree into memory. To lighten this process, XML processors for mobile terminals such as TinyTree(OSTG, 2004b) and DTM (Document Table Model)(Apache Project, 2004) have been developed. By expanding XML document as tree or array structure in the memory using these XML processors, it is more efficient to deal with difference data. In addition, the proposed method needs only XSLT engine, different from DUL (Delta Update Language) (OSTG 2004a) in which special language processing module is needed.

La Fontaine (2001) and Curbera (1999) described methods to generate difference data from arbitrary pairs of XML documents. These methods compare nodes of the original and the revised XML DOM trees from root to leaf. If a unique node is detected, all descendant nodes from that node are regarded as difference. They can not detect the most appropriate difference and no mention was made of this issue. On the other hand, the proposed method resolves this issue and so can extract the differences most effectively. It similarly compares the nodes of the original and revised XML DOM trees from root to leaf. When a unique node is detected, the corresponding node is regarded as difference if its descendant nodes are common. Therefore it is able to accurately detect the difference between original and revised XML documents.

6   Conclusion

We proposed an automatic method of generating differential XSLT stylesheets from arbitrary pairs of XML documents. The proposed method consists of difference detection, difference extraction and difference representation; we proposed algorithms for each process. We have implemented prototype software and showed it to be effective using special contents such as stock price and news flash. We also proposed new XSLT function.

In future work, we will investigate processing time to generate differential XSLT stylesheet and continue to work on improving the performance of our algorithm. Future work includes quantitatively evaluating the proposed method in the case of general XML content. We will also confirm the effectiveness of the proposed XSLT function.

References

Bray, T., el al.: Extensible Markup Language (XML) 1.0, 2nd edn. W3C Recommendation (2000)

Baker, M., et al.: XHTML Basic. W3C Recommendation (2000)

Mogul, J.C., et al.: Potential benefits of delta-encoding and data compression for HTTP. In: Proceeding of SIGCOMM 97. (1997)

Mogul, J.C., et al.: Delta Encoding in HTTP. RFC3229. The Internet Engineering Task Force (2002)

Clark, J.: XSL Transformations (XSLT) Version 1.0. W3C Recommendation (2000)

Le Hors, A., et al.: Document Object Model (DOM) Level 2 Core Specification Version 1.0. W3C Recommendation (2000)

Clark, J.: XML Path Language (XPath) Version 1.0. W3C Recommendation (1999)

The, GNU: Project (2002) Diffutils [Software]. Version 2.8.1.(Accessed 25 January 2005) Available from, http://www.gnu.org

Open Source Technology Group: diffxml [software] Version 0.92A. SourceForge.net.(Accessed 25 January 2005) (2004a) Available from, http://diffxml.sourceforge.net/

Open Source Technology Group (2004b) SAXON [software]: version 8.2. SourceForge.net. (Accessed 25 January 2005) Available from: http://saxon.sourceforge.net/

The Apache Software Foundation (2004) xalan-J [software] version 2.6.0. www.apache.org [Accessed 25 January 2005] Available from http://www.apache.org/dyn/closer.cgi/xml/xalan-j

La Fontaine, R.: A Delta Format for XML: Identifying Changes in XML Files and Representing the Change in XML. In: XML Europe 2001 (2001)

Curbera, F.P., et al.: Fast Difference and Update of XML Documents. XTech'99 held in San Jose (1999)

Ishikawa, N., et al.: Automatic Generation of a Differential XSL Stylesheet From Two XML Documents. In: Proceeding of WWW Conference 2002 held in Hawaii. WWW Conference 2002 (2002)

Appendix A: XSLT Template Mapping for Accordance, Delete and Change Node

TYPE	Mapping to XSLT (No continuing process to descendant of pattern)	Mapping to XSLT (Continuing process to descendant of pattern)

Accordance	No template	`<xsl:template match="XPath of its own position">`
		`  <xsl:copy>`
		`    <xsl:apply-templates/>`
		`  </xsl:copy>`
		`</xsl:template>`

Delete	`<xsl:template match="XPath of its own position">`
	`</xsl:template>`
		`<xsl:template match="XPath of its own position">`
		`  <xsl:apply-templates/>`
		`</xsl:template>`

Change	`<xsl:template match="XPath of its own position">`
	`  <Data of Changed node/>`
	`</xsl:template>`
		`<xsl:template match="XPath of its own position">`
		`  <Data of Changed node>`
		`    <xsl:apply-templates/>`
		`  </Data of Changed node>`
		`</xsl:template>`

Appendix B: XSLT Template Mapping for Addition Node

TYPE	Mapping to XSLT (No continuing process to descendant of pattern)	Mapping to XSLT (Continuing process to descendant of pattern)

Addition node in Parent	`<xsl:template match="XPath of a pattern node">`
	`  <Parent addition node>`
	`    <xsl:copy/>`
	`  </Parent addition node>`
	`</xsl:template>`
		`<xsl:template match="XPath of its own position">`
		`  <Parent addition node>`
		`    <xsl:copy>`
		`      <xsl:apply-template>`
		`    </xsl:copy>`
		`  </Parent addition node>`
		`</xsl:template>`

Addition node in Child	`<xsl:template match="XPath of a pattern node">`
	`  <xsl:copy>`
	`    <Child addition node/>`
	`  </xsl:copy>`
	`</xsl:template>`
		Same as left template

Addition node in elder brother	`<xsl:template match="XPath of a pattern node">`
	`  <Elder brother addition node/>`
	`  <xsl:copy/>`
	`</xsl:template>`
		`<xsl:template match="XPath of a pattern node">`
		`  <Elder brother addition node/>`
		`  <xsl:copy>`
		`    <xsl:apply-templates/>`
		`  </xsl:copy>`
		`</xsl:template>`

Addition node in younger brother	`<xsl:template match="XPath of a pattern node">`
	`  <xsl:copy/>`
	`  <Younger brother addition node/>`
	`</xsl:template>`
		`<xsl:template match="XPath of a pattern node">`
		`  <xsl:copy>`
		`    <xsl:apply-templates/>`
		`  </xsl:copy>`
		`  <Younger brother addition node/>`
		`</xsl:template>`

Appendix C: XSLT Template Mapping for Addition Node with Descendant Templates

TYPE	Mapping to XSLT (No continuing process to descendant of addition node)	Mapping to XSLT (Continuing process to descendant of addition node)

Additio n node	`<Addition node/>`	`<Addition node>`
		 `<xsl:apply-template select="XPath of lower pattern"/>`
		 `</Addition node>`

Mining Architectural Patterns in Specific Contexts and Its Application to e-Finance

Feras T. Dabous[1] and Fethi A. Rabhi[2]

[1] College of Engineering and Computer Science
Abu Dhabi University, P O Box 59911, United Arab Emirates
feras.dabous@adu.ac.ae
[2] School of Information Systems, Technology and Management
The University of New South Wales, Sydney NSW 2052, Australia
f.rabhi@unsw.edu.au

Abstract. The success of today's enterprises is critically dependant on their ability to automate the way they conduct business with customers and other enterprises by means of e-business applications. However, developers are confronted with a large number of alternatives when considering the design and implementation of e-business applications such as deciding on whether or how legacy system integration should be performed. Identifying the set of possible architectural design alternatives for a given problem context is not trivial since it requires architects to have extensive experience in a specific domain and its existing information systems. Moreover, determining the alternatives that corresponds to good architectural practices and selecting the most appropriate one for a given e-business application would have critical impact on participating enterprises. This chapter discusses a two-phase systematic framework for the determination of a range of alternative architectural designs for e-business applications and for making these alternatives evolve into either formal architectural patterns or anti-patterns. Such a framework is investigated based on a specific problem context in the e-finance domain with some requirements and assumptions that are based on experience working in that domain. The concepts presented in this paper are demonstrated using a real life context specification example derived from capital markets trading.

Keywords: Patterns, e-Business Applications, Architectural Design, Legacy Systems, e-Finance, Design Environments.

1 Introduction

The concept of e-business applications has been used extensively in the literature to refer to a range of applications. This range encompasses B2C interactions (e.g. simple Web-based client/server applications) and B2B interactions either as an intra-enterprise workflow or as an inter-enterprise distributed application. In this paper, we use the term Business Process (BP) to refer to any of such applications.

This chapter proposes a framework that can systematically aid in identifying architectural patterns for e-business applications in a specific context. Such a context must be identified based on domain experience and thorough knowledge of the architecture of key legacy systems. The proposed framework comprises two phases. The first one is the

J. Filipe, J. Cordeiro, and V. Pedrosa (Eds.): WEBIST 2005/2006, LNBIP 1, pp. 69–83, 2007.

identification of candidate patterns. This phase relies on the concept of a decision tree that can be constructed systematically based on identified set of design decisions' alternatives. The latter one is the candidate patterns evolution phase into formal patterns or anti-patterns. This phase is a long term one and relies on quality-based architecture selection approaches. This chapter illustrates both phases with a realistic example derived from the e-finance area.

In related work (Dabous, 2005), we identified and formalised a number of architectural patterns based on practical experience is a specific context in the domain of e-finance. These patterns address a similar problem context and therefore constitute alternative architectural approaches for such a problem context. We also presented quantitative models for patterns consequences estimations that are used in conjunction with the AHP (Anderson et al., 2002) method in ranking architectural patterns appropriateness for a given problem context.

2 Basic Assumptions and Concepts

This section presents the basic assumptions made in this paper and introduces the different concepts used such as functionality, legacy systems and BPs together with a selected application domain. The assumptions and concepts discussed are based on several architectural analysis, benchmarking studies, and e-business applications development such as (Rabhi et al., 2003) that have been conducted on a number of legacy systems.

2.1 Problem Context

The problem context considered in this paper is far from being an accurate representation of reality. Its purpose is only to give some idea on the number and type of business processes in the area of interest, the legacy systems in use and the most important non-functional requirements for stakeholders. The models used here are pragmatic in nature and have been based on several architectural analysis and benchmarking studies conducted on a number of legacy systems. We define three important concepts[1]:

- functionality: corresponds to an activity within a business process that performs a specific job (i.e. it is part of the business logic). We use the notion $F^{all} = \{f_i : 1 \leq i \leq |F^{all}|\}$ to represent the set of all functionalities that belong to a particular domain. The definition of the set F^{all} does not tell anything about the implementation of any functionality.
- equivalent functionalities: refers to a group of functionalities that have similar business logic. Our assumption here is that we cannot have two exact implementations of the same functionalities. Two "similar" implementations usually implement two equivalent (yet slightly different) functionalities. We use the notion $Q = \{q_i : 1 \leq i \leq |Q|\}$ to represent the set of all groups of equivalent functionalities. Each $q_i \subset F^{all}$ is the ith set of a number of equivalent functionalities such that $|q_i| \geq 1$ and $q_a \cap q_b = \phi : a \neq b$ and $\bigcup_{i=1}^{|Q|} q_i = F^{all}$.

---

[1] These concepts may be defined differently elsewhere but for the sake of consistency, we provide our definitions here.

- business process (BP): describes the requirements of an e-business application in terms of the activity flow of its constituent functionalities. An activity diagram is associated with every bp_i where the nodes represent functionalities and the arcs determine the execution flow across the functionalities. We use the set $BP = \{bp_i : 1 \leq i \leq |BP|\}$ to represent all BPs and the function $activities(bp_i) \subseteq F^{all}$ to identify the set of functionalities that are required by a bp_i (i.e. it returns the set of all nodes in a bp_i's activity diagram). We also assume that every $f \in F^{all}$ has at least one corresponding $bp_i \in BP$ such that $f \in activities(bp_i)$. In other words, $\bigcup_{i=1}^{|BP|} activities(bp_i) = F^{all}$.
- legacy system: refers to an existing architectural component that supports the implementation of a number of functionalities. We assume that the design team has not played a role in the development of the legacy systems and therefore has no access rights to the source code. Interaction with a legacy system can only be achieved through their defined interfaces. We use the notation $F^{au} \subseteq F^{all}$ to represent functionalities contained in all legacy systems and $LG = \{l_i : 1 \leq i \leq |LG|\}$ as the set of legacy systems identified in that particular domain. Every $l_i \subset F^{au}$ and $l_a \cap l_b = \phi$ when $a \neq b$. There is no instance of two equivalent functionalities within the same legacy system meaning that if $f_x, f_y \in l_i$ then $\{f_x, f_y\} \nsubseteq q_k \forall q_k \in Q$.
- access method: refers to the way an architectural component is being accessed. All access methods belong to a set AC and are ranked according to different abstraction levels. By definition, using a low-level access method is faster than using a high-level access method. In contrast, the development time of a client program is likely to take much more time in the case of a low-level access method than in the case of a high-level access method.

In (Dabous, 2005), we define the following 4 classes of access methods:

- AC1: includes communication at the network protocol level such as using TCP/IP packets.
- AC2: includes the use of facilities offered by the operating system(s) and Remote Procedure Calls (RPCs)
- AC3: includes the use of distributed object technology interfaces such as CORBA IDL and Java RMI.
- AC4: includes the use of service-oriented standards such as Web Service standards.

Therefore, a problem context is defined as a tuple $context$ denoted by $< F^{au}, F^{all}, Q, LG, BP >$.

2.2 Example Context Specification

The selected application domain is in the area of e-finance. We focus on capital markets which are places where financial instruments such as equities, options and futures are traded. Trading in capital markets comprises a cycle of a number of phases which are: pre-trade analytics, trading, post-trade analytics, settlement and registry. At each phase of this cycle, one or more legacy systems may be involved. Therefore, a large number of BPs that span through different stages of the trading cycle exist within this domain.

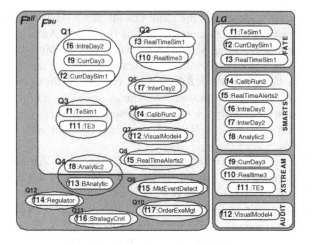

Fig. 1. Selected application domain

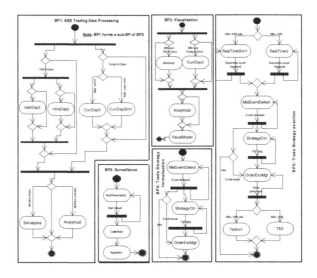

Fig. 2. Activity diagrams of the BPs

The implementation of these BPs is challenging for many of the reasons outlined in our problem context (e.g. legacy systems are owned by different companies and can only be accessed through a low-level access method). We have provided a visual representation of our problem context in figure 1. We focus on four legacy systems that have been customised around Australian Stock Exchange (ASX) practices. These systems are (see www.financeit.unsw.edu.au): FATE, SMARTS, XSTREAM , and AUDIT Explorer. The functionalities supported by each system (i.e. those relevant to the BPs in this problem context) are illustrated in the left part of the figure. There are five BPs of interest in this paper for which corresponding activity diagrams are shown in figure 2:

BP1 (ASX trading data processing) is related to analysing market-related data and generating some metrics that can be used by market analysts. The data can be related to historic trading activities on the ASX over a single day (intra-day data) or over a long period (inter-day data). It could also come from an ASX market simulator when experimenting with hypothetical situations.

BP2 (Visualisation of ASX trading data) is related to pre-processing of ASX market data to be used by a number of visualisation modules.

BP3 (Reporting surveillance alerts) is related to listening for a specific type of real-time market events (called surveillance alerts). Once an alert is detected, a market analyst performs a calibration run to verify the seriousness of the alert, then possibly reporting the alert to the regulatory authorities.

BP4 (Trade strategy simulation) is related to analysing a simulated market and searching for a specific type of market events (called trading opportunity alerts). Once such an event is detected, it is analysed possibly resulting in some action being taken on the simulated market to take advantage of the trading opportunity. This BP is usually followed by an evaluation of the simulated trading strategy (by looking at the overall profit made for example).

BP5 (Trade strategy execution) is an extension of BP4 which deals not only with a simulated market but also a real one. In the latter case, trading opportunity alerts have to be detected and acted upon in real-time.

Additional details about this example can be found in (Dabous, 2005).

3 Target Architecture Description

The purpose of the common architecture notation is to support a unified architectural description for the patterns generated by the framework. In particular, it embodies design decisions being made and facilitates the development of models that estimate the architecture's impact on the non-functional requirements. In this notation, an architecture is described in terms of a set of distributed components $Comp = \{X_i : 1 \leq i \leq |Comp|\}$. A component $X_i \in Comp$ is described according to four essential features: (1) the 'tasks' that are supported by the component, (2) the set of components accessed by this component, (3) the set of components that access this component, and (4) the method by which each component is accessed. Therefore, we can describe each entry $X_i \in Comp$ by the tuple $< tasks(X_i), conTo(X_i), invBy(X_i), access(X_i) >$ where:

1. $tasks(X_i)$: is a function that identifies the set of tasks that are supported by the component X_i. Each task can be one of three types.
   - The first one is the implementation of a functionality $f \in F^{all}$ that is denoted by $C(f)$ and is used in three different cases. The first one is when $f \in F^{au}$ refers to an existing functionality within a legacy system. The second one is when $f \in F^{au}$ refers to redeveloping (i.e. reengineering) an existing functionality. The third one is when $f \in (F^{all} - F^{au})$ i.e. f is a new functionality that is not implemented in any of the legacy systems.
   - The second type of tasks correspond to the implementation of a wrapper for a functionality f, denoted by $CW(f)$. It is used when X_i masks out the actual component that embeds $C(f)$ using a higher level access method.

- The third type of tasks correspond to implementing the logic of a business process bp, denoted by $CBL(bp)$. We will use the term 'business process enactment' to refer to the implementation code of the business logic.

Therefore, each task corresponds to implementation code resulting from applying one of the task constructors C, CW, or CBL on its parameters.

2. $conTo(X_i) \subset Comp$: is a function that returns the set of components that X_i invokes while executing its tasks.

3. $invBy(X_i) \subset Comp$: is a function that returns the set of components that invoke X_i while executing their tasks.

4. $access(X_i)$: a function that returns the access method used by the component X_i. Meaning that $accessType(access(X_i)) \in AC$ (see section 2.1).

For simplicity, we refer to an architecture XLG as the one in which every legacy system is represented as a component. This architecture is constructed using the following algorithm:

ConstructXLG (LG)

- For each $l_x \in LG$ Do:
    - X_x = createNew(); /* creates and initialised a new component*/
    - $access(X_x) = legacyAccess(l_x)$; /* see section 2.1*/
    - $tasks(X_x) = \{C(f_k) : f_k \in l_x\}$;
    - $XLG = XLG \cup \{X_x\}$ /* add X_x to XLG */

Where the $createNew()$ function invocation creates a new component X_x and initialises its four features to nil (i.e. $access()= tasks()= conTo()= invBy() = \phi$). The set XLG still represents an incomplete architecture as other tasks (such as those for BPs enactment) have not yet been created.

4   Phase I: Candidate Patterns Identification

This phase (see figure 3) considers the identification of possible architectural descriptions that correspond to candidate patterns. It presumes the existence of a common architectural description (see section 3). This phase consists of the following steps:

1. Given a set of *design strategies* denoted by the set DS (see section 4.1) such that each strategy is formalised using the common architectural description, identify a set of design decisions denoted by the set DD (see section 4.2). Each design decision $ds_i \in DD$ has a number of predefined alternatives.

2. Construct a decision tree using the algorithm described in section 4.3.

3. For every path pth in the decision tree that starts from the root note to a leaf node, do the following:
    (a) If pth is validated by the decision tree construction algorithm, (see section then a candidate pattern is recognised. The candidate pattern description denoted by $arch_{pth}$ is generated by combining the architectural description algorithms for all participating design alternatives along pth from the root to leaf node. For example, if pth is "$a_1 \to\sim a_2 \to a_3 \to a_4$" then the $arch_{pth}$ consists of the application of the construction algorithms of a_1, a_3, then a_4.

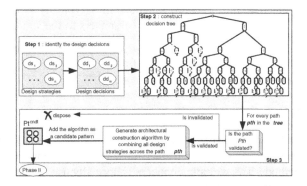

Fig. 3. Phase I: candidate patterns identification

(b) The architectural description $arch_{pth}$ is added to the set of candidate patterns denoted by Pt^{cndt} (i.e. $Pt^{cndt} = Pt^{cndt} \cup \{arch_{pth}\}$).

(c) If pth is invalidated by the decision tree construction algorithm, then pth is discarded because the combination of its participating design strategies cannot generate a complete architectural description.

At any time, the introduction of a new design strategy in DS would have an impact on either the alternatives of existing design decision in DD or on introducing a new design decision (see (Dabous, 2005) for more details for examples of both cases). Consequently, this would enforce the regeneration of the decision tree in a way the preserve existing validated paths in addition of possible generation of extra valid path and therefore extra candidate patterns.

4.1 Design Strategies

In this framework, we use the concept of 'design strategy' as a basic architectural construct into the pattern identification process. we present five simple design strategies that are particularly suited to the problem context and described algorithmically based on the target architectural notation. We use the notion $DS = \{Reuse, Automate, Wrap, Migrate, MinCoordinate\}$ as the set of design strategies used in this chapter. More complex design strategies are presented in (Dabous, 2005).

Reuse. This design strategy emphasises on the importance of leveraging the functionalities embedded in existing legacy systems and allowing them to be shared across BPs. It simply creates $|LG|$ entries in $Comp$ which correspond to the set $XLG \subset Comp$ defined in section 3. The corresponding algorithm is:

Reuse()
- For each $X_i \in XLG$:
    - $Comp = Comp \cup \{X_i\}$

Automate. This design strategy creates $|F^{all} - F^{au}|$ components each of which supports a single new functionality (i.e. required functionality that does not exist in any of existing legacy systems). This strategy suggests that all new components provide a unified access method for these new functionalities (typically a high-level access method). This access method is given as a parameters to the strategy. The corresponding algorithm is:

Automate(am) /*am is the access method used by the new components */

1. For each $f_k \in (F^{all} - F^{au})$:
   - X_x = createNew ();
   - $access(X_x)$ = am;
   - $tasks(X_x) = \{C(f_k)\}$;
   - $Comp = Comp \cup \{X_x\}$;

Wrap. Remotely accessing the functionalities of legacy systems is not simple and requires significant programming effort since most of such systems provide low-level access type methods. The wrapping concept is normally used to provide a higher-level method for remotely accessing legacy functionalities. This design strategy creates a total of $|F^{au}|$ new components in $Comp$, each of which corresponds to a wrapper component. This wrapper redirects all calls from component's interface (high-level) to the legacy system's interface (low-level). The corresponding algorithm is:

Wrap (am)

1. For each $X_i \in XLG$ such that $X_i \in Comp$ do:
   - For each $C(f_k) \in tasks(X_i)$:
     - X_x = createNew();
     - $access(X_x)$ = am;
     - $tasks(X_x) = \{CW(f_k)\}$;
     - $invBy(X_i) = X_x$
     - $conTo(X_x) = X_i$
     - $Comp = Comp \cup \{X_x\}$

Migrate. In cases when existing legacy systems are expected to be discarded in the near future, the corresponding functionalities can be redeveloped from scratch in a process that we refer to as 'migration'. There are different possibilities of rearranging the redeveloped functionalities into new components. This design strategy implements one possible migration technique that treats all functionalities equally whether they are legacy or new functionalities. It groups each set of equivalent functionalities $q \in Q$ in one component. Each new component contains a task $C(f_k)$ for each $f_k \in q$. This design strategy also uses a uniform access method across all new components (typically a high-level access method). The corresponding algorithm is:

Migrate(am)

1. For each $q_i \in Q$:
   - X_x = createNew ();
   - $access(X_x)$ =am;
   - $tasks(X_x) = \{C(f_k) : f_k \in q_i\}$;
   - $Comp = Comp \cup \{X_x\}$

MinCoordinate. All previous strategies only deal with how to implement functionalities. This one is specifically about enacting BPs. It works in situations where BPs of interest are unrelated and do not interact with each other. The Minimum Coordinate (MinCoordinate) design strategy gives the responsibility for the enactment of every $bp \in BP$ to a dedicated component X. For every functionality required in the BP, there are two cases. The first case is when the functionality is already supported by another existing component Y. In this case, a *link* is created between the components X and Y. The second case is when the functionality is not implemented by

Table 1. Design decisions and alternatives vs. design strategies

	Alternatives	
Design decisions	1st alternative	2nd alternative
DD1	Use 'Reuse'	Use 'Migrate'
DD2	Use 'Wrap'	Do not use 'Wrap'
DD3	Use 'Automate'	Do not use 'Automate'
DD4	Use 'MinCoordinate'	

the other components of the architecture. In this case, a local task will be created on X to support that functionality (hence the word "Minimum" which means the strategy only creates one new component). The corresponding algorithm is:

MinCoordinate()

1. Let BpComp $=\phi$ /* An empty set of same type as $Comp$*/
2. For each $bp_j \in BP$:
   (a) X_x = createNew ();
   (b) $tasks(X_x) = \{CBL(bp_j)\}$;
   (c) **For** every $f_k \in activities(bp_j)$ **DO**:
   - **IF** ($\exists X_i \in Comp$: /* When f_k already exists */
     $(CBL(q) \in tasks(X_i), f_k \in q)$ /*f_k is part of a $q \in Q$*/
     or $(CW(f_k) \in tasks(X_i))$ /*f_k has a wrapper and not in a $q \in Q$*/
     $(C(f_k) \in tasks(X_i))$ /* f_k already exists with no wrapper and not part of a $q \in Q$ */
     – $conTo(X_x) = conTo(X_x) \cup \{X_i\}$;
     – $invBy(X_i) = invBy(X_i) \cup \{X_x\}$;
     – $BpComp = BpComp \cup \{X_x\}$;
   - **ELSE** $tasks(X_x) = tasks(X_x) \cup \{C(f_k)\}$; /*develop local copy of f_k*/
3. $Comp = Comp \cup BpComp$;

4.2 Design Decisions

Each of the design strategies considered earlier can be regarded as the outcome of an architectural design decision. Design decisions include whether to reuse or discard existing legacy functionality, whether to wrap existing legacy functionality or leave it as it is, implementing new functionalities using separate components or embedding them with the component that implements BPs enactment etc. We use the notion DD = {DD1, DD2, DD3, DD4} whose corresponding alternatives that have been considered so far are summarises in table 1.

The table shows that each of DD1, DD2, and DD3 has two alternative designs (two different design strategies in DD1, and using/not using a design strategy in both DD2 and DD3). On the other hand, DD4 has only one alternative given in this chapter. Introducing a new design strategy can correspond to an alternative design for either an indetified or new design decision.

4.3 Decision Tree Construction Algorithm

A binary decision tree can be constructed in which each node corresponds to a design alternative in a design decision. The construction algorithm for such a tree is based on two types of input: design decisions processing order and conflicting design alternatives pairs.

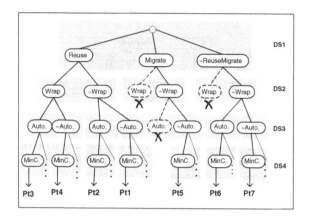

Fig. 4. Application of the decision tree construction algorithm

4.3.1 Algorithm Inputs

Design decisions procession order. We classify the design decisions into groups depending on the order in which the design decisions are considered for constructing the tree. We use the notion $order_i$ to correspond to the set of design decisions that can be made at level i ($i < j$ means that $d \in order_i$ is a decision made closer to the root of the tree than $d' \in order_j$).

When considering the design decisions identified so far in this chapter, we have the following procession order sets:
$order_1 = \{DD1\}$
$order_2 = \{DD2, DD3\}$
$order_3 = \{DD4\}$

We extend on table 1 to have an alternative in each design decision that corresponds to not using any of the alternatives strategies in that particular design decision (i.e. corresponds to not using that particular design decision at all). Therefore, the four design decisions alternatives are:
$DD1 = \{\text{Reuse, Migrate,} \sim \text{ReuseMigrate}\}$
$DD2 = \{\text{Wrap,} \sim \text{Wrap}\}$
$DD3 = \{\text{Automate,} \sim \text{Automate}\}$
$DD4 = \{\text{MinCoordinate,} \sim \text{MinCoordinate}\}$

Note that the alternative '$\sim$ReuseMigrate' $\in$ DD1 corresponds to neither using 'Reuse' nor 'Migrate'.

Conflicting design alternatives pairs. There are some certain cases when two alternatives that belong to different design decisions result in an invalid architecture. We use the set $conflicts = \{(alt_a, alt_b) : alt_a \in dd_n, alt_b \in dd_m, dd_n \neq dd_m\}$ to record all conflicting pairs.

When considering the alternatives of the design decisions identified so far in this chapter, we can have two pairs of conflicting alternatives:

- The first one is not using 'Reuse' alternative of DD1 that is represented by '$\sim$ReuseMigrate' and the alternative 'Wrap' of DD2. This is because 'Wrap' is intended to support a high level access method for the legacy functionalities. In this case using 'Wrap' would be inappropriate because there are no legacy functionalities in the architecture as a result of not using 'Reuse' alternative.

- The second one is 'Migrate' of DD1 and 'Automate' of DD3. This is because 'Migrate' involves developing both the legacy and new functionalities. In this case 'Automate' is inappropriate because it would generate another copy of the new functionalities.

As a result,

$$conflicts = \{(\sim \text{ReuseMigrate}, \text{Wrap}), (\text{Migrate}, \text{Automate})\}$$

4.3.2 Algorithm

Definitions and initialisation:

    typedef Decision; /* *each decision a set of alternatives*/

    typedef Alternative; /**each alternative is using/not using design strategies*/

    typedef Node{ /**decision tree node structure*/

        Alternative value, /**the value of the node*/

        Node Set children; /* *the set of children nodes*/

        }

    Let Decision $dd = [dd_1, dd_2, \dots, dd_n]$ be the list of all n design decisions such that:

        $dd_x \in order_i$ and $dd_{x+1} \in order_j$ if and only if $i \leq j$.

        dd_x design decision is a set of alternatives.

Tree construction call:

    Node $root$ = buildTree(dd_1, nil)

Node buildTree(Decision dd_i, Alternative alt) {

    Node $node$ = **new** Node;

    $node.value = alt$;

    If dd_i does not exist **then** {

        - $node.children = \phi$;

        - **return** $node$;}

    For every $a \in dd_i$ {

        - $child$ = buildTree(dd_{i+1}, a);

        - **if** $\exists(a, b) \in conflicts$: b is the value of a node cut along any path starting from $child$, **then** $cut.children = \phi$;

        - $node.children = node.children \cup \{child\}$;

        - mark the node cut as 'invalid'; /* *so that the path from root to cut is not considered*/

    }

}

The previous algorithm uses recursive calls to construct decision sub-trees. The root of each sub-tree is an alternative to a design decision $d \in order_i$. The children of each sub-tree root represent the alternatives of a design decision $d' \in orders_j$ such that $i \leq j$. Whenever a sub-tree is constructed, the algorithm checks for conflicting alternatives along the path from the tree root to the leaves of the created sub-tree. Figure 4 shows the generated tree by applying this algorithm on the four decisions mentioned earlier.

4.4 Candidate Patterns

In a particular decision tree, the nodes along each path from the root to a leaf correspond to either a complete architecture that we refer to as 'valid path' or incomplete architecture that we refer to as an 'invalid path'. We consider each valid path as a candidate pattern. Given a problem context, a candidate architecture implementation starts with an empty architecture (i.e. $Comp = \phi$). Then, the algorithm for each design strategy that is used as a design alternative across the candidate pattern path is applied on the given problem context; therefore the current architecture is constructed incrementally with a new set of tasks and components.

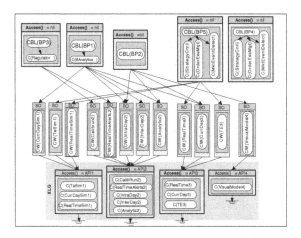

Fig. 5. Pt4 applied on the example context specification

Now we briefly discuss the architectural description of the five candidate patterns. Details of their forces and consequences are discussed thoroughly in (Dabous, 2005). We provide our naming convention for each pattern as follows:

Reuse+MinCoordinate (Pt1). This pattern considers generating invocations to the required functionalities across legacy system by direct invocations through the APIs of these systems. On the other hand, each BP implements its local program code for each of its activities that have no corresponding functionality in any of the legacy systems.

Reuse+Automate+MinCoordinate (Pt2). This pattern considers generating an invocation to the required functionalities across legacy system by direct invocation through the APIs of these systems. It also considers implementing all activities of BPs that have no correspondence in any of the legacy systems as global e-services.

Reuse+Wrap+Automate+MinCoordinate (Pt3). This pattern considers providing a unified interface to every particular functionality across legacy systems. This provision is achieved by developing wrappers. It also considers implementing all activities of BPs that have no correspondence in any of the legacy systems as global e- services.

Reuse+Wrap+MinCoordinate (Pt4). This pattern considers providing a unified interface to every particular required functionality across legacy systems. This provision is achieved by developing wrappers. On the other hand, each BP implements its local program code for each of its activities that have no corresponding functionality in any of the legacy systems.

Migrate+MinCoordinate (Pt5). This pattern considers the disposal or abandoning existing legacy systems. Therefore, starting from scratch, this pattern migrates the implementation of required functionalities through a re-engineering/automation process into global e-services with advertised service-based interface. In this process, each group of equivalent functionalities are reengineered within a single program that supports one interface.

MinCoordinate (Pt6) and Automate+MinCo. (Pt7). are more likely to evolve into anti-patterns because they promote the isolation and standalone BP implementation that is obsolete and does not correspond to current practices.

Figure 5 illustrates Pt4 generated architecture when implemented on the example problem context. In the following is the corresponding content of $Comp$: $Comp^{Pt4} = \{$

$x_1 < \{C(f_1), C(f_2), c(f_3)\}, \phi, \{x_5, x_6, x_7\}, api1 >,$

$x_2 < \{C(f_4), C(f_5), C(f_6), C(f_7), C(f_8)\}, \phi,$

$\{x_8, x_9, x_{10}, x_{11}, x_{12}\}, api2 >,$

$x_3 < \{C(f_9), C(f_{10}), C(f_{11})\}, \phi, \{x_{13}, x_{14}, x_{15}\}, api3 >,$

$x_4 < \{C(f_{12})\}, \{x_{16}\}, \phi, api4 >,$

$x_5 < \{CW(f_1)\}, \{x_1\}, \{x_{21}\}, so >,$

$x_6 < \{CW(f_2)\}, \{x_1\}, \{x_{17}\}, so >,$

$x_7 < \{CW(f_3)\}, \{x_1\}, \{x_{21}\}, so >,$

$x_8 < \{CW(f_4)\}, \{x_2\}, \{x_{19}\}, so >,$

$x_9 < \{CW(f_5)\}, \{x_2\}, \{x_{19}\}, so >,$

$x_{10} < \{CW(f_6)\}, \{x_2\}, \{x_{17}, x_{18}\}, so >,$

$x_{11} < \{CW(f_7)\}, \{x_2\}, \{x_{17}\}, so >,$

$x_{12} < \{CW(f_8)\}, \{x_2\}, \{x_{17}, x_{18}\}, so >,$

$x_{13} < \{CW(f_9)\}, \{x_3\}, \{x_{17}, x_{18}\}, so >,$

$x_{14} < \{CW(f_{10})\}, \{x_3\}, \{x_{21}\}, so >,$

$x_{15} < \{CW(f_{11})\}, \{x_3\}, \{x_{21}\}, so >,$

$x_{16} < \{CW(f_{12})\}, \{x_4\}, \{x_{18}\}, so >,$

$x_{17} < \{CBL(bp_1), C(f_{13})\}, \{x_6, x_{10}, x_{11}, x_{12}, x_{13}\}, \phi, nil >,$

$x_{18} < \{CBL(bp_2)\}, \{x_{10}, x_{12}, x_{13}, x_{16}\}, \phi, nil >,$

$x_{19} < \{CBL(bp_3), C(f_{14})\}, \{x_8, x_9\}, \phi, nil >,$

$x_{20} < \{CBL(bp_4), C(f_{15}), C(f_{16}), C(f_{17})\}, \phi, \phi, nil >,$

$x_{21} < \{CBL(bp_5), C(f_{15}), C(f_{16}), C(f_{17})\}, \{x_5, x_7\}, \phi, nil >, \}$

5   Phase II: Evolution into Formal Patterns

This phase (see figure 6) considers the evolution opportunities for the candidate patterns in Pt^{cndt} into either formal patterns denoted by the set Pt^{frml} or anti-patterns denoted by the set Pt^{anti}. Theoretically, this evolution process would result in $Pt^{cndt} = Pt^{frml} \cup Pt^{anti}$. However, in reality, the evolutionary process for any candidate pattern may take several years and depends mostly on frequent use for that candidate pattern in practice with different problems to generate either successful solutions that push forward into formal pattern or unsuccessful solutions that push forward into anti-pattern. This phase consists of the five main steps:

1. Instantiate the architectural description for each identified candidate pattern in Pt^{cndt} on a given application domain problem that is formalised with accordance to the notations in section 2.1. Section 4.4 discussed the candidate patterns instantiations on the application domain example.
2. Apply the quality attributes estimation models on the given application domain specifications so that estimation per model for each pattern architecture is generated. In (Dabous et al., 2005; Dabous, 2005), we derived models for performance,

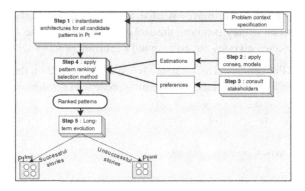

Fig. 6. Phase II: evolution into formal patterns

development effort, and maintenance effort. Other patterns consequences that correspond to other important quality attributes can be incorporated in this process by investigating suitable models or simply by utilising a hybrid method as discussed in (Dabous, 2005).

3. Investigate the stakeholders' preferences on the required quality attributes that correspond to the patterns' consequences.

4. Apply a pattern selection algorithm based on steps 1, 2, and 3 using Multiple-Attribute Decision Making (MADM) methods (Yoon and Hwang, 1995) such AHP (Svahnberg et al., 2003). More complicated methods can be utilised such as Bayesian Network based technique (Zhang and Jarzabek, 2005) and Integer Programming (IP) based technique (Al-Naeem, 2006). The outcome of such a selection method is an appropriateness rank for each pattern' architecture in Pt^{cndt}.

5. The last step is to investigate possibilities of the evolution of each candidate pattern. A candidate pattern would gradually evolve into a formal pattern in Pt^{frml} if it has been occupying one of the higher ranks and successful stories have been reported about its usage in practice. Otherwise, such candidate pattern would gradually evolve into an anti-pattern in Pt^{anti} if it has been occupying lower ranks and/or unsuccessful stories have been reported about its usage in practice. While evolving, each candidate pattern documentation in Pt^{cndt} would also be enriched with all ranks and experiences obtained with different problem context specifications.

The application of steps 2, 3, and 4 of this phase on the given domain context example is described in (Dabous, 2005).

6   Conclusion

In this chapter, we presented and discussed the basic components of a framework for identifying patterns during the architectural design of applications that fit in a specific context. We have demonstrated this framework through an application in the e-finance domain. This work is motivated by three factors (Dabous, 2005). The first one is the availability of architectural patterns that are identified and formalised based on practical experience in developing e-business applications in a particular domain. The second one is the possibility of building models for estimating the qualities of generated architectures. The third one is the utilisation of selection methods such as the AHP for identifying optimal designs.

The proposed framework is systematic and extensible. It is systematic since the formalisation of the design strategies, the candidate patterns and the quality models uses the same target architectural description. It is also extensible since the identification of each extra design strategy can trigger extra candidate patterns. In (Dabous, 2005), we showed that introducing two additional strategies led to identifying more candidate patterns.

Current work focuses on providing tool support for defining candidate patterns in a domain context, instantiating these patterns for a given application specification and finally ranking these patterns according to the estimations provided by the quality models and the preferences for such quality attributes provided by stakeholders.

References

Al-Naeem, T,: A quality-driven decision-support framework for architecting e-business applications. Phd thesis, School of Computer Science and Engineering, The University of New South Wales, Australia (2006)

Anderson, D.R., Sweeney, D.J., Williams, T.A.: An Introduction to Management Science: Quantitative Approaches to Decision Making. South-Western Educational Publishing (2002)

Dabous, F. T,: Pattern-Based Approach for the Architectural Design of e-Business Applications. Phd thesis, School of Information Systems, Technology and Management, The University of New South Wales, Australia (2005)

Dabous, F.T., Rabhi, F.A., Yu, H., Al-Naeem, T.: Estimating patterns consequences for the architectural design of e-business applications. In: 7th International Conference on Enterprise Information Systems (ICEIS'05), Miami, USA, pp. 248–254 (2005)

Rabhi, F.A., Dabous, F.T., Yu, H., Chu, R.Y., Tan, G.E., Trong, T.: SMARTS benchmarking, prototyping & performance prediction. Technical Report Project #CRCPA5005, Capital Markets crc (CMCRC) (2003)

Svahnberg, M., Wohlin, C., Lundberg, L., Mattsson, M.: A quality-driven decision-support method for identifying software architecture candidates. International Journal of Software Engineering and Knowledge Engineering 13(5), 547–573 (2003)

Yoon, K.P., Hwang, C.-L.: Multiple attribute decision making: An introduction. Saga Publications (1995)

Zhang, H., Jarzabek, S.: A bayesian network approach to rational architectural design. IJSEKE 15(4)

Knowledge Management for Adapted Information Retrieval in Ubiquitous Environments

Angela Carrillo-Ramos, Marlène Villanova-Oliver, Jérome Gensel, and Hervé Martin

LSR Laboratory, SIGMA Team, 681 rue de la Passerelle,
38402 Saint Martin D'Hères, France
{carrillo,gensel,villanov,martin}@imag.fr

Abstract. *PUMAS* is a framework based on agents which provides nomadic users with relevant and adapted information. Using *PUMAS*, information delivered to nomadic users is adapted according to, on the one hand, their preferences and history in the system and, on the other hand, the limited capacities of their *Mobile Devices* (*MDs*). This framework is composed of four *Multi-Agent Systems* (*MAS*, *Connection MAS*, *Communication MAS*, *Information MAS* and *Adaptation MAS*) for handling adaptation. In this paper, we illustrate how the *PUMAS* agents augment user queries with information about her/his characteristics and those of her/his *MD* and, how the *Router Agent* (which belongs to the *Information MAS*) redirects the user queries towards the different *Web based Information System* (*WIS*) which contain all or part of the information for answering them and which execute on servers or *MDs*.

Keywords: Agents, Knowledge Management, Query Routing, Adaptation.

1 Introduction

Ubiquitous Computing is defined by the *W3C* (*http://www.w3.org/TR/webont-req/*) as an emerging paradigm of personal computing characterized mainly by the use of *Mobile Devices* (*MDs*). The term *MD* refers generally to small, handheld and wireless computing devices, used to access *Web based Information System* (*WIS*). *WIS* are systems which enable collecting, structuring, storing, managing and diffusing information, like traditional *Information Systems* (*IS*) do, but over a Web infrastructure. *WIS* provide users with complex functionalities which are activated through a Web browser in a hypermedia interface. *WIS* designers must be provided with mechanisms and architectures that cope with the reduced capabilities of the *MDs,* in order to efficiently retrieve and deliver data using these devices. The *WIS* must provide users with useful information retrieved from an *intelligent search* and presented in a *suitable* way. We believe that the *agent paradigm* is an interesting approach for this purpose. The *Multi-Agent System* (*MAS*) approach is defined in (El Fallah-Seghrouchni *et al.*, 2004) as a credible paradigm to design distributed and cooperative systems based on the agent technology.

The interest of *MAS*, when the Internet is used to access and exchange information through *MDs* (that they call "*smart devices*"), is shown in (Ramparany *et al.*, 2003). In this case, agents can be useful to represent user characteristics inside the system

J. Filipe, J. Cordeiro, and V. Pedrosa (Eds.): WEBIST 2005/2006, LNBIP 1, pp. 84–96, 2007.

and the *MDs* can work like *"cooperative devices"*. The *W3C* defines an *agent* as *"a concrete piece of software or hardware that sends and receives messages"*. In our context, these messages can be used to access a *WIS* and to exchange information.

The *MD* applications require network architectures able to support automatic and ad hoc configuration which consider features of the *ubiquitous computing environment* such as heterogeneity, mobility, autonomy, high distribution, etc. Such *environment* is defined in (Pirker *et al.*, 2004) as a dynamic distributed network of embedded devices and systems that can interact with humans to satisfy their requirements and provide a variety of information, communication, and collaboration services.

In order to provide nomadic users only with the *most relevant information* (i.e. *"the right information in the right place at the right time"*), a *MD* application must embed mechanisms for propagating the user queries towards the *"right"* information sources (stored in one or several devices) which can answer these queries considering user preferences, features of her/his *MDs*, her/his location, etc. This is the main purpose of the *Query Routing* process. (Xu *et al.*, 1999) define this process as the general problem of, on the one hand, evaluating the query using the most relevant data sources and, on the other hand, integrating results returned from data sources. In order to optimize the *Query Routing* process, (Agostini *et al.*, 2004) and (Park *et al.*, 2004) propose to use some metrics related to the trustworthiness of the information sources, their capability to satisfy user information needs and their timeliness of information delivery.

PUMAS (Carrillo *et al.*, 2005a) is a framework for retrieving information distributed between several *WIS* and/or different types of *MDs*. The architecture of *PUMAS* is composed of four *MAS* (*Connection MAS, Communication MAS, Information MAS* and *Adaptation MAS*), each one encompassing several *ubiquitous agents* which cooperate to achieve the different tasks handled by *PUMAS* (e.g., *MD* connection/disconnection, communications between agents, information exchange, storage and retrieval, etc.). In this paper, we present the activities of representation and data exchange of the *PUMAS* agents (activities based on *XML* files). Through *PUMAS,* the final objective is to build and propose a framework which additionally to the management of accesses to *WIS* performed through *MDs*, is also in charge of performing an adaptation of information according to user profiles (which refers to their needs, preferences, histories in the system, current location, etc.) and, the technical capabilities of her/his *MD*. This paper focuses on the representation of knowledge managed by *PUMAS* agents (to achieve the adaptation tasks and support the *Query Routing* process executed by the *Router Agent*) in order to redirect queries formulated by users towards the different *WIS*. We show here how the *Knowledge Bases* (*KBs*) managed by *PUMAS* agents are used by this process. We also explain and illustrate each activity of the *Query Routing* process using as example an airport *WIS* and a scenario we briefly describe:

A passenger equipped with her/his MD must take a plane. Let us suppose that she/he must arrive three hours before for checking in and that she/he also must buy some gifts at the duty free shops. Let us assume that, at the airport, each airline and shop has a WIS which provides customers with information about their services (e.g., departure and arrival schedule) and their products (e.g., sales, new products). The passenger wants to know the closest duty free shops to the departure gate of her/his flight which sell each article of her/his gift list (at the lowest price). Let us suppose that several shops sell the same products (e.g., souvenirs, books, post cards, liquors) which correspond to what the user would like to buy.

The paper is organized as follows. We present in section 2, the goal and the architecture of the *PUMAS* framework. We describe more particularly the data representation and data exchange of the agents and their managed information. In section 3, we present *Knowledge Management*, especially that performed by agents which belong to the *Information* and *Adaptation MAS* for adaptation purposes. In section 4, through the example scenario described above, we explain the *Query Routing* process performed by the *Router Agent*. Finally, we present some related works before we conclude in section 6.

2 The PUMAS Framework

The architecture of *PUMAS* is composed of four *Multi-Agent Systems* (*MAS*) which will be explained in the following subsections (see Figure 1).

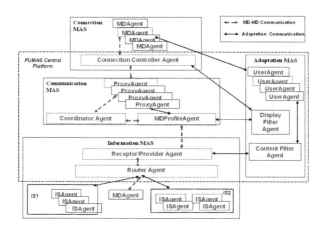

Fig. 1. The PUMAS Architecture

The *PUMAS* framework has been extended compared to the architecture presented in (Carrillo *et al.*, 2005a). We have introduced in (Carrillo *et al.*, 2005b) a new *MAS*, called the *Adaptation MAS*, in the architecture of *PUMAS*. The agents belonging to the *Adaptation MAS* have as responsibilities to manage specific *XML* files which contain information about the user and her/his *MD*. Its knowledge allows selection and filtering of information for users. This paper focuses, on the one hand, on the managed knowledge and the exchanged information between agents of *PUMAS*, especially, those belonging to the *Information* and the *Adaptation MAS* for adaptation purposes, and on the other hand, on the strategies followed by the *Router Agent* in order to perform the *Query Routing* process. The following subsections give a short description of each *MAS*, focusing on the information exchanged between *PUMAS* agents. A detailed description of the *Connection MAS*, the *Communication MAS* and the *Information MAS* can be found in (Carrillo *et al.*, 2005a) while the *Adaptation MAS* is presented in detail in (Carrillo *et al.*, 2005b).

2.1 The Connection MAS

This *MAS* includes several *Mobile Device Agents* and one *Connection Controller Agent*.

A **Mobile Device Agent** is executed on the user's *MD*. This agent manages the *Device Profile XML* file, located on the user's *MD*, which describes the characteristics of the *MD*, using *OWL* (*Ontology Web Language, http://www.w3.org/2004/OWL/*) in order to define a common ontology for all agents which share this information (e.g., the *DisplayFilterAgent* which belongs to the *Adaptation MAS*, see section 2.4). This file contains some information about hardware and software requirements, network status, type of hypermedia files supported by the *MD*, conditions for disconnecting (i.e. finishing sessions), etc. A **Mobile Device Agent** also manages the *Session XML* file which describes characteristics of the user sessions: who is the user connected, when the session begun and what *MD* is connected. This file will be exchanged with the *UserAgent* (belonging to the *Adaptation MAS*).

The **Connection Controller Agent** executes on the central platform of *PUMAS*. This agent checks connections established by users and agent status (e.g., connected, disconnected, killed, etc.). It also gets the user's location and the *MD* type (e.g., *PDA*) from the *User Location XML* file (which contains physical and logical location features) and from the *Device Profile XML* file (which contains *MD* features). Both files are provided by the *Mobile Device Agents* and locally managed by the *Connection Controller Agent*.

The *XML* files (i.e., *User Location, Session* and *Device Profile XML* files) managed by the *Mobile Device Agent* and the *Connection Controller Agent* have been defined using *OWL* and the extensions introduced by (Indulska *et al.*, 2003) to *CC/PP*. These extensions include some user characteristics like location (physical and logical location), requirements of available applications (hardware, software, browser and *WAP* requirements), characteristics of sessions (user, device, application) and user profiles (general user's requirements, preferences).

2.2 The Communication MAS

This *MAS* is composed of several *Proxy Agents*, one *MDProfile Agent* and one *Coordinator Agent*. These agents are located in the central platform of *PUMAS*.

There is one **Proxy Agent** for each connection from a *Mobile Device Agent*. The main task of this agent is to represent a *Mobile Device Agent* within the system and has the same properties and behaviour as the *Mobile Device Agent* except those concerning the connection.

The **MDProfile Agent** has to check the user profiles according to her/his *MD*. This agent shares information about specific *MD* features for user session with the *DisplayFilterAgent* (which belongs to the *Adaptation MAS*).

The **Coordinator Agent** is in permanent communication with the *Connection Controller Agent* in order to verify connection status of the agent which searches for information. This agent knows all agents connected in the system using a yellow pages mechanism. If there are some problems with the *Connection Controller Agent* (e.g., if the *Connection Controller Agent* fails or, if there is a lot of connections), the **Coordinator Agent** can play the role of the *Connection Controller Agent* up until problems are fixed. At that moment, the *Connection Controller Agent* and the *Coordinator Agent* must synchronize information about the connected agent and check current connections.

2.3   The Information MAS

The *Information MAS* is composed of one or several *Receptor/Provider Agents*, one or several *Router Agents* and one or several *ISAgents*.

The **Receptor/Provider Agents** which are located in the central platform of *PUMAS* own a general view of the whole system. They receive requests that are transmitted from the *Communication MAS* and redirect them to the *Router Agents*. Once a query has been processed by the *ISAgents*, a *Receptor/Provider Agent* checks whether the query results consider the user profile according to her/his preferences, history in the system, etc.

In order to redirect a query to the "*right*" *WIS*, the **Router Agent** applies a *strategy* which depends on one or several criteria (see section 4). This agent also compiles results returned by the *ISAgents* and analyzes them (according to defined criteria in the user preferences) to decide whether the whole set of results or only a part of it has to be sent to the *Receptor/Provider Agents*.

An **ISAgent** associated with a *WIS* (and which executes on the same device that the *WIS*) receives user queries from the *Router Agent* and is in charge of searching for information. Once a result for a query is obtained, the **ISAgent** returns it to the *Router Agent*. An **ISAgent** can execute a query by itself or delegate this task to the adequate *WIS* component.

2.4   The Adaptation MAS

This *MAS* is composed of one or several *UserAgents*, one *DisplayFilterAgent* and one *ContentFilterAgent*. They are located in the central platform of *PUMAS*.

Each **UserAgent** manages a *User Profile XML file* (defined using *OWL*) which contains personal characteristics of a user (e.g., user *ID*, location, etc.) and her/his preferences (e.g., the user wants only video files). This file is obtained by means of the *Mobile Device Agent* (which executes on the user's *MD*). There is only one **UserAgent** which represents a user at the same time and centralizes all the characteristics of the same user who can have several sessions opened. The **UserAgent** communicates with the **ContentFilterAgent** to send the *User Profile XML* file in order to update user preferences.

The **DisplayFilterAgent** manages a *Knowledge Base* which contains general information about the characteristics of different types of *MDs* (e.g., format files supported) and knowledge acquired from previous connections (e.g., problems and capabilities of networks according to data transmissions).

The **ContentFilterAgent** manages a *Knowledge Base* which contains preferences and characteristics of the users. It communicates with the *UserAgent,* asking for user preferences defined for a specific session (e.g., the current session).

3   Knowledge Management in PUMAS

In this section, we describe the *knowledge* managed by agents of the *Information* and the *Adaptation MAS* of *PUMAS* to achieve their adaptation tasks and support the *Query Routing* process. This knowledge is stored in *Knowledge Bases* (*KBs*) in the shape of pieces of knowledge called "*facts*" and defined using *JESS* (which is a rule engine and scripting environment for building Java applications which has the capacity to "reason" using knowledge supplied in the form of declarative rules. *http://herzberg.ca.sandia.gov/jess/*). We declare these facts as instances of *JESS Templates* in order to represent user preferences, features of the *MD*, the *WIS*, etc. as described in the following subsections.

3.1   Knowledge of the Information MAS

The *Router Agent* stores in its *KB* a *fact* for each *WIS*. This agent exploits these facts to redirect user queries. A fact which represents a *WIS* describes characteristics of the *WIS* like its name, managed information, the type of device where it is executed (e.g., server, *MD*) and the *ISAgent* associated with the *WIS* (i.e., the *ISAgent* which execute on the *WIS* and can be asked for information and consequently answers queries). The following template defines a *WIS*:

```
(deftemplate WIS
(slot name)
(slot agentID)
(slot device)
(multislot info_items)) ; fact (1)
```

The following fact (instance of the template defined above) represents the *WIS* of a store. The *WIS* is called *StoreWIS* and executes on a *server*. The *ISAgent* which executes on this *WIS* is called *StoreISA*. The *StoreWIS* contains information (a list of *info_items*) about the *articles, sales,* and *new products* which are sold in the store:

```
(assert (WIS
(name StoreWIS)(agentID StoreISA)
(device server)
(info_items "articles" "sales" "new products")))
```

3.2   Knowledge of the Adaptation MAS

The *ContentFilterAgent* (*CFA*) manages a *KB* which contains user preferences. These preferences are represented as *facts* defined as follows:

```
(deftemplate User_Preference
(slot userID)
(slot required_info)
(multislot complementary_info)
(multislot actiontodo)
(slot problem)
(multislot actionforrecovering))) ;  fact (2)
```

The *User_Preference* fact is composed of a *userID* (which identifies the owner of this preference), required information (*required_info*) and *complementary_info* which is added to the *User_Preference* definition by the *CFA* and is inferred from queries of previous sessions (i.e. information frequently asked simultaneously with the *required_info*). This fact is also composed of information about what and how the user would like the system to present results (list of *actionstodo* for displaying information to her/him) and in the case of problems, what the system has to do (*actionsforrecovering*).

We consider that queries also depend on several criteria (criteria managed by the *CFA*): user location, her/his history in the system, activities developed during a time period, etc. Such *Criterion* is defined as:

```
(deftemplate Criterion
(slot userID)(multislot criteria)
(multislot attributes)) ; fact (3)
```

Here is an example of *Criterion* which expresses that all of *John Smith*'s queries depend on his *location*, especially if he is in the *airport*:

```
(assert (Criterion
(userID "John Smith")
(criteria location)
(attributes "airport" )))
```

In the next section, we describe the *Query Routing* process which is performed by the *Router Agent* exploiting the knowledge we have described in this section.

4   Query Routing in PUMAS

The *Query Routing* (*QR*) process in *PUMAS* is achieved by the *Router Agent* (*RA*) which receives queries together with user characteristics and those of their *MDs*. In order to redirect a query to the "*right*" *WIS*, the strategy chosen by the *RA* depends on several criteria: user location, peer similarity, time constraints, preferences, etc. The strategy can lead to sending the query to a specific *WIS*, or to sending the query through broadcast, or to splitting the query in sub-queries, each one being sent to one or several *ISAgents* (*ISAs*, agents which belong to the *Information MAS* and execute on the *WIS*). The *RA* is also in charge of compiling results returned by the *ISAs* and of analyzing them (according to the defined criteria for the queries, see section 3.2) to decide whether the whole set of results or only a part of it will be sent to the user.

In *PUMAS*, the *QR* process consists of three activities, based on the work of (Xu *et al.*, 1999) which are described and illustrated in the next subsections, using the airport scenario presented in introduction.

4.1   Analyzing the Query

This activity is related to the possible split of a query into sub-queries. The *RA* analyzes the complexity of a query. A query is considered as *simple* if it can be answered by only one agent and *complex* if several agents are required. This analysis is more precisely based on facts, stored in the *KB* of the *RA*, about the *WIS* (which notably contains knowledge about information managed by this *WIS*). The *RA* also analyzes criteria of a query (e.g., location, user's activities, etc.), knowledge of the query receivers (e.g., if the query is directed to specific known receivers), etc. After this analysis, the *RA* decides whether it has to divide a query in sub-queries or not.

For the scenario, the *RA* must split the query (*"all the shops which sell the articles of my gifts list"*) in several sub-queries (*"all the shops which sell each article of my gifts list"*). The number of sub-queries depends of the number of articles. If there is only one article, the query is *simple* (only one agent will answer). Otherwise, the query is *complex*. The *RA* must also consider two criteria: *proximity* of the departure gate and *price* of the article in the shop. For that, the *RA* asks the *CFA* for the user preferences and criteria of the query (i.e., fact (2,3) and its instances; see section 3.2). The *RA* could receive from *CFA* facts as the following which expresses that when the passenger *"John Smith"* consults the *"closest shops"*, he also wants those which sell their products at the *"lowest prices"*:

```
(assert (User_Preference
(userID "John Smith")
(required_info "closest shops")
(complementary_info "lowest prices")
(actiontodo show)
(problem "empty list of shops")
(actionforrecovering cancel)))
```

4.2 Selecting the Information Sources

A query could be directed to a specific agent or to a group of agents; if the query receivers are known, the selection is simple (the potential information sources are the specific agents). Otherwise, the *RA* selects information sources and computes the *network of neighbours*, based on ideas of (Yang *et al.*, 2004). These authors propose an efficient *QR* approach for information retrieval in unstructured *P2P* networks. The *QR* policies are utilized to determine to how many nodes and to which nodes, the query should be forwarded in the network. This work introduces the *Routing Guide* (*RG*) concept which is based on results returned for queries previously processed, and is used to determine routing directions for queries. In the information retrieval process in *P2P* systems, each node owns a collection of data that is shared with other nodes. When a user submits a query, her/his node becomes the source of the query (requestor). Such node may send query messages to any number of its neighbours. Then any neighbour receiving the query message firstly processes the query over its local information. If the node finds some results, it sends back its address to the requestor node so that it fetches data directly.

In our proposal, a peer is *neighbour* of some others if it satisfies a set of characteristics (criteria defined in user preferences of an application). For example, close location, same activities, same role, similar knowledge, colleagues who work in group. The characteristics are not restricted to proximity criteria.

We can consider several cases for composing a network of neighbours in which each node is an information source:

First case, there could be one or several agents which answer the same query. The simplest way of composing this network is to group all these agents. This gathering is useful, for example, when the *RA* does not have information about the sources or when it is the first time that the *RA* works with the neighbours. In order to avoid unnecessary, redundant or useless communications and select the most relevant neighbours, the *RA* applies criteria of dependency of the query. For instance, if the criterion is *location*, the network is composed of the *nearest neighbours*; if user queries depend on her/his *previous queries*, the *RA* must redirect them to the *most trusted neighbours*; if the criterion is *similarity*, the network could be composed of the neighbours with a *similar profile, tasks*, etc. If no criteria are established, the *RA* analyzes the trust level of these neighbours. The *RA* associates a trust level to each neighbour from answers to previous queries, based on the work of (Agostini *et al.,* 2004). In these authors' work, when a peer receives a query, it analyzes the result of its queries and increases the trust of those peers who reply with more appropriate semantic contents. This work explains the process for sending queries from a peer to other ones. After query formulation, a peer named "*seeker*" checks what peers are connected ("*active*") and chooses, among those connected, which peers send the query. A query session is then opened to manage the answer from each peer, or from peers that are connected with the peer in charge of solving the query. The strategy used by the seeker in order to select a provider and referrals from providers to solve the query is a *Trust and Reputation Strategy*.

The *Trust and Reputation Strategy* proposed by (Agostini *et al.*, 2004) consists of the following process: the *seeker* faces the problem of selecting which one among the peers is able to solve a query Q with highest probability, or who makes the most progress towards solving the query. To decide, the *seeker* constructs and manages a list $<p1, p2,...pk>$ of trusted peers to which submit the query. The list is conventionally ordered according to decreasing trust level. The *seeker* strategy of query resolution is the following: first, it asks $p1$, then $p2$, and continues up to pk until it receives relevant answers from previous peers in the list. It is important to note that the list of trusted peers evolves with the system. The *Trust* of a peer is acquired by its *Reputation*.

Second case, a query could be only answered by one agent which is known. The *RA* uses its *KB* (describing what are the *WIS*, their *ISAs* and their managed information) to contact the *WIS* from which it could obtain the answer to this query. This is a specialization of the first case.

Third case, the query has been split in several sub-queries in the analysis step. The *RA* analyzes which agents can answer each one. The *network of neighbours* is then composed by the agents which could answer the sub-queries. The process applied in order to select information sources (*ISAs*) for each sub-query is the same that the process defined in the first case. Finally, the *network of neighbours* is composed of the union of the different sub-networks generated for each sub-query.

For the scenario, the *RA* could include in the *network of neighbours* all *ISAs* executing on *WIS* of the *duty free shops* which sell the products she/he searches (based on fact (1) and its instances; see section 3.1). The *RA* must also analyze the trust level associated with these neighbours (e.g., the first shop which answers). If it is the first time that the *RA* executes this query or that works with these *ISAs*, the *RA* sends the query to them through a broadcast message. The *RA* must compose the *network of neighbours* of the agents which could answer the sub-queries of the query ("*the closest shops to the departure gate which sell the wanted article at the lowest price*"). In order to select the *WIS* of those shops, the *RA* must apply criteria for the queries (based on fact (3) and its instances; see section 3.2), in this case, the *proximity* of the shops to the departure gate and the *lowest price* for the articles. For this case, the *RA* could store facts in its *KB* like the ones presented below. These facts express that all queries from passenger "*John Smith*" depends on both his *location*, particularly if he is at the airport, and, the *proximity* of the departure gate:

```
(assert (Criterion
(userID "John Smith")
(criteria location)
(attributes "airport" )))

(assert (Criterion
(userID "John Smith")
(criteria proximity)
(attributes "departure gate" )))
```

4.3 Redirecting the Query

Once the *RA* has identified potential information sources (*neighbours*), it redirects the query, sending a message which includes the query to its *neighbours*. The *RA* can use an oriented message (for specific receivers) or broadcast it to all neighbours (e.g., waiting for the first one to reply, obtaining all the answers and analyzing which are the most trusted ones). If the *RA* has a trust schema for the agents which compose the *network of neighbours*, the *RA* could send the message in a sequential way, starting with the most trusted one. If it answers, the process is finished. Otherwise, the *RA* has to continue sending messages until the least trusted agent has been contacted, according to the ideas of (Agostini *et al.*, 2004).

For the scenario, the network is composed of *ISAs* which execute on the *WIS* of the *duty free shops*. If there is only one shop *WIS*, the *RA* sends it the query. Otherwise, the *RA* sends the query to each *ISA*, beginning with the most trusted one.

If the *RA* knows that *neighbor1* can answer *sub-query1*, *neighbor2* can answer *sub-query2* and so on, it sends the oriented messages to each neighbour (based on fact (1) about the *WIS* and its instances; see section 3.1). For example, if the passenger would like to know if her/his flight is on time, the *RA* sends the query to the *ISA* which executes on the *WIS* of the airline (for this example, we call it "*OneISA*") and to the *ISA* which executes on the *WIS* of the airport and manages flight departure and arrival schedules (for this example, we call it "*DAFlightsISA*"). In this case, we can find in the *KB* of the *RA* the following facts which allow it to redirect the query to the *OneISA* and the *DAFlightsISA*:

```
(assert (WIS
(name AirlineOneIS)(agentID OneISA)
(device server)
(info_items "departures" "arrivals" "prices")))

(assert (WIS
(name AirportIS)(agentID DAFlightsISA)
(device server)
(info_items "departures" "arrivals")))
```

The *RA* must then compile answers obtained from different agents and select the most relevant ones according to the established dependency criteria. The mechanisms for compiling results are not explained in this paper.

5 Related Works

We present here some agent-based architectures or frameworks for adapting information to users.

CONSORTS Architecture (Kurumatani, 2003) is based on ubiquitous agents and designed for a massive support of *MDs*. It detects user locations and defines user profiles to adapt their information. The *CONSORTS* architecture proposes a mechanism to define the relations that hold between agents (e.g., communication, hierarchy, role definition), with the purpose of satisfying user requests. Unlike *PUMAS*, it does not consider distribution of information between *MDs* (which could improve response time) nor user preferences.

The work of (Gandon *et al.*, 2004) proposes a Semantic Web architecture for context-awareness and privacy. This architecture supports automated discovery and access of a user's personal resources subject to user-specified privacy preferences. Service invocation rules along with ontologies and profiles enable identification of the most relevant resources available to answer a query. However, it does not consider that information which can answer a query can be distributed between different sources.

The *PIA-System* (Albayrak *et al.*, 2005) is an agent-based personal information system for collecting, filtering and integrating information at a common point, offering access to information by *WWW*, e-mail, *SMS*, *MMS* and *J2ME* clients. It combines *push* and *pull* techniques in order to allow the user on the one hand, to search explicitly for specific information and, on the other hand, to be informed automatically about relevant information. However, the *PIA System* only searches information in text format. It does not consider the adaptation of different kinds of media to different *MDs*, nor user location.

(Sashima *et al.*, 2004) propose an agent-based coordination framework for ubiquitous computing. It coordinates services and devices to assist a particular user in receiving a particular service in order to maximize her/his satisfaction. This framework chooses proper resources from numerous sources, coordinates those resources on behalf of users and assists them in accessing resources of ubiquitous computing environments. These authors take into account the contextual features of nomadic users, especially, the location. Unlike *PUMAS*, this framework does not consider the adaptation of information according to the access devices nor the possible distribution of data among devices.

6 Conclusions and Future Work

In this paper, we have described knowledge managed and exchanged by the *Information* and the *Adaptation MAS* of *PUMAS* to support the adaptation capabilities and the *Query Routing* process. *PUMAS* is a framework which retrieves adapted information according to user profiles and technical capabilities of *MDs* used to access the *Web Information Systems* (*WIS*). We have also described the strategies followed by the *Router Agent* to perform the *Query Routing* process. In *PUMAS*, this process is composed of three activities: *analysis of the query, selection of the information sources* and *redirection of the query*. Finally, we have presented each activity and we have also illustrated them through a scenario supported by a *WIS* in an airport.

We are currently implementing and testing each *MAS* of *PUMAS*. For this purpose, we have chosen *JADE-LEAP* (*http://jade.tilab.com/*), a *FIPA* compliant platform. We intend to define, on the one hand, algorithms for each activity of the *Query Routing* process and, on the other hand, extensions of an *Agent Communication Language* (*ACL, http://www.fipa.org/specs/fipa00061/SC00061G.html*) in order to consider nomadic user characteristics like location and connection time. For this purpose, we want to introduce in *ACL*, primitives like *query-when*, *query-where*, *query-close*.

Acknowledgements

The author *Angela Carrillo-Ramos* is partially supported by the *Universidad de los Andes* (Colombia). She thanks *Nicolas Lopez-Giraldo* for his comments.

References

Agostini, A., Moro, G.: Identification of Communities of Peers by Trust and Reputation. In: Bussler, C.J., Fensel, D. (eds.) AIMSA 2004. LNCS (LNAI), vol. 3192, pp. 85–95. Springer, Heidelberg (2004)

Albayrak, S., Wollny, S., Varone, N., Lommatzsch, A., Milosevic, D.: Agent Technology for Personalized Information Filtering: The PIA-System. In: Preneel, B., Tavares, S. (eds.) SAC 2005. LNCS, vol. 3897, pp. 54–59. Springer, Heidelberg (2005)

Carrillo-Ramos, A., Gensel, J., Villanova-Oliver, M., Martin, H.: PUMAS: a Framework based on Ubiquitous Agents for Accessing Web Information Systems through Mobile Devices. In: Preneel, B., Tavares, S. (eds.) SAC 2005. LNCS, vol. 3897, pp. 1003–1008. Springer, Heidelberg (2006a)

Carrillo-Ramos, A., Gensel, J., Villanova-Oliver, M., Martin, H.: A Peer Ubiquitous Multi-Agent Framework for providing nomadic users with adapted information. In: Despotovic, Z., Joseph, S., Sartori, C. (eds.) AP2PC 2005. LNCS (LNAI), vol. 4118, pp. 166–179. Springer, Heidelberg (2005b)

El Fallah-Seghrouchni, A., Suna, A.: CLAIM: A Computational Language for Autonomous, Intelligent and Mobile Agent. In: Dastani, M., Dix, J., El Fallah-Seghrouchni, A. (eds.) PROMAS 2003. LNCS (LNAI), vol. 3067, pp. 90–110. Springer, Heidelberg (2004)

Gandon, F., Sadeh, N.: Semantic Web Technologies to Reconcile Privacy and Context Awareness. Journal of Web Semantics 1(3) (2004) (Retrieved Nov. 9, 2005). http://www.websemanticsjournal.org/ps/pub/2004-17

Indulska, J., Robinson, R., Rakotonirainy, A., Henricksen, K.: Experiences in Using CC/PP in Context-Aware Systems. In: Chen, M.-S., Chrysanthis, P.K., Sloman, M., Zaslavsky, A. (eds.) MDM 2003. LNCS, vol. 2574, pp. 247–261. Springer, Heidelberg (2003)

Kurumatani, K.: Mass User Support by Social Coordination among Citizen in a Real Environment. In: Kurumatani, K., Chen, S.-H., Ohuchi, A. (eds.) IJCAI-WS 2003 and MAMUS 2003. LNCS (LNAI), vol. 3012, pp. 1–16. Springer, Heidelberg (2004)

Park, J., Barber, S.: Finding Information Sources by Model Sharing in Open Multi-Agent System. In: UbiAgents04, Workshop on Agents for Ubiquitous Computing. (Retrieved November 9, 2005) (2004). http://www.ift.ulaval.ca/~mellouli/ubiagents04/

Pirker, M., Berger, M., Watzke, M.: An approach for FIPA Agent Service Discovery in Mobile Ad Hoc Environments. In: UbiAgents04, Workshop on Agents for Ubiquitous Computing. (Retrieved November 9, 2005) (2004). http://www.ift.ulaval.ca/~mellouli/ubiagents04/

Ramparany, F., Boissier, O., Brouchoud, H.: Cooperating Autonomous Smart Devices. In: sOc'2003, the Smart Objects Conference, pp. 182–185 (2003)

Sashima, A., Izumi, N., Kurumatani, K.: Bridging Coordination Gaps between Devices, Services, and Humans in Ubiquitous computing. In: UbiAgents04, Workshop on Agents for Ubiquitous Computing. (Retrieved November 9, 2004). http://www.ift.ulaval.ca/~mellouli/ubiagents04/

Xu, J., Lim, E., Ng, W.K.: Cluster-Based Database Selection Techniques for Routing Bibliographic Queries. In: Bench-Capon, T.J.M., Soda, G., Tjoa, A.M. (eds.) DEXA 1999. LNCS, vol. 1677, pp. 100–109. Springer, Heidelberg (1999)

Yang, D., Xu, L., Cai, W., Zhou, S., Zhou, A.: Efficient Query Routing for XML Documents Retrieval in Unstructured Peer to Peer Networks. In: Yu, J.X., Lin, X., Lu, H., Zhang, Y. (eds.) APWeb 2004. LNCS, vol. 3007, pp. 217–223. Springer, Heidelberg (2004)

Ontology-Based Integration of XML Data

Schematic Marks as a Bridge Between Syntax and Semantic Level

Christophe Cruz and Christophe Nicolle

Laboratoire LE2I, UMR CNRS 5158, Université de Bourgogne,
BP 47870, 21078 Dijon Cedex, France
christophe.cruz@u-bourgogne.fr, cnicolle@u-bourgogne.fr

Abstract. This paper presents an ontology integration approach of XML data. The approach is composed of two pillars the first of which is based on formal language and XML grammars analysis. The second pillar is based on ontology and domain ontology analysis. The keystone of this architecture which creates a bridge between the two pillars is based on the concept of schematic marks introduced in this paper. These schematic marks make it possible to establish the link between the syntactic level and the semantic level for our integration framework.

Keywords: XML, XML schema, Ontology, Integration, Semantic.

1 Introduction

Data integration consists in inserting a data set into another data set. In the context of the Web, document integration consists in creating hypermedia links between the documents using URL. Associated documents are multimedia documents which can be text, pictures, videos, sounds or any other file format. In the context of database integration, integrated data coming from several information systems makes information more complete and more relevant with a more global objective use. For example the biomedical data source is known to be hyper-linked because the description of objects suggests several hyperlinks, allowing the user to "sail" from one object to another in multiple data sources. Indeed there are on the Web more than one hundred genetic databases, two hundred twenty-six data sources of molecular biology, etc. (A. Baxevanis, 2000), (D. Benson et al., 2000). A second example of activity which is more and more based on the use of complex data source integration is the field of geographical information management. Just as biological and medical data, geographical data are heterogeneous and distributed. These data are for example weather (France: www.meteofrance.com) or cartographic (road maps: www. viamichelin.com). In fact data integration of various sources will thus make it possible to carry out more complex, precise requests and improve the various information systems available. The objective of data integration is to benefit from the diversity of information available and to benefit from the rise of new Web technologies. Moreover the re-use of data and services make it possible to optimize the costs for the acquisition and the maintenance of information. Finally, the

J. Filipe, J. Cordeiro, and V. Pedrosa (Eds.): WEBIST 2005/2006, LNBIP 1, pp. 97–110, 2007.

management and the cost of the data-processing resources are distributed among the whole of the data suppliers.

2 Background

In the context of the Web, XML technologies became a headlight technology for data structuring and data exchanges. Many systems using XML as databases integration have a mediation approach (A. Pan et al.,2002), (D. Draper et al., 2001), (M. J. Carey et al., 2000), (A. Cali et al., 2001). The evolution of the Web technologies changed the integration problem of information. In fact the XML contribution to define not only integration schemas but also the definition languages of the corresponding models reduced considerably the problems related to the structural and the syntactic heterogeneity. The contribution of the Web technologies related to the service oriented architectures solved partially the problems of the localization and the data access allowing the design of interoperability architectures on a greater scale (K. Aberer et al., 2001). Nevertheless, during the integration data process and the integration services there remain many problems related to semantic heterogeneity.

In order to support the action of agents, knowledge has to represent the real world by reflecting entities and relations between them. Therefore knowledge constitutes a model of the world and agents use their knowledge as a model of the world. On the one hand the integration of different entities is possible when the semantic of the entities and the relations is identical. In addition, to model the semantic of knowledge as well as the structure where this knowledge is stored, it is necessary to reach a higher conceptual level. For that knowledge representation is independent of knowledge use. Thus knowledge representation and inferential mechanisms are dissociated (N. Guarino et al., 1994). On the other hand, domain conceptualization can be performed without ambiguity only if a context of use can be given. In fact a word or a term can designate two different concepts depending on the particular context of use (B. Bachimont et al., 2000). The semantic of knowledge is strongly constrained by the symbolic representation of computers. Therefore N. Guarino (N. Guarino, 1994) introduced an ontological level between the conceptual level and epistemological level. The ontological level forms a bridge between interpretative semantics in which users interpret terms and operational semantics in which computers handle symbols (T. Dechilly and B. Bachimont, 2000). In fact the problem consists in defining an upper conceptual level to handle the semantic in XML documents for their integration. This level will define a semantic framework leading to the integration of XML data by the use of an ontology.

The implementation of an ontology is a mapping stage between the system elements and their ontological "counterparts". Once this mapping has been carried out, the representation of elements in the ontology is regarded as a meta-data diagram. The role of a meta-data diagram is double (B. Amann and D. Partage, 2003). On the one hand it represents an ontology of the knowledge shared on a domain. On the other hand it plays the role of a database schema which is used for the formulation of requests structured on meta-data or to constitute views. This principle is applied to ontology based data integration using domain ontology to provide integration structures and request processes to these structures. According to (I. F. Cruz et al., 2004),

(M. Klein, 2002), (L. V. Lakshmannan and F. Sadri, 2003) data integration consists in defining rules of mapping between information sources and the ontological level. The principle consists in labeling source elements and thus providing semantic definition to elements compared to a consensual definition of the meaning. This phase is inevitably necessary because this information was not added to the document during its creation. Moreover an XML schema defines only the structure of associated XML documents. However, an XML schema contains tacit knowledge that can be used to define ontology by extracting a set of elements and properties whose meaning will be defined for a more global use.

Section 3 describes a general view of our method based on two pillars (ontology and formal language). The keystone of our method is the concept of schematic marks. This section describes this concept by a formal way. Section 4 defines a set of integration rules based on the schematic marks.

3 Method Overview

Our integration solution consists in connecting various levels of semantic and schematic abstraction. This solution is articulated in two stages. The first stage relates to the semantic formalization of the writing rules to define an XML grammar. This formalization will enable us to define the components of a generic ontology. The second stage relates to the definition of the ontologization mechanisms of the semantic elements from a specific XML grammar to obtain an ontology of domain. The concepts and the relations of the domain ontology are then defined starting from the elements of the XML schema. These mechanisms make it possible to identify some concepts and relations common to several XML schemas. Consequently ontology makes it possible to link the concepts and the relations by amalgamating the attributes of the common elements which are semantically identical. The domain ontology will be extended and then modified to represent the semantic of several XML schemas relating to a particular domain. To specify the "semantic elements" of an XML schema it is first necessary to identify and mark them. We call these schematic marks. They will be used to establish links between the structure of an XML document and its semantic definition. Those schematic marks represent the structural level of the integration system (e.g. Fig. 1).

Fig. 1. The two pillars and the keystone of our method

To specify the semantic of the XML schema elements it is necessary to identify and mark them using schematic marks. These marks will be used to establish links between the structure of the XML document and its semantic definition. This section presents first of all the formalization of XML documents using formal languages. In addition this section outlines a formalization of XML grammars using the formal languages on which the principle of schematic marks is based. This underlines the fact that XML grammars generate languages of Dyck. According to definite properties of Dyck languages the concepts of factor and schematic mark are defined.

3.1 XML Document Formalization

An XML document is composed of text and opening tags associated to closing tags. Some of these tags are at the same time opening and closing tags. In fact, empty tags define the sheets of the XML trees. One of the properties of an XML canonical document is to be composed of only opening or closing tags. Empty tags can be exchanged by opening and closing tags without any problems for the XML parser. Consequently, any XML file having empty tags has an equivalent without empty tags. This property is syntactic because it does not appear in the grammatical rules formalizing the structure of the document. Starting from this information some definitions are expressed.

Definition 1: An *alphabet* is a finite set of symbols recorded Σ. These elements are called *letters*. In this paper most of the time it will be written: $\Sigma = \{a, b, \ldots\}$. The *size* $|\Sigma|$ of an alphabet Σ equals the number of its elements.

Definition 2: A *word* or a *sentence* on Σ is a sequence of letters coming from this alphabet. The word « wall » is a sequence of letters from the alphabet $\Sigma = \{a, b, \ldots, z\}$. It is said by convention that the word *empty* is the null size word. It is written: ε. The set of all words that are possible to be written on the alphabet Σ is written: Σ^*. $\Sigma^+ = \Sigma^* - \{\varepsilon\}$.

Definition 3: A *formal language* L is a set of words on Σ^*. A *language* L on the alphabet Σ is called regular (A regular language is a language of kind 3 in the Chomsky hierarchy) only if it is generated on the alphabet Σ and if it is defined by a regular expression. It means that the set of regular languages on Σ is exactly the set of languages recognizable by finite state automaton on Σ. In others words for each finite state automaton it is possible to associate regular expressions that define identical languages recognized by the same automaton and reciprocally.

We have just seen that a language L is made of words generated starting from an alphabet. If in an XML document we just consider the tree structure without taking into account the values of the tags' attributes, then the set of the XML documents which it is generable from a XML schema define a language. Moreover the set of the tags of XML documents defined by XML schema represents a part of the alphabet on the language. It defines only one part because the alphabet can contain letters not used by the language.

Definition 4: A formal grammar can be defined as a mathematical entity on which we can associate an algorithmic process to generate a language. It is defined as a quadruplet $G = \langle N, T, P, S \rangle$ in which:

- T written also Σ is the terminal alphabet on G.
- N the non terminal alphabet on G.
- $V = N \cup T$ is an alphabet composing the whole symbols of G.
- P is a set of production rules or regular expressions.
- $S \in N$ is the start symbol on G.

$$N = \{S, A\} \quad T = \{a, b\}$$

$$P = \{(S \rightarrow AA), (S \rightarrow \varepsilon), (A \rightarrow aa), (A \rightarrow bb)\}$$

$$S \rightarrow AA \mid \varepsilon$$

$$A \rightarrow aa \mid bb$$

$$G_1 = \langle N, \Sigma, P, S \rangle$$

Example 1: G_1 grammar.

Example 1 shows a grammar for which the generated words are «aaaa» «aabb» «bbaa» «bbbb» and «». The language is composed of four words and the empty word.

3.2 Formal Grammar and XML Grammar

We saw in the preceding section the concept of regular language and that of formal grammar. This section presents formal grammars and XML grammars by making connections between them. These grammars have the characteristic to have a final vocabulary composed of opening tags and closing tags.

Definition 5: For a given set A composed of opening tags and corresponding closing tags, an XML document is a word composed from the alphabet $T = A \cup \overline{A}$.

For the moment we just take into account the syntactic structure. An XML document x is well formed if only one tag is root and if the tags are correctly imbricated.

Definition 6: A document x is well formed if x is generated by production rules from a language of Dyck on $T = A \cup \overline{A}$. A language of Dyck is a language generated by a context-free grammar where $a_n \in A$ and $b_n \in \overline{A}$:

$$S \rightarrow SS \mid \varepsilon \mid a_1 S b_1 \mid a_2 S b_2 \mid ... \mid a_n S b_n \ with \ n \geq 1$$

This definition corresponds to the terminology and the notation used in the XML community. A language is indeed a set of XML documents which can be generated starting from a grammar. These grammars of XML languages are called "Document Type Definition" (DTD). The axiom of grammars is qualified DOCTYPE and the whole of the production rules is associated to a tag ELEMENT (Example 2). A tag ELEMENT is made up of a type and a model. The type is simply the name of the tag and the model is the regular expression for the element.

$$P = \left\{ \left(S \to a \left(S \mid T \right) \left(S \mid T \right) \overline{a} \right), \left(T \to b T \overline{b} \right), \left(T \to b \overline{b} \right) \right\}$$

```
<?xml version="1.0" encoding="UTF-8"?>
<!ELEMENT a ((a | b), (a | b))>
<!ELEMENT b (b*)>
```

Example 2: Similarity between a grammar and a DTD.

All of the production rules corresponding to the grammar can also be represented using a XML schema which can be translated out of a DTD (Example 3). DTD only defines the relations between the various components of a document contrary to the XML schema that defines also data types.

```
<?xml version="1.0" encoding="UTF-8"?>
<!ELEMENT ROOT (A | (B, C))>

<?xml version="1.0" encoding="UTF-8"?>
<xsd:schema
xmlns:xsd="http://www.w3.org/2001/XMLSchema"
elementFormDefault="qualified">
  <xsd:element name="A"/>
  <xsd:element name="B"/>
  <xsd:element name="C"/>
      <xsd:element name="ROOT">
          <xsd:complexType>
              <xsd:choice>
                  <xsd:element ref="A"/>
                  <xsd:sequence>
                      <xsd:element ref="B"/>
                      <xsd:element ref="C"/>
                  </xsd:sequence>
              </xsd:choice>
          </xsd:complexType>
      </xsd:element>
</xsd:schema>
```

Example 3: Similarity between DTD and W3C XML schema.

In this section we saw reminders on the formal languages by making parallels between a formal grammar and an XML schema. We know that an XML schema is a formal grammar that generates a language of Dyck and that it has consequently the properties of a language of Dyck. The following section describes the properties of grammars that generate languages of Dyck and introduces the definition of schematic marks.

3.3 Factor and Schematic Marks

The properties of the languages of Dyck were the subject of studies undertaken by J Berstel (J. Berstel and L. Boasson, 2000). By drawing parallels between XML grammar and the languages of Dyck, J Berstel defines the concept of factor. According to the lemma 3.3 of J.Berstel if G is an XML grammar on $T = A \cup \overline{A}$ generating a language L with a non terminal vocabulary X_a and $a \in A$ then for each $a \in A$ the language generated by X_a is a set of factors of words in L which are languages of Dyck starting by the letter $a : L_G(X_a) = F_a(L)$.

A given language: $L = \left\{ ca(b\overline{b})^{n_1} \overline{a}a(b\overline{b})^{n_2} \overline{a} \ldots a(b\overline{b})^{n_k} \overline{a}\overline{c} \mid n_{1,2\ldots_k} > 0 \right\}$

then $F_c(L) = L$, $F_b(L) = \left\{ b\overline{b} \right\}^*$, $F_a(L) = \left\{ a(b\overline{b})^* \overline{a} \right\}$

Example 4: Factors of the language L.

This means that a language is factorizable in an under language and a factor of a language of Dyck is a language of a language of Dyck. Consequently an under tree of an XML document can be generated by a factor of the language of Dyck to which the XML document belongs.

According to the corollary 3.4 of J. Berstel there is only one factor for an XML grammar $F_a(L) = L$. This means that there is only one 'father' tag for all others. This tag is the root. Consequently there is only one factor $F_a(L) = L$ where a is the root.

According to the same corollary 3.4: For a given word w of the language L there is a unique factorization $w = au_{a_1} u_{a_2} \ldots u_{a_n} \overline{a}$ with $u_{a_i} \in D_{a_i}$ for $i \in 1, \ldots n$.

D_{a_i} is a language of Dyck starting by a_i and $D_{a_i} \subset D_A$. The *trace* of a word w is defined by a word $a_1 a_2 \ldots a_n$. The *surface* $a \in A$ in the language L is a set $S_a(L)$ of all traces of the words of the factor $F_a(L)$. The notion of surface is used by Berstel to demonstrate the following proposition:

Proposition 1: For each XML language L there is only one reduced XML grammar generating L.

This means that all the languages of an XML grammar are generated by the same reduced XML grammar. This independently of the values of tag's attributes in the documents. And if we only take into account the syntactic structure of XML documents. This proposal implies that if a factor were defined on an XML language then this factor would correspond to a production rule of the reduced grammar XML generating this language. This proposal makes it possible to introduce the concept of schematic mark (e.g. Fig. 2). A reduced grammar does not have any useless non terminal vocabulary which is, in general, not the case for grammars generating languages of Dick. But an XML schema does not use unnecessary tags, so an XML schema does not use unnecessary non terminal vocabulary.

Definition 7: A schematic mark is a mark on an XML schema to identify a production rule.

Fig. 2. Definition of a schematic mark for the floor

Those schematic marks allow to make links between an XML schema element and a factor in a corresponding XML language and, as a result, all XML documents that can be generated by the XML schema. In the following example the elements which are marked define a concept. Consequently, the schematic marks allow to provide links between the concept and these instances. Thus, the schematic marks can also mark a relational element and an attribute element. Those concept elements, relational elements and attribute elements are used to define the domain ontology of the XML schema. The schematic marks are used to link the component of the ontology and the element of the XML schema (e.g. Fig. 3). At the ontology level the schematic marks are said to be the semantic definition of the XML schema elements that allow to identify the elements that have a tacit semantic and are not defined formally.

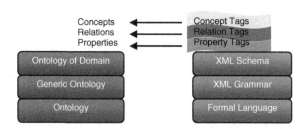

Fig. 3. Definition of schematic marks

The following section shows that several schematics marks of various XML schemas can have the same semantics defined by a common ontology. In this case, the element properties corresponding to the schematic marks are integrated within the same concept defined in ontology. It is called semantic integration of XML schema.

4 Integration Rules

This section is outlined in three parts. The first part presents the formalization of the XML grammar construction rules. This formalization enables us to release a set of terms which will be used to build our generic ontology. This generic ontology allows to define the elements of the domain of each XML schema to be integrated. The second part presents the definition of generic ontology. This generic ontology is used as model to create domain ontologies. This formal structure makes it possible to index the tacit knowledge contained in the XML schema. This knowledge is then explicit because it raises any ambiguity on the interpretation of the XML document terms generated starting from an integrated XML schema.

4.1 Schematic Formalization

This section presents a set of definitions and rules to formalize the construction of XML grammars and to define the concepts, relations and attributes of our generic ontology.

Definition 8: The Factor $F_a(L)$ of a language L is a *conceptual factor* if it defines a concept. For example, the factor $F_{Building}(L)$ is a concept because it defines the concept *Building*.

Rule 1: If the conceptual factor $F_a(L_1)$ of a language L_1 and the conceptual factor $F_b(L_2)$ of a language L_2 handle the same semantic of a common concept then the intension of the concept is define with the help of the conceptual factors $F_a(L_1)$ of L_1 and $F_b(L_2)$ of L_2.

Definition 9: The Factor $F_a(L)$ of a language L is a *relational factor* if it defines a relation. For example, if a wall contains a door then the relational factor $F_{Contain}(L)$ is a relation because it defines a relation between a wall and a door.

Rule 2: If the factor $F_a(L_1)$ of a language L_1 and the factor $F_b(L_2)$ of a language L_2 handle a common semantic of a relation then the intension of the relation is define with the help of the relational factors $F_a(L_1)$ of $F_b(L_2)$ of L_2.

Definition 10: The Factor $F_a(L)$ of a language L is an *attribute factor* if it defines one or several proprieties of a concept or a relation. For example, if a wall has a geometrical shape then the attribute factor $F_{Geometry}(L)$ is an attribute because it defines the geometry of a wall.

Rule 3: If the factor $F_a(L_1)$ of a language L_1 is an *attribute factor* then it is integrated in the intension of the concept or the relation. For example if a wall has a thermical propriety the geometry attribute factor $F_a(L_1)$ is integrated in the intension of the concept *wall*. The attribute factor can be integrated in several intensions of concept and relation.

The rules and definitions 8, 9 and 10 make it possible to define the conceptual factors, the relational factors, and the factor attributes of a language. These factors correspond to schematic marks carried out the elements of an XML grammar. A schematic mark in an XML grammar corresponds to a factor in the language. By defining these factors as conceptual, relational or as attributes, we give them a semantic. This semantic is already carried by the elements but this marking allows to make it explicit. Moreover, the definition of their attributes constitutes the intension of the concept or the relation and thus this improves their definition. By amalgamating the attributes of the diagrammatic marks of various XML schemas through the same concept or the same relation we carry out an integration of concepts or relations. This integration constitutes the integration of an XML schema. The following rules and definitions define the particular cases.

Rule 4: If $F_a(L)$ is a relational factor of a language L then $F_a(L)$ links a conceptual factor 'father' to a set of conceptual factor 'sons'.

Rule 5: If the trace of a conceptual factor $F_a(L)$ is composed of a conceptual factor $F_b(L)$ then the link between the two conceptual factors $F_a(L)$ and $F_b(L)$ is a relational factor $F_{rab}(L)$. For example if the conceptual factor *wall* has a conceptual factor 'son' *door* then there is a relational factor between the conceptual factor *wall* and the conceptual factor *door*.

Rule 6: If the trace of a conceptual factor $F_a(L)$ is composed of a conceptual factor set $F_\alpha(L)$ with $\alpha \in A$ (alphabet $T = A \cup \overline{A}$) and if the semantic of the relation is the same then the link between $F_a(L)$ and the set $F_\alpha(L)$ is a relational factor $F_{r\alpha}(L)$, having for conceptual factor 'father' $F_a(L)$ and for conceptual factor 'son' set $F_\alpha(L)$. For example the conceptual factor *floor* has a conceptual factor *wall*, a conceptual factor *column*, a conceptual factor *beam* and a conceptual factor *slab*. If the signification of the link between a floor and the elements *wall*, *column*, *beam* and *slab* is the same then the relational factor between the element *wall* and the other elements are of the same kind.

Definition 11: The intension of a concept is composed of a set of schematic marks on XML grammars. Those schematics marks are connected to several conceptual factors of the language generated by the grammars.

Definition 12: The extension of a concept is composed of set of instances. In the present case those instances are called semantic elements having a trace which is a set of XML trees.

Definition 13: The intension of a relation is composed of a set of schematic marks on the XML grammars. Those schematic marks are connected to a relational factor of the language generated by the grammars.

Definition 14: The extension of a relation is composed of a set of instances. In the present case those instances called relational elements have a trace which is a set of XML trees.

Definition 15: A factor defines a concept or relation or an attribute of an element from an XML schema. Consequently, a mark is a conceptual factor or a relational factor or an attribute factor.

Rule 7: If two instances of a concept represent the same object or the same relation then they can be identified as equal. For example, an object *wall* has a set of thermical properties and another object *wall* has a geometrical shape definition. Those two walls are the same object if they have an identifier that allows to identify them as the same object.

These definitions and rules give a set of vocabulary that composes the taxonomy of our system. This vocabulary is composed of the following words: *concept, relation, attribute, conceptual factor, relational factor, attribute factor, semantic element,* and *relational element.* Each word defines a concept of our generic ontology and is linked to a class.

- The class *concept* is defined by properties represented by its intension which is composed of a list of conceptual factors.
- The class *relation* is defined by properties represented by its intension which is composed of a list of relational factors.
- The *semantic* and *relational elements* are classes allowing the instantiation of objects coming from XML documents.
- The whole object of the class *semantic element* linked to an instance of the class concepts represents the extension of the instance of *concept.*
- The whole object of the class *relational element* linked to an instance of the class *relation* represents the extension of the instance of *relation.*
- The instances of the class *conceptual factors* and the class *relational factors* are references to the schematic marks on XML grammars. Those marks are XML documents extracted from XML grammars. The traces are XML documents extracted from XML documents to integrate.

We saw until now the definitions and the rules for the integration of XML schemas using a generic ontology. These rules make it possible to share the properties of various XML schemas. This level of integration is called schema integration level because it gathers in the heart of the same concept or relation various properties defining the intension of a concept or a relation. On this level of integration follows a second level of integration. This level is called data integration level. The first level defines the concepts, the relations, and the attributes which will be instanced on the second level of integration using the schematic marks.

4.2 Generic Ontology

Previous sections have presented a partial formalization of XML grammars which makes it possible to build a generic ontology (e.g. Fig. 4). This generic ontology allows to define a set of domain ontologies corresponding to various integrated XML schemas.

Fig. 4. Def. of the generic concepts of our generic ontology

Once implemented this generic ontology makes it possible to define the concepts, the relations, and the properties of several domain ontologies.

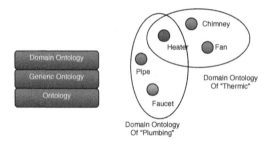

Fig. 5. Definition of two domain ontologies and integration of the concept "heater"

In the example figure 5 the concept *Heater* is common to both domain ontologies coming from two different XML schemas. The pooling of this concept in two domain ontologies makes it possible to integrate two XML schema.

Among the languages of representation developed at the conceptual level there are three principal types of models: languages containing frame (M. Kifer et al., 1995), logics of description (D. Kayser, 1997), and the model of the conceptual graphs (J. Sowa, 1984). To define our ontology we chose the language containing frame because the development related to the Web services which will be used in our architecture is carried out in the programming language directed for JAVA objects.

5 Conclusion

After a syntactic approach of XML data this paper presented an ontology based on the semantic approach of data XML. The study of the semantic structure of XML grammars and ontologies has inspired the construction of classes representing an integration ontology of data generated by XML grammars. This cognitive structure has many advantages of which the most important one is to be evolutionary as well on the level of the data as of the definition of the data structures. The field of ontologies made it possible to achieve the goal which is an integration structure of XML data. Nevertheless, the treatment of XML grammars for the semantic extraction of knowledge realized by the user in a manual way thanks to the knowledge of XML schema is not without defects. This extraction causes problems in the decomposition of the XML schemas. How to choose the level of granularity by limiting the problem of the redundancy of information? This case is rather current in complex XML schema where tags refer to tags having an identifier. In this manner a tag can have two 'fathers' so that these tag 'fathers' compete with each other (A. Dekhtyar, 2003). In this case if these links are not factorized the information of the link is duplicated for each semantic element which are referenced. These cases are easily detectable and it is then as easy to help the user to remove this redundancy of information.

Our method was tested in a static way on a set of XML grammar schema as well as a set of documents XML associated with each XML schema. The future objectives of development are double. On the one hand we wish to develop a complete system allowing the integration of XML schema and XML data in a dynamic manner through a graphic interface. This tool will include also tools allowing requests to the system according to our previous work. In addition, we wish to test this method for the integration of Web Services. The Web services are defined using an XML schema defining the contents of SAOP documents. Consequently, our architecture would make it possible to carry out semantic requests on a set of Web Services.

References

Baxevanis, A.: The Molecular Biology Database Collection. Nucleic Acids Research 28(1), 1–7 (2000), http://nar.oupjournals.org/cgi/content/full/27/1/1

Benson, D., Karsch-Mizrachi, I., Lipman, D., Ostell, J., Rapp, B., Wheeler, D.: GenBank. Nucleic Acids Res. 1, 15–18 (2000), http://www.ncbi.nih.gov/Genbank/

Pan, A., Raposo,J., Álvarez,M. , Montoto, P. , Orjales, V., Hidalgo, J., Ardao, L., Molano, A., Viña,Á.: The Denodo Data Integration Platform, VLDB, Hong Kong, China, 2002

Draper, D., HaLevy, A.Y., Weld, D.S.: The Nimble XML Data Integration System. In: IEEE International Conference on Data Engineering, April 02-06, Heidelberg, Germany (2001)

Carey, M.J., Kiernan, J., Shanmugasundaram, J., Shekita, E.J., Subramanian, S.N., XPERANTO: Middleware for Publishing Object-Relational Data as XML Documents. The VLDB Journal, 646–648 (2000)

Cali, A., De Giacomo, G., Lenzerini, M.: Models for Information Integration: Turning Local-as-View into Global-as-View. In: Proceedings of the International Workshop on Foundations of Models for Information Integration (2001)

Aberer, K., Cudre-Mauroux, P., Hauswirth, M.: A framework for semantic gossiping. SIGMOD Record 31(4) (2002)

Guarino, N., Carrara, C., Giaretta, P.: An ontologie of meta-level categories. In: Doyle, F.S.J., Torano, P. (eds.) Principles of Knowledge representation and Reasonning, pp. 270–280. Morgan-Kauffman, San Francisco (1994)

Bachimont, B.: Engagement sémantique et engagement ontologique: conception et réalisation d'ontologie en ingénierie des connaissances. In: Charlet, J., Zackland, M., Kessel, G., Bourigault, D. (eds.) Ingénierie des connaissances: évolution récentes et nouveaux défis, Eyrolles, pp. 305–323 (2000)

Guarino, N.: The ontological level. In: Casati B, S, R., White, G. (eds.) Philosophy and the cognitive sciences, Hölder-Pichler-Tempsky, (1994)

Dechilly, T., Bachimont, B.: Une ontologie pour éditer des schémas de description audiovisuels, extension pour l'inférence sur les descriptions. In: Actes des journées francophones d'Ingénierie des Connaissances (IC'2000) (2000)

Amann, B.: Du Partage centralisé de ressources Web centralisées à l'échange de documents intensionnels, Documents de Synthèse (2003)

Cruz, I.F., Xiao, H., Hsu, F.: An Ontology-based Framework for Semantic Interoperability between XML Sources. In: Eighth International Database Engineering & Applications Symposium (IDEAS 2004) (July 2004)

Klein, M.: Interpreting XML via an RDF schema. In: ECAI workshop on Semantic Authoring, Annotation & Knowledge Markup SAAKM, Lyon, France (2002)

Lakshmannan, L.V., Sadri, F.: Interoperability on XML Data. In: Proceeding of the 2nd International Semantic Web Conference (ICSW'03) (2003)

Kifer, M., Laussen, G., Wu, J.: Logical foundations of object-oriented Land frame-based languages. In: Kifer, M., Laussen, G., Wu, J. (eds.) journal of the ACM, ACM, New York (1995)

Kayser, D.: La représentation des connaissances, Hermès (1997)

Sowa, J.: Conceptual structures: information processing in mind and machine. Addison-Wesley, London, UK (1984)

Dekhtyar, A., Iacob, I.E.: A Framework for Management of Concurrent XML Markup, International Conference on Conceptual Modeling. In: Olivé, À., Yoshikawa, M., Yu, E.S.K. (eds.) ER 2003. LNCS, vol. 2784, pp. 311–322. Springer, Heidelberg (2003)

Berstel, J., Boasson, L.: XML Grammars. In: Nielsen, M., Rovan, B. (eds.) MFCS 2000. LNCS, vol. 1893, pp. 182–191. Springer, Heidelberg (2000)

Extending an XML Mediator with Text Query

Clément Jamard and Georges Gardarin

Laboratoire PRiSM, Université de Versailles, 45 avenue des Etats-Unis,
78000 Versailles, France
clement.jamard@prism.uvsq.fr, georges.gardarin@prism.uvsq.fr

Abstract. Supporting full-text query in an XML mediator is a difficult problem. This is because most data-sources do not provide keyword search and ranking. In this paper, we report on the integration of the main functionalities of the emerging XQuery Text standard in XLive, a full XML/XQuery mediator. Our approach is to index on keywords virtual documents in views. Selected virtual documents are on demand mapped to data source objects. Thus, the mediator selection operator is efficiently extended to support full-text search on views. Keyword search and result ranking are integrated. We rank results using a relevance formula adapted to XPath, based on number of keywords in elements and distance from the searched nodes.

Keywords: XML, mediation, indexing technique.

1 Introduction

As XQuery becomes the standard for querying XML, new needs appear to perform full-text search in XML. A task force, Buxton and Rys (2003), is currently specifying new full-text search predicates and functions to be included in XQuery, so as to express searching on multiple keywords, ranking results on relevance, searching on suffix or prefix of terms, etc. TexQuery, Amer-Yahia (2004), can be seen as a precursor of the future language.

Some text search functionalities are very common and present in most DBMSs, such as single keyword search. Data from distributed system has to be recomposed before applying text search; important functionalities often required by applications are not possible with distributed systems. These concern ranking query results, multiple conjunctive keywords searches, and searches dealing with stemming, prefix or suffix on terms. An increasing number of XQuery-based information integration platforms are available like BEA (2004), IBM DB2 (2004), Papakonstantinou (2003) or XQuare (2005). They are mostly based on a global as view architecture and support a significant subset of XQuery. At the best of our knowledge, none of them support fully XQuery Text. However, many data integration applications are full-text oriented and requires full support.

The goal of a mediator is to federate sources around an integrated architecture fulfilling the lacks of some sources. Most data sources support single word search, some multi-keyword search, but most mediated systems have different capabilities for searching full text. For example, the XLive mediator can currently query Google as a

J. Filipe, J. Cordeiro, and V. Pedrosa (Eds.): WEBIST 2005/2006, LNBIP 1, pp. 111–124, 2007.

(large) virtual XML collection through a Web service wrapper. This search engine is very powerful in multi-keyword search and in ranking results, compared to common relational databases. We also federate Xyleme, Abiteboul (2002), an XML native database system that supports efficiently multi-keyword searches. All these systems have some capabilities, but none propose the full set of XQuery text functionalities. Thus, there is a strong need to integrate uniform full-text search on all sources. Moreover the integration of the ranking systems is very difficult, as all integrated system have their own ranking scheme.

In this paper, we address the problem of extending an XML mediator for querying text-oriented sources using XQuery Text. We base our implementation on XLive, Dang-Ngoc and Gardarin (2003). The XLive system integrates and query relational or XML sources in XQuery. A large subset of XQuery is supported including FLWR expressions and nested queries. Sources are wrapped in a subset of XQuery. The query runtime is dataflow-oriented and built around an extended relational algebra for XML, known as the XAlgebra. The basic idea of this algebra is to model XML documents as tuples of paths referencing virtual DOM trees, called XTuples. The mediator evaluates query plans of XAlgebra operators on collections of XTuples and constructs XQuery results.

Data retrieved through XLive are distributed on multiples sources. An important issue in integrating full-text search in XLive is the management of sources capabilities. We propose to unify these capabilities through views. The mediator defines views of distributed XML data and provides XQuery Text support through these views. The mediator does not materialize the views to avoid replicating sources data; but, it indexes their contents and structures. Several indexing schemes have been proposed in centralized systems for fast retrieval of elements on keywords. The interested reader can find a survey in Gardarin and Yeh (2003). We propose an efficient distributed indexing scheme that relies on a viewguide, an invariant abstract DTD-like summary derived from the query defining the view. This index scheme is particularly adapted for text search over distributed data.

XQuery/IR, Bremer and Gertz (2002), is an efficient integration of information retrieval techniques within XQuery. It uses an indexing scheme adapted to XML tree structures allowing solving tree pattern queries. Such a system does not provide a solution for our mediation context as data structures are centralized and homogeneous. Another approach to support XQuery Text query is to define function operators. TexQuery, Amer-Yahia (2004), uses Boolean operators on XML data flows to determine the presence of keywords in elements and distance between keywords. Scores functions are also defined as operators to rank results. Such operators are not easy to adapt to mediation; the mediator has to manipulate a huge amount of data through complex operations. Both systems do not provide solutions to reconcile data coming from different sources before applying text search functions. Numerous works focus on reducing index size in centralized systems (Chen and al. 2003, Chung and al. 2002, Cooper and al. 2001, Milo 1999 or Kaushik and al. 2002). In summary, although functional and efficient solutions have been studied for supporting XQuery Text, they are not easily applicable to mediation systems.

Managing view requires integration of data available in different schemas. Relationship (mappings) between schemas must be specified, to determine correspondence between elements in source schemas and elements in target schemas. A lot of work has been done on unifying source schemas under a target schema. A survey can be found in Rahm and Bernstein (2001). Defining rules mapping paths from one schema to paths of another is a simple but effective approach. Our system provides for this kind of mapping techniques to create integrated views.

This paper is organized as follows. Section 2 presents the integration of indexed views to support full-text search in XLive. Section 3 develops the query processing algorithm for querying views and ranking results. Section 4 gives some experimental results of our system. Section 5 summarizes the contributions and introduces future work.

2 Indexing Virtual Views

The key question in a mediation context is how to integrate a keyword path indexing technique within the distributed architecture. In mediation systems, views are often used to focus the search on relevant data source parts. To combine the power of views with keyword search, a key decision of our design is to index virtual views of sources by keywords.

We choose to index the view content. Through the index, the mediator knows the locations of terms, which helps in answering text queries efficiently. Indexing important terms avoids replicating entire sources in the mediator. It avoids huge data transfer between sources and the mediator. The index determines relevant results, which avoids complex full text search operation on data in the mediator. A compact and fast index is the focus of our approach in order to avoid managing large data sets in the mediator.

Identifiers used in index entries are mapped to objects in sources through additional structures maintained at the mediator and source layers. We use these additional structures that determine where data composing a document in the view are located. It helps in recomposing the document efficiently.

2.1 Index Overview

We choose to index view content at creation time and to maintain index when view sources are updated. Term positions in the view are memorized in the index at mediator level. The index determines relevant elements addresses; it avoids huge data transfer between source and mediator; only relevant data are transferred. Thus, the mediator does not manipulate the whole data, through complex information retrieval operations.

Identifiers used in our index reference objects on sources using intermediate structures managed by wrappers. These structures allow view data localization, extraction, and reconstruction from sources. When an update occurs on a source, the source reports to the mediator in order to update index identifiers. Triggers or periodic polling is used to detect updates on sources. The reporting functionality depends on the source wrapper.

2.2 Location of Words in Views

To index content of the view, the position of a word has to be identified precisely. A word is located by a path and a document instance of the view. We propose our own numbering scheme to encode this position. We now detail the index structure used for determining and locating the relevant view instances.

2.2.1 Numbering Scheme

We first introduce the numbering scheme implemented for identifying virtual nodes in a view. Any element in a view instance is addressed by a global document identifier (GDID) plus a node identifier (NID) determining the path reaching the element.

Global document identifier (GDID): Unique integer allocated by the mediator identifying a virtual document instance of a view.

Node identifier (NID): Unique identifier of a node element in a document determined by the view definition.

To encode a NID, we make use of a *Viewguide* summarizing the structure of a view.

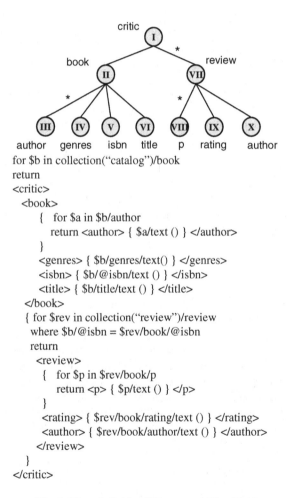

```
for $b in collection("catalog")/book
return
<critic>
  <book>
      {  for $a in $b/author
         return <author> { $a/text () } </author>
      }
      <genres> { $b/genres/text() } </genres>
      <isbn> { $b/@isbn/text () } </isbn>
      <title> { $b/title/text () } </title>
  </book>
  { for $rev in collection("review")/review
    where $b/@isbn = $rev/book/@isbn
    return
      <review>
        {  for $p in $rev/book/p
           return <p> { $p/text () } </p>
        }
        <rating> { $rev/book/rating/text () } </rating>
        <author> { $rev/book/author/text () } </author>
      </review>
  }
</critic>
```

Fig. 1. View definition XQuery and ViewGuide

Viewguide: Tree giving the common structures of all documents in a view, whose nodes correspond to elements or attributes and edges to simple or multi-valued (marked with*) imbrications of elements.

Attributes are treated as elements with a name prefixed by @. All children of a node have different names as duplicates are removed. In addition, edges are marked by the maximum cardinality of the element (1 by default, and * if multiple). Thus, each distinct path of the view is represented once and only once in the viewguide.

The viewguide is somehow similar to a DataGuide (Widom and al), but: (i) It is a pure structural summary. (ii) It is derived from a view definition (i.e., the query defining the view) and not from instances. (iii) It is annotated with cardinalities of elements. It is used to assign a compact and stable unique node identifier (NID) to each element of an instance of a view. Viewguide nodes are numbered by means of a pre-order traversal (see figure 1). We select this structure as it is easy to derive from a query with a fully specified return clause. View definitions are restricted to fully specified return clauses, as detailed in the sequel.

To facilitate logical operation and XPath encoding, we implement a structure for NIDs. A NID is composed of a prefix and an optional suffix:

- The *prefix* is the node number assigned to the node in preorder traversal of the viewguide.
- The *suffix* corresponds to the cardinality of the traversed multi-valued elements from the root to the node.

The document identifier determines a document instance in the view while the node identifier encodes the path to reach the node from the document root. Then a <GDID-NID> pair identifies a unique element in the view.

For example, an element identified by the XPath *critic/review/p* is assigned the path I/VII/VIII. Only the leave number is kept as node identifier, i.e., VIII. Nodes with edges marked with multiple occurrences are additionally identified by a suffix added to the identifier. Therefore the path *critic/review[1]/p[2]*, which corresponds to the numbering I/VII[1]/VIII[2] is encoded as VIII[1,2]. We keep suffixes only for multi-valued elements; a mono-valued element has no suffix, for example *critic/book/title* is encoded as VI. Such identifiers are compact and do not change while the view definition does not change. The <GDID-NID> pair identifying the position of the *author* of the second *review* in the second document of the view is *<2-X[2]>*.

To translate XPath expressions selecting several nodes in path identifiers, we introduce the concept of identifier pattern (NID pattern called NIP). This structure is used further for query processing.

Node identifier pattern (NIP): Profile of node identifier with * in place of indices, meaning that any indice is valid.

A node identifier pattern is simply a node identifier in which stars replace one or more indice of the suffix. A star in a suffix means that any number is valid. For example, the path *critic/review/p[1]*, selecting the first *p* element in any *review* of a *critic* will be encoded VIII[*,1].

2.2.2 Word Index

The mediator stores words positions in the view in the Word Index.

Word Index: B-tree structure giving for each keyword the virtual addresses of the nodes containing these keywords.

The *Word Index* is a classical inverted list addressing element locations in virtual documents. An address is a <GDID-NID> pair determined by our numbering scheme. Keywords are determined by a thesaurus giving important words to be indexed, which can be used in queries. It is populated with location of all words at view creation time. In a more detailed way, entries of the word index are pairs (term, position record). The position record is a table with column GDID, NID prefix, sorted list of NID suffix. Each tuple corresponds to an element containing the term with possibly multiple instances if the element is multi-valued. Table 1 illustrates two position records. This structure has been selected for fast evaluation of intersection and union operations detailed further in query processing section.

Table 1. Two position records, rec1 and rec2

GDID	Prefix	Suffix list	GDID	Prefix	Suffix list
120	VIII	(1,4) (3,5)	120	IV	-
120	IX	(2)	120	VI	-
121	VI	-	120	VIII	(1,2) (2,3) (2,5)
121	VIII	(3,4) (4,1)	120	IX	(1)

2.3 Location on Data Sources

The Source Map maintains the mapping between a global document in the view and local documents in the sources used to compose the view instance. More precisely, we refer local documents through local document identifiers. This local identifier is associated to an extraction data operation.

Source Map: Mapping structure on the mediator mapping a GDID to a set of LDID composing the document.

Local document identifier (LDID): Number allocated by a wrapper allowing retrieving a part of a document in the source.

At view creation time, the view definition query is decomposed into atomic queries (queries referring to a single collection of XML documents). Each concerned wrapper rewrites the atomic query(ies) according to its local schema(s). Mapping between global schema (defined by atomic queries definition) and local schema can be given by a human or can be determined semi-automatically by schema matching algorithms. Mapping techniques used are not detailed here for lack of place.

Each local source wrapper extracts and provides data to the mediator respecting the target view schema (viewguide). The view creation framework is detailed in figure 2. The *Plan Generator* defines an *Execution Plan*, which constructs view documents from data retrieved by wrappers. Data is then indexed by the *View Indexer,* which populates the Word Index and Source Map.

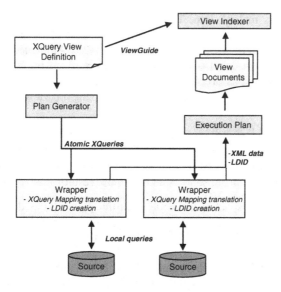

Fig. 2. Framework for creating an Indexed View

For each document on a local source, a LDID is created. An LDID maintains a reference to data on the local source and a reference to the mapping used to extract data. The LDID mapping depends on the wrapper. For a file wrapper, the LDID can be simply the file URI. For an XML database, it is generally a document identifier, for example a URL in Xyleme. For relational databases, it can be a reference to an SQL/XML or XQuery query allowing mapping table rows to XML. The mapping associated to each LDID determines the way to query and recompose data on local sources.

In the view example, two atomic queries corresponding to *book* and *review* are generated from the view definition. Wrappers corresponding to these collections of entities are retrieved, queries are rewritten according to local mapping, and data are extracted.

From any LDID identifier, wrappers are able to query the source to retrieve the local part of document participating in the view. Finally, the mediator uses the view definition to recompose the whole document.

3 Text Query Processing

The query processing algorithm first retrieves the index entries corresponding to a textual search (e.g., search on keyword list with ranking of results). Then, it uses the retrieved node identifiers to extract from the sources the relevant elements from the view. We detail how to search the index and recompose results after querying the source. We also propose an efficient way to rank results by relevance in the context of distributed heterogeneous sources.

A multi-keyword search over semi-structured data relies on two parameters: the structural search space and a keyword list (k1, k2... kn). The structural search space defines the elements to look into. Typically, it is expressed as an Xpath. We first concentrate on conjunctive queries in which the relevant elements shall contain all keywords. Predicates in queries are of the form A1/A2.../Am[. Ftcontains k1 && k2 &&... kn], where Ai are labels (or attribute names prefixed by @) and ki are keywords. Regular expressions are allowed, i.e., Ai can be * or empty (wildcards). A typical query is "find all books in the critics view having a review dealing with XML and databases".

Steps performed by a search are:

1. Determine the search space.
2. Compute the set of entries containing each term of the keyword list.
3. Extract documents from sources and compose results.

We define the search space using node identifier pattern(s) as define above. NIPs are derived from the Xpath expression by a viewguide traversal from the root. Notice that an Xpath query searches for all elements when the position is not specified for a repetitive element.

On the example, we rewrite the predicate Xpath in pattern *critic/review[*]*. Then, we encode the Xpath, which results in VII,(*). Thus, we obtain the root(s) of the subtree(s) interesting for the query. However, we need to access the full contents of these subtrees, to look for other keywords inside (keywords may be contained in any element among *comments, comment, p, author* or *rating*. To retrieve efficiently the ancestors or descendants of a node, we maintain the ancestor-descendant matrix (ad-matrix): it is a compact Boolean matrix in which element $C_{ij} = 1$ if element i is an ancestor of element j in the viewguide. This matrix provides an immediate method to retrieve the relationship between two identifiers in the viewguide.

The search space for our example query is an interval of nodes identified between VI(*) and X(*).

We query the word index to compute the set of entries containing each term of the keyword list. The strategy consists in accessing the B-tree entries (position record) for each keyword k_1 to k_n. We then intersect these lists of identifiers for conjunctive queries; the element searched must contain at least one or more occurrences of each keyword. The intersect operation determines the first common ancestor between two or more nodes. Each valid intersection (i.e., remaining in the search space) will be kept as a result.

To reduce the number of comparisons, the intersection algorithm processes intersection on entries respecting these three conditions:

1. GDID equality, i.e., keywords are in the same document. It is a trivial condition avoiding intersecting position contained in different documents.
2. NID prefixes are descendant of the NIP search space, i.e., keyword positions out of the search space are not considered.
3. NIDs suffixes are not already computed.

Figure 3 sketches the intersection algorithm. It computes every valid intersection between list of identifiers in a given search space. Condition 1 is checked on lines 8 and 12-13 to select identifiers of same documents. Condition 2 is applied when asking for next element with the search space on lines 1, 5, 13, 27. Each next element is chosen only among lines of position record corresponding to the search space. Last condition is applied on line 21-22, by checking if the current intersection remains in the last result (descendant of that result).

Entries are ordered by NID suffix in position records, which avoids skipping intersection when scanning each list. Therefore condition on line 30 always selects the minimum NID of list to intersect.

```
ALGORITHM INTERSECT
INPUT              : List(n)
                      n list of keyword position
VARIABLES :        intersect, current_id, test_id, tmp_res
                      type:identifier<GDID-NID>
                   search_space
                      type:NIP filter
                   result
                      type:list of result
1. current_id = List(0).nextElement(search_space)
2. WHILE( List(0).hasNextElement(search_space) ) DO
3.      intersect = NULL;
4.      FOR EACH LIST DO
5.          test_id = list().nextElement(search_space)
6.          /* No element intersecting in same document
7.          Repeat process on the next element */
8.          WHILE ( test_id.GDID > current_id.GDID )
9.              current_id = test_id;
10      FOR EACH LIST DO
11          /* Find next element with same GDID */
12          WHILE (test_id.GDID < current_id.GDID) DO
13              test_id = list().nextElement(search_space);
14          /* Intersection in a given search space */
15          tmp_res =
16              ancestor(test_id,current_id,search_space);
17.         /* Valid intersection ->
18.             search in the next list */
19.         /* Invalid intersection ->
20.             same process on next element */
21.         IF (tmp_res != NULL &&
22.                 !tmp_res.descendantOf(result.last))
23.             intersect = tmp_res;
24.         ELSE
25.             intersect = NULL;
26.             IF (current_id.suffix > test_id.suffix)
27.                 current_id =
28.                     list().nextElement(search_space);
29.             break;
30.
31.     /* Keep the resulting intersection */
32.     if(intersect != NULL)
33.         result.add(intersect);
34.         last_res = intersect;
35.         current_id = list().nextElement(search_space);
```

Fig. 3. Intersection algorithm

The algorithm can be applied to position record list of table 1 with the search space of our query as a NIP: VII(*). For GDID 120 only lines VIII and IX are selected. We obtain valid intersection for IX(1) records1 and VIII(1,4) records2, VIII(2,3) records1 and IX(2) records2. These are VII(1) and VII(2). Other intersections for GDID 120 are not leading to a valid intersection (in the search space, or an intersection already found). Entries of other GDID are processed in the same way.

4 Xquery Text Capabilities

4.1 Full Text Search

A full-text search may use the position of keywords inside the document. This position can be expressed in two metrics. The position as element means that only the path from the root of the document determines the criteria. The position inside an element means the path and the position among the other words in the element determine the criteria.

The index presented before allows answering any full-text search dealing with position expressed as element. Other functionalities like term distance, window, order or result ranking require additional information, the word offset inside an element. The offset is added to position records as needed by these operations. Full functionalities are available in Buxton and Rys (2003).

4.2 Ranking Results

A ranking method associates a relevance weight to each result. In a mediator, we have to rank results coming from different sources and to merge results for delivery to the user in correctly ranked order. Our architecture provides a way to pre-rank results, i.e., virtual results are ranked before source extraction; we compute the relevance score of each result when querying the word index. The weighting formula has to be accurate but simple enough to be computable with information contained in the word index.

We determine the weight of a result by adding the weights of each node containing directly one or more keywords. Our ranking approach is based on the specificity of each result. The ranking method gives more influence to element nodes close to the root of the search space. Thus, words close to the root weight more than words deeply hidden in the result tree. Such an approach is a bit simplistic, as ranking weights are attributed independently of keyword position in relation with each other.

We also give more influence to element nodes containing several keywords of the search. The percentage of keywords in a node is used as a polynomial factor to adjust the weight. Finally, the following formula computes the weight of a node:

$$We = \frac{Ni^{\beta}}{N} \sum_{i=0}^{n} \left(\frac{Wi}{(1+\alpha)^d} \right)$$

Wi is the weight of the keyword (tf.idf), N is the total number of keywords in the query, Ni is the total number of keywords in the node, and d is the distance to the root of the sub-graph (number of edges). The constant α is designed to give more influence to the distance from the root to the word position (in edges). β is a polynomial factor used to increase the weight of an element containing several keywords. The total weight of a result is the sum of each node weight containing one or more keywords.

An advantage of the implemented ranking system is the formula modularity. It may be extended or replaced. The mediator may integrate any formula relying on information contained in the word index (tf.idf, distance). The ranking formula is application adjustable.

Some other systems propose concrete solutions to rank results of a keyword–based query. XRANK, Lin and al. (2003), proposes a ranking algorithm relying on the *elemRank* of an XML element. This rank is computed using the number of outgoing and incoming edges (inter and intra documents). It contrasts with our approach, which focuses first on keywords distribution and second on links, by applying a tf.idf based formula on element contents. Moreover, the proximity factor proposed in XRANK is not fully adapted to XML tree structures; XRANK uses the minimum containing window (containing all keywords) as proximity metric. It is a global proximity; our system rather uses a proximity factor computed at the element granularity, i.e., not globally on the full result sub-graph. Thus, our approach is more precise on content. XRANK also uses a decreasing factor for less specific results (far from the sub-graph result root).

The XXL system, Theobald and Weikum (2002), uses relevance ranking focused on a vagueness operator, which computes a similarity score for every result. It compares the structure of the result with the structure of the query, by applying ontological rules. This kind of ranking is not easily adaptable to XQuery Text in the context of mediation, as it is not based on a specific search space. However, it could be interesting to consider ontology-based similarity for integrating heterogeneous sources.

XIRQL, Norbert and Kai (2001), extends IR functionalities to XML, like relevance-oriented search, looking for XML objects satisfying a content search. Weighting formulas are applied to objects (i.e., sub-graphs) defined in the schema at the type level and in the index at the instance level. Composed objects are weighted with the sum of the composing objects. Content queries are processed by combining relevance of objects according to the logical search conditions. Only the relevant objects are returned ranked by weights. A tf.idf computation and the specificity of the position of keywords are used to adjust the weight of the objects. This approach is difficult to apply in a mediation architecture where objects are not defined for each source.

5 Experiments

We experiment index search on three different data sets stored in an XML repository. The data sets are presented in table 2. The size is the total size of the view after creation. Each data set is structured as the *critic* view definition given above. Collections are stored on different sources. We measure search time through the index for three queries:

(**q01**) critic/review [. ftcontains "k1" && ... "kn"]
(**q02**) critic [. ftcontains "k1" && ... "kn" without content .//title]
(**q03**) critic [. ftcontains "k1" && ... "kn"]

The queries are searching documents containing a conjunctive set of keywords. The search space includes different elements of the view. q01 searches in the review element, q02 in the *review* element without *title*, and q03 in the full document. Queries are executed on the same Pentium 4 with 512K memory configuration. The numbers of keywords in queries vary from 2 to 26. The measures presented here are an average of ten executions.

Table 2 presents the execution time of q01 searching for 5 keywords. For each data set, we measure the execution time with an indexed view, and without index (the mediator handles the search operation). The time for the view includes the index search time (both Word Index and Source Map), the query plan execution in the mediator, and the result construction. The time without indexed view includes the plan execution and the result construction times. As planned, index speeds up the execution time as only relevant results are requested from the sources and complex content search operations are avoided on huge text data at the mediator layer. For each data set, the execution through the indexed view brings out a significant ratio averaging 3, for a low selectivity of queries (from 60 % to 68 % of the documents are selected).

Table 2. Data sets

	Docs	Byte Size
ds1	100	607 855
ds2	250	1 556 052
ds3	500	3 029 990

Table 3. q01 execution time and index search time

Execution Time		Intersection		
View	Mediator	5 words	15 words	25 words
1042.1	2917.6	1.6	3.1	4.6
1976.5	5969	6.3	15.6	21.9
5949	18501	17.2	65.6	86

Index search times for query Q01 are presented in table 3. The index search does not increase significantly the execution time; it represents less than 1% of the overall execution time. These preliminary results validate our approach.

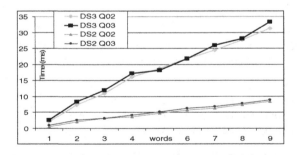

Fig. 4. q02 and q03 evaluation for DS2 and DS3

Figure 4 illustrates the index search time difference between q03 and q02. Due to the identifiers ordering scheme, q02 always executes faster than q03 as fewer elements are considered in the search space.

6 Conclusion

In this paper, we have reported on the integration of XQuery Text in an XML mediator. The main difficulty is to integrate sources with little capabilities in full-text search. We propose to use indexed virtual views to support such sources. The views are indexed inside the mediator using a sort of structural dataguide derived from the view definition, called a viewguide. Nodes identifiers and path expressions are encoded through the viewguide, which yields to algorithms to process efficiently the mediator basic selection operator involving XPaths and keywords. A parameterized ranking formula taking into account relevance and deepness of elements is proposed to integrate result relevance.

Further work remains to be done. Notably, a better support of source capabilities would be desirable. When a source can support a subset of XQuery, we should be able to build limited views at the wrapper to integrate it in distributed query processing. Thus, functionalities should be divided in multiple stages, e.g., concrete local views combined with global virtual views. Also, local ranking of results from a view or a capable source (e.g., Google) seems easy, but global ranking with pertinent formulas remains to be experienced in details on real applications. The propagation of updates must also be studied. Indexing structures should be automatically updated when inserting and deleting objects in data sources. A basic approach could be detecting updates at wrapper level and propagate them at the different index structures.

References

Abiteboul, S., Cluet, S., Ferran et, G., Rousset, M.C.: The Xyleme project. Computer Networks 39(3), 225–238 (2002)

Amer-Yahia, S., Botev, C., Shanmugasundaram, J.: TeXQuery: A Full-Text Search Extension to XQuery, WWW'04 (2004)

BEA: Liquid data for WebLogic 1.1 (2004) http://e-docs.bea.com/liquiddata/docs11/

Bremer J. M., Gertz, M.: XQuery/IR: Integrating XML Document and Data Retrieval, WebDB (2002)

Buxton, S., Rys, M.:(eds.): XQuery and XPath Full-Text Requirements, W3C Working Draft 02 (May 02, 2003). http://www.w3.org/TR/xquery-full-text-requirements/

Chen, Q., Lim, A., Ong, K.W.: D(k)-index: An adaptive structural summary for graph-structured data. In: Proc. of SIGMOD (2003)

Chin-Wan, C., Min, J., Shim, K.: APEX: an adaptive path index for XML data. In: SIGMOD Conference 2002, pp. 121–132 (2002)

Cooper, B., Sample, N., Franklin, M.J., Hjaltason, G.R., Shadmon, M.: A Fast Index for Semistructured Data. VLDB, 341–350 (2001)

Dang-Ngoc, T.-T., Gardarin, G.: Federating heterogeneous data sources with XML. In: Proc. of IASTED IKS Conference, Scottsdale, USA, pp. 193–198 (2003)

Fuhr, N., Großjohann, K.: XIRQL: A Query Language for Information Retrieval in XML Documents. SIGIR, 172–180 (2001)

Gardarin, G., Yeh, L.: Treeguide Index: Enabling Efficient XML Query Processing, Bases de Données Avancées, Montpellier (Octobre 2005)

IBM: DB2 Information Integrator for Content (2004), http://www-306.ibm.com/software/data/eip/

Kaushik, R., Shenoy, P., Bohannon, P., Gudes, E.: Exploiting local similarity for indexing paths in graph-structured data. In: Proc. of ICDE (2002)

Lin, G., Shao, F., Botev, C., Shanmugasundaram, J.: XRANK: Ranked Keyword Search over XML Documents. In: SIGMOD Conference, pp. 16–27 (2003)

Milo, T., Suciu, D.: Structures for Path Expressions. In: Beeri, C., Bruneman, P. (eds.) ICDT 1999. LNCS, vol. 1540, pp. 277–295. Springer, Heidelberg (1998)

Papakonstantinou, Y., Borkar, V., Orgiyan, M., Stathatos, K., Suta, L., Vassalos, V., Velikhov, P.: XML queries and algebra in the Enosys integration platform. Data Knowl. Eng. 44(3), 299–322 (2003)

Rahm, E., Bernstein, P.A.: A survey of approaches to automatic schema matching. VLDB journal, 334–350 (2001)

Theobald, A., Weikum, G.: The Index-Based XXL Search Engine for Querying XML Data with Relevance Ranking. In: Chaudhri, A.B., Unland, R., Djeraba, C., Lindner, W. (eds.) EDBT 2002. LNCS, vol. 2490, pp. 477–495. Springer, Heidelberg (2002)

Widom, J., et al.: Lore, a DBMS for XML, http://www-db.stanford.edu/lore/

XQuare: The XQuare project: open source information integration components based on XML and XQuery (2004), http://xquare.objectweb.org/

Instances Navigation for Querying Integrated Data from Web-Sites

Domenico Beneventano[1], Sonia Bergamaschi[1], Stefania Bruschi[1],
Francesco Guerra[2], Mirko Orsini[1], and Maurizio Vincini[1]

[1] DII - Università di Modena e Reggio Emilia
via Vignolese 905, 41100 Modena
[2] DEA - Università di Modena e Reggio Emilia
v.le Berengario 51, 41100 Modena
`lastname.firstname@unimore.it`

Abstract. Research on data integration has provided a set of rich and well understood schema mediation languages and systems that provide a meta-data representation of the modeled real world, while, in general, they do not deal with data instances.

Such meta-data are necessary for querying classes result of an integration process: the end user typically does not know the contents of such classes, he simply defines his queries on the basis of the names of classes and attributes.

In this paper we introduce an approach enriching the description of selected attributes specifying as meta-data a list of the "relevant values" for such attributes. Furthermore relevant values may be hierarchically collected in a taxonomy. In this way, the user may exploit new meta-data in the interactive process of creating/refining a query. The same meta-data are also exploited by the system in the query rewriting/unfolding process in order to filter the results showed to the user.

We conducted an evaluation of the strategy in an e-business context within the EU-IST SEWASIE project. The evaluation proved the practicability of the approach for large value instances.

Keywords: Semantic integration, wrapper HTML, query manager.

1   Introduction

Integration of data from multiple sources is one of the main problems facing the database research community. One of the most common approach for integrating information sources is to build a mediated schema as synthesis of them. By holding all the data collected in a common way, such mediated schema allows the user to pose a query following a global perception. The system answers translating the query into a set of sub-queries for the involved sources by means of automatic unfolding-rewriting operations taking into account the mediated and the sources schemas. Results from sub-queries are then unified by exploiting data reconciliation techniques.

Research on data integration has provided a set of rich and well understood schema mediation languages and systems, which may be classified as the global-as-view (where

J. Filipe, J. Cordeiro, and V. Pedrosa (Eds.): WEBIST 2005/2006, LNBIP 1, pp. 125–137, 2007.

the mediated schema is defined as a set of views over the data sources) and the local-as-view (where the contents of data sources are described as view over the mediated schema) formalisms (Halevy, 2003).

Following the GAV approach, we developed MOMIS (Mediator envirOnment for Multiple Information Sources) (Bergamaschi et al., 2001; Beneventano et al., 2003), a framework to perform information extraction and integration from both structured and semi-structured data sources, plus a query management environment to take incoming queries and process them through the exploitation of the mediated schema.

Two kinds of users interact with MOMIS: the integration engineer and the end user (or client/web service applications). The integration engineer is responsible for the integration process (the operation is performed by means of the MOMIS - Ontology Builder) giving rise to a Global Virtual View (GVV) of selected information sources; the end user queries the GVV classes (created by the integration engineer) aiming at obtaining a unified answer from the involved sources.

Several approaches emerged about the user supporting in querying. Such approaches may be summarized in three different schools (Broder et al., 2005): (a) the search-centric schools that guided navigation is superfluous since users can satisfy all their needs via simple queries; (b) the taxonomy navigation school claims that users have difficulties expressing informational needs; (c) the meta-data centric school advocates the use of meta-data for large sets of results.

In this paper, we describe a method for supporting users in querying by providing meta-data about attributes of integrated GVV classes. Our approach aims at showing to the user semantic, synthesized and meaningful information emerged directly from the data. We claim such meta-data are necessary for querying classes result of an integration process: the end user typically does not know the contents of the GVV classes, he simply defines his queries on the basis of the names of classes and attributes. Such labels may be generic: the synthesis operation narrows in few classes data "semantically similar" coming from different sources. Consequently the name/description for a global class is often unspecific, especially for web sources where the user is highly involved in choosing the label for the elements descriptions. For example the integration of two local classes "T-Shirt" and "Trouser" could be a unique Global Class called "Dress". Such name does not allow a user to know which specific kinds of dresses are stored.

We proposed a partial solution to these issues in (Beneventano et al., 2003) where a semantic annotation of all the Global Classes with respect to the WordNet lexical database[1] provides each term with a well- understood meaning.

Our goal is now enriching the description of selected attributes specifying as meta-data a list of the "relevant values" for such attributes. Furthermore relevant values may be hierarchically collected in a taxonomy. In this way, the user may exploit new meta-data in the interactive process of creating/refining a query. The same meta-data are also exploited by the system in the query rewriting process in order to filter the results showed to the user.

Exploiting such new kind of meta-data is an interesting challenge: the literature about integration systems mainly focuses on creating/representing structures for

---

[1] http://wordnet.princeton.edu/

heterogeneous data sources (Buneman et al., 1997; Nestorov et al., 1997; Halevy, 2004). Only recently, some techniques for combining data structure and data management were developed (Chaudhuri et al., 2005). The work closest to our is the "Malleable Schema" (Dong and Halevy, 2005), where a middle point between a collection of schemas/DTDs in a domain and a single strict schema for that domain is offered. In contrast with malleable schemas, our approach models a domain with a fixed semistructured model (ODM_{I^3}) where meta-data derived from extensional analysis are added.

Next section describes the MOMIS approach to data integration, section 3 defines our technique to calculate relevant values for selected attributes, section 3.2 shows the impact of relevant values in the querying process and section 4 gives an example of relevant values calculated for a real domain. Finally section 5 sketches out some conclusions.

2   The MOMIS Approach

The framework consists of a language and several semi-automatic tools:

- The ODL_{I^3} language is an object-oriented language, with an underlying Description Logic; it is derived from the standard ODMG. ODL_{I^3} extends ODL with the following relationships expressing intra- and inter-schema knowledge for the source schemas: SYN (synonym of), BT (broader terms), NT (narrower terms) and RT (related terms). By means of ODL_{I^3} only one language is exploited to describe both the sources (the input of the synthesis process) and the GVV (the result of the process). The translation of ODL_{I^3} descriptions into one of the Semantic Web standards such as RDF, DAML+OIL, OWL is a straightforward process. In fact, from a general perspective an ODL_{I^3} concept corresponds to a Class of the Semantic Web standard, and ODL_{I^3} relationships are translated into properties.
- Information integration is performed in a semi-automatic way, by exploiting the knowledge in a Common Thesaurus (semi-automatically defined from the structural and lexical analysis of the information sources) and ODL_{I^3} descriptions of source schemas with a combination of clustering techniques and Description Logics. This integration process (performed by means of the MOMIS - Ontology Builder) gives rise to a GVV of the underlying sources. The GVV consists of a set of Global Classes, each of them made up of Global Attributes. Mapping rules connect the GVV with the original information sources and integrity constraints are specified to handle heterogeneity.
- The MOMIS Query Manager is the coordinated set of functions which take an incoming query, decompose the query according to the mapping of the GVV onto the local data sources relevant for the query, send the sub-queries to these data sources, collect their answers, perform any residual filtering as necessary, and finally deliver the answer to the requesting user. The unfolding and rewriting process is based on the full disjunction operation (Galindo-Legaria, 1994) and it is described with details in (Beneventano and Lenzerini, 2005).

2.1   The MOMIS Ontology Builder

The MOMIS integration process, shown in Figure 1, has five phases:

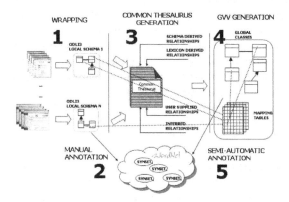

Fig. 1. Functional representantion of the MOMIS Ontology builder

1. **Local source schemata extraction.** Wrappers analyze sources in order to extract (or generate if the source is not structured) schemas. Such schemas are then translated into the common language ODL_{I^3} .
2. **Local source annotation with WordNet.** The integration designer defines a meaning for each element of a local source schema, according to the WordNet lexical ontology. A tool supports the integration designer: some WordNet synsets are suggested for each source element.
3. **Common thesaurus generation.** Starting from the annotated local schema, MOMIS constructs a set of relationships describing inter- and intraschema knowledge about classes and attributes of the source schemata.
4. **GVV generation.** The MOMIS methodology, applied to the common thesaurus and the local schemata descriptions, generates a global schema and sets of mappings with local schemata. The Global Schema is made up of a set of global classes. Several global attributed belong to a global class.
5. **GVV annotation.** Exploiting the annotated local schemata and the mappings between local and global schemata, the MOMIS system semi-automatically assigns name and meaning to each element of the global schema.

The Ontology Builder Tool supports the integration designer in all the GVV generation process phases.

2.2   Local Source Schemata Extraction

To enable MOMIS to manage web pages and data sources, we need specialized software (wrappers) for the construction of a semantically rich representations of the information sources by means of a common data model. A wrapper logically converts the source data structure into an ODL$_{I3}$ schema. The wrapper architecture and interfaces are crucial, because wrappers are the focal point for managing the diversity of data sources. For conventional structured information sources (e.g. relational databases), schema description is always available and can be directly translated. For web content, this is mainly available in the form of HTML documents: such documents do not separate data from presentation and are ill-suited for being the target of database queries and most other forms of automatic processing. This problem has been addressed by much work on so-called Web wrappers, programs that extract the relevant information from HTML documents and translate it into a more machine-friendly format such as XML. The wrapping problem has been addressed by a substantial amount of work: in our approach we used Lixto (Gottlob et al., 2004) to translate the website data in XML format. The main feature of Lixto is its graphics intuitive interface that interactively guides the wrapper designer's intervention. The lixto wrapper is coupled with an XML wrapper, we developed, generating for each XML representation of a web-site the related XML Schema (an XSD file) and loads the XML data into a relational database. In this way, we are able to structure and query web-site sources. Our XML wrapper is based on MS .net framework and automatically updates the data extracted from the web by means of script daemons into the relational database.

3   Providing Information About Relevant Values of Attributes

A global class contains data collected from different local sources by means of an integration process, and consequently its name (and the associated annotations) may not perfectly fit in its contents. Thus, a query written only on the basis of this information name may be misleading. Moreover, ignoring the values assumed by a global attribute may generate mistaken queries: a user that does not know the granularity of an attribute may write an exceedingly selective query, or a selection clause that does not really produce any result because semantically improper for that context. On the other hand, to know all the data collected from a global class is not possible for a user: databases contain large amount of data which a user can not deal with.

For these reasons, we present a technique to provide the end user with the knowledge of the "relevant values" for global attributes selected by the integration designer in the GVV building phase.

Given an attribute At of a global class C, a *relevant value* RV for At is a pair $RV = \langle RVN, RVI \rangle$ where RVN is the *name* of the relevant value and RVI is a set of values assumed by At, i.e., $RVI \subseteq \prod_{A_t}(C)$.

A *set of relevant values* SRV is a set $SRV = \{RV_1, RV_2, ..., RV_v\}, n > 0$, such that $\bigcup_{RV_i \in SRV} RV_i = \prod_{At} C$

The relevant values may be classified in a taxonomy by means of ISA relationships: RV_1 ISA RV_2; a taxonomy need to be *consistent*: if RV_1 ISA RV_2 then $RVI_1 \subseteq RVI_2$.

A relevant value $RV = \langle RVN, RVI \rangle$ is *representative* of all the associated values RVI: at the level of query management a condition $At=RVN$ will be transformed in the equivalent condition At IN RVI.

Such relevant values are calculated by means of a semi-automatic process composed of the following steps:

1. **Identification of the relevant values:** The set of relevant values SRV is calculated by applying clustering techniques to $\prod_{At} C$.

   There are different algorithms in literature to be applied for clustering values. For example in (Gibson et al., 2000) a proposal for clustering values that cannot be naturally ordered by a metric (i.e. categorical data) is described. Nevertheless, we claim that one single algorithm may not work in any domain. Therefore our goal is to develop and propose to the user a pool of techniques for selecting the most suitable method (or the combination of different methods) for the specific domain. In MOMIS, we developed a syntactic algorithm particularly customized for dealing with classifications of services and goods. It is a typical topic of the e-commerce, where enterprises propose their products by means of web-sites. In such sites, products are often grouped by means of categories called in different sites in different ways. Moreover categories are typically collected in taxonomies on the basis of specific criteria.We observed that the names of these categories are often qualified with multiple attributes in order to describe specific products. The proposed method exploits such features by means of the "Contains" function that shows if a single value for the selected attribute is contained in another one. We choose this function because typically implemented in RDBMS and anyhow easily developed. The list of relevant values is obtained by a stemming process on the $\prod_{At} C$ elements and applying the "Contains" function to the attribute values repeatedly until the achievement of a fixed point. In section 4 we show an example of relevant values set obtained by applying the algorithm on four web-sites.

2. **Identification of the name of a relevant value:** The name associated to the relevant value is typically the most general value among the collected values, i.e. given $RV = \langle RVN, RVI \rangle$, RVN is the most general value of RVI. The name choice may be result of the clustering algorithm applied to identify the relevant values. Otherwise, the system proposes a name that has to be confirmed by the user. The method proposed in MOMIS, based on the "Contains" function, allows defining for special string domains a set of relevant values $SRV = \{RV_1, RV_2, ..., RV_v\}$, where in each RVI_i there is a "most general value" which can be used as name of the relevant value RV_i (see section 4).

3. **Hierarchy definition:** Relevant attributes may be exploited for summarizing categories and classifications. In this context, data sources (e.g.: information systems, web-sites) typically provide partial/total hierarchies for supporting users in the querying phase. Our goal is exploiting such original hierarchies by applying to the SRV the hierarchical relationships being among the values RVI_i belonging to the RVI (see section 4 for an example). In addition, the MOMIS system provides a graphical interface helping users in the manually execution of this process.

3.1 Relevant Values Representation

The set of relevant values is represented according the proposal of the Ontology Engineering and Patterns Task Force in the Semantic Web Best Practices and Deployment

Working Group (N. Noy, 2005), where five different approaches are suggested to represent OWL classes as property values on the Semantic Web. In particular, with reference to the first representation , OWL classes are directly used to describe the different relevant values belonging to the selected global attribute A_t. This assumption allows modeling an hierarchy of relevant values by means of the   rdfs:subClassOf property. According to this approach, we represent each RVN as an OWL Class and the set of values $v_j, j : 1, ..., k$ of RVI as instances of RVN; finally each RVN (i.e. an OWL class) is then generalized by a root OWL Class (called as the A_t name) that becomes the property value of the A_t attribute.

For example, referring to the example domain described in Section 4 (Table 1), the Moulding relevant value is modeled as follows:

```
<owl:Class rdf:ID="CategoryName">
 <rdfs:subClassOf
   rdf:resource=
   "http://www.w3.org/2002/07/owl#Class"/>
</owl:Class>

<owl:Class rdf:ID="Moulding">
 <rdfs:subClassOf
   rdf:resource="#CategoryName"/>
</owl:Class>

<Moulding rdf:ID="Moulding" />
<Moulding rdf:ID=
   "Compression injection moulding" />
<Moulding rdf:ID="Insert moulding" />
<Moulding rdf:ID="Normal moulding" />
<Moulding rdf:ID="Intrusion moulding" />
<Moulding rdf:ID="Deep moulding" />
```

3.2   Querying Relevant Values

The MOMIS system provides the end user with a graphical interface where the global classes, the global attributes, the primary and foreign keys are shown (see figure 2). This interface enables the end user to write a query. The interface shows on the left the complete GVV with an E/R like formalism and a tree representation. By selecting a class, its WordNet annotations (i.e. the synsets associated to the class) are visualized on the bottom panel. Right on the top a box allows inserting the query.

On the basis of the knowledge about relevant values, the queries may exploit selection clauses fitting in the data:

1. **The user is interested to the instances assuming a specific known value:** Relevant values do not improve the querying process, but, if an attribute value is called in different sources in different ways, the results may not include interesting instances.
2. **The user queries an attribute with relevant values:** The user expresses a query, by using the graphical interface, containing a relevant value, i.e. a condition of the form At = RVN. As stated before, this condition is equivalent to the condition At IN RVI. The discussion about how this query is executed is out of the scope of this paper; intuitively:
   - In a naive approach the condition At = RVN is rewritten into a local source L (for simplicity, we suppose that the global attribute At corresponds to the same local attribute At in the local sources L) as $\bigvee_{value \in RVI} At = value$.

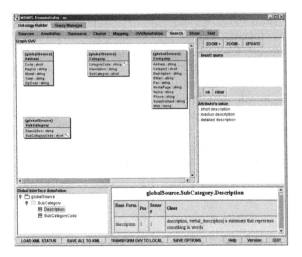

Fig. 2. Screenshot of the MOMIS Query Manager

- On the other hand, if the function Contains is *executable/supported* by the local source L (this is a frequent case if the local source is a database), the condition At = RVN may be rewritten into L as Contains(At,RVN) = *true*.

4   Evaluation on a Real Domain

Within the EU SEWASIE project (IST-2001-34825), we collected information about enterprises working on the mechanical sector. Our goal was to integrate information coming from specialized web sites.

4.1   Building the GVV and a Relevant Attribute Set

Four portals containing data about italian companies were analyzed:

- www.subforn.net: provides access to a database containing more than 6.000 subcontractors of eight italian regions. Companies are classified on the basis of their production. Mechanichal and mould sectors are divided into 53 different categories. For each category, several specific kinds of production (almost 1000) are defined.
- www.plasticaitalia.net: the plasticaitalia database contains more than 12.000 italian companies. For each company, several kinds of production are indicated: this classification is based on a three levels hierarchy specializing each kind of production in more than 300 cases.
- www.tuttostampi.com: contains 4000 italian companies categorized in 58 different kinds of services.
- www.deformazione.it: more than 2000 companies are catalogued on the basis of 39 different sectors.

```
Company(id, name, address, email, fax,
        telephone_number, country,
        foundation_year, ... )
Category(id, name)
List_categories(company_id, category_id)
```

Fig. 3. Some of the Global Classes for the mechanical GVV

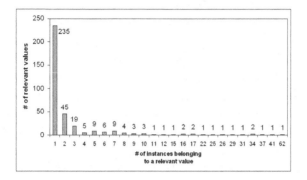

Fig. 4. Attributes distribution in the relevant values set

Table 1. An example of some relevant values

Castings	Castings, Casting zinc and its alloys, Casting with pouring under pressure, Cast iron casting, Steel casting, Casting titanium and its alloys, Aluminum and magnesium casting, Casting copper and its alloys, Casting other metals, ...
Moulding	Moulding, Compression injection moulding, Insert moulding, Normal moulding, Intrusion moulding, Dip moulding, ...
Windings	Windings,Filament winding reinforced plastic, Transformer windings, Motor windings, Coil windings

By means of the MOMIS system, a GVV representative of the four web sites was built. The simple structure of the original information sources generates a generic GVV composed of two main global classes: one storing data about companies, the second one containing all the production categories (see figure 3 where a third table allows mapping companies into categories).

According with this representation, it is very difficult for a user querying for companies producing on a specific sector: the user does not have any idea about the more than 1000 possible categories (the union of all the different categories used in the four web-sites) and indicating a specific category may be misleading: similar categories may

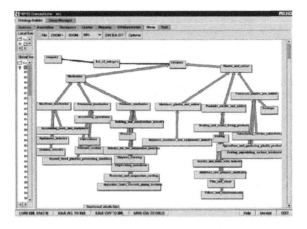

Fig. 5. Part of the hierarchy of the relevant values for the category name attribute

be called in different sources in different ways (and then the user will have no result or a partial result from his query) or the user may be interested to a result with a larger granularity. For example, if the user searches for companies producing "mould", the result will not include companies classified as producing "Plastic castings", that could be interesting for the user. For these reasons, we apply the "Contains" technique to the global attribute name of the global class category. The result was a set of 355 relevant values. Figure 4 shows the dimension of the obtained relevant values: 34% of the relevant values (120) represents 80% (845) of the instances of the selected attributes, while 235 relevant values contain only one instance. Table 1 shows some significant relevant values and the instances belonging to them.

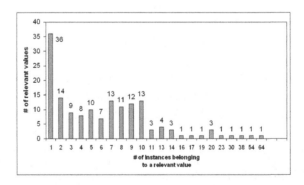

Fig. 6. Attributes distribution in the relevant values set for the SEWASIE project

The high number of relevant attributes made up of only one instance suggested to us to improve our technique by considering some semantic knowledge extracted from the original web-sites. E-commerce web-sites classify their products on the basis of hierarchical classifications. By automatically exploiting these taxonomies with customized wrappers, it is possible to build a relevant values set taking into account the semantic grouping of services and goods made in the original sources. In SEWASIE, the result was the identification of 135 relevant values. By exploiting again the original taxonomies, such relevant values were then classified in a three levels hierarchy. Figure 5 shows parts of the hierarchy: the first level divides the categories in two parts: the mechanical sector and the plastic and rubber sector; then, each sector is specialized in specific topics. For example, the "mould_making" relevant value is contained in the class "plastic_and_rubber_processes" that is part of the "plastic_and_rubber" sector. Moreover, the "mould_making" relevant value stands for 54 values in the local sources, for example large size moulds, castings, mould manufacturing, ... Figure 6 shows the dimension and the number of obtained relevant values.

4.2   Querying the GVV by Means of the Relevant Attribute Set

We suppose that an end user is searching for enterprises by using the MOMIS system applied to this domain. His query may assume different forms:

- The user is looking for enterprises without specifying their kinds of production. The result is a set of almost 30,000 enterprises and the related productions (several enterprises belong to more than one category).
- The user is looking for enterprises belonging to a specific category (e.g.:mould). The corresponding query is:

```
select *
from Company C, List_categories L,
     Category Cat
where C.id = L.company_id
and L.category_id = Cat.id
and Cat.name like 'mould'
```

The result is a set of 89 companies.
- The user is interested to enterprises working on a category mould manufacturing by exploiting the relevant values set (e.g.: the moulding relevant value). In this case he has to simply indicate the selected relevant value and the selection clause of the query automatically changes including as predicate all the instances belonging to the relevant value. The choice of the moulding relevant attribute generates a selection clause "... Cat.name in ('Moulding', 'Compression injection moulding', 'Insert moulding', ...)". The result of this query is 943 companies if the relevant values set is calculated by the algorithm described in section 3, 1459 companies if relevant values set is calculated by means of the "semantic" version (i.e., by using the mould making value).

5   Conclusions and Future Work

In this paper we proposed a method to identify the relevant values of selected global attributes. These values may be provided to the end user (classified in a hierarchy when it possible) in order to ease him having the knowledge about a Global Class and writing a query. There are few critical issues to be pointed out:

- the method is based on a data analysis. Working with instances is a limit of such technique: if data change, relevant values and the consequent hierarchy has to be updated. In specific contexts (databases not frequently updated, e.g. databases for e-commerce storing the products catalog for a company), data are almost static and then the calculus has to be only occasionally re-done. Nevertheless, the MOMIS wrappers were modified in order to periodically check the sources for verifying the relevant values consistency.
- the relevant values identification is a critical aspect: the integration engineer has to define a set of relevant values covering all the possible kinds of values, with a limited number of different values to be easily visualized and known by the end user. Otherwise, the end user does not know the Global Class contents and does not find the required information to write a query.
- the method allows a user to write specific queries having an organized knowledge of the sources contents.

The future work will be addressed on three directions:

1. to improve the relevant values selection by proposing to the user a multi-strategic approach for obtaining the most suitable relevant values set: for this goal, we think of it is possible to use industrial standards for classification of services and goods (e.g. UNSPSC, ecl@ss, NAICS, ...) inside specific domains both for creating the most suitable set of relevant values and for creating an automatic hierarchy of these attributes;
2. to calculate relevant values of multiple global attributes;
3. to improve the Query Manager graphical interface allowing users to query the GVV without writing any query.

Acknowledgements

This work started in the EU SEWASIE project (IST-2001-34825). Now the research activity continues within the Italian MIUR PRIN WISDOM project (2004-2006). Further information at http://www.dbgroup.unimo.it/wisdom.

References

Beneventano et al., 2003. Beneventano, D., Bergamaschi, S., Guerra, F., Vincini, M.: Synthesizing an integrated ontology. IEEE Internet Computing Magazine, 42–51 (2003)
Beneventano and Lenzerini, 2005. Beneventano, D., Lenzerini, M.: Final release of the system prototype for query management. Sewasie, Deliverable D.3.5, Final Version (2005), available at http://www.dbgroup.unimo.it/pubs.html
Bergamaschi et al., 2001. Bergamaschi, S., Castano, S., Beneventano, D., Vincini, M.: Semantic integration of heterogeneous information sources. Data & Knowledge Engineering, Special Issue on Intelligent Information Integration 36(1), 215–249 (2001)

Broder et al., 2005. Broder, A.Z., Maarek, Y.S., Bharat, K., Dumais, S.T., Papa, S., Pedersen, J., Raghavan, P.: Current trends in the integration of searching and browsing. In: WWW (Special interest tracks and posters), pp. 793 (2005)

Buneman et al., 1997. Buneman, P., Davidson, S., Fernandez, M., Suciu, D.: Adding structure to unstructured data. In: Afrati, F.N., Kolaitis, P.G. (eds.) ICDT 1997. LNCS, vol. 1186, pp. 336–350. Springer, Heidelberg (1996)

Chaudhuri et al., 2005. Chaudhuri, S., Ramakrishnan, R., Weikum, G.: Integrating db and ir technologies: What is the sound of one hand clapping. In: Proceedings of the Second Biennial Conference on Innovative Data Systems Research, Asilomar, CA, USA, pp. 1–12 (2005)

Dong and Halevy, 2005. Dong, X., Halevy, A.Y.: Malleable schemas: A preliminary report. In: Proceedings of he Eight International Workshop on the Web & Databases (WebDB 2005), Baltimore, Maryland, USA, pp. 139–144 (2005)

Galindo-Legaria, 1994. Galindo-Legaria, C.A.: Outerjoins as disjunctions. In: Snodgrass, R.T., Winslett, M. (eds.) SIGMOD Conference, pp. 348–358. ACM Press, New York (1994)

Gibson et al., 2000. Gibson, D., Kleinberg, J., Raghavan, P.: Clustering categorical data: an approach based on dynamical systems. VLDB Journal 8(3-4), 222–236 (2000)

Gottlob et al., 2004. Gottlob, G., Koch, C., Baumgartner, R., Herzog, M., Flesca, S.: The lixto data extraction project - back and forth between theory and practice. In: Proceedings of the Twenty-third ACM SIGACT-SIGMOD-SIGART Symposium on Principles of Database Systems, Paris, France, pp. 1–12 (2004)

Halevy, 2003. Halevy, A.: Data integration: a status report. In: Proceedings of the German Database Conference, BTW-03, Leipzig (2003)

Halevy, 2004. Halevy, A.Y.: Structures, semantics and statistics. In: Proceedings of the 30th International Conference on VLDB, Toronto, Canada, pp. 4–6 (2004)

N. Noy, 2005. Noy, N., Uschold, M.C.W.: Representing classes as property values on the semantic web. Semantic Web Best Practices and Deployment Working Group, part of the W3C Semantic Web Activity (2005), http://www.w3.org/TR/swbp-classes-as-values

Nestorov et al., 1997. Nestorov, S., Abiteboul, S., Motwani, R.: Inferring structure in semistructured data. SIGMOD Record 26(4), 39–43 (1997)

Web Federates – Towards A Middleware for Highly Scalable Peer-to-Peer Services

Ingo Scholtes and Peter Sturm

University of Trier
Department of Computer Science, Systemsoftware and Distributed Systems,
D-54286 Trier, Germany
{scholtes,sturm}@syssoft.uni-trier.de

Abstract. Starting from the classical Client/Server paradigm, in the last couple of years Peer-To-Peer approaches have evolved and proven their power. Currently we see an evolution from the distributed object access paradigm represented e.g. by middleware architectures like CORBA, DCOM or RMI towards Service Oriented Architectures (SOA), entailing a retrogression to the Client/Server paradigm. In this paper we want to present how Peer-To-Peer Applications can to a large extend benefit from intrinsic Web Service properties like loose coupling, declarative interface definition and interoperability, thus incorporating advantages from SOA and the Peer-To-Peer approach, opening new fields of application to both of them. For this purpose, WebFederate, a prototype middleware based on Microsoft's .NET Framework has been implemented and will be presented in this paper.

Keywords: Web Service, Peer-To-Peer, Web Federate, WSDL, SOAP, Middleware, Message Exchange Patterns, Code Generation, Request/Response, One-Way, Solicit/Response, Notification, Publish/Subscribe, Scalability, Light-Weight Hosting, Service Oriented Architecture.

1 Introduction

Starting from the classical Client/Server paradigm, in the last couple of years Peer-To-Peer approaches have evolved into a serious alternative. Prominent examples like Skype or notorious file-sharing applications but also scientific prototypes like Freenet (Clarke et al., 2000) or Oceanstore (Rhea et al., 2003) show the power of this approach in regard to scalability and availability. While these accomplishments of the Peer-To-Peer paradigm are widely accepted, currently one can see an evolution from classical distributed object access technologies like CORBA, DCOM and RMI towards Service Oriented Architectures (SOA), entailing a retrogression to the Client/Server paradigm. This retrogression is to a large extend based on the idea, that Web Services are hosted by heavy-weight Web or Application servers, which automatically results in an asymmetric relationship between caller and callee. Apart from that this deployment model usually implies, that Web Service providers are passive, reacting only to requests from active service consumers. These properties are however no intrinsic characteristics of the underlying standards. Light-weightiness and usability in a decentralized distributed

J. Filipe, J. Cordeiro, and V. Pedrosa (Eds.): WEBIST 2005/2006, LNBIP 1, pp. 138–149, 2007.
© Springer-Verlag Berlin Heidelberg 2007

environment are two key design goals which have been respected in the definition of the SOAP standard. Apart from simple Web Service usage scenarios adopted today - Web Services being mainly used as interconnection between back-end servers and presentation front-end - which primarily use the Client/Server paradigm, the SOAP standard defines the SOAP Intermediary role which is suitable for multihop scenarios. These are very likely to be applied when Web Services will need to be deployed in global scale.

Furthermore, the WSDL standard, in addition to the commonly used One-Way and Request/Response message exchange patterns, also defines two others: Solicit/Response and Notification. In most Web Service implementations however, these additional message exchange patterns remain unused for reasons which will be discussed in a separate section.

Regarding declarative service description, loose coupling, late binding and interoperability, Peer-To-Peer applications can to a large extend benefit from these intrinsic Web Service qualities, henceforth incorporating advantages from Service Oriented Architectures and the Peer-To-Peer approach and opening new fields of application to both of them. One fundamental step towards this goal is a light-weight way to create, deploy and host Web Services.

The remainder of this paper is organised in the following way: Section 2 discusses the Solicit/Response and Notification message exchange patterns, reasons why these are commonly unused, some code generation technique and related multicast considerations. Having examined scalability issues of the general Web Service technology in section 3, section 4 presents work in progress on a prototype middleware, which remedies Web Services from the aforementioned deficiency of asymmetric role association. Finally, after having done a presentation of related work in section 5, a conclusion will be drawn along with an outlook to future work. For the course of this paper we introduce the term "Web Federate", which henceforth denotes a computing node running applications based on this middleware, since these nodes may act in the roles of service provider and consumer simultaneously and swarms of them may federate in order to host superordinate services collaboratively.

2   Solicit/Response and Notification Message Exchange Patterns

There are several reasons why most Web Service implementations do not use the Solicit/Response and Notification message exchange patterns:

- The WSDL-To-Code mapping is more complicated than for the Request/Response or One-Way patterns
- They require service providers to become active, a behavior not foreseen in most container deployment models
- They require some kind of Publish/Subscribe model
- They do not scale in the number of subscribers due to the lack of multicast communication schemes available on the public Internet
- They exhibit concurrency difficulties at the service consumer side
- The most widely used HTTP protocol binding does not make use of Solicit/Response and Notification
- Requirement R2303 of WS-I Basic Profile 1.0 and 1.1 precludes their usage

One reason why these additional message exchange patterns are currently not supported by the WS-I Basic Profile, is that one can describe them also at the consumer's side in terms of Request/Response or One-Way. Although a Notification operation certainly can be seen as a reverse One-Way operation and a Solicit/Response operation is nothing more than a Request/Response from the callee's point of view, it does however make sense to use them. In Peer-To-Peer application scenarios we are addressing, a peer may not know what kinds of notifications are available and what it is interested in beforehand. It does however know which notifications it can provide. So it seems natural to describe such a service at the side of the notification provider in terms of a Notification rather than describing it at the service consumer's side in terms of a One-Way pattern. A similar argument is true for Solicit/Response operations. At the time when a peer needs a service there may e.g. be no appropriate peer providing such a service in terms of Request/Response. The peer searching for a service however does know what he desires thus he can ask for it explicitly by exposing a Solicit/Response operation, so accessory peers which are able to satisfy this desire will learn about it. Admittedly the term "service provider" may be misleading in this case, as in the case of a Solicit/Response operation, the actual service (in the sense of an attendance) is done by the service consumer. So in many cases the usage of a Solicit/Response service may require some form of altruism on the consumer side in order to use it.

2.1   Code Generation Techniques

As mentioned before, the mapping from WSDL document to proxy and stub code is more complicated for the Solicit/Response and Notification message exchange patterns than for Request/Response or One-Way which can be mapped to (possibly void) methods in a very natural and straight-forward way. Regarding a WSDL document mixing Request/Response, Notification and Solicit/Response message exchange patterns the primary reason for this additional complexity is the fact, that the clear division in proxy and stub code gets lost. At the service provider side, instead of having a stub class with abstract methods to be implemented by the application programmer, due to Solicit/Response and Notification schemes stub classes may now contain additional method implementations that need to be callable by the user. This naturally precludes the container deployment model from being used. Regarding proxy classes at the service consumer side, the deprivation of this division is even more painful, as these become abstract too.

Traditional code generation techniques can however be applied, if middleware tools are allowed to generate several classes for a single service. Instead of the straight-forward approach described above, tools might also generate:

- a traditional proxy class for Notification and Solicit/Response operations at the service provider side
- a traditional stub class for Request/Response and One-Way operations at the service provider side
- a traditional stub class for Notification and Solicit/Response operations at the service consumer side
- a traditional proxy class for Request/Response and One-Way operations at the service consumer side

An example for a Web Service framework which makes use of this code generation technique is LEIF[1], a C++ framework for service-oriented applications which supports all message exchange patterns defined in WSDL, including Solicit/Response and Notification.

Apart from generating proxy and stub code from WSDL documents, state-of-the art middleware also allows automatic generation of WSDL documents from service implementations. In case of the Request/Response and the One-Way message exchange pattern application programmers commonly simply provide a service implementation inheriting a service's base class, tagging methods they want to expose as service operations (e.g. the WebMethod attribute in the .NET context) - the Middleware can then generate the WSDL document along with the code, which actually receives SOAP envelopes, unmarshals the arguments and invokes the methods provided by the application programmer.

Using the Solicit/Response and Notification patterns, the situation is again more complicated as it requires application programmers to provide an abstract class with some abstract methods. Code generation tools would now need to create a class which inherits the user's abstract class and provides implementations for all abstract methods. In these implementations, marshalling of arguments and the actual sending to the subscribers needs to be done. As the subscribers list has to be known in order to actually send notifications and soliciting requests, there need to be means of making this list available to the middleware.

Comparing the aforementioned abstract service class from which middleware shall generate a WSDL document and the stub code that would have been generated from the same WSDL document, `abstract` qualifiers are transposed. Actually this transposition becomes evident, if one looks at an `abstract` qualifier as a "request for implementation" for this method. Starting with a WSDL description, in the case when a stub class has been generated from the WSDL document, the middleware requests the application programmer to provide service operation implementations it can not provide itself. In the latter case, starting with the implementation, a WSDL document being generated from it, the application programmer requests the middleware to provide marshalling operations he does not want to provide himself.

2.2 Achieving Multicast Communication

As the public Internet lacks true multicast communication schemes, the sending of Notification and Solicit/Response messages to a large number of subscribers does not scale. One possible solution to overcome this problem in case of the Notification message exchange pattern is the usage of distribution trees, playing on the federate role of the subscribers. Instead of shipping a Notification message to all subscribers, the service provider sends it to a constant number of federates, these redistributing messages in an overlay distribution tree. This allows the shipping of notifications to all subscribers with only a constant number of subscriptions per federate although it induces additional latency depending on the position of a federate in the tree. A similar scheme has been implemented in the ATLAS Event Monitoring System, which will be used in order to distribute collision event data among physicists' monitoring processes in a scalable manner

---

[1] http://www.roguewave.com/products/leif/

at CERN's forthcoming LHC particle accelerator experiment. A more detailed discussion and evaluation of this content distribution scheme can be found in (Scholtes, 2005) and (Kolos and Scholtes, 2005).

In case of Solicit/Response message exchange patterns the solution is however not that simple, as response messages have to be routed back to the service provider, thus leading to an implosion problem. Data aggregation techniques may find application along the path in order to solve this problem, presumably requiring domain-specific knowledge.

3   Web Service Scalability

Today mostly major companies like Amazon, Google or eBay are involved in large-scale deployment of Web Services and a lot of time and effort is being put into making them scale. Although vulnerability for attacks and sabotage as well as laborious scalability and fault tolerance are intrinsic properties of centralised Client/Server architectures, for the reasons set forth in section 1 it is the one which is most widely spread in the context of Web Services. In his recent article (Birman, 2005) Ken Birman argues, that in the future all sorts of companies and organisations will be interested in deploying Web Services at a large scale. Many of those will not have the means Amazon, eBay or Google have.

While also big players might benefit from Peer-To-Peer approaches, relieving them from cost-intensive scalability and fault tolerance efforts, Peer-To-Peer technology is likely to become inevitable for smaller institutions willing to deploy Web Services at large scale. The success of a small start-up company like Skype[2] could hardly have ever been imagined if rather than relying on Peer-To-Peer technology they had had to set up cost-intensive network infrastructure in the first instance. Similar scenarios are also imaginable for Web Service technologies. Furthermore, regarding a scenario of Web Services becoming the primary communication architecture across the Internet, even individuals might want to offer scalable Web Services. Today, Weblogs are one example of Web Service technology that is already used by a still-growing number of millions of individuals. While currently for example RSS feeds are implemented using pull model technology simulating a push model behavior, technologies like Trackback also today make use of a push model similar to WSDL's Notification communication scheme, requiring Weblogs of individuals to offer and consume Web Service in a federate manner.

Taking into account the tremendous increase in bandwidth, computing power and storage capacity observable in home computing devices over the past couple of years, today the application of Peer-To-Peer technology appears more promising than ever. Future technologies like network filesystems similar to prototypes like Oceanstore (Rhea et al., 2003) but also mobile devices with limited storage and computing power are therefore very likely to rely on Peer-To-Peer technology and the means provided by Web Services.

Apart from mere scalability, in the future Web Services might find application in critical domains which require a high level of immunity against failures and deliberate breakdowns. Regarding scalability and decentralism being intrinsic properties of Peer-To-Peer approaches and interoperability being a key characteristic of Web Services, it seems to

---

[2] http://www.skype.com

be evident that a marriage between these techniques is about to happen. Power-law obeying overlay networks similar to those used in today's Peer-To-Peer applications might be utilised in the future to create swarms of Web Federates providing superordinate services in a fault-tolerant, self-organising and scalable way. For this purpose means like those introduced in (Devlin et al., 1999) seem to be appropriate.

4   WebFederate Middleware

In order to empower developers to achieve the goals presented above, a prototype middleware based on Microsoft's .NET Framework and Microsoft's Web Services Enhancement Toolkit has been implemented, which provides the following key functionality:

- Lightweight and stateful in-process hosting of Web Services
- Lightweight and stateless container model hosting of Web Services
- Dynamic Web Service discovery, proxy-generation and invocation at run-time
- Dynamic Composition of Web Services at run-time
- Automatic exposition of a simple discovery service on start-up
- Automatic service discovery of Web Federates accessing a service

4.1   Overall Architecture

The middleware prototype consists of three libraries: WebFederate, WebFederate.Visualization and Cassini. The purpose of these libraries will be described in the following paragraphs.

WebFederate Visualization Library. This library may be used in order to visualise Web Federates along with the services they expose in a graphical manner. It is used by the example application presented in 4.2 in order to illustrate the middleware's dynamics and allow GUI driven interaction with Web Services and Web Federates.

WebFederate. The public application programmer's interface of the library's main class `WebFederate` is shown in figure 1. Lightweight Web Service hosting is achieved by using a library which has been implemented on top of Microsoft's shared-source Cassini project, Web Service hosting capabilities offered by ASP.NET and the in-process Web Service hosting provided by Microsoft's Web Service Enhancements (WSE3). Web Services are published using SOAP's TCP and/or HTTP binding according to the application programmer's settings.

The Cassini project is an easy-to-use Web Server library with a small memory footprint published as a shared-source project by Microsoft[3]. Along with ASP.NET it is used for lightweight and stateless Web Service hosting following the container model and using HTTP as transport. Similar lightweight hosting approaches can be found in the UNIX world e.g. using combinations of lightweight Web Server implementation like abyss [4] or NanoHTTP [5] and the eSOAP[6] toolkit. As ASP.NET Web Service hosting follows the

---

[3] http://www.asp.net/Projects/Cassini/Download/Default.aspx
[4] http://www.aprelium.com
[5] http://www.cwc.oulu.fi/nanoip/
[6] http://esoap.ultimodule.com

Fig. 1. The WebFederate API

container model using a per-request instance creation, it is per-default stateless leaving state management to the application programmer.

Stateful Web Service hosting is provided by using Microsoft's Web Service Enhancements (WSE), which in this regard pretty much allows a glance at Microsoft's upcoming service-oriented Communication Foundation (codename Indigo). Rather than creating object instances on a per-request basis as done by ASP.NET, instantiation is done on application start-up, the lifetime of object instances being managed by the WebFederate middleware. Federate Services using this hosting facility are therefore inherently stateful. Apart from TCP and HTTP which can be used as transport mechanisms according to the application programmer's preference, the usage of a UDP transport for true asynchronous communication schemes is at the planning stage.

The development procedure commonly used for Web Service implementations and Web Service consuming applications is, even though WSDL offers declarative service descriptions, to a large extend still influenced by distributed object access middleware like CORBA or DCOM. Stub and skeleton classes are generated from a WSDL service description by WSDL parsers (like the `wsdl` tool in Visual Studio, `WSDL2Java` tool in AXIS or the `leifgen` tool in LEIF) at - or actually even before - compile-time, functionality then being added to these generated stubs and skeletons by the application programmer, just like it used to be done with traditional IDL compilers in the distributed object access middleware approaches mentioned above. In order to allow dynamic invocation, creation of and binding to Web Services at run-time, the WebFederate middleware presented in this paper makes use of the declarative service description and .NET's reflection and run-time compile facilities. At run-time proxy code will be generated from the WSDL description of a Web Service, the resulting proxy code will be dynamically compiled and invoked in the background. A wrapper class offers dynamic access to the Web

Fig. 2. The FederateService interface

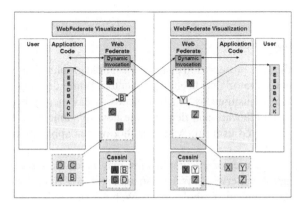

Fig. 3. Middleware Architecture

Service methods, which are queried from the generated proxy via the reflection mechanism. All of the above steps are done transparently for the application programmer, so all he has to specify is the WSDL document's URI or the IP address of the Web Federate machine along with the name of the service, enabling him to obtain an object instance at run-time which he may utilise in order to use a service.

In order to discover Web Services running at a Web Federate computing node, on installation-time a straightforward discovery Web Service is automatically created, which in the prototype simply returns a list of all services hosted by a Web Federate. This list can then be used by the requesting Web Federate application in order to dynamically create a specific Web Service proxy as described above. As this discovery service is exposed using a preassigned service name, it can easily be accessed by other Web Federate applications. In emphasis of the symmetric role of Web Federates, hooks have been embedded into the discovery service which will trigger an event whenever a Web Federate performs a discovery request, so the users of the middleware can immediately discover and make use of services provided by the calling federate.

The prototype middleware offers a dynamic deployment mechanism of Web Services. C# Code can be submitted to the middleware, which will try to compile, instantiate and publish the service immediately at run-time. For this purpose a class library along with an asmx file is produced, providing the WSDL description of the new Web Service. The service itself is then published by instantiating the service class and registering it with Microsoft's WSE runtime. In order to simplify service development, an abstract class FederateService may be used as base class for custom services, it's public interface being shown in figure 2.

The high-level architecture of the middleware can be seen in figure 3.

Apart from traditional service implementations, application programmer's may use the abstract service base class FederateService for dynamic Web Service implementations which call back application code on request. The connection between Web Service implementation and application code is achieved making use of .NET's delegate/event mechanism. The implementer of applications based on the middleware may register event handlers dynamically which will be called on reception of requests. The application code handler can then satisfy the request itself or even pass it on to the user.

4.2 Example Application

On top of the middleware presented in chapter 4 a simple graphical test application, the "Web Federate Demonstrator" has been implemented. While this application does not serve a special purpose justified by practical needs, it has mainly been implemented in order to test the middleware and demonstrate how dynamic Web Services can be implemented and deployed using it. A screen shot of this application can be seen in figure 4.

In the address box, a user of this application may enter the URI of a Web Federate or a conventional Web Service's WSDL document. If a WSDL document's address has been entered, a graphical symbol for this Web Service will appear in a panel, if

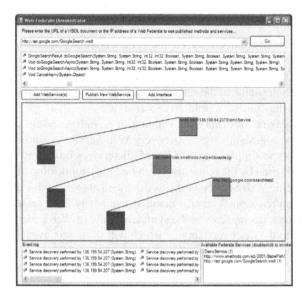

Fig. 4. Screen shot of the Web Federate Demonstrator Application

a Web Federate's IP address has been entered a service discovery will be performed, showing all available services on the selected Federate. The user may then select services and add graphical symbols for them to the panel. In order to interact with Web Services added earlier, users may add so-called interface nodes to the panel, connecting them to Web Services dynamically and graphically for invocation using the above-mentioned `WebFederate.Visualization` library. Web Services can simply be published by pushing a single button and completing a service skeleton based on the `FederateService` class. When an interactive Web Service has been published by the Web Federate node and a request to this service has been performed which requires a user's feedback, a window pops up, asking for the user's response and delivering this response to the caller. Using the Web Federate Demonstrator application, it is a question of only a minute to implement e.g. a simple chat application at run-time in a graphical manner.

4.3   Usage Scenarios

In this section some example usage scenarios for middleware approaches like WebFederate will be presented.

E-Learning. Although not being the original intention, the "Web Federate Demonstrator" application presented in section 4.2 can be used right-away as an E-Learning application for introductory programming courses. One might think of a scenario where the lecturer assigns a task to his students, every student using a computer running the "Web Federate Demonstrator" application. In order to solve the task a Web Service has to be implemented at a specific Web Federate which provides a certain given functionality. It is the student's job to collaboratively compose this service possibly combining publicly available Web Services and services they need to implement themselves just as described in the above paragraph. Taking into account the wide variety of Web Services which are publicly available at no charge e.g. listed by (Fan and Kambhampati, 2005), comprehensive and expedient yet feasible tasks can be easily defined. This scenario boosts the student's domain decomposition, teamwork and programming skills and it early introduces collaborative thinking, distributed programming and the RPC paradigm without needing knowledge about the technical details this usually requires. The early introduction of Web Service programming in CS1/CS2 classes has been earlier proposed by (Lim et al., 2005).

Scalable Web Services. As pictured in section 3, in the future Peer-To-Peer approaches will become more important in the context of Web Services. This requires special middleware architectures which are capable of providing a self-organisational and scalable infrastructure. The WebFederate middleware represents one step towards this goal as it provides basic techniques for light-weight Web Service hosting and dynamic invocation.

Ubiquitous Computing. Light-weight Web Service hosting techniques are crucial for ubiquitous computing scenarios, regarding small devices with their very limited processing power and memory layout. Although the WebFederate middleware is based on Microsoft .NET and provides Web Service hosting with a very small memory footprint, it can not be used for .NET enabled mobile devices right-away as it relies on the hosting capabilities of the ASP.NET framework, which are not included in the .NET Compact framework available for these appliances. In the future, investigation shall be done how to overcome this deficiency as the availability of such a middleware for mobile devices might enforce the emergence of ubiquitous computing applications.

5   Related Work

(Harrison and Taylor, 2005a) and (Harrison and Taylor, 2005b) introduce WSPeer, a JAVA-based Web Service middleware for Peer-To-Peer applications. Just like the middleware presented in this paper, in WSPeer deployment of Web Services does not follow the container model or require a Web Server. As it relies on the classic RPC paradigm, it does however not support advanced message exchange patterns like Solicit/Response or Notification. Regarding ubiquitous computing application scenarios, some research on light-weight means of Web Service hosting for embedded devices has been made by (Pratistha et al., 2003), proposing the Micro-Services framework. EIRI, a JAVA based approach for a lightweight Web Service deployment framework from the year 2002 as presented by (Gergic et al., 2002), does not make use of standards like SOAP or WSDL and therefore lacks interoperability. Today however the term Web Service is commonly associated with these standards. Besides that, asymmetry is an intrinsic feature of the framework, as it has been designed in order to support information retrieval of light-weight devices like PDAs, telephones or information terminals from heavy-weight back end database systems. Apache's Web Service Invocation Framework (WSIF) and the AXIS toolkit from the Java world allow dynamic proxy generation and invocation of Web Services. Furthermore WSIF supports Solicit/Response and Notification message exchange patterns at the service consumer side.

6   Conclusion and Future Work

In this paper we argue that Peer-To-Peer scenarios can be of great use for Web Services. In order to investigate means for light-weight Web Service hosting based on currently available techniques, a simple and generic Peer-To-Peer middleware has been implemented and - along with some use cases - presented. In a future version of this middleware the usage of SOAP intermediaries for the creation of highly scalable and self-organising Web Service Federate networks which act like a single superordinate service provider will be investigated. It seems to be evident, that forthcoming technologies like Microsoft's Windows Communication Foundation middleware (codename Indigo) will boost the emergence of Web Federates, as they will propagate simple-to-use and light-weight techniques for in-process Web Service hosting. While it is common to look at Web Services as the next generation distributed object access, SOAP being a new declarative RPC protocol, we think that this reduction to the RPC paradigm is a fatal underestimation of the standard's potential. RPC-like communication schemes provide only a small portion of the Web Service standards' capabilities and - as they often make assumptions about the underlying implementation - even are counterproductive regarding the original intention of Service Oriented Architectures.

An important fact presented in this paper is, that Web Services are not inherently associated with the Client/Server paradigm, just because they are commonly hosted by Web or Application servers in a traditional 3-tier architecture that separates program logic, data and presentation. In order to build highly scalable systems, Peer-To-Peer approaches to Web Services are required and can actually be implemented using state-of-the-art techniques as proven by the WebFederate middleware prototype.

References

Birman, K.P.: Can Web Services Scale Up? IEEE Computer 38(10), 107–110 (2005)

Clarke, I., Sandberg, O., Wiley, B., Hong, T.W.: Freenet: A distributed anonymous information storage and retrieval system. In: Workshop on Design Issues in Anonymity and Unobservability, pp. 46–66 (2000)

Devlin, B., Gray, J., Laing, B., Spix, G.: Scalability terminology: Farms, Clones, Partitions, Packs, Racs and Raps. CoRR, cs.AR/9912010 (1999)

Fan, J., Kambhampati, S.: A snapshot of public Web Services. SIGMOD Record 34(1), 24–32 (2005)

Gergic, J., Kleindienst, J., Despotopoulos, Y., Soldatos, J., Patikis, G., Anagnostou, A., Polymenakos, L.: An approach to lightweight deployment of Web Services. In: SEKE, pp. 635–640 (2002)

Harrison, A., Taylor, I.: Dynamic Web Service Deployment Using WSPeer. In: Proceedings of 13th Annual Mardi Gras Conference - Frontiers of Grid Applications and Technologies, pp. 11–16. Louisiana State University (2005a)

Harrison, A., Taylor, I.: WSPeer - an interface to Web Service hosting and invocation. In: HIPS Joint Workshop on High-Performance Grid Computing and High-Level Parallel Programming Models. To be published (2005b)

Kolos, S., Scholtes, I.: Event Monitoring Design. Technical report, CERN (2005)

Lim, B.B.L., Jong, C., Mahatanankoon, P.: On integrating web services from the ground up into CS1/CS2. In: SIGCSE, pp. 241–245 (2005)

Pratistha, I.M.D.P., Nicoloudis, N., Cuce, S.: A micro-services framework on mobile devices. In: ICWS, pp. 320–325 (2003)

Rhea, S.C., Eaton, P.R., Geels, D., Weatherspoon, H., Zhao, B.Y., Kubiatowicz, J.: Pond: The OceanStore prototype. In: FAST (2003)

Scholtes, I.: A reimplementation of the CORBA-based Event Monitoring System for the ATLAS LHC Experiment at CERN. Diploma thesis, University of Trier (2005)

Part II

Web Interfaces and Applications

Modeling Preferences Online

Maria Cleci Martins[1] and Rosina Weber[2]

[1] College of Businees, Brazilian Lutheran University R. 15 de Novembro,
253 Novo Hamburgo, RS 93315 Brazil
gelog@ulbra.tche.br
[2] College of Information Science & Technology, Drexel University 3141 Chestnut Street
Philadelphia, PA 19104 USA
rosina.weber@drexel.edu

Abstract. The search for an online product that matches e-shoppers' needs and preferences can be frustrating and time-consuming. Browsing large lists arranged in tree-like structures demands focused attention from e-shoppers. Keyword search often results in either too many useless items (low precision) or few or none useful ones (low recall). This can cause potential buyers to seek another seller or choose to go in person to a store. This paper introduces the SPOT (Stated Preference Ontology Targeted) methodology to model e-shoppers' decision-making processes and use them to refine a search and show products and services that meet their preferences. SPOT combines probabilistic theory on discrete choices, the theory of stated preferences, and knowledge modeling (i.e. ontologies). The probabilistic theory on discrete choices coupled with e-shoppers' stated preferences data allow us to unveil parameters e-shoppers would employ to reach a decision of choice related to a given product or service. Those parameters are used to rebuild the decision process and evaluate alternatives to select candidate products that are more likely to match e-shoppers' choices. We use a synthetic example to demonstrate how our approach distinguishes from currently used methods for e-commerce.

Keywords: E-Commerce, Discrete choices, Stated preferences, Personalization, Ontologies, User modelling.

1 Introduction

The search for an online product that matches e-shoppers' needs and preferences can be frustrating and time-consuming. Information about products and suppliers is usually accessed from database servers using either list browsing or keyword search. However, the amount of information available in those databases has substantially increased the cognitive effort required for e-shoppers to make their choices. Browsing large lists, arranged in tree-like structures can be time consuming, while keyword search often results in too many useless items and too few actually useful (or none) being returned. Thus, instead of facilitating the choice (and the sale), the Internet makes the e-shopper's choice decision-making process more difficult. Such difficulty is frustrating and is detrimental to online sales.

Addressing customers' needs is crucial for e-commerce. E-commerce systems should be able to facilitate the customers' choice process by offering alternatives that

J. Filipe, J. Cordeiro, and V. Pedrosa (Eds.): WEBIST 2005/2006, LNBIP 1, pp. 153–165, 2007.
© Springer-Verlag Berlin Heidelberg 2007

are more likely to satisfy their preferences. This would generate less frustration and potentially increase revenues, service level and customer's satisfaction.

Personalization is an approach that uses characteristics of individual users to select information to be searched and displayed to users (Cotter & Smyth 2000). Recommender systems for e-commerce (e.g., Ardissono & Godoy 2000; Domingue et al. 2002, Burke 2000) address the personalization issue by filtering the amount of non-requested products to be showed to the e-shopper in a given session. Recommender systems can be collaborative, content-based, demographic, utility-based, and knowledge-based (Burke 2002).

Recommender systems are useful when customers do not know exactly what product or service they need, or when the company wants to introduce different products to the user. However, when customers roughly know their needs and the type of product or service to address those needs, the problem is to find the best available online option according to the user's viewpoint. This problem is typically addressed only by utility-based recommender systems (Burke 2002). As a comparison, in a physical store, the shopper would be able to use other senses (e.g. vision, touch) to recognize available products and compare them before choosing one, or ask a sales person for advice. On the Internet, however, they have to rely on their decision-making skills and the available information to choose the best option.

This paper proposes the use of the economic theory on discrete choices (Ben-Akiva & Lerman 1985) to help e-shoppers find the best match for their needs from what is available on the Internet. In this sense, it can be categorized as an utility-based recommender. *Our approach is to elicit from e-shoppers how they make choices, build a model of their choice behaviour, and use it to refine the search and show products and services that meet their preferences.*

Discrete choice modeling has been largely used in the transportation field to forecast travel demand from disaggregate data on individual choices (Ben-Akiva & Lerman 1985; Fowkes & Shinghal 2002). For example, it is used to forecast demand by finding the likelihood that a travel mode is chosen given certain characteristics such as travel time, comfort, and headway. The rationale for using discrete choice modeling is that it is a mature methodology to uncover users' decision-making processes without asking them directly.

The mathematical model – Logit is very robust and it is likely that the user's decision-making model found is the best possible (Ben-Akiva & Lerman 1985). Alternative methods (e.g. non-linear) are computationally more complex, more demanding to the user, and their result has been shown to be only marginally better (De Carvalho, M. 1998).

Section 2 reviews methods used in this work: discrete choice modeling, stated preference, ontologies, and personalization. The SPOT methodology is described in Section 3, followed by a demonstration that uses statistics-based simulation in Section 4; Section 5 is a discussion and Section 6 concludes.

2 Methods

2.1 Discrete Choice Theory

The term *choice* refers to the cognitive process of a consumer who, after evaluating the alternatives in a *choice set*, decides to select one of them (Louviere 1988).

Discrete choice modeling is a well-known and mature methodology (Ben-Akiva & Lerman 1985) to investigate that process. The main feature of discrete choice data is that the observed response (i.e. the dependent variable) is discrete: the method only determines whether or not customers choose one alternative option.

Discrete choice models can use compensatory or non-compensatory rules. Compensatory models allow offsetting changes in one or more attributes to compensate for a change in a particular attribute (implying simultaneous consideration of all attributes). For instance, a roomier seat can compensate for a higher price in air travel. By contrast, non-compensatory models do not permit trade-offs between attributes; comparisons are made on a sequential consideration of each attribute. The last decision is often based on a compensatory model to compare final options (if more than one). This is the decision-making situation faced by e-shoppers on the Internet.

Discrete choice modeling is based on the economic utility theory for compensatory models with the following four assumptions about the consumer behaviour.

1. Products or services can be represented in vectors of feature-value pairs (attributes), e.g. cost, brand.
2. Customers are optimizers and they compare options based on the value of their attributes.
3. Customers make trade-offs between attributes of a product/service to reach their decision, e.g. in transport service, less comfort can be accepted if the fare is reduced.
4. Customers are maximizers and they always choose the best perceived option within a knowledge domain.

2.2 Stated Preference

Stated Preference (SP) is a technique used to collect data on individual's discrete choices (Pearmain & Kroes 1990). It can be understood as a simulation game where individuals are asked to state their preferences for a set of possible options (i.e. choice set). A choice set is composed of at least two alternatives e.g. a trip can be characterized by the attributes cost and in-vehicle travel time. A choice set would consider the transportation modes car and train, each mode being represented by its respective cost and travel time. The number of choice sets is developed according to the number and levels of attributes to be considered.

The design of a SP collection must consider trade-offs between attributes of the product or service. Respondents should be given choice sets with possible options, but it is not necessary to know exactly which options are available and the exact values of the attributes; the attribute values should be as close to reality as possible. An Internet collection can be designed at runtime (e.g. using the support of a knowledge base).

A desired property of a SP collection is orthogonality (zero correlation between attribute values and alternatives), so that separate effects on choices can be estimated, as well as possible interaction effects of their combinations. For the sake of demonstration (Section 0) we are employing a full factorial design that guarantees orthogonality (Kocur et al. 1982). On a real situation, fractional designs have to be employed to reduce the respondents' fatigue. Factorial design provides a way to investigate the interaction effects between attributes, such as price and travel time. To measure all interaction effects one should use a full factorial design, which is a problem that grows exponentially. Fractional factorial designs are employed to reduce dimension and the number of alternatives users have to analyse. In that case, some minor interaction effects are ignored in the experiment.

In our proposed approach, customers' stated preference data is used to calibrate a Logit model (Ben-Akiva & Lerman 1985) that will unveil the parameters (weights) that the e-shopper would use to evaluate and choose one online option.

2.3 Logit Modeling

Logit modeling assumes that options are represented by a function (U_i) composed of unobserved variables (β_j), which are somehow associated with characteristics (X_{ij}) of the product (i) and a random term (ε)(See Equation 1). The function U might be continuous or not, depending on the type of the attributes. If price is continuous and colour is discontinuous, then a function with both these variables would necessarily be discontinuous at some point. The values of the coefficients are found from data containing trade-offs between attributes that are therefore incorporated into the modeling.

$$U_i = f(\beta_j X_{ij}, \varepsilon) \tag{1}$$

The coefficients (β) on the observed characteristics (X_{ij}) in the utility function (U_i) are estimated with an optimization procedure such as Newton-Raphson (Ben-Akiva & Lerman 1985). The exponential behaviour (e) is employed to explain predicted probabilities (P_i) of a particular response ("buy" or "not buy") regarding an alternative "i" (See Equation 2) belonging to the choice set with "J" options. Thus, the likelihood that an alternative is chosen is expressed as a function of its attributes and the other options available in the choice set.

$$P_i = \frac{e^{Ui}}{\sum_j e^{U_j}} \tag{2}$$

As maximizers, individuals place their preferences in the alternative they recognize as having the highest utility value ($U_i > U_j$). The analyst uses the modeling approach to be able to find the likely coefficients underneath the decision that has determined the choice. Considering that some of the variables influencing the choice might not have been accounted for, a random term is added to the model. In case of Logit, Luce (1959) has shown that the random term is independent and identically distributed according to the Weibull distributions. This means that alternatives are uncorrelated and also independent. We will use this characteristic of the model as the base to create synthetic data and demonstrate our approach (Section 4).

2.4 Web Personalization

Web personalization is concerned with schemes that select the type and quantity of content to be shown to the e-user based on individual profiles. Personalization applications for e-commerce usually show products and services the e-shopper did not ask for, hoping that some of them will catch his or her attention.

Content-based filtering makes recommendations based on comparisons between resources and the user's profile. Results retrieved are based on their similarity to what the e-shopper has previously shown interest. Collaborative filtering selects products or services that are recommended or used by the e-shoppers' peers by identifying groups of users with similar characteristics and interests (Cotter & Smyth 2000).

The approach in this paper can be considered both utility and knowledge-based. Utility-based because it models utilities of an option; knowledge-based because it proposes the use of ontologies for representing knowledge related to online shopping. Ontologies are knowledge models that retain conceptualizations that are explicit, consensual, and conceptual (Gruber 1993). ALICE (Domingue et al. 2002) is an example of an ontology-based recommender system.

3 Spot Methodology

The Stated Preference Ontology Targeted (SPOT) methodology (Figure 1) for web personalization uses the implicit user's decision function to find the product or service with the highest likelihood of being considered by the e-shopper in a given e-session. While keyword search methods use words to find related information, SPOT uses the individual's decision function (i.e. utility) to search the web space and find appropriate offers. Figure 2 is a pictorial representation of the search space, i.e. data points and extrapolation points. One can understand those points as choice possibilities or products. The approach suggested in this paper builds a user profile based on the individual's utility curve, instead of those based on isolated points whose matching product options might not exist.

The core of the methodology is stated preference: the technique employed to collect individual data on discrete choices (i.e. how individuals make decisions). Once enough data is collected, the model is calibrated using Logit modeling. The results are coefficients relating product attribute values and their importance to the users. Those coefficients are then used to rebuild the utility function for each alternative of product available online. Those with the highest likelihood value should be shown to the user. The two main modules in SPOT are the knowledge base and the mathematical module. The knowledge base retains ontologies, (e.g. products, customers' profiles, communities); the mathematical module manipulates algorithms for modeling the discrete choice data, and for analysis of the results.

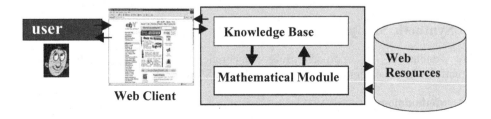

Fig. 1. The SPOT methodology

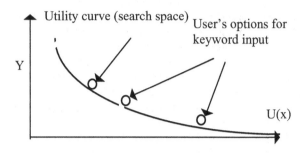

Fig. 2. Pictorial representation of utility function (U(x))

3.1 Knowledge Base

We are assuming that within the semantic web, products and services will be described using product ontologies. Standards for defining and classifying goods have already been developed, such as ISO 10303 (step) and can be used as the basis of products ontologies. Such ontologies will contain links to web pages of those companies providing the service, and to product attributes that customers might consider important (and therefore use in their decision-making).

The ontology-based recommender system ALICE (Domingue et al. 2002) includes ontologies for customer, products, typical shopping tasks, and the external context. Ontologies are populated as they are linked to the company's databases. Two important ontologies in ALICE are Customers and Products. Customers ontology defines slots about customers (their typology, how they use the product, which attributes are important, etc.). The Product ontology contains information about the product, such as type and attributes.

As product ontologies grow, so does the need for more sophisticated methods to select products to offer to users. The SPOT methodology can be implemented on top of e-commerce systems such as ALICE (ibid) to address the selection problem. E-shoppers' preferences and information about their decision-making processes would be part of the customer's ontology.

Another characteristic of incorporating knowledge bases to e-commerce systems is the potential to systematically discover knowledge from collected data. Kozinets (1999) suggests the identification of true communities of consumption by clustering information on individuals' profiles i.e. gathered in their buying decision-making processes.

4 Synthetic Study

We demonstrate our approach using a theoretical example of an online search situation where we compare keyword search with SPOT.

4.1 Methodology

A factorial design was used to gather choice answers for a simulated customer. The full factorial design guarantees that calibration results are significant. Alternative options were built with the purpose of showing how the proposed methodology compares with the traditional database search. The data contains choice sets with three alternatives each, which are evaluated in three attributes (Table 1: Attributes 1, 2, and 3). For instance, a transport option could be characterized by its cost, travel time, and headway. High and low (Table 1) indicate extreme ranges for the options.

Table 1. Attribute levels for the 512 choice scenarios

	Alternative 1		Alternative 2		Alternative 3	
	low	high	low	high	low	high
Attribute 1	30	80	40	100	50	120
Attribute 2	20	45	15	30	10	40
Attribute 3	30	15	60	20	70	30

The synthetic data is created based on a full factorial design so that our simulated customer made 512 hypothetical discrete choices. Of course, in a real situation there are other methods (Fowkes & Shinghal 2002) that can be employed to reduce this number to an acceptable value and still show good calibration performance.

The simulation approach is based on the fact that we *know* the deterministic part of the utility function used by decision makers in a choice situation. The random term is the unknown part of the utility but we know its distribution mean and standard deviation. The total utility for each alternative is found by adding the random term (Weibull distributed) to the deterministic utility component (see Equation 1). A linear function that adds the option attribute values by its respective weight is employed to find the deterministic component. The probabilistic part is simulated using the method of the inverse function. Thus pseudo-random numbers are created according to the inverse of the Weibull probability distribution (Equation 4) and used as the behaviour of our simulated individual regarding his choices. Following is a brief explanation of the Weibull probability distribution as the base to create data that follows Logit assumptions.

4.1.1 Weibull Probability Distribution

The random part of the utility refers to unknown variables influencing the choice process, from the analyst point of view. For instance, taste variation. Logit modeling is based on the assumption that such random term is Weibull (or Extreme Value) distributed (Luce 1959) as in Equation 3. Therefore, knowing the inverse of the cumulative Weibull distribution function (Equation 4), it is possible to recreate a SP experiment synthetically. This procedure allows one to compare methodologies on the bases of what the answers would be.

$$F(\varepsilon) = e^{-e^{-\mu(\varepsilon - \eta)}} \tag{3}$$

Assuming $\eta=0$, the inverse of that function (Equation 4) results in a random number (ε) which is Weibull distributed. This number would account for the uncertainties in the modeling a process analysts do not know (though known by the decision-maker).

$$\varepsilon = \frac{-\ln(-\ln(u))}{\mu}, \qquad \mu = \frac{\pi}{\sqrt{6} * \sigma} \qquad (4)$$

Where u = a uniformly random number; σ = standard deviation; η = location parameter.

Table 2. Calibration results for SP discrete choice data

Likelihood	-176.7801
Rho-Squared	0.6857
N. iterations	7
Coefficients	
Attribute 1	-0.03697 (-9.2)
Attribute 2	-0.03057 (-12)
Attribute 3	-0.03032 (-5.5)

The synthetic data (composed of 512 choice scenarios and the choice) is then used to calibrate a Logit model that reveals the weights the customer used to make the choice. The performance of the calibration is investigated using a well-known econometric test, Rho squared. Results from calibrating our synthetic data are shown in Table 2. Rho squared is quite high and coefficients are significant, as expected (since we are using data that follows Logit modeling).

Table 3. Choice options and respective utility values

Option	Attr. 1	Attr. 2	Attr. 3	Utility*
1	30	20	15	-7.6779
2	30	45	30	-15.7752
3	30	45	30	-15.7752
4	30	45	30	-15.7752
5	30	45	30	-15.7752
6	100	30	20	-13.4744
7	40	15	60	-7.8835
8	120	40	30	-17.574
9	50	10	70	-7.0279
10	50	10	30	-5.8151
11	50	40	70	-16.1989
12	50	40	30	-14.9861

Additionally, coefficients used to create the data could be roughly recovered. Therefore, we are using these coefficients to evaluate the alternative options in Table 3. Observe that in our special case we know the true coefficients employed to create the data. In real situations those coefficients are only known employing a mathematical model. A major advantage of using synthetic data is that we know beforehand the deterministic part of the utility function and the parameters used to create the random part. Then, we can evaluate the results comparing them with the known function used to create the data. The following tables show the results from calibrating the SP synthetic dataset.

4.2 Results

Table 3 shows for each option (1 to 12) their attribute values and their respective utilities. For instance, the values of Attributes 1, 2 and 3 for Option 1, are 30, 20 and 15, respectively. In case of a transport option it could be 30 minutes travel time, 20 minutes waiting time, and price of 15 USD, or nominal values. Table 3 is the database of available options for a searching system.

Given the database of 12 possible choices shown in Table 3, we examine Situation 1 and Situation 2, where we employ respectively keyword search and SPOT. Results are shown in Tables 4 and 5.

Situation 1: The user inputs a keyword that matches at least one of the available options. For instance, value of 40 to Attribute 1.

Table 4. Results for Attribute 1 = 40

Method	Result shown to the user
Keyword search	Alternative 7 (40, 15, 60)
SPOT	Alternatives 9, 10 and 1

Keyword search shows Alternative 7 as its own possible match. SPOT methodology using the value of the utility of all alternatives, would show three results corresponding respectively to 1st, 2nd, and 3rd places.

Situation 2: The same user inputs a keyword that does not match any of the available options (quite common on the Internet for travel services like car rental). For instance, value of 60 to Attribute 1.

In Situation 2, the keyword search method does not return any possibility. On the other hand, SPOT methodology returns 3 possible alternatives. In this case, we are employing a compensatory model and the three attributes are evaluated at once. However, a non-compensatory model can also be employed to perform a pre-selection of maximum or minimum attribute values. As an example, the user would not accept to pay more than US$ 50 for the trip.

Table 5. Results for Attribute 1 = 60

Method	Result shown to the user
Keyword search	None
SPOT	Alternatives 9, 10 and 1

Given results shown on Table 3, the best choice from the customer decision-process viewpoint would be Option 10 (the highest utility), which is highlighted.

In this theoretical example, we illustrated how using knowledge about the user's decision-making process can improve the quality of the online search results. For instance, in case of Situation 1, only one alternative would be shown to the user (Option 7 in Table 3). This alternative would not even be considered by the user as there are others with higher utility value (Table 3). On the other hand, Situation 2 would show no results to the user; as the criteria do not match any of the alternatives in the database (Table 5). This is quite a common situation in e-commerce sites.

5   Discussion

A recommender system is one that, based on certain criteria, recommends products or services. Current personalization schemes are mainly focused on delivering contents that are either similar to users' profiles (i.e. content-based) or are recommended by their peers (i.e. collaborative). Information on e-shoppers (e.g., history, profile, preferences) is used to feed the personalization scheme. A comprehensive review of recommender systems is given by Burke (2002). Being utility-based, this paper addresses a slightly different problem: *how to help the e-shopper decide between the choices available on the Internet.*

Usually, the information gathered over the Internet from recommender systems is not used for other purposes than to feed the personalization scheme. These schemes do not address ways to improve the company's decision strategies (such as product design), or how it could help the e-shopper's choice decision-making process. Helping the e-shopper in this decisive moment has the potential not only to increase the company's sales but also to improve the knowledge about their customers' values. That is often a strategy used in physical stores where the sales person often has a decisive impact on the choice.

Figure 3 illustrates a real situation of online car rental pictured on a shopbot web page. Shopbot is an e-commerce portal where users have access to different web service providers and can compare their offers as well as buy them. In this web site, the e-shopper begins the search process filling out a form with some parameters (e.g., car size, pick-up day, pick-up location). Those parameters are used to search the server database for available options. Quite often the search is unsuccessful at the first time. There are different reasons for that. For example, the specific supplier may not have branches on the pick-up location, or the requested car size is not available. Eventually, the user has to change the search parameters a couple of times in order to find one offer. When the user finally manages to find some offers, she or he has to reason and decide for one of them or none. It might be the case that by evaluating the choices available, the user considers that all offers are overpriced compared to the prices of the cars and decides not to buy the service. Therefore, instead of hiring a car, the individual might decide to use local public transport, or a taxi service. Note that decision processes vary according to the individual and the situation. Whether the individual is shopping for himself or for a company may change the decision model.

From the perspective of the car rental company, it could be a lost sale. If only the car-rental company new how individuals evaluate the different attributes of the service, they would try to show alternative options from the customer perspective. Maybe showing an offer with a better car would give the correct balance between the price of the car and the rental value.

Fig. 3. Online car rental shopbots

In the example above, we are assuming that the user evaluates the car rental options considering the price of the vehicle being hired and alternative ways of transport (such as public transport and taxi). Other decision models for this service would consider car-size within an acceptable price-range. In the car rental business, companies are often bounded to specific carmakers. Moreover, they have prices tied to combination offers that force the consumer to purchase at least two services. A web portal offering such car rental services would benefit from the SPOT approach, as it would *always* show options regarded by the user as relevant. With currently used methods, the search usually has to be repeated a couple of times with different keywords before a reasonable option comes up as a result.

Furthermore, the SPOT methodology is based on knowledge about how customers evaluate product characteristics, e.g. what sort of decision process they perform, which attributes and variables they consider. This is an application with potential to take full advantage of the semantic web infrastructure. It can search semantic information on products (i.e. from products ontology) and service information, and populate ontologies on customers' profile. Although ontologies are seen as the core of the semantic web, actual applications are still in their infancy. An initiative for transforming knowledge about products and services into a world common ontology is ISO 10303, an International Standard for product data representation and exchange. However, there is still need for technologies that enable application systems to exchange and share data about technical products. Their product classification cannot be used as a complete ontology, as the definitions tend to be semantically weak.

6 Conclusion

The SPOT methodology discussed in this paper uses the evaluation of the online alternatives based on the e-shopper decision process. This personalization scheme will prompt advantageous options that the e-shopper would not find otherwise. The main purpose of SPOT is not to make recommendations on products that users may or may not be interested in. SPOT's main contribution is to help the user with the decision-making on products he needs but have difficulties choosing between the large amounts available on the Internet. This approach has the potential to substantially improve the relevance of the results shown to the e-shopper in an e-commerce session and therefore increase the likelihood of a sale. Even though the user would be anonymous during the session, results from the system allow the company to know the trade-offs individuals make between the characteristics of a product or service and use them to forecast online demand, improve products, etc.

This paper discusses a methodology that uses economic theory on discrete choices to link e-shoppers' decision-making process to available online options. The approach suggested in this paper builds a user profile based on the individual's utility curve, instead of isolated points (the user's criteria) whose options might not exist.

The main input to the proposed methodology is the discrete choice data, which is collected from interactive Stated Preference "games" that the e-shopper agrees to participate. The data is then used to calibrate a Logit model that will reveal the trade-offs the e-shopper employed in his or her choice decision-making process. Afterwards, these results are employed to search for the available options and calculate their values as the customer himself would. Options with high utility value are then shown to the e-shopper.

The benefits of using the methodology are twofold. First, it has the potential to increase customer satisfaction and therefore the likelihood of sales and revisits. Second, the information on customer's choice decision-making process gives the company insights on how to improve the business (such as product design and sales). The implementation of this methodology requires investigation of the user's decision-making process for each product and the development of friendly interfaces to reduce the time to collect stated preference data online.

The major challenge of implementing SPOT is the data gathering. The approach's input is data from an interactive SP game that demands customers' time. Customers have to be convinced that providing answers to the interactive game will give them a better service. A friendly interface can help overcome this problem by reducing the cognitive effort needed for the task.

Another alternative would be to insert an additional reasoning step and try to match a current e-shopper with a previously recorded decision-making model. This match could be based on similarity (i.e. using case-based reasoning) and would reduce the number of required questions to elicit the e-shopper's preferences.

We should also consider that customers may not be interested in wasting time to take part in a SP game that evaluates low priced products or services. This requires an analysis of the customer's value of time to discover the threshold from which they would be willing to compare options further. As a guideline, the company could employ this methodology only to the most profitable or high priced 20% products, which often represents approximately 80% of the company's profit.

References

Ardissono, L., Godoy, A.: Tailoring the Interaction with Users in Web Stores. User Modeling and User-Adapted Interaction 10, 251–303 (2000)

Ben-Akiva, M., Lerman, R.: Discrete Choice Analysis. MIT Press, Cambridge (1985)

Burke, R.: Knowledge-Based Recommender Systems. In: Kent, A. (ed.) Encyclopedia of Library and Information Systems, 69, 32, Marcel Dekker, New York (2000)

Burke, R.: Hybrid Recommender Systems: Survey and Experiments. User Modeling and User-Adapted Interaction 12(4), 331–370 (2002)

Cotter, P., Smyth, B.: PTV: Intelligent Personalised TV Guides. In: Proceedings of Innovative Applications of Artificial Intelligence, pp. 957–964. AAAI Press/ The MIT, Stanford, California, USA (2000)

Carvalho, M, D.: A Comparison of Neural Networks and Econometric Discrete Choice Models in Transport. Institute for Transport Studies, University of Leeds, UK (PhD-thesis) (1998)

Domingue, J., Martins, M., Tan, J., Stutt, A., Pertusson, H.: Alice: Assiting Online Shoppers through Ontologies and Novel Interface Metaphors. In: Gómez-Pérez, A., Benjamins, V.R. (eds.) EKAW 2002. LNCS (LNAI), vol. 2473, pp. 335–351. Springer, Heidelberg (2002)

Fowkes, T., Shinghal, N.: The Leeds Adaptive Stated Preference Methodology (In Danielis, R. (ed.) Freight Transport Demand and Stated Preference Experiments, F. Angeli, Milan) (2002)

Gruber, T.R.: A Translation Approach to Portable Ontology Specifications. Knowledge Acquisition 5(2), 199–220 (1993)

Kocur, G., Adler, T., Hyman, W., Aunet, B.: Guide to Forecasting Travel Demand with Direct Utility Assessment. Report No. UMTA-NH-11-0001-82, Urban Mass Transportation Administration, US Department of Transportation, Washington, DC (1982)

Kozinets, R.V.: E-Tribalized Marketing: the Strategic Implications of Virtual Communities of Consumption. European Management Journal 17(3), 252–264 (1999)

Luce, R.D.: Individual Choice Behavior, New York. John Wiley & Sons, West Sussex, England (1959)

Louviere, J.J.: Analyzing Decision Making: Metric Conjoint Analysis. Sage Publications, Newbury Park, CA (1988)

McGinty, L., Smyth, B.: Comparison-Based Recommendation. In: Craw, S., Preece, A.D. (eds.) ECCBR 2002. LNCS (LNAI), vol. 2416, pp. 575–589. Springer, Heidelberg (2002)

Pearmain, D., Kroes, E.: Stated Preference Techniques: a Guide to Practice. Steer Davies & Gleave, UK (1990)

Efficient Information Access from Constraint Wireless Terminals

Exploiting Personalization and Location-Based Services

Hans Weghorn

Faculty for Information Technology, BA-University of Cooperative Education,
Rotebühlplatz 41, Stuttgart, Germany
weghorn@ba-stuttgart.de

Abstract. Today, the success of data services used from small mobile devices, like digital phones or PDAs, appears very limited. Different reasons can be identified, which prevent the average customer from broadly using wireless data services. At first, the user has to deal with very uncomfortable devices in terms of UI ergonomy, and on the other hand, the costs for wireless data communication are extremely high. These restrictions can be overcome by employing a system concept, which is built up on two main components: A personalized display software allows simplifying the information access on the wireless terminal, while an intermediate agent residing on the Internet takes care of mining the desired contents from the open Web. In addition to the improved UI handling, this concept offers a reduction of access costs and an increase in retrieval speed. Real-world experiments with an information system on actual train departures are reported for measuring and demonstrating the benefit of the described system concept.

Keywords: Personalization, Wireless Internet, Wireless JAVA, Location-based Services, Information Management.

1 Introduction

Up to now, a common use of data services accessed from mobile terminals could not establish very well. Due to their broad market distribution, digital mobile phones for cellular networks would yield a very interesting platform for data services, e.g. information retrieval on traffic situation on lanes and public transportation. Unfortunately, the user of these devices today faces a couple of constraints, which prevent a wide acceptance of such wirelessly accessed data services.

Considering first the handling of mobile devices, it has to be stated that software tools are usually very uncomfortable. Most tools do not sufficiently respect the constraints of small mobile devices (Johnson, 1998), because the user often has to enter information, e.g. lengthy Web paths, account information, or selection information. The costs for the wireless transfer of data contents represent another critical aspect. For instance in Germany, a comparison of the tariffs of land line networks (e.g. ADSL technology) and cellular phone networks shows that transferring data amounts wirelessly is roughly 10^4 times more expensive.

J. Filipe, J. Cordeiro, and V. Pedrosa (Eds.): WEBIST 2005/2006, LNBIP 1, pp. 166–176, 2007.

Furthermore, the wireless data rates are slower in the order of $10^2 - 10^3$. WLAN (Riezenmann, 2002) seems to be an alternative wireless access technology, which can overcome these back draws. Unfortunately, it is not truly feasible for a seamless information retrieval, because it does not supply roaming and requires more complicate hardware. E.g., a laptop computer linked to a WLAN hot spot is good for reading e-mails in a restaurant or at an airport terminal, but it cannot conveniently be used for accessing current departure information on, e.g., trains or planes while walking or traveling to the station or airport.

A system concept, which was developed and reported during the recent years (Weghorn, 2003; Weghorn, 2004-1), is presumed to overcome these restrictions. The concept bases on two components (Fig. 1): One part is personalized display software for the wireless terminal, which minimizes the required inputs from the user and which optimizes the presentation of the results. And the other part is a data-mining agent running on a central server on the Internet, which appropriately collects, examines and prepares the desired information content for a transfer to the wireless display terminal, as soon as the user remotely commands this. Since this system collects customer specific contents on base of customized tools, the name C2C was defined for this mechanism.

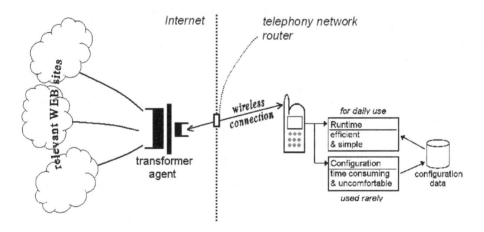

Fig. 1. Construction concept of the customized information service

The user interacts with the C2C information retrieval system through the wireless terminal (Fig. 1). During this, the terminal executes specialized display software, which directs information queries to a central service agent residing on the Internet. The display software has to be constructed in the following manner:

- The required user input actions have to be minimized.
- The results have to be output in a reasonable presentation.
- Preferences of the user (e.g. passwords, account information) have to be remembered automatically, or should be editable by the user.
- The terminal software retrieves the desired information from the Internet agent by its activation with the appropriate settings and user preferences.

The counterpart to the display tool is the mining agent. The agent has to be permanently available on the Internet, and it is in charge of sourcing the addressed contents – in many cases from the open Web. For instance, there exist many Web sites, which provide current information on traffic situation on highways and other main routes, and these could be used for a traffic information system. As other example, a mining agent could be employed to collect e-mail messages (or concise parts of it) for a remote display.

This kind of middleware should be a more generalized approach than wrapper or mediator services, which were reported earlier (Mahmoud, 2002; Wang et al., 2003), because in the new concept here the mining agent sources information from different sites in parallel, and retrieves by that a measure of the quality of information (Weghorn, 2004-2). Depending on the situation, the agent can already decide which information finally should be the correct one. In the end, the user will receive on the terminal the desired output together with a reliability score.

Clearly, for many cases, the user could do the same actions through WAP browsing manually, but of course, the automation of these procedure speeds up the information access, reduces the access costs, offers the user a very compact and efficient handling, and allows finally an appropriate display of the querying results. The fully programmed solution (instead of the manual use of standard tools like WAP browsers) allows also to apply compacted coding schemes on the expensive and slow wireless data link between the mobile terminal and the mining agent, which should additionally increase access speed and the effect of cost saving. In the reports about the different development stages of the C2C concept (Weghorn, 2004-1) the investigations mainly were derived from computer simulations of the wireless access. A considerable advance of this research presented in the following sections here is an extended real-world application for a specific information access system on public transportation.

2   Key Technologies for Efficiency Improvments

2.1 Personalization

Personalization can be used as key for simplifying the user handling of wireless terminals. For instance, if the user wants to access e-mail from a handheld device, all account information (server settings, user name and password, filter definitions for mail retrieval) need to be entered only once into the terminal software, and these settings can be used automatically from this point. After initial configuration, the user can launch the e-mail inspection efficiently by pressing only a few buttons or – depending on the capabilities of the terminal – even by one single press of a so-called hot key. This concept renders possible, because handheld devices usually are treated as personal belongings. This means that a mobile phone rarely is lent to a colleague or another person, and hence, the information on these mobile devices can be considered as protected contents.

People, who are daily commuting between their living home and their working place (office, school place, University, or similar) are also prospective candidates for using this kind of personalized information systems, because most societies today face continuous traffic problems in terms of delays of public transportation or traffic jams. For a person, who is using public transportation like trains, the information query parameters, which have to be defined once, would be the departure, changing and destination stations, and probably the kind of train that is used. Another person, who usually goes by car to the office, will drive on a certain routing of roads and highways, and exactly this routing list of streets will represent the configuration set for an information query on traffic jams or other traffic messages.

2.2 Automated Personalization with Location-Based Services

One very recent research topic is the application of location-based services (Schiller, and Voisard 2004). This could be used in the here described information systems as well, since for the commuting sample, the travel direction changes each day. Hence, the direction represents also a parameter for the information collection. Introducing the geographical location into the information retrieval process, allows the system automatically detecting the travelling direction: When a commuting person is inside or close by the office, the information system knows implicitly, which station the next departure place of the daily used train link will be.

Unfortunately, accessing this geographical information in general will require additional high efforts, for instance a GPS receiver inside the handheld terminal. Theoretically, each cellular phone terminal knows the communication cell, where it is registered, and this cell, which is identified by some kind of index value, could be resolved into a geographical location. How such a translation process can be implemented is discussed, e.g., in (Roth, 2003). The inconvenience today in the software structure of wireless devices is that this cell broadcast content (its regularly broadcasted information, which does not require any retrieval costs) is not always accessible from add-on wireless application software. The chance is that all cell broadcast information will be available in future through standardized APIs, and then the location-based concepts can directly help to improve the described information systems without introducing new restrictions or requirements.

More recent communication technologies also would allow location-based control of information retrieval. Again for the commuting sample, Bluetooth communication can be applied for automatically determining the position of user: In particular, when the user is inside the office, the fact that the wearable device is registered in a local Bluetooth communication cluster can be used as location measure. For this, no application communication with the wireless device is required, but only the presence of the hand held terminal in the Bluetooth cell has to be detected, which can be done automatically and periodically from a host computer inside the office. If the user enters during the day once the office, this method provides already a feasible indicator for switching the travelling direction in the information system. As other example, an e-mail forwarding concept was reported already at a time (Weghorn, 2001), when programming of handheld devices was not available for cellular phones openly to the market. Today due to the before described technologies and applicable development systems like wireless JAVA programming (Piroumian, 2002), also this forwarding of important e-mail contents can be automatically controlled by the before described location detection mechanisms.

3 Sample System for Train Departure Querys

3.1 Information Retrieval Mechanism

After some prior concept design and simulation of an information system on train actual departures, an information access system was developed, which is truly executable on JAVA-enabled wireless devices (Piroumian, 2002). The intermediate agent is implemented as JAVA servlet (Hall, and Parr 2001), and it handles a query about a certain train connection route. This tool uses a public Internet page, which is operated by the railway company (Fig. 2), and translates the Web coded contents into a format (Fig. 3) that is feasible for transfer and display on a wireless terminal (Fig. 3). Depending on the query parameters, the original information source will have sizes of 300 kilobytes and more, which obviously shows that a direct access to this information by mobile browsing does not make any sense. Truly, the same railway company operates a WML page server for WAP access to the information (Fig. 2), but the contents presented there are only a fraction of the Web version; in particular, if the reader doesn't know the train code, the system is more or less worthless, because intermediate train destinations are not displayed. For a personalized application, the WAP solution provides the wrong subset of information, at least for the indicative sample of daily commuting. Another problem is that it is obviously working incorrectly (Fig. 2), but this is not a fundamental problem.

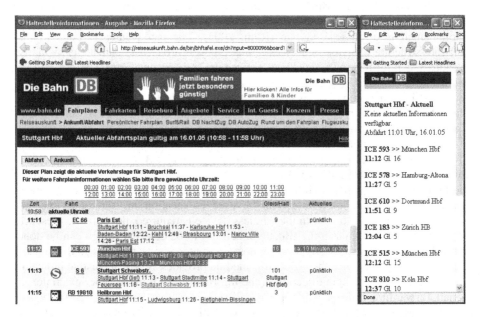

Fig. 2. The railway company, which is used for the investigations, provides a Web site, from which departure tables for all main stations can be downloaded (left browser frame). In parallel to that, also information pages for WAP download are available, but the herein contained information is reduced for size reasons (right frame). Both content pages were retrieved at the same time, and as seen in this sample, the WAP service also is not accurate, because it does not report the information about the delayed train to Munich ("München").

Fig. 3. The personalized service filters all connections of interest out of the generalized Web departure table, which is seen in Fig. 2. The debug mode of the mining agent (left browser frame) shows the intermediate steps of this analysis, and the result will be displayed by the terminal software part (right frame) of the described information system.

3.2 UI Design for the Terminal Client

The minimization of required inputs is one aim for the proposed information system. Therefore, the normal operation mode in the train departure query application is that after launching the terminal software, the information retrieval will start automatically. For overcoming the necessity of an additional configuration tool, the train query application starts with a welcome screen, which dismisses after a defined short time delay (Fig. 4). If the user doesn't want to run the default query, the welcome screen can be interrupted by a keyboard press. In this case a selection menu will appear next, and the user can modify the configuration for the favourite query, or place a manual query. The latter feature of performing individual queries shall make the information system more flexible, and it can casually be of interest, e.g., for use during business travels. The first launch of the application after its installation on the terminal requires one special additional UI mode: During this, the customer is informed about the regular behaviour of the information tool, and is then directly switched to the configuration menu.

The system was tested on six different physical devices: First, a Palm IIIc PDA computer, and a Siemens SL45i with B+W display screen belong to the first generation of JAVA-enabled handheld devices, which appeared on the market; next, the devices Erricson T630, Erricson P900, Nokia 6600, and Siemens SX-1 represent the recent generation on the market, while the latter three smart phones are based on the open operating system Symbian (www.symbian.com). The implementation and the tests showed that the different phone vendors do have individual interpretations about the operation of the standardized JAVA API. Therefore, several adoptions were required to produce terminal software, which is sufficiently working on all the test devices, although the first implementation was working cleanly in Sun's simulation environment.

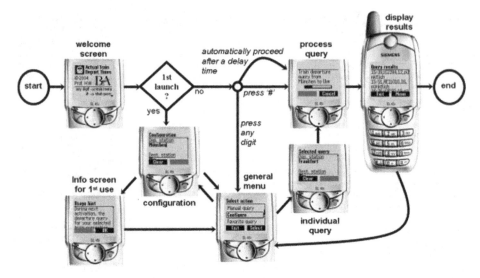

Fig. 4. UI chart of the information channel on actual train departure times for a certain (personalized) travelling route. The direction of travelling is determined by a configurable switching time. If the user doesn't interfere, the query process proceeds automatically through the direct path between the markers for "start" and "end". This sample shows that this kind of application is feasible for a use on simple-styled phones, which are equipped with small B+W screens only.

To give samples of this disturbing behaviour, four of the devices do not display the defined program icons, which would make the handling more convenient for the non-technical user. Another of the devices couldn't display graphical images, which were produced with standard UNIX imaging tools. The alternatively used desktop software produced images files, which were displayed correctly on all devices, but the coding length of these images was bigger, which leads to a waste of memory on the terminal.

For automatically determining the travelling direction, an additional time parameter is defined and used in the system. The user can set a time, e.g. noon, from which the system assumes that the user will travel home, which means that the departure and the destination stations are exchanged for the departure table query. This sample shows how the requirement for knowing the geographical location can be overcome. Although this doesn't represent always an accurate measure, it will in most cases be a feasible strategy for replacing the detection of the geographical location.

With the P900 smart phone it can be demonstrated how convenient the use of the proposed information tool can be, because on this device JAVA applications can be placed for a quick start on top menu level. The actions for running the tool are opening first the keyboard cover, and next pressing with the touch pen the appropriate icon. Following this, the query launches automatically, and the user can read after a few seconds delay the result about the train connections of interest.

3.3 Performance Measurements in Phone Networks

The train information system was used with different network operators and networking modes for investigating the efficiency of the tool. In general, in Europe data services can be used through the wireless telephony network (GSM) as traditional modem connection and with GPRS with enhanced data communication. Understanding the tariffs of the different network operators is not straight forward, and hence the produced costs for the information retrieval were also measured (Table 1).

In the standard GSM data link, the customer has to pay for the time duration of the connection, while with GPRS the customer has to pay theoretically for the transferred data amount. The latter paying method was too low for the network operators, and they invented additional charges for GPRS, some are billing an extra monthly charge of five Euros for using GPRS, others bill for each day of use an additional service charge (e.g. 19 Eurocents). This all complicates the calculation, what the retrieval of a dedicate information will cost, but exactly this confusion may be of strategic business interest for the network operators. As consequence, it is in general not possible to specify the precise billing amount for a single information access, e.g., one retrieval on train departures.

In summary, it can be derived that running one information query can in average cost down to 10 Eurocent with GPRS, while with the old modem connection at least twice this amount is charged. The required time for retrieving the information is an important factor for the user handling. With the GSM standard data link, the entire access will take approximately one minute. With GPRS the overall time depends on the fact, whether the mobile terminal has already registered the GPRS link. In this mode, most time is consumed for setting up the data link (~ 15 sec), while the information transfer from the application takes only a few seconds.

4   Consideration of Experimental Results

4.1 Discussion of Benefits for the Customer

For qualifying the benefit of the proposed information access concept, its handling has to be compared to alternative methods. Traditionally, one could use a desktop computer with an Internet connection or a phone voice service. Due to the structure of current operating systems, the use of a desktop computer will consume much more time, because it has to be booted, the user has then to log on to the operating system, and afterwards to launch the Internet connection. After this, the information retrieval can be invoked, and finally the whole computer system has to be shut down. This will take several minutes, and of course, the data terminal is not wearable. With a laptop computer this process can be accelerated, but in the end it will also take considerably longer for accessing the information. In addition to that, the laptop computer solution is not conveniently applicable in many situations, e.g. walking, going by public bus, or driving in a car.

With voice telephony services, it is like there is no possibility of personalization. Hence, if the user wants to obtain information about current train departure, always a voice-controlled navigation through an access tree will be required, which consumes time and produces network costs. The situation is comparable to Web browsing without bookmark links. Summarizing, it can be stated that the personalized access is much more efficient than traditional alternatives, because it can be performed in almost any situation and it will take one minute or with the proper configuration only a fraction of a minute. Each information access typically will cost around 10 Eurocent, which may be more expensive than with other systems.

4.2 Run-Time Behaviour of J2ME Devices

Besides the above-discussed difficulties with the operation of J2ME standard UI elements, there arise also problems with networking on the J2ME-enabled devices manufactured by different companies. This applies especially when using the standard GSM data link instead of the enhanced GPRS mode. On some devices, a network data link can be established from the J2ME application, but it cannot be terminated under application control. It is closed down only after exiting the JAVA sub menu in the phone UI. The consequence is that the user is charged in background additional costs, e.g., when the results of an information query are displayed, although no data needs to be transferred any more. Methods for closing down the physical layer connection, which are available in the standard JAVA system, are missing in J2ME. Interestingly, this kind of operation is present in Sun's sample implementation for Palm OS handheld computers, and it seems to be inherited by other devices. Even worth appears the fact that some newer devices are incapable at all of establishing a HTTP connection with the standard data link. These devices are working well with GPRS, but it depends on the phone contract, whether GPRS mode is available. For cost control reasons, and for reliability reasons the recommendation for a non-technical customer can only be using J2ME data networking only with GPRS.

In general, the data networking configuration is non-trivial, and therefore most devices are delivered today with all possible configurations for the different network operators. Unfortunately, it can be observed that on some devices these settings interfere with each other, and in the end there were several cases detected, for which the data networking was non-functional. After removing the unusable configurations, these devices started working correctly, but form this experience it can be derived that also in GPRS mode non-expert customers might be incapable of using the information access software due to general constraints of the device handling

4.3 SW Engineering and XML Coding of Contents

The original approach of the concept was that low level coding (= binary exchange of information contents) should improve the overall performance of the wireless information system. From the experiments (Table 1), it can be deducted that this is not fully true, because in particular the transfer of the content in the data communication consumes only a small fraction of the overall access time. Hence, coding the data packet according to established software engineering philosophies (in particular in XML: Bradley, 1998) would be acceptable with GPRS for the transfer time and costs as long as the content packet size remains in the order of one kilobyte. Despite these measurement results, there arises still some impact of inefficiency on the terminal side, since XML coded contents will require a more complicate parsing

Table 1. Representative measurements of information access time and costs for different networking modes

Experiment no.	Network Operator	Mode	Open URL	Time for content transfer	Costs	Remarks
1	T-Mobile	GPRS	9,2 sec	31 ms	19 ct	
2	T-Mobile	GPRS	3,5 sec	<1 ms	19 ct	
3.1	T-Mobile	GPRS	16,28 sec	<1 ms		one
3.2	T-Mobile	GPRS	3,00 sec	<1 ms	28 ct	GPRS
3.3	T-Mobile	GPRS	3,39 sec	15 ms		session
3.4	T-Mobile	GPRS	3,44 sec	31 ms		
4	Vodaphone	GSM std	22,25 sec	7564 ms	19 ct	
5	Vodaphone	GSM std	17,56 sec	5377 ms	19 ct	
6	Vodaphone	GSM std	20,96 sec	5146 ms	35 ct	
7.1	T-Mobile	GPRS	9,70 sec	31 ms	28 ct	one GPRS
7.2	T-Mobile	GPRS	3,11 sec	<1 ms		session
8.1	Vodaphone	GSM std	20,87 sec	6770 ms	35 ct	performed
8.2	T-Mobile	GPRS	3,47 sec	<1 ms	n/a	at the same
8.3	T-Mobile	GPRS	3,50 sec	140 ms	n/a	time

in the wireless software part. Of course, this can be obtained by using standard library packages (Setiawan, 2001), but this will increase considerably the code size of the handheld application.

On the other hand, thinking forward of PUSH technologies (Ortiz, 2003), XML coding of contents still is not recommended, because an SMS, which can be used for this technology, will not be capable of carrying that content size.

5 Conclusion

A new information access system for truly mobile access was conceptually designed and developed during the recent years. In our former investigations on this, the concept, which shall customers provide an efficient and convenient access, was tested and developed mainly on base of simulations. The advance of the work presented here is the application of the information retrieval system in true networks under real conditions. On base of these experiments, it can be derived that the claimed properties, like increased access speed and improved handling, can be achieved with the proposed kind of information access structure.

Future work will stepwise regard quality of information by means of AI, and it shall further aim to reduce the information access costs, e.g. by applying AI controlled proactive PUSH mechanisms. Although the wireless JAVA platform defines a standard API, the experience with true devices is that it is not a straightforward task to develop applications, which are running truly sufficiently on all devices. Extra effort is required for achieving this, and therefore alternative technologies, e.g. C++-based software on Symbian devices, shall be investigated in future for obtaining best overall performance.

Also the application fields shall be expanded. Besides information on public transportation and car traffic, we are working in actual projects on weather channels for a customized retrieval of local recent information and forecasts. Furthermore, we are currently investigating how Web service technology (Aleksy and Gitzel, 2004) can contribute to an improvement of the described information access systems.

References

Aleksy, M., Gitzel, R. (eds.): Workshop on Web Applications and Middleware (WAM2004). In: GI-Edition Lecture Notes in Informatics(LNI) - Proceedings, Köllen Druck+Verlag GmbH, Bonn, Germany, pp. 264–286 (2004)
Bradley, N.: The XML Companion, 1st edn. Addison-Wesley, London, UK (1998)
Hall, M., Parr, M.: Core Servlets and JAVA Server Pages, 2nd edn. Sun Microsystems Press, Prentice Hall PTR. Dorchester (2001)
Johnson, P.: Usability and Mobility: Interactions on the move. In: First Workshop on Human Computer Interaction with Mobile Devices, Glasgow, May 1998. GIST Technical Report G98-1, Department of Computing Science, University of Glasgow (1998)
Mahmoud, Q.H.: Accessing and using Internet services from JAVA-enabled handheld wireless devices. In: Braz, J., et al. (eds.) 4th International Conference on Enterprise Information Systems, Ciudad Real, April 2002, ICEIS Press (2002)
Ortiz, E.: The MIDP 2.0 Push Registry (2003). http://wireless.java.sun.com/midp/articles/pushreg/
Piroumian, V.: Wireless J2ME Platform Programming, Prentice Hall. Palo Alto, 1st edition (2002)
Riezenman, M.J.: The ABCs of IEEE 802.11. IEEE Spectrum Online (September 2002), http://www.spectrum.ieee.org/WEBONLY/resource/sep02/802ABCs.html
Roth, J.: Flexible Positioning For Location-Based Services. IADIS International JournalWWW/Internet 1(2), 18–32 (2003)
Schiller, J., Voisard, A. (eds.): Location-Based Services. Morgan Kaufmann Publishers, San Francisco, USA (2004)
Setiawan, T.: The Use of J2ME with a Campus Portal for Wireless Devices, Master Thesis, Faculty of Engineering, San Jose State University. San Jose, USA (2001)
Wang, F., et al.: An E-Commerce System Integrating Data Mining Functionalities. In: Palma dos Reis, A., Isaías, P. (eds.) e-Society 2003, Lisbon, IADIS Press (2003)
Weghorn, H.: Notification and routing of electronic mail to mobile phone devices. In: Miranda, P., et al. (eds.) 2nd International Conference on Enterprise Information Systems, Setúbal, July 2001, 2nd edn. ICEIS Press (2001)
Weghorn, H.: Teaching Wireless JAVA at the University of Cooperative Education. In: Mahmoud, Q.H. (ed.) 2nd International Workshop on Wireless Information Systems WIS 2003, Angers, April 2003, ICEIS Workshop Proceedings (2003)
Weghorn, H.: 2004-1. In: Isaías, P., et al. (eds.) IADIS International Conference on e-Society, vol. I, IADIS Press (2004)
Weghorn, H.: 2004-2. Employing the C2C Principle for Making the Use of Data Services on Mobile Phones More Attractive. In: Ascenso, J., et al. (eds.) 1st International Conference on E-Business and Telecommunication Networks, Setúbal, August 2004, vol. 3, ICEIS Press (2004)

An Algorithm to Use Feedback on Viewed Documents to Improve Web Query

Enabling Naïve Searchers to Search the Web Smartly

Sunanda Patro, Vishv Malhotra, and David Johnson

School of Computing, Pvt Box 100, University of Tasmania, Hobart TAS 7001 Australia
spatro@postoffice.utas.edu.au, vishv.malhotra@utas.edu.au,
dgjohnso@utas.edu.au

Abstract. This paper presents an algorithm to improve a web search query based on the feedback on the viewed documents. A user who is searching for information on the Web marks the retrieved (viewed) documents as relevant or irrelevant to further expose the information needs expressed in the original query. A new web search query matching this improved understanding of the user's information needs is synthesized from these text documents. The methodology provides a way for creating web search query that matches the user's information need even when the user may have difficulty in doing so directly due to lack of experience in the query design or lack of familiarity of the search domain. A user survey has shown that the algorithmically formed query has recall coverage and precision characteristics better than those achieved by the experienced human web searchers.

Keywords: Web searching, Information need, Boolean query, Relevance feedback.

1 Introduction

Quality of the links returned in a web search depends on how well the query embodies the user's information needs. An erudite user is able to state a web search query using appropriate terms and jargon to obtain links to the valuable resources. A user searching for information in a new or unfamiliar domain faces difficulties. The difficulties are caused by the searcher's inability to provide suitable terms and synonyms, or not being able to combine them suitably to express the information needs accurately. An unsatisfactory query may return an overwhelming majority of links to resources of no interest to the searcher or may fail to identify useful resources. The former problem is called a *precision* problem and the latter a *recall* problem.

Information foraging (Aula, Jhaveri and Kaki, 2005) is an unusual but apt description of the common web search behavior. It suggests that a typical searcher aims to *maximize the amount of valuable information they gain in a unit time*. This attitude manifests in many well-known observations; for example, few queries have more than three terms; use of operators in the web queries is rare; and only a small number of links appearing at the top of links returned by a search engine are viewed

J. Filipe, J. Cordeiro, and V. Pedrosa (Eds.): WEBIST 2005/2006, LNBIP 1, pp. 177–189, 2007.

by the searchers (Jansen, Spink, Bateman and Saracevic, 1998), (Hölscher and Strube, 2000). Indeed, the search strategy used by the web searchers simply mimics well-known Artificial Intelligence heuristic called *hill-climbing* (Kopec and Marsland, 1997). In turn, like the heuristic, a search may end in a sub-optimal local maximum. The searcher misses to retrieve the best documents matching the information needs. Some of these searches fail to even retrieve a satisfactory document, leaving the searchers frustrated and believing that appropriate resources do not exist on the Web for their needs.

As a user views documents on the Web, useful examples of documents that user considers somewhat relevant as well as those that are irrelevant are generated. Few browsers make use of this information to improve the quality of the search. Previously, Cohen et al. (1996) and Malhotra et al. (2005) have described algorithms to generate Web search queries from example documents. These algorithms have relied on established techniques in text-categorization to construct queries to select relevant examples and reject irrelevant examples. The generated Boolean expressions have good recall and precision characteristics but the query can be too large to be effectively processed by a search engine. Suggested approach of breaking a single query into a series of queries is not effective; few searchers bother to access more than a few documents let alone try a sequence of queries. Thus, the onus is on the query synthesis algorithm to provide a single query that meets the user's information needs well when a searcher asks for help. This paper gives such an algorithm to generate a query. Only an integrated query provides access to resources that meet all aspects of the user's information needs as opposed to some aspects of the needs.

Oyama et al. (2004) have suggested a different approach to improve the quality of the web search experience. They identify a domain specific *keyword spice* to augment query terms so that only the resources from the relevant domain are targeted by the search. They illustrate their technique by searching for beef cooking recipes. While a single word query *beef* returns few links to the useful resources, the keyword spiced query *beef & ((ingredients & !season & !description) | tablespoon)* has good success in meeting the user's information needs. The main limitation of the approach is that one needs to develop a keyword spice for each information domain a user may be interested in. Even if such a collection of keyword spices could be developed, the problem remains unabated as the users need to select correct keyword spices for their information needs.

This paper presents an algorithm to construct web queries that fit the query interface of Goolge search engine. The algorithm uses Incremental Learning (IL) algorithm (Sanchez, Triantaphyllou, Chen and Liao, 2002) as modified in Malhotra et al. (2005) to define an initial set of minterms. These minterms collectively select all relevant examples and each minterm rejects examples marked as irrelevant by the viewing searcher. The algorithm chooses and organizes these minterms to devise query that accesses the best resources as measured by the precision and recall characteristics and yet are small to meet the size limit of the search engine. Cohen et al. (1996) also generate a set of minterms using a rule-learning technique RIPPER (Cohen, 1995). However, the RIPPER expressions are already optimized to minimize misclassification errors. This makes the expression less amenable to further transformations to reduce their sizes to meet limitations of search engine query interfaces.

In section 2, we briefly introduce relevance feedback approaches used in text-categorization and explain why we have chosen to use Boolean expression based query synthesis approach. The section also summarizes IL algorithm to construct a set of minterms. This set of minterms constitutes the primary input for our query synthesis algorithm described in Section 3. The main goal of the algorithm would be to synthesize web query that fits the query interface of the search engine without unduly compromising its access to the best web resources. Section 4 presents results from a user survey to establish the effectiveness of the synthesized queries. In section 5 we conclude with a description of planned work to integrate the algorithm with a browser and also other applications.

2   Related Background

Relevance feedback has been studied extensively in the context of text categorization (Baeza-Yates, 1991, Sebastiani, 2002). Given a corpus of documents, certain terms are chosen as discriminators. A query is a vector assigning weights to the terms. Relevance feedback and query expansion are used to adjust the terms and their weights so that query is more aligned to documents considered relevant and avoids documents considered irrelevant (Ruthven and Lalmas, 2003).

Notwithstanding their success and usefulness in text-categorization the vector based queries are little used for web searching. Vector queries do not express information needs in a way humans can easily interpret. Thus, search engines use Boolean expression based user interface for web searching. Vector based approaches also use a large number of terms in a query. On the other hand, it is important for the search engines to limit the terms in queries to deliver results efficiently and within an acceptable time frame.

A web query also differs from the text categorization in regards to its aims. An ideal text categorization query for an information need is required to locate all relevant documents without retrieving any irrelevant document. The practical algorithms – for example, RIPPER – aim for misclassification minimization using a cost model for errors. A web searcher typically views only a few (usually, one) documents – clearly, one would like these documents to meet the information need perfectly.

A *web search query* is a list of terms (words) punctuated by Boolean operators AND (&), OR (|) and NOT (!). Following on from Google conventions, AND is an implied operator and not explicitly written. Operator NOT applies to a single term and has highest precedence. The operator AND (&) has lowest precedence. For a set of textual documents, D, and a search query, Q, expression $D \, \sigma \, Q$ denotes the results of search by query Q over the document set D with the following interpretation:

Case Q is *term*	{doc | doc $\in D$ and *term* occurs in document doc}
Case Q is *!term*	{doc | doc $\in D$ and *term* does not occur in document doc}
Case Q is *(R & S)*	$(D \, \sigma \, R) \, \sigma \, S$
Case Q is *(R | S)*	$(D \, \sigma \, R) \cup (D \, \sigma \, S)$

We shall assume the readers familiarity with the standard terminology related to Boolean expressions (Aho and Ullman, 1992) especially the terms minterm, maxterm, Conjunctive Normal Form (CNF), and Disjunctive Normal Form (DNF).

Quality of a query is a subjective notion. Information retrieval systems measure the quality through two objective measures precision (P) and recall (R). Suppose a given collection of N documents containing I irrelevant documents is searched by a query that returns r relevant and n non-relevant documents. Precision (P) and recall (R) of the query are defined as follows: $P = r/(r+n)$ and $R = r/(N - I)$.

These definitions require knowledge of the various parameter values: N, I, n and r. The Web is large and ever expanding collection of documents. Therefore, it is impossible to know these values for a web search. We therefore use other measures, P@20 and C@20 to model precision and recall respectively (Patro and Malhotra, 2005). P@20 is defined as fraction of top 20 links returned by query that the searcher finds relevant. C@20 is defined based on the estimated number of documents (say, E) in the search engine database matching the query. C@20 is defined as $min(log_2(E \cdot P@20)/20, 1)$. Briefly, $E \cdot P@20$ is the number of relevant documents the query is able to find in the search engines database. Logarithmic scale caters for reduced marginal utility of the larger sets. It can be easily noticed that for specific information need, a query with better recall returns higher C@20 value. We shall combine the two measures through harmonic mean to define a metric for quality of a query Q@20: $Q@20 = 2/(1/P@20 + 1/C@20)$.

2.1 Building Blocks of a Query

For the sake of completeness, in this section, we briefly describe the algorithm to generate minterms needed to synthesize the queries. Further details of the algorithm can be found in (Patro, 2006).

We assume that a searcher seeking help to improve query has used an initial query to retrieve and view a few documents. As the documents are viewed the user divides them into two sets: *Relevant* containing documents that have some information of interest to the user; and, *Irrelevant* containing documents that have little information to interest the user.

The query synthesis algorithm makes use of the initial query and a set of minterms derived from documents in sets *Relevant* and *Irrelevant* to synthesize a new query. To construct this set of minterms, the algorithm first constructs a series of maxterms. Each maxterm is derived by selecting a series of terms from the documents in set *Relevant*. This selection of the terms to augment maxterms is facilitated by computing selectivity of the terms. The selectivity for term t in construction of $(i+1)^{st}$ maxterm is defined as follows (In the following $\texttt{maxterm}^p$ denotes a partially constructed $(i+1)^{st}$ maxterm):

TR = *Relevant* − (*Relevant* σ maxterm^p);
TR$_t$ = TR σ t;
TIR = *Irrelevant* σ (maxterm$_1$ &...& maxterm$_i$));
TIR$_t$ = TIR σ t;
selectivity (t) =
$((|TR_t|)(|TIR|-|TIR_t|))/((|TR|-|TR_t|+1)(|TIR_t|+1))$.

A maxterm selects all documents in set *Relevant* and reject one or more documents in set *Irrelevant*. When enough maxterms have been found such that each irrelevant document is rejected by at least one maxterm, a Boolean expression is formed by taking conjunction of initial user query and constructed maxterms. The expression is simplified to its DNF form. Minterms that do not select any relevant document are dropped from this expression. The set of remaining minterms constitute the required set of minterms for query synthesis algorithm described in the next section.

The construction process ensures that each minterm rejects every irrelevant document viewed by the searcher. Collectively the minterms in the set select every relevant example identified by the searcher. This set of minterms is called *MSet*.

We illustrate this with an example. Suppose the following prose describes information need of a student.

We are to search information about plant Eucalyptus.

A page containing any one of the following criteria in a brief description is treated as relevant:

• A relevant page should contain the herb information or description of the plant.

• The page should provide information relating to its use or growing of the plant.

The page containing the word Eucalyptus but not related to above criteria may be treated as irrelevant.

The student uses keyword *eucalyptus* to retrieve a number of documents and mark them as relevant and irrelevant based on the information needs described above. The student viewed 71 text documents and marked 23 relevant and 48 irrelevant documents. We will continue to pretend, for the sake of example, that the student used them to devise a better search query. During a test run of the algorithm, five maxterms were constructed before all retrieved irrelevant documents could be rejected by at least one maxterm. The resulting CNF Boolean was as follows: *(eucalyptus) (fruit | tall | cream | drought | asthma) (tree | evergreen | alcohol) (gum | south | blue | book) (white | found | green) (plant | long | ground | index)*. In turn, DNF expression had 720 minterms of which 634 were found to be non-redundant. These 634 minterms define the MSet for synthesizing the query.

3 Query Synthesis

The minterms in a non-redundant DNF query collectively select all documents in set *Relevant*. However, a document may be selected by several minterms. For example, the query concerning eucalyptus has 23 relevant documents, but has 634 non-redundant minterms in the Boolean expression. No more than 23 minterms are needed to select 23 documents.

A minimal set of minterms that selects each document in set *Relevant* is all that is needed to derive a complete search query. As the minimization problem is NP-hard, we use a heuristic to construct a compact cover for set *Relevant*. The query is derived from this DNF expression.

The main idea used in the implemented algorithm is to add one minterm into an incomplete cover set at a time. At each augmentation step, for each candidate minterm function *gain* is computed based on the number of new relevant documents that the minterm selects and its effect on query size. The minterm providing maximum gain is added to the cover set.

To construct a Google query from a given set of minterms the algorithm determines a term that occurs most frequently in the minterms. The term is factored out of the minterms using the following equivalence rule: (A B) | (A C) ≡ A (B | C).

The application of this rule partitions the original set of minterms in two sets of minterms. The first set of minterms is comprised of the minterms that do not include the term. The second set of minterms is created as the result of factoring of the term from minterms which included the factored term. The algorithm is applied recursively to two sets of minterms to achieve further reduction in the size of the query.

3.1 Trading Precision for Query Size

Many queries generated by the algorithm are small to fit the constraints imposed by the search engines. The oversize query for our example was (assuming old Google limit of 10 terms in a query): *eucalyptus ((tall white) | (gum (green | alcohol)) | (evergreen blue) | (fruit south) | (cream found))*. The oversized queries need to be trimmed in size. The trimming, however, would adversely affect the recall or precision of the query.

The preservation of recall rather than the precision is preferred as it generates a query that integrates the aspects of the documents in set *Relevant* into the synthesized query. The property is useful as the synthesized query benefits from all examples, even those that only partially satisfy the user's information needs. A precision-centric approach would require each document in set *Relevant* to be fully satisfying user's information needs causing an obvious paradoxical demand on the user.

Each minterm used to construct the web query rejects every document in set *Irrelevant*. Thus, each minterm has terms to reject every document in set *Irrelevant*. A minterm can be reduced in size, by dropping one or more of these terms from it. Such a transformation, affects the minterm in two ways: (i) A reduced-size minterm either selects the same set of relevant documents as the original minterm or selects some additional documents from set *Relevant*. (ii) The reduced-size minterm selects some documents from set *Irrelevant*. The original minterm selected no document from this set.

In turn, a search query constructed from the reduced-size minterms is affected as follows:

- A search query may need a smaller number of reduced-size minterms to cover all documents in set *Relevant*.
- The search query is composed of minterms with fewer terms in them.
- The search query fails to reject all documents in set *Irrelevant*.

Thus, the size of the constructed query will be smaller but will be of lower precision.

The query synthesis approach uses the reduced-size minterms that have best benefit-to-cost ratios. The cost is measured by the number of irrelevant documents selected by the reduced-size minterm and the benefit is measured by reduction in the number of terms in the constructed query.

A *quality* value – roughly representing a reciprocal of the cost – is assigned to each minterm to measure its ability to avoid irrelevant documents. The *quality* of minterm *mt* is defined by fraction: |*Relevant* σ *mt*| ∧ |*Irrelevant* σ *mt*|. The *quality* of a set of minterms is defined by the minimum *quality* of a minterm in the set.

The *benefit* is represented by the (incremental) change in the query size for each new relevant document selected. Since small query sizes are desired, synthesis algorithm used a reciprocal function *gain*. For minterm *mt*, gain is defined as *(number of new relevant documents selected by mt for the query)/ (change in the query size resulting from the introduction of mt in the query)*.

The set of all reduced-size minterms (called, *RSet*) is derived from set *MSet* by taking a minterm from *MSet* at a time. The reduced-size minterms are added to *RSet* by deleting one or more (but not all) terms from the selected minterm. Thus, each minterm will add 2^n-1 reduced-size minterms in set *RSet*, where n is the number of terms in the minterm.

Finally, we systematically construct a series of search queries till we obtain one that meets the size constraint of the search engine. At each stage, we choose a cut-off value for attribute *quality*. The first cut-off value chosen is infinity, representing the case where the original *MSet* is used as the set of minterms to construct the query. In the subsequent runs, minterms exceeding the chosen *quality* cut-off are chosen from *RSet* to define minterm set for input to query synthesis algorithm. The set is cleaned first to remove dominated minterms. A minterm is dominated if another minterm with a smaller number of terms selects all relevant documents selected by the dominated minterm. If the synthesized query is not suitable for the search engine, the next lower value for attribute *quality* is chosen to construct another candidate query.

To illustrate the procedure with *eucalyptus* example:

- The first query synthesized at quality level infinity was: *eucalyptus ((tall white) | (gum (green | alcohol)) | (evergreen blue) | (fruit south) | (cream found))*. Clearly this query with 12 words is an oversized query for Google search engine.
- Selecting the next highest *quality* value which is 12.0, the query obtained is: *eucalyptus ((fruit | (tall white) | (evergreen (gum | blue)) | (alcohol gum) | (cream found)))*. This query has 11 words, which is again an oversized query for Google search engine.
- The next lower *quality* value is 11.0. At this *quality* value, the synthesized query is: *eucalyptus (fruit | tall | (gum (white | alcohol) | (evergreen blue))*. This query with 8 words is acceptable to the Google search engine.

4 Results and Discussion

A web search query synthesized from only a few relevant documents is not expected to be precise. The deficiency results as small number of available relevant documents may not train the CNF Boolean expression adequately. As the number of relevant documents used to train the Boolean expression increases the precision of the synthesized query improves. The recall also benefits from the increase in the number of relevant example documents available for query synthesis. Different relevant documents tend to use different vocabulary. The diversity in vocabulary introduces new terms, including synonyms and related words, to the synthesis process.

Our initial experience suggests that query synthesized from six relevant documents gives a precision of about 50%. This level is satisfactory as several surveys have pointed that a successful web search is followed by an access to only one document (Jansen, Spink, Bateman and Saracevic, 1998). Queries synthesized from sets of 8 or more relevant documents out-perform experienced human searchers.

4.1 User Survey

To compare the effectiveness of the synthesized queries against human queries we conducted 39 search sessions involving 25 topics. For each topic, the intended information need was described in a form similar to one illustrated for eucalyptus example in Section 2. Documents for the first 70 links returned by Google when searched using (single-word) topic title as keyword were downloaded. Our goal was to get some 10 to 20 relevant text documents for each topic to synthesize queries. Since many of these 70 links where defunct or non-text documents, for each topic a different number of usable text documents remained for query synthesis. For each topic, available text documents were classified manually by the authors. The number of relevant documents for topics ranged from 2 to 44 with average of 17 documents a topic. Average number of irrelevant documents for a topic was 38. These collections were used to synthesize queries.

Table 1. Statistical summary of the performances of user defined queries and synthesized queries on precision (P), coverage (C) and quality (Q) metrics

Metrics	User query			Synthesized query		
	P	C	Q	P	C	Q
Min	0.50	0.42	0.50	0.60	0.63	0.65
Average	0.75	0.72	0.72	0.91	0.79	0.84
Max	1.00	1.00	0.91	1.00	1.00	0.98
Median	0.75	0.70	0.72	0.95	0.74	0.84
Std. Dev.	0.14	0.14	0.11	0.09	0.13	0.09

The survey volunteers were all university students and staff with extensive experience with the web searching. For a chosen topic, a volunteer devised a web query based on the description given to them. The volunteer formed the query interactively and used web search to test queries as they formed them before identifying their best query. We then gave the volunteer the synthesized query. Using the volunteer's query and the synthesized query separate set of 20 top documents were retrieved. These documents were then classified by the volunteer based on their understanding of the information need presented in the description statement. The arrangement overcomes bias in classification due to interpretation of the information need or influence from the classifications made by the authors in forming the synthesized queries.

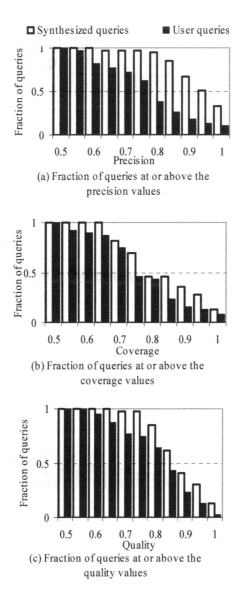

Fig. 1. Distribution of performance metrics for precision, coverage and quality metrics for user devised and synthesized queries from survey sessions

The statistical summary of data collected during the survey is presented in Table 1. Figure 1 shows cumulative distributions of precision (P@20), coverage (C@20) and quality (Q@20) of user devised (volunteer) queries and synthesized queries. It is clear from the figure that for any specified precision, coverage and quality threshold fraction of synthesized queries performing better than human queries is better.

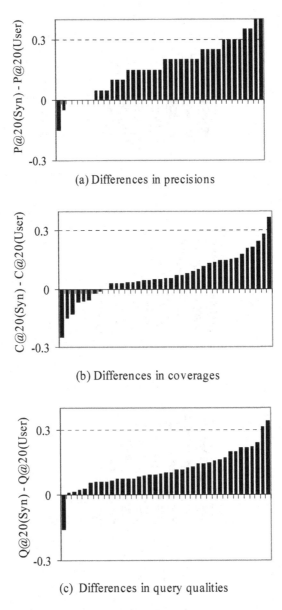

(a) Differences in precisions

(b) Differences in coverages

(c) Differences in query qualities

Fig. 2. Performance differences between user and synthesized queries noticed in survey sessions. Each metrics is sorted independently.

Figure 2 shows the same data but compares data for user and synthesized query from the same survey session. The bars shown in the graphs represent differences in performance of two queries (user and synthesized) on the chosen metrics. Again synthesized queries have performed better more often than the volunteers' queries.

Hypotheses tests on paired data confirm that the synthesized queries perform better than the user queries on precision and quality metrics at 99.99% confidence. The confidence level judging the better performance for synthesized query on coverage metrics is lower at 99%. It is worth stressing that coverage without a supporting precision does not make a query better – an inane query *TRUE* has 100% coverage but 0% precision for every search.

4.2 Discussion

Only in two survey sessions human queries performed better than the synthesized queries on precision metrics. One of these sessions searched for information on Australian marsupial *Kangaroo*. The synthesized query reads: *kangaroo ((tail pouch) | (feet found) | (user grass))*. The human query that gave better precision was *kangaroo (macropodiade | animal)*. The precision of the synthesized query was 0.85 and of the user query 0.9. The coverage for the two queries was 0.928 for the human query, and 0.678 for the synthesized query. The search was repeated in another session. In the latter search, the human devised query was *(kangaroo animal Australia)* with precision 0.7 and coverage 0.827. The synthesized query had a precision of 0.9 and coverage of 0.677 in this session.

In our post survey analysis, it was noted that there are a large number of business and commercial web-sites using term *kangaroo*. The synthesized query has correctly abstracted the nature of the desired information from the given relevant documents. The first volunteer has avoided these business sites using an uncommon but a Kangaroo specific term. The second searcher has been less successful. The combined harmonic mean score, Q@20, for the first volunteer query (0.914) correctly rates it better than the other two queries with scores of around 0.76.

The other case giving better precision by a human query *(ostrich bird struthio neck)* over a synthesized query *ostrich ((((bird largest) | neck) world) | ((neck | (bird brown)) ground)* searched for information about Ostrich. Precision for the human query was 1.0 and coverage 0.545. The synthesized query had precision 0.85 and coverage 0.699. A different volunteer used query *(ostrich Africa flightless largest)*. This gave the precision of 0.85 and coverage of 0.601. However, both human queries are narrowly focused and are less general than the synthesized query. One of them is focused exclusively on *neck* and the other on size *(largest)* of the bird.

It is interesting to note that keywords *macropodiade* and *struthio* are not common vocabulary of a typical web searcher. We believe that these volunteers were very motivated, knowledgeable persons in the topic of their search. Anecdotally, both these searches occurred in the earlier stages of the survey when volunteers had many topics available to choose from. We believe these volunteers searched topics that were close to their interests and knowledge.

The algorithm was developed and tested through survey using the old Google limit of 10 terms in a query. The limit has since been raised to 32. The concession, however, does not make the part of the algorithm that reduces query size unnecessary. Compact query is necessary for good precision and recall. Well targeted terms in the query help the ranking algorithms in the search engines to order the links well. Shorter queries are also easily understood by the human searchers.

5 Concluding Remarks

The synthesized queries have performed better than queries that humans could devise. The links returned by the synthesized queries are different and much expanded collection from those used in the synthesis. The links to the documents used in synthesis are not easily located in those returned by the new query. The correctness of the learned abstraction is evident by the high precisions achieved by the synthesized queries.

Figure 3 gives a brief outline for integrating the algorithm with a web browser. All traffic between the browser and the Internet flows through a proxy that records the documents and the user's feedback. The proxy augments the displayed document with additional buttons for interaction with the searcher.

A criticism of our approach could be made based on the perception that the searchers may not be willing to spend time and effort the documents. We acknowledge that the majority of searches will be satisfactorily and efficiently serviced through the standard search engine interfaces. However, the hard and frustrating searches, albeit uncommon, do need help. We believe that our approach provides a mechanism for such searches without reducing the experiences of the searches that do not require this help.

The algorithm described in this paper has other applications too. It can provide a convenient way for locating related emails. Other application area includes search for all related files on a file system using tools like Google Desktop.

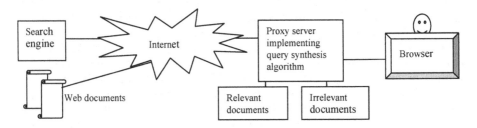

Fig. 3. Architecture for integrating query synthesizer with web browser

References

Aho, A.V., Ullman, J.D.: Foundations of Computer Science. Computer Science Press, NY (1992)

Aula, A., Jhaveri, N., Kaki, M.: Information Seach and Re-Access Strategies of Experienced Web Users. In: The intl. World Wide Web (WWW2005) conf. ACM Press, New York (2005)

Baeza-Yates, R., Riberio-Neto, B.: Modern Information Retrieval. Addison-Wesley, Reading, Ma (1991)

Cohen, W.W.: Fast Effective Rule Induction. In: 12th Intl. Conf. on Machine Learning (1995)

Cohen, W.W., Singer, Y.: Learning to Query the Web. In: AAAI-96 Workshop on Internet-Based Information Systems, AAAI Press, Menlo Park, CA (1996)

Hölscher, C., Strube, G.: Web Search Behavior of Internet Experts and Newbies. In: Proc. of the 9th intl. World Wide Web conf. on Computer networks: the intl. journal of computer and telecommunications networking, North-Holland, Amsterdam (2000)

Jansen, B.J., Spink, A., Bateman, J., Saracevic, T.: Real Life Information Retrieval: A Study of User Queries on the Web. SIGIR Forum 32(1), 5–17 (1998)

Kopec, D., Marsland, T.A.: Search. The CRC Press, Inc (1997)

Malhotra, V., Patro, S., Johnson, D.: Synthesise Web Queries: Search the Web by Examples. In: 7th Intl Conf. on Enterprise Information Systems (ICEIS2005), vol. 2, INSTICC, Portugal (2005)

Oyama, S., Kokubo, T., Ishida, T.: Domain-Specific Web Search with Keyword Spices. IEEE Transaction on Knowledge and Data Engineering 16(1), 17–27 (2004)

Patro, S., Malhotra, V.: Characteristics of the Boolean Web Search Query: Estimating Success from Characteristics. In: 1st intl. conf. on web info. systems and technologies (WEBIST2005). INSTICC, Portugal (2005)

Patro, S.: Synthesising Web Search Queries from Example Text Documents. Master of Science Thesis, School of Computing, University of Tasmania, Launceston. (2006) Website: eprints.comp.utas.edu.au

Ruthven, I., Lalmas, M.: A Survey on the Use of Relevance Feedback for Information Systems. Knowledge engineering Review 18(2), 95–145 (2003)

Sanchez, S.N., Triantaphyllou, E., Chen, J., Liao, T.W.: An Incremental Learning Algorithm for Constructing Boolean Functions from Positive and Negative Examples. Computers and Operations Research 29(12), 1677–1700 (2002)

Sebastiani, F.: Machine Learning in Automated Text Categorization. ACM Comp. Surveys 34(1), 1–47 (2002)

Web User Interaction
Comparison of Declarative Approaches

Mikko Pohja[1], Mikko Honkala[1], Miemo Penttinen[2], Petri Vuorimaa[1],
and Panu Ervamaa[2]

[1] Telecommunications Software and Multimedia Laboratory, Helsinki University of Tehcnology
P.O. Box 5400, FI-02015 HUT, Finland
`mikko.pohja@hut.fi, mikko.honkala@hut.fi,`
`petri.vuorimaa@hut.fi`
[2] Frantic Media Arabianranta 6,
FI-00560 Helsinki, Finland
`miemo.penttinen@frantic.com,`
`panu.ervamaa@frantic.com`

Abstract. The World Wide Web is evolving from a platform for information access into a platform for interactive services. Several applications are already used through Internet and Web browsers. User interface of such an application is defined by HTML. However, HTML has its deficiencies when used as a general UI description language. Several parties have addressed this problem by defining specific UI description languages. Thus, for instance, a web browser could be used as a user interface for any application. We have revised the requirements for a UI description language from literature and evaluated two XML-based UI description formats against the requirements through use cases.

Keywords: Web User Interface, XForms, XUL.

1   Introduction

Commerce and communication tasks, such as using e-mail, are common today in the World Wide Web (WWW). Also, there is a trend to realize higher interaction tasks, such as information authoring, over the WWW. Therefore, WWW is transforming from a platform for information access into a platform for interactive services (Hostetter et al., 1997). Traditionally, application User Interfaces (UI) were programmed as stand-alone clients using procedural programming languages, such as Java or C++ and component toolkits. WWW changed that; any browser can be used as the client when accessing applications in the Web, and the application UI is written in platform independent HTML.

Unfortunately, some of the technologies used in the Web are outdated and, in fact, were not originally designed for the complex use case scenarios of today's applications. For instance, HTML forms are used as the main interaction definition, even though they were not designed to describe complex, higher-interaction UIs. Their usage (along with client-side scripting) has led to bad usability, maintainability, re-use, and accessibility. Therefore, a new paradigm for the Web is needed: the declarative UI. Declarative

J. Filipe, J. Cordeiro, and V. Pedrosa (Eds.): WEBIST 2005/2006, LNBIP 1, pp. 190–203, 2007.

UI languages have usually a higher semantic level while traditional programming languages have more expressive power. Declarative languages, in addition to being modality and device independent, are more easily processed by accessibility and other tools, therefore fixing many of the problems found in the approaches with lower semantical level (e.g., HTML forms and scripting). For practical reasons, it is essential that a balance between semantical level and expressive power is found.

In this paper, we study two UI description languages and how they suit to Web applications. The languages are XForms (Dubinko et al., 2003) and XUL (Hyatt, 2001). They are selected, because they can be used to build cross platform applications and have already several implementations. The research work has been conducted by doing a literature study of related work, defining requirements for a UI description language, and defining and implementing use cases with selected languages. The results are comprised of evaluation of the languages against the requirements and heuristics analysis of the use case implementations.

The main contributions of this paper are the following:

- Based on literature, a set of requirements for a web user interface definition language is derived.
- Three descriptive use cases are designed and implemented in two different languages, XForms and XUL.
- XForms and XUL are evaluated based on the derived requirements and the use cases.
- We propose an extension to XForms language for navigating and editing recursive structures.

The paper is organized as follows. The next Section gives background to the topic and reviews the related work. Section 3 discusses the research scope and the problem. In addition, it defines use cases. Results of the work are presented in Section 4. Finally, Section 5 concludes the paper.

2   Background

2.1   Related UI Languages

The focus of this paper is UI languages, whose cross-platform implementations are readily available. Because of this, some research-oriented UI languages, such as XIML (Puerta and Eisenstein, 2002) and UIML (Abrams et al., 1999), are outside of the scope. In addition to the UI languages reviewed in this paper (XForms and XUL), there exists a whole array of XML-based UI definition languages, whose implementations can be verified. Those are reviewed in related research (Souchon and Vanderdonckt, 2003; Trewin et al., 2004). In addition, there exists numerous XML-based languages for the desktop GUI, including Glade[1], and Microsoft XAML (Rector, 2003), while InfoPath addresses office applications (Hoffman, 2003).

---

[1] Glade. Available at: http://glade.gnome.org/

2.2 XForms

XForms 1.0 Recommendation (Dubinko et al., 2003) is the next-generation Web forms language, designed by the W3C. It solves some of the problems found in the HTML forms by separating the purpose from the presentation and using declarative markup to describe the most common operations in form-based applications (Cardone et al., 2005). It can use any XML grammar to describe the content of the form (the instance data). Thus, it also enables to create generic editors for different XML grammars with XForms. It is possible to create complex forms with XForms using declarative markup, without resorting to scripting.

XForms is an abstract user interface description language. One of its design goals was not to mandate a certain modality. Therefore, it can be suited to describe user interfaces, which are realized in different modalities, such as the GUI and Speech.

Several XML vocabularies have been specified in W3C. Typically, an XML language is targeted for a certain purpose (e.g., XHTML for content structuring or SVG for 2D graphics). Moreover, XML languages can be combined. An XML document, which consists of two or more XML languages, is called compound document. A compound document can specify user interface of an application. In this paper, XForms is combined with XHTML+CSS level 2 to realize the use cases. XForms 1.0 includes other W3C specifications directly: XML Events, XPath 1.0, XML Schema Datatypes, and XML 1.0.

2.3 XUL

Mozilla has developed a UI description language called XML User Interface Language (XUL) (Hyatt, 2001). The markup consists of widget elements like buttons, menus, etc. XUL applications are based on several W3C standards. Those include HTML 4.0; Cascading Style Sheets (CSS) 1 and 2; Document Object Model (DOM) Levels 1 and 2; JavaScript 1.5, including ECMA-262 Edition 3 (ECMAscript); and XML 1.0.

The goal of XUL is to build cross platform applications. The applications can be ported to all of the operating systems on which Mozilla runs (e.g., Linux, Windows, Windows CE, and Mac OS X). The layout and appearance of XUL applications are separated from the application definition and logic. Moreover, the application can be localized for different languages and regions independently of its logic or presentation.

XUL can be complemented by few technologies introduced by Mozilla. *The eXtensible Bindings Language (XBL)* is a markup language that defines new elements for XUL widgets. *Overlays* are XUL files used to describe extra content for the UI. *XPCOM* and *XPConnect* enable the integration of external libraries with XUL applications and, finally, *XPInstall* provides a way to package XUL application components with an install script. (Bojanic, 2003).

2.4 Requirements

Souchon and Vanderdonckt have reviewed XML-compliant user interface description languages in (Souchon and Vanderdonckt, 2003). The paper compares the general properties and the UI description capacities of the languages. XIML is found out most expressive language whereas UIML has best software support. XUL is found to be less expressive. XForms has not been evaluated in the paper.

Four XML languages for abstract user interface representation are examined in (Trewin et al., 2004). The languages are UIML, XIML, XForms, and AIAP. The paper defines requirements for the representations. Those include high level requirements like applicability to any target and any delivery context, personalization, flexibility, extensibility, and simplicity. In addition, they have defined technical requirements, which consist of separating purpose from presentation, characteristics of interface elements and functions, flexibility in inclusion of alternate resources, compatibility with concrete user interfaces, support for different interaction styles, and support for remote control. XForms and AIAP fulfill best the requirements. Especially, in terms of separation of data from presentation and flexibility in resource substitution.

Requirements for a generic user interface description format are discussed in (Simon et al., 2004). They also present an implementation of an integrated description of user interfaces for both graphical and voice modality. The proposed requirements are device independence, modality independence, and customizability concerning layout without restricting device independence.

3   Research Scope and Methods

The research area of the paper is *Web user interaction models*.

Because of the huge variance in interaction scenarios and technologies (ranging from natural language speech interaction to 3D interaction with immersive displays), the research is tightly scoped. The scope for the research is desktop-style user interaction in WWW environment.

The research steps are enumerated in the following list. The scoping, which is defined above, applies to all of the research steps.

1. The Web application use cases are selected.
2. Requirements of a UI description format from literature are collected.
3. XForms and XUL are evaluated against the requirements.
4. The use case implementations are evaluated through heuristic analysis (Nielsen, 1994).

3.1   Use Cases

The selected use cases are from an existing content management system, which is used to manage the content of an Internet magazine. The application is used through Web and is originally implemented with HTML and CSS. We selected three user interfaces from the system, which are difficult to realize properly with HTML. First, the wireframe models of the use cases were drawn. The models were designed using general usability guidelines without taking account possible restrictions of the languages. Users are mainly journalists, who have experience in using typical word processing program and are familiar with concepts like *copy-paste*.

The design of the user interfaces in this paper is based on usability best practices (Cooper, 1995) and user interface design patterns (Tidwell, 2005) and (Laakso, 2003). The usability of the interfaces has been validated by usage simulation (Preece et al., 2002) and heuristic analysis (Nielsen, 1994).

Document Editor. The purpose of this user interface is to create and modify simple structural documents, which could, e.g., be displayed as a web page. The type of data in the document is limited to text, pre-existing images and pre-existing tables (created, e.g., by the Table Editor user interface). Wireframe model of the Document Editor is shown in Figure 1.

Fig. 1. Wireframe model of the document editor

The structure of the document can be modified by marking text blocks with different existing styles (e.g., heading 1, heading 2, text paragraph, notice, etc.). The marking is targeted to a selected text box. For the sake of simplicity, all styles are block-level styles, i.e., they are always attached to the whole text block.

To keep the focus on the structure of the document in the interface, the images and tables cannot be modified in the document editor interface. A possible use case for the document editor is: a journalist creates a review of a laptop and completes it with images of the laptop and a table about its features.

Table Editor. The purpose of this user interface is to create and modify simple tabular data, which can be displayed, e.g., in a web page. The type of data in the table is limited to characters and numbers. Wireframe model of the Table Editor is shown in Figure 2.

The user can also edit the structure of the tabular data by marking some of the columns or headers as headings and by entering a header text for the whole table. The number of rows and columns in the table is user-editable.

For the sake of simplicity, table cells are not allowed to span multiple columns or rows. Possible use cases for the table editor are: the user wants to create a table

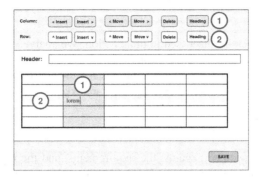

Fig. 2. Wireframe model of the table editor. (1) Active column is color coded to match the coloring of the buttons for manipulating the column. (2) Active row is color coded to match the coloring of the buttons for manipulating the row.

documenting the average monthly temperatures in four different locations during one year; or the user wants to create a table presenting the costs estimate for purchasing a new computer setup.

Tree Editor. The purpose of this user interface is to create and modify a tree structure where the nodes of the tree have multiple editable attributes. In this paper, we use the nodes to represent web site areas for a site of a magazine. However, the nodes and attributes could represent anything. The tree Editor is depicted in Figure 3.

The user is able to create new nodes, edit the attributes, move nodes around in the tree and delete nodes. A possible use case for the tree editor is: managing the structure of an online magazine.

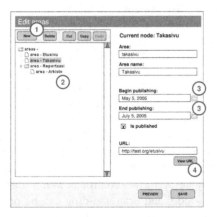

Fig. 3. Wireframe model of the tree editor. (1) Creates a new area as a child to the currently selected node. Data for the newly created area is entered from the form in the right. (2) Moving nodes in the tree is done by drag-and-dropping them. (3) Opens a calendar widget for selecting the date. (4) Opens the URL in a browser.

4   Results

The results of the paper are discussed in this Section. We analyzed how the languages fulfill the requirements of a UI description language presented in the literature. In addition, we introduce the use case implementations and the heuristic analysis we did for them. Finally, model differences of the languages are explained.

4.1   Requirements

The languages were evaluated against the requirements, and the results are shown in Tables 1-3. The general requirements in Table 1 are from (Simon et al., 2004). They are device and modality independence and customizability. Both languages meet the requirements. XForms has abstract UI description. Thus, the concrete UI is totally device independent. Also, the UI description of XUL does not restrict the selection of devices. XForms uses data types, which makes it easy to utilize different modalities. For instance in voice modality, grammar based recognition can be made more specific. XUL widgets can also be transferred to other modalities, but lack of data types makes it more difficult. Both XForms and XUL provide control over layout and graphical appearance. In XUL, the customization is easier because of specific UI elements.

The requirements in Table 2 are represented in (Trewin et al., 2004). In the paper, XForms is evaluated against the requirements among three other languages. XForms, along with Alternative Interface Access Protocol (AIAP), was found best suited to meet the requirements defined in the paper. Especially, regarding to separation of data from presentation and flexibility in resource substitution.

The interface elements are not separated from their presentation in XUL. In XForms, the data model can be accessed through separate binding layer. In both languages, the interface elements can have dependencies. However, in XUL, the dependencies have to be realized through scripts. XForms is also easier to use in any target since its UI description is more abstract. XForms supports data types, whereas XUL does not.

The presentation can be grouped well with both languages. XForms provides explicit way to include labels and help texts, while in XUL they can be realized with normal text. Providing an alternative presentation is possible with both formats. Local computations (e.g., data validation) and data serialization are easier to provide with XForms, which has current state always available. They must be realized through scripts in XUL. These differences are discussed in more detail in Subsection 4.6.

The requirements found from the literature were extended with a more detailed *typical interaction patterns* requirement set from the application scenario (c.f. Table 3). Repeating structures (repeat) and paging and dialogs (switch, message) are natively supported by XForms, while in XUL they require some script programming. Nested constructs are supported by the XUL tree control as well as our proposed XForms tree module. Copy-paste, undo-redo, and drag-and-drop can be programmed with scripts in XUL, while in XForms only copy-paste is possible to implement. As a summary, XUL handles the typical interaction patterns better, since it has more desktop-oriented focus.

Table 1. The requirements of the UI description language (Simon et al., 2004)

Requirement	XForms	XUL
General requirements		
Device Independence	Good	Possible
Modality Independence	Good	Possible
Customizability	Possible	Good

Table 2. The requirements for universal interaction (Trewin et al., 2004)

Requirement	XForms	XUL
Separation of Interface Elements from Pres.		
Separation of Data/Pres.	Good	Possible
Interface Elements		
Dependencies	Good	Possible
Any Target	Good	Possible
Data Types	Good	No
Presentation Related Information		
Logical Groupings	Good	Good
Labels & Help Text	Good	Possible
Presentation Replacement	Possible	Possible
Run Time and Remote Control		
Local Computation	Good	Possible
Serialization	Good	Possible

Table 3. The proposed extensions to requirements

Requirement	XForms	XUL
Typical Interaction Patterns		
Paging & Dialogs	Good	Good
Repeating constructs	Good	Possible
Nested constructs	Good[*]	Good
Copy-paste	Possible	Possible
Undo-redo	No	Possible
Drag-and-drop	No	Possible

[*] using the proposed tree extension.

4.2 Use Case Implementations in XForms

The XForms implementations of the use cases were done using the XForms 1.1 Working Draft (Boyer et al., 2004) (W3C Work In Progress), which is implemented in the X-Smiles browser (Vuorimaa et al., 2002). XForms 1.1 has several features, which make it possible to minimize scripting. The main features from XForms 1.1, which were

Fig. 4. XForms Tree Editor

utilized, are duplicate and destroy actions, and mediatype-aware output rendering. Otherwise these features would have required the use of scripting.

XForms language was extended with a tree module, since in XForms 1.1, there is no way of selecting nodes from a recursive structure. We also implemented the tree module, as a proof of concept, in the X-Smiles XForms implementation.

The user interface state is completely contained in the XForms model, and can therefore automatically be serialized and submitted to a server without any additional scripting.

Document Editor. The document editor relies on XForms repeat, and dynamic UI bindings. It requires few XForms 1.1. features, which it utilizes heavily, namely destroy and duplicate, and output@mediatype. This UI has no scripting.

Tree Editor. The tree editor (cf. Fig. 4) uses the proposed XForms Tree extension. All other dynamic features are done using XForms UI bindings. This UI has no scripting.

Table Editor. This table editor UI is written in XForms 1.1, but it has a small script to insert, delete and move columns. This could be avoided if XForms had repeating and conditional action containers (such as *for* and *if*).

4.3   Proposed XForms Extension: Tree Module

We have extended the XForms 1.0 specification with a tree module *xforms:tree* and a corresponding XPath extension function *nodeindex*.

This form control displays a tree, which corresponds to the instance tree rooted at the bound node. It must have an id attribute. The item element's label (executed with the context of corresponding node) is used to determine the label of each node.

The XPath function *nodeindex* takes an idref of an tree widget, as an argument and returns the instance node, which corresponds to the currently selected node in a tree widget.

```
<instance>
  <data>
    <folder name="xxx">
      <folder name="xxx">
        <file name="xxx" description="xxx"/>
      </folder>
    </folder>
  </data name="xxx">
</instance>

<tree ref="/data/folder" prune="true"
    id="folders">
  <label>The directory document</label>
  <item><label ref="@name"/></item>
</tree>

<group ref="nodeindex('folders')">
  <group
    ref="self::node()[localname()='folder']>
    <label>Folder</label>
    <input ref="@name"/>
  </group>
  <group
    ref="self::node()[localname()='file']>
    <label>File</label>
    <input ref="@name"/>
    <input ref="@description"/>
  </group>
</group>
```

Fig. 5. Example of tree widget usage

A code example of the tree element's usage is shown in Figure 5. It would display a tree of folders and files. When a user selects a node, an editor for that node is shown in the relevant group.

4.4   Use Case Implementations in XUL

In addition to the wireframe model designs, XUL enabled to use context menus in Document and Tree Editors. Also, Document editor has a real time preview of a document. It is remarkable that XUL interfaces require a lot of scripts. All the button functionalities, drag-and-dropping, and focusing of elements have to be realized through scripts. The XUL Document editor is depicted in Figure 6.

4.5   Heuristic Analysis

We did the heuristic analysis according to the heuristics defined by Nielsen (Nielsen, 1994). We did not find any major problems from the interfaces. Mainly,

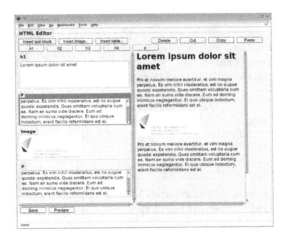

Fig. 6. XUL Document Editor

because the wireframe models were already designed according to the heuristics. Nevertheless, we were able to identify some problems from all the interfaces. Common deficiencies were lack of undo-redo and help operations. Of course, these should have been considered already in the design phase.

XForms Document Editor does not have drag-and-drop functionality. In addition, the preview function is a bit problematic in XForms editors, because user has to always save the form before previewing it. However, saving is not always desired when previewing. Finally, selected column or headers cannot be highlighted in XForms Table Editor.

4.6   Model Differences Between XUL and XForms

Although, in the selected use cases on a desktop computer, the usability between the XForms and XUL user interfaces does not differ, we have noticed a difference in the user interface development model. Like XUL, most of the XML-based user interface definition languages are widget based. This means that they are quite concrete, and the author works by adding widgets, such as buttons and text areas to the user interface. It is therefore very easy to graphically create a user interface layout, but all user interface logic has to be programmed using a programming or scripting language, though. In contrast, XForms starts by defining a XML data model, and all operations are done to the datamodel using declarative actions and XPath expressions, while user interface is automatically kept up-to date with a dynamic dependency tracking.

Maybe the biggest difference is the communication between the user interface and the back-end system. For the communication, the user interface state has to be serialized for transmission. Vice versa, after getting serialized reply from the server, it has to be deserialized into application state. In XForms (cf. Fig. 7), that serialization is automatic, since the datamodel is a live XML document object model, which is automatically serialized and de-serialized.

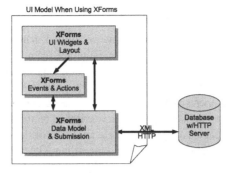

Fig. 7. UI Model using XForms

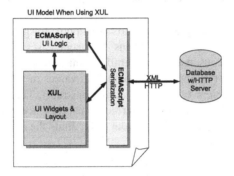

Fig. 8. UI Model using XUL

On the other hand, in XUL there is no explicit datamodel, and communication between a backend process and the user interface have to be reimplemented using ECMAScript for each user interface, as shown in Fig. 8. This is true also for HTML forms and its derivatives, such as Ajax[2]. For example, when the server sends an updated structured content back, there has to be a script, which updates the corresponding XUL DOM, respectively. This means, that authoring and maintaining XUL-based applications is more complicated than XForms.

It is noteworthy that XUL has a templates mechanism, which allows to use RDF as the datamodel to some extent. Since RDF is more complicated than XML (graph vs. tree), and we would have to serialize the RDF datamodel anyway into the XML document model either at server or client, it was not used in this paper. Using XBL (Hyatt, 2000) combined with XUL should allow the use of XML datamodels, thus removing the need of serializing and de-serializing communications. All user interface logic has to be still written in ECMAScript, though XBL encapsulates the operations in a reusable manner. It is still unknown, whether XUL+XBL removes the need for any serialization and deserialization in the selected use cases.

---

[2] Ajax: A New Approach to Web Applications, http://adaptivepath.com/publications/essays/archives/000385.php

5   Conclusion

In this paper, two UI description languages were studied, namely XForms and XUL. We collected requirements for a UI description language from literature, extended them with typical interaction patterns, and evaluated the languages against the requirements. In addition, we selected three use cases, which are typical to Web application UIs, but are difficult to realize properly with HTML. First, we designed wireframe models of the use cases according to the usability guidelines. Based on those, we implemented the use cases with both languages, and did heuristic analysis for the implementations.

XForms fulfilled the requirements slightly better than XUL. On the other hand, with XUL, the use cases could be realized more strictly according to the wireframe models, since, for instance, drag-and-drop is not supported in XForms. As a conclusion, the differences between XForms and XUL+XBL on desktop are not big. We do expect that major differences can arise in device independence and multimodal usage scenarios, where XForms is better.

Also, we feel that both languages should add support for general undo-redo, copy-paste, and drag-and-drop interaction patterns. In special cases, it is possible to support these, but for instance, copy-paste between different types of data input and outputs is not usually supported (for instance, copying the values in a repeating spreadsheet-type of table into a different type of repeating construct). These interaction patterns are so widely available in current user interfaces, that they need to be supported in the Web user interface languages as well, in order to facilitate the deployment of these user interfaces on the Web.

References

Abrams, M., Phanouriou, C., Batongbacal, A.L., Williams, S.M., Shuster, J.E.: UIML: an appliance-independent XML user interface language. In: WWW '99: Proceeding of the eighth international conference on World Wide Web, New York, USA, pp. 1695–1708. Elsevier, North-Holland, Inc. (1999)

Bojanic, P.: The Joy of XUL (2003), http://www.mozilla.org/projects/xul/joy-of-xul.html

Boyer, J., Landwehr, D., Merrick, R., Raman, T.V.: XForms 1.1. W3C Working Draft (2004)

Cardone, R., Soroker, D., Tiwari, A.: Using XForms to simplify web programming. In: WWW '05: Proceedings of the 14th international conference on World Wide Web, pp. 215–224. ACM Press, New York, NY, USA (2005)

Cooper, A.: About Face: The Essentials of User Interface Design. John Wiley & Sons, West Sussex, England (1995)

Dubinko, M., Klotz, L.L., Merrick, R., Raman, T.V.: XForms 1.0. W3C Recommendation (2003)

Hoffman, M.: Architecture of microsoft office infopath 2003. Microsoft Developer Network (2003)

Hostetter, M., Kranz, D., Seed, C., Terman, C.S.W.: Curl, a gentle slope language for the web. World Wide Web Journal (1997)

Hyatt, D.: XBL - extensible binding language 1.0. Netscape (2000)

Hyatt, D.: XML user interface language (XUL) 1.0. Mozilla.org (2001)

Laakso, S.: User Interface Design Patterns. Available online (2003). http://www.cs.helsinki.fi/u/salaakso/patterns/

Nielsen, J.: Ten Usability Heuristics. Available online (1994). `http://www.useit.com/papers/heuristic/heuristic_list.html`

Preece, J., Rogers, Y., Sharp, H.: Interaction Design, chapter 13, 1st edn. Wiley, Chichester (2002)

Puerta, A., Eisenstein, J.: Ximl: a common representation for interaction data. In: IUI '02: Proceedings of the 7th international conference on Intelligent user interfaces, pp. 214–215. ACM Press, New York, NY, USA (2002)

Rector, B.: Introducing "longhorn" for developers. Microsoft Developer Network (2003)

Simon, R., Kapsch, M.J., Wegscheider, F.: A generic UIML vocabulary for device- and modality independent user interfaces. In: WWW Alt. '04: Proceedings of the 13th international World Wide Web conference on Alternate track papers & posters, pp. 434–435. ACM Press, New York, NY, USA (2004)

Souchon, N., Vanderdonckt, J.: A review of XML-compliant user interface description languages. In: Jorge, J.A., Jardim Nunes, N., Falcão e Cunha, J. (eds.) DSV-IS 2003. LNCS, vol. 2844, Springer, Heidelberg (2003)

Tidwell, J.: Designing Interfaces: Patterns for Effective Interaction Design. O'Reilly Media, Inc. 1st edn. (2005)

Trewin, S., Zimmermann, G., Vanderheiden, G.: Abstract representations as a basis for usable user interfaces. Interacting with Computers 16(3), 477–506 (2004)

Vuorimaa, P., Ropponen, T., von Knorring, N., Honkala, M.: A Java based XML browser for consumer devices. In: The 17th ACM Symposium on Applied Computing, Madrid, Spain, ACM Press, New York (2002)

Enabling Vocal Interaction in a Web Portal Environment

Federico Bergenti, Lorenzo Lazzari, Marco Mari, and Agostino Poggi

Dipartimento di Ingegneria dell'Informazione, Università degli Studi di Parma
Parco Area delle Scienze 181/A, 43100, Parma, Italia
bergenti@ce.unipr.it, lazzari@ce.unipr.it, mari@ce.unipr.it,
poggi@ce.unipr.it

Abstract. The growing request of innovative, multimodal interfaces for mobile users and the need of different navigation paradigms for impaired Internet users are promoting and driving nowadays research on multimodal interactions. In this paper we present our experiences in the integration of vocal components in a portal engine, namely Apache Jetspeed. First, we discuss the reasons why the integration of a full-featured portal brings significant advantages to the development of a vocal platform. Then, we describe two complementary approaches for enhancing portals with vocal capabilities, and we compare them under various standpoints. The first approach that we investigate is based on a server-side speech synthesizer, while the second relies on client-side technologies, X+V and the SALT markup languages. For each of these approaches we present some examples and we discuss advantages and drawbacks.

Keywords: Web portals, Vocal interaction, Human-computer interaction.

1 Introduction

In last few years the development of the Internet has brought a great amount of information and services to an enormous number of users. At the same time, mobile devices and wireless networks have significantly widened their capabilities from simple voice calls to the hybrid, converged services and fast navigation of the Internet that third generation UMTS devices support. The necessary convergence of the technologies for wireline and wireless networks has provided users with the capability of accessing information and services from anywhere, at anytime. In this scenario, the differences between input/output devices of desktop computers, mobile phones and PDAs are pushing researchers to define new interaction methods, beyond traditional interaction with keyboard and mouse, capable of overcoming such differences. An important example of these efforts is the formation of the W3C Multimodal Interaction Activity, with the aim of extending the user interface of the Web to allow multiple modes of interaction, e.g. vocal, visual and tactile. Moreover, the research in new interaction methods raises to a higher level of importance in consideration of the utility of such methods for the navigation of impaired Internet users, thus increasing the accessibility of the Web to people with visual or other disabilities.

J. Filipe, J. Cordeiro, and V. Pedrosa (Eds.): WEBIST 2005/2006, LNBIP 1, pp. 204–213, 2007.
© Springer-Verlag Berlin Heidelberg 2007

Taking into account the requirements of mobile navigation and accessibility of multiple, personalized contents, portal technologies occupy a key role in future development of ubiquitous and integrated applications. A portal is a central hub that can simplify and personalize access to heterogeneous services, applications and information. These characteristics turn a portal into an ideal gateway to the Internet for impaired navigators. Moreover, everyday portal engines facilitate the access to their contents from mobile devices, and they also provide transparent adaptation of such contents to the characteristics of end users' devices, as we will see in the following section.

In this paper we present our experiences in the direction of enhancing the interaction methods offered by a portal system, namely Apache Jetspeed, in order to provide users with a vocal interface. In Section 2 we discuss some related work, while in Section 3 we summarize the key features of the portal engine that we used and we explain why a portal engine can facilitate the development of a vocal or multimodal platform. In sections 4 and 5 we describe in detail the two complementary approaches that we followed to integrate voice capabilities into the portal. Finally, section 6 is dedicated to a comparative discussion of these two approaches and to an outline of our future work.

2   Existing Standards and Related Work

2.1   EMMA, X+V and SALT

The starting point for investigating the actual status of multimodal technologies is without any doubt the W3C Multimodal Interaction Activity home page. The main objective of this workgroup is to extend the Web to allow users to dynamically select the most appropriate mode of interaction on the basis of their current needs, while enabling developers to provide an effective user interface for whichever modes the user selects. The modes that the W3C Multimodal Interaction Activity considers for input are speech, handwriting and keystrokes, while output can be presented via displays, pre-recorded and synthetic speech, audio, and tactile mechanisms, e.g., mobile phone vibrators and Braille strips. An important result of the W3C Multimodal Interaction Activity workgroup is the recent definition of EMMA (Extensible MultiModal Annotation Markup Language), a language used to represent human input to a multimodal application. An example of interpretation of a user input that EMMA facilitates is the transcription into words of a raw signal, for instance derived from speech, pen or keystroke input.

The specification of EMMA is so recent that it is not yet possible to find tools supporting this new language. However, waiting for EMMA-compliant tools, we can still test multimodal (in particular vocal) applications using two standards that have provided a strong contribution to EMMA: X+V and SALT.

X+V (XHTML + Voice) has the aim to integrate two mature standards, i.e., XHTML and VoiceXML, to bring spoken interaction to the Web, i.e., creating multimodal dialogs that combine the visual input mode and speech input and output. X+V is sustained by a consortium comprising IBM, Motorola and Opera Software.

The SALT (Speech Application Language Tags) Forum groups different companies, which includes Microsoft, Intel and Cisco, sharing a common interest in developing and promoting speech technologies for multimodal and telephony applications. SALT specification extends existing mark-up languages, i.e., HTML, XHTML and XML, enabling multimodal and telephony access to the Web.

2.2 Related Work

Multimodal and vocal interaction means are a longstanding research problem. Already in 1992, Cohen (Cohen, 1992) suggested that the focus should not only be on building interfaces that make available two or more communication modalities, rather on developing integrated interfaces in which the modalities forge a productive synthesis, using the strengths of one modality to overcome weaknesses of another.

It is possible to distinguish three kinds of reason (Sharma et al., 1998) for using a multimodal interface in human computer interaction (HCI):

- Practical: traditional HCI systems are unnatural and cumbersome. Moreover, redundant or alternative input sources can help impaired users to access computer applications.
- Biological: human beings, as well as other animals, integrate multiple senses. This strongly suggests that the use of multimodality in HCI would be desirable, especially if the goal is to incorporate the naturalness of human communication in HCI.
- Mathematical: it is statistically advantageous to combine multiple observations from the same source because improved estimates are obtained using redundant observations. In this way, the concurrent use of two or more interaction modalities may improve system reliability.

Multimodality can be defined from human and technology perspectives (Baber et al., 2001). From the human point of view, people can exchange information using different sensory modalities, and so a multimodal system would support more than one sensory and response modality. From the technology point of view, computer systems can receive and present information using different modes, and so multimodality is the capability of a system to allow combination of modes to operate concurrently. Given these definitions, we can point out one of the main problems of multimodality: the design of systems capable of fully supporting concurrent, alternative modes.

Several research works aim to define multimodal interfaces combining different interaction modes. Moran presents an agent-based interface that focuses on voice and pen input, and supported by a gestures-recognition engine (Moran et al., 1997). Again, the SmartKom system (Wahlster et al., 2001) merges three paradigms: spoken dialogue, graphical user interfaces and gestural interaction. For the two latter paradigms, SmartKom does not use a traditional WIMP (Windows, Icons, Menus, Pointer) interface combined together with gesture recognition; instead, it supports natural gestural interaction combined with facial expressions. Another valuable characteristic of SmartKom is that it spans across a number of different platforms and application scenarios: the kernel functionalities are portable to a wide range of devices. MOUE (Lisetti et al., 2003) is a system whose main characteristic is the ability to build a model of user's emotions by observing the user via multi-sensory devices, i.e., camera, microphone and wearable computer. This system can have a wide range of applications, like tele-monitoring and healthcare. MEDITOR system (Bellik, 1997) applies multimodal interfaces, including speech recognition, synthesis, and Braille terminals, to provide improved computer access to blinds.

Thus some portal solutions (e.g.: IBM WebSphere Portal) offer support for multimodal applications, and despite the amount of research in this field, to the best of our knowledge this is the first paper to discuss the integration of a vocal mode in a portal engine (both for the interface and the contents). The benefits of such a solution will be described in detail in the next section.

3 Portal Engines

In our vision, the research in innovative and multimodal interaction paradigms has two main goals: *(i)* to facilitate the navigation for impaired users; and *(ii)* to improve the usability of ubiquitous applications. In both cases, the integration of a portal engine can bring significant advantages. In fact, a portal acts as a common layer on which it is possible to integrate heterogeneous applications and contents in a personalized way, without exploring several, different sites, and thus facilitating the navigation for both mobile and impaired users. Moreover, the adaptation of portal pages to the characteristics of mobile devices is easier than the adaptation of generic Web pages because a portal engine provides natively a set of tools for performing such adaptation almost transparently. This last argument has already been discussed in a previous paper (Mari et al., 2004), so in this section we only summarize the reasons why a portal is an ideal platform for providing contents to mobile devices:

- Content adaptation applies to single portlets, not to entire portal pages. Portlets are the base components of a portal, the elements that process a request and generate dynamic contents. Therefore, the content of a portlet is generally shorter and easier to adapt than the content of a whole page.
- The design of the user interface (and therefore the usability of the portal) is separated from the content it presents, therefore a different interface can be specified for each class of devices.
- The disposition of the portlets on the page is separated from the content they present and a different disposition can be provided for each class of devices.
- The portal can easily be extended with the support for new classes of devices.

Therefore, a portal provides an environment in which it is possible to create and adapt separately the contents, the user interface and the content disposition.

Another relevant advantage portals provide is suggested by the works of Dybkjaer (Dybkjaer et al., 2004) and Walker (Walker et al., 2004). The conclusion section of Dybkjaer et al. discusses the benefits of a user modelling facility, in order to adapt the behaviour and the dialogues generated by the system, while in Walker et al. the generation of answers for users is fully tailored on the basis of user profiles. A portal engine always includes a user database that can contain all relevant information for this profiling. Moreover, this database can be updated on the fly, following a possible change of user preferences during system navigation (e.g., a user enters a portion of the portal in which vocal interaction is not desirable).

The portal we used in our research is Jetspeed 1.5, an open source implementation of an enterprise information portal. Jetspeed is part of Portals, a top-level project of the Apache Software Foundation (ASF). Jetspeed provides portal view customization and access to information on the basis of user capabilities: it acts as the central hub where information from multiple sources is made available in an easy to use manner. Therefore, each user can access to a subset of the information/applications available and select the part which she/he is interested in.

The off-the-shelf version of Jetspeed can only serve content to PCs and WAP devices. In a past work, we developed (Mari et al., 2004) an add-on for Jetspeed that provides the portal with the capability of supporting other mobile devices, i.e., PDAs and I-Mode terminals (I-Mode is the Internet access system offered by the Japanese operator NTT DoCoMo). This add-on is useful to test the results of our research on various platforms, both emulators and real devices. We are also developing an add-on that provides real-time user profiling, analyzing user actions and changing the system behaviour on the basis of user preferences.

4 Enabling a Vocal Mode

The first approach we entailed to enhance the portal navigation experience with voice was to add a vocal mode to all portal content. In this way, each part of the portal can be read or heart by the user. For this purpose, we integrated a speech synthesizer in a servlet, then we created a tool to access the synthesizer from the portal, and finally we modified the portal structure to make the new functionality available transparently to all portlets.

Before describing in more detail this work, it is important to remember that the content of a portal is composed by portlets, and from each single portlet it is possible to access external applications, RSS feeds, Web services, corporate contents, and so on.

4.1 FreeTTS

After an accurate analysis of the available speech synthesizers, we decided to develop the speech synthesis module of our add-on to Jetspeed using FreeTTS. FreeTTS is a speech synthesis engine written entirely in Java and it is based on Flite, a small runtime speech synthesis engine developed at Carnegie Mellon University. FreeTTS has been developed by the Speech Integration Group of Sun Microsystems Laboratories and it is distributed with an open source, BSD-style licence. The main reasons that brought us to the choice of FreeTTS are:

- Support for JSAPI 1.0 specification. JSAPI are the standard Java interfaces for incorporating speech capabilities in a Java program. Moreover, FreeTTS provides its own libraries with added functionalities, e.g., the direct redirection of audio sources to a remote client.
- Being a Java program and an open source project, it is easy to adapt and to integrate in the architecture of our project. Jetspeed is structured as a servlet, and so the best solution is to also have the speech synthesizer available in the servlet itself.
- Among the suggested uses, authors included a sample remote TTS server, whose behaviour is similar to our requirements: FreeTTS can act as a back-end text-to-speech engine that works with a speech/telephony system.
- The internal speech synthesis engine has been recently enhanced to provide optimal performances.

Fig. 1. The vocal mode in the Web user interface of Jetspeed

FreeTTS has been integrated in a servlet, and all synthesizer configurations (i.e.: the voice selections) are made available through a Web interface. The integration has been tested with the Apache Tomcat servlet engine, giving good results and performances.

4.2 Portal Integration

For providing text-to-speech functionalities to Jetspeed, we developed a portal module called TextToSpeech Service. This module is designed as a pluggable service of Turbine, the framework on which Jetspeed is built. This service is a set of classes, based on the Singleton design pattern, with utility methods that can be called from every part of the portal. It is worth noting that the architecture of this service is not tied to FreeTTS, so, in the future, we could provide implementations of our service on the basis on other synthesizers.

Having the text-to-speech functionalities available, next step was to introduce the vocal mode in the portal core features. Jetspeed defines a set of standard modes for each portlet: view, customize, info, print, minimize and maximize. On the basis of the portlet type and of the administrator policies, a portlet can have one or more modes available, while the user can select in which the portlet is displayed. A new mode has been defined: the vocal mode. In the Web user interface, the vocal mode is presented as a new icon near the portlet title (see figure 1). As for the other modes, the portlet can declare in its registry if the vocal support is provided. From a functional point of view, the introduction of the vocal mode means that the user can trigger another type of action. This action was defined in the interfaces and in the abstract classes that describe the portlet state and methods. A detailed description of the modifications in Jetspeed code is beyond the scope of this paper. When the user triggers the vocal action, the portlet generates a call to the TextToSpeech service, the service in his turn activates the FreeTTS synthesizer, passing the portlet content to the speech synthesis engine.

By default, the vocal mode is activated only when the user selects the corresponding icon, but it is possible to force the activation whenever a user interacts with a vocal portlet.

4.3 Example Portlets

As an example of vocal-enabled portlet, we implemented the vocal mode for two of the most common portlet types of Jetspeed: RSS (Rich Site Summary) and Velocity.

RSS portlets are used to retrieve news from remote sources: they take an RSS feed from a remote server, apply an XSLT transformation to the feed content and present the result in the portal screen. The sample RSS portlets provided with Jetspeed are BBC Front Page news, ApacheWeek and XMLHack. When a user clicks on the vocal icon, the TextToSpeech service synthesizes the content of the news and sends the audio stream to the client device.

Apache Velocity is a simple, yet powerful, template engine used to develop Web applications following the MVC (Model-View-Controller) model. All Jetspeed screens and most portlet templates are written using Velocity. When a Velocity portlet generates its content, it looks for a template according to the media type of the user (e.g., HTML and WML). Thanks to the new vocal support, developers can also write templates for the vocal mode. The content of Velocity templates is inherently dynamic, and therefore the audio stream sent to the user is not a static description of the portlet, rather it follows the user-portal interaction. For example, the speech can present the results of a query to a database, or it can answer to the inputs of a user compiling a form.

5   A Deeper Interaction Using Markup Languages

Although the vocal mode provided by a simple speech synthesizer like FreeTTS can significantly improve the navigation experience of the user, a more complete vocal interaction between the user and the portal is achieved only with a dedicated markup language. For this reason, our second approach was to include in Jetspeed the support for X+V and SALT: the integration procedure is similar for both languages, and it is described in the next section.

5.1   New Media in the Portal

The presentation of portal pages is strongly dependent on the media type associated with the client browser. On the basis of the media type, the portal selects what portlets can be shown and it finds out the templates to use with such portlets. For example, a portlet could not be suitable for mobile devices, or it could use different templates for desktop computers and PDAs.

All portal elements (portlets, media types, clients, etc.) are stored in local XML registry files. Jetspeed associates the client browser with a media type after analyzing the browser description in the registry. For this reason, we changed the portal registry with the descriptions of three browsers supporting X+V and/or SALT. We have then added two media types, called X+V and SALT, to the registry, and we linked browsers descriptions with the corresponding media types. At this point, it is possible to build the portal for the new media types, creating portal pages and portlets with fragments of X+V or SALT markup in their templates.

5.2   Testing

As a matter of facts, neither X+V nor SALT, are widely accepted standards and they are not supported by everyday browsers. For example, in order to test SALT with Internet Explorer, it is necessary to download the Microsoft Speech Application Software Development Kit, that requires a previous installation of Internet Information Services and of the .NET Framework. We decided to test the portal with three products available free of charge and based on browsers used by a large community:

- Opera Beta 8: it is the first version of a widely used browser that comes with the support for vocal interaction. The support is activated downloading an add-on that enables X+V management.
- Access NetFront for Pocket PC: this version of NetFront supports X+V markup, and it is the result of a partnership between Access and IBM. Thanks to this browser, we succeeded in testing vocal portal navigation from a mobile device.
- OpenSALT: this open source project makes available a SALT compliant browser based on Mozilla.

We have tested the new media added to Jetspeed by including in all portal pages a set of testing portlets. These portlets have been built from the examples provided by the three browsers', developers and by X+V and SALT specifications. The new portlets enable vocal interaction with users: a user fills the fields of a form using its voice, and the portlet can answer with instructions or comments. A portal screen with vocal portlets is shown in figure 2. All tests have been positive, the portal preserves the original behaviour of the examples, and, above all, the results of the interaction (e.g.: the contents of a form) are available from the portlet classes. In this way it is possible to develop complex portlet applications based on the vocal interaction between user and portal.

Fig. 2. Portal screen with sample multimodal portlets

6   Conclusions and Future Work

In this paper we presented two approaches for providing a portal engine with the capability to communicate and to receive inputs using voice. This vocal interaction is a first, significant, step to reach a more complete multimodal interaction. We believe that the introduction of multimodality will play a significant role in the future of human computer interaction, mainly for two reasons: the growing request of innovative interfaces for mobile devices and the need of different interaction paradigms for the navigation of impaired Internet users.

We focused our research on portal engines, rather than on more generic Web sites, because of their capability of integrating heterogeneous applications and contents, without the need for users to explore manually several, different sites, and thus facilitating the navigation for both mobile and impaired users. Moreover, portal contents are easily adapted to mobile devices, and the interaction with users can be tailored on the basis of user profiling functionalities that portals normally provide.

The two approaches that we followed for enabling the vocal interaction are complementary, and each of them has advantages and drawbacks. The first approach generates an audio stream on the server and sends it to the client, so that the vocal interaction is possible only from the portal to the user. This process drains server resources and bandwidth, but our tests demonstrated that a synthesizer like FreeTTS can grant good performances also with several users connected. The main advantage of this approach is that it does not require a dedicated client, it works with every browser that can receive audio streams. The second approach is based on markup languages designed for client-side vocal interaction: it is the best way to enable a bidirectional vocal communication between portal and user, and it does not employ extra server resources or bandwidth. The drawbacks lie in the need of dedicated, uncommon browsers and in the higher computational power required to the client devices. Taking into account advantages and drawbacks, we believe that both approaches can coexist in the same portal: the user selects his preferred method, according to the characteristics of the client device and of the connection.

Our future research includes the extension of this work to the EMMA language, as soon as EMMA-enabled browsers would be available. We also intend to provide portal users with other interaction modalities, e.g., pen input and gesture recognition. Moreover, we want to include in the portal engine some tools that can facilitate the multimodal interaction, e.g., an enhanced user profiling system and an improved procedure for adapting contents and interface to mobile devices. Finally, we are planning to port all our work to the new released Jetspeed 2 portal. Jetspeed 2 is compliant with JSR (Java Specification Request) 168, a standard that has enabled interoperability between portal servers and portlets (JSR 168, 2003). In this way, most of our work won't be hooked on Jetspeed, but it will be available to all portals that follow the JSR 168 specification.

Acknowledgements

This work is partially supported by MIUR (Ministero dell'Istruzione, dell'Università e della Ricerca) through the FIRB WEB-MINDS project.

References

UMTS Forum Home Page. Available from http://www.umts-forum.org

Multimodal Interaction Activity Home Page from http://www.w3.org/2002/mmi/

EMMA Working Draft Home Page. Available from http://www.w3.org/TR/emma/

X+V Specification. Available from http://www.voicexml.org/specs/multimodal/x+v/12/

SALT Forum Home Page. Available from http://www.saltforum.org/

Cohen, P.R.: The Role of Natural Language in a Multimodal Interface. In: Proc.of the 5th annual ACM symposium on User interface software and technology pp. 143–149, Monteray, California, United States (1992)

Sharma, R., Pavlovic, V.I., Huang, T.S.: Toward Multimodal Human-Computer Interface. Proc. IEEE special issue on Multimedia Signal Processing 86(5), 853–859 (1998)

Baber, C., Mellor, B.: Using Critical Path Analysis to Model Multimodal Human-Computer Interaction. Int. Journal Human-Computer Studies 54, 613–636 (2001)

Moran, D.B., Cheyer, A.J., Julia, L.E., Martin, D.L., Park, S.:: Multimodal User Interfaces in the Open Agent Architecture. In: Proc. of the 1997 International Conference on Intelligent User Interfaces (IUI97), pp. 61–68 (1997)

Wahlster, W., Reithinger, N., Blocher, A.: SmartKom: Towards Multimodal Dialogues with Anthropomorphic Interface Agents. In: Proc. of International Status Conference, Human Computer Interaction, pp. 23–34 (2001)

Lisetti, C., Nasoz, F., LeRouge, C., Ozyer, O., Alvarez, K.: Developing Multimodal Intelligent Affective Interfaces for Tele-Home Health Care. Int. Journal Human-Computer Studies 59, 245–255 (2003)

Bellik, Y.: Multimodal Text Editor Interface Including Speech for the Blind. Speech Communication 23 (1997)

Mari, M., Poggi, A.: A Transcoding Based Approach for Multi-Device Portal Contents Adaptation. In: Proc. WWW/Internet 2004 (IADIS International Conference 2004), pp. 107–114, Madrid, Spain (2004)

Dybkjaer, L., Bernsen, N.O., Minker, W.: Evaluation and Usability of Multimodal Spoken Language Dialogue Systems. Speech Communication 43, 33–54 (2004)

Walker, M.A., Whittaker, S.J., Stent, A., Maloor, P., Moore, J., Johnston, M., Vasireddy, G.: Generation and Evaluation of User Tailored Responses in Multimodal Dialogue. Cognitive Sciences 28, 811–840 (2004)

Apache Jetspeed 1 Home Page. Available from http://portals.apache.org/jetspeed-1/

I-Mode Home Page. Available from http://www.nttdocomo.com/corebiz/imode/index.html

FreeTTS Home Page. Available from http://freetts.sourceforge.net/docs/index.php

Flite Home Page. Available from http://www.speech.cs.cmu.edu/flite/

JSAPI Home Page. Available from http://java.sun.com/products/java-media/speech/

Apache Turbine Home Page. Available from http://jakarta.apache.org/turbine/

Apache Velocity Home Page. Available from http://jakarta.apache.org/velocity/

Opera Browser Home Page. Available from http://www.opera.com

Access NetFront Home Page. Available from http://www.access.co.jp/english/

OpenSALT Home Page. Available from http://hap.speech.cs.cmu.edu/salt/

JSR 168 Specification. Available from (2003), http://www.jcp.org/en/jsr/detail?id=168

M-FIRE: A Metaphor-Based Framework for Information Representation and Exploration

Matteo Golfarelli, Andrea Proli, and Stefano Rizzi

DEIS, University of Bologna
Via Risorgimento 2, Bologna, Italy
{mgolfarelli,aproli,srizzi}@deis.unibo.it

Abstract. An open problem in the construction of an environment for visualizing and navigating information in the context of the Semantic Web is to guarantee a satisfactory compromise between expressivity and domain-independence. In this paper we first introduce M-FIRE, a configurable framework for instantiating visualization and navigation systems based on the adoption of custom metaphors: metaphors drive the process for obtaining a visual representation of a given piece of information and define how queries are generated upon user actions. Then, the paper describes in detail how presentation is achieved. The possible applications for our framework range from semantic browsing to ontology-enabled Web site design.

Keywords: Ontology, visualization, navigation, metaphor, RDF.

1 Introduction

The Semantic Web vision is built upon the ability of formally defining and processing the semantics of knowledge. Knowledge definition languages of increasing expressivity, allowing for increasingly sophisticated (and computationally complex) reasoning, have been developed by the W3C organization: they are structured as a layered tower of languages, where each layer builds on the lower one as its *semantic extension* (W3C, 2004). At the bottom of the tower is RDF, which allows for the assertion of *statements* about *resources* and their *properties*.

Since expressive languages like RDF Schema (RDFS) and OWL are semantic extensions of RDF, RDFS and OWL documents share the same syntax and structure of RDF documents. Though the syntax of RDF is designed to be human-readable, most end-users are not familiar with it, and (most important) neither they are with the semantics of abstract concepts like 'restriction', 'specialization', 'cardinality', and so on: because of this, they should be provided with tools that (1) translate low-level statements into easy-to-interpret visual renderings and (2) translate user actions performed on those visual renderings into low-level queries over the underlying knowledge base.

An open problem in the field of visualization and navigation of RDF documents is to guarantee a satisfactory compromise between expressivity and domain-independence. The former is meant as the capability of delivering an intuitive representation of knowledge and some tailored navigation primitives to end-users working in a given application domain, while the latter is aimed at accomplishing a high degree of reusability.

J. Filipe, J. Cordeiro, and V. Pedrosa (Eds.): WEBIST 2005/2006, LNBIP 1, pp. 214–227, 2007.

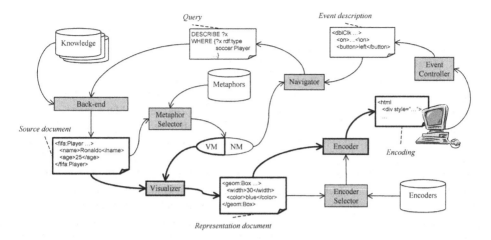

Fig. 1. Overall functional architecture of M-FIRE

Most existing tools favor domain-independence, and represent entities in a way that is closer to the abstract form used to formally define them: in fact, they adopt visual items to represent things – such as classes, properties, specializations, and instantiation relationships – that are familiar to knowledge engineers (a narrow category of end-users) but not to domain experts. Indeed, though domain-specific formalisms have a lower degree of reusability, they provide graphically richer constructs allowing for a representation that is closer to how entities appear in the application domain.

An approach to address this issue is to decouple the mechanism for transforming RDF documents into an expressive representation from the criteria that drive the representation itself. In this paper, we present M-FIRE, an original, configurable framework for easily instantiating visualization and navigation systems for RDF-based knowledge, relying on the adoption of custom *metaphors*. Metaphors drive the process through which visual representations are obtained for a given document, and define how queries are generated upon user actions. This allows users to perform semantic browsing by relying on intuitive concept representations and to interact in a simple manner with complex knowledge.

The overall functional architecture of our framework is sketched in Figure 1. First of all, we postulate the existence of a *back-end* module that, given a query in a supported query language, returns a result as an RDF document (from now on, the *source document*). The *metaphor selector* component takes the source document and returns the best suited metaphor for its visualization (*visualization metaphor*, VM in Figure 1) and navigation (*navigation metaphor*, NM in Figure 1); many criteria could drive this choice, for instance the vocabulary of the source document. The chosen visualization metaphor is then given as input to the *visualizer* module, which applies the directives contained in the visualization metaphor to generate a *representation document* for the source document; the representation document describes the visualization to be produced in an abstract form, independently of any implementation detail. Then, a properly chosen *encoder* translates the representation document into a concrete form, called *encoding* (e.g., an HTML document), which can be given as input to the end-user's visualization program (e.g., a Web browser). The choice of the best suited encoder for a given representation document is carried out by the *encoder selector* and could depend, again, on different decision criteria. The reason for this two-layer visualization architecture (visualization followed by encoding) is to obtain flexibility and independence with respect to any visualization device, program, and language.

Once rendering has been completed by the visualization program, end-users are allowed to interact with the produced visualization. Events generated by user actions are captured by the *event controller*, which creates an *event description* in the form of an OWL document describing the occurred event (for instance, a user's double click on an icon representing a soccer player). The event description is then given as input to the *navigator* module together with the chosen navigation metaphor. In the same way as the visualization metaphor tells the visualizer which representation must be produced for a given RDF document, the navigation metaphor tells the navigator which query must be formulated for a given event. The resulting query is then forwarded to the back-end, and the process is repeated.

In this paper we focus on presentation, meant as the process through which an encoding is generated starting from the source document returned by the back-end. Such path is tracked in Figure 1 by means of thick lines.

2   Related Work

Several general-purpose tools currently exist, that highlight the semantics of a few basic terms from the RDF(S) or OWL vocabulary only (e.g., instances of rdfs:subClassOf, instances of rdfs:Class, and so on) and allow users to perform simple navigation actions, mainly resulting in graph node expansion. This is a reasonable limitation if we consider that those formalisms are intended to give a presentation for a wide range of RDF-based documents, no matter what their application domain is. However, they fail in offering end-users intuitive representations of the described objects and concepts, thus missing the main goal of our approach. The front-ends of well-known ontology management systems such as KAON (Volz et al., 2003), Spectacle (Harmelen et al., 2001), Ontolingua (Farquhar et al., 1995), Ontosaurus (Swartout et al., 1996), Ontorama (Furnas, 1986), and WebOnto (Domingue et al., 1999) all fall into this category; the same also applies to Protégé plug-ins for ontology visualization and navigation, except for Jambalaya (Storey et al., 2001).

Jambalaya is a significant step toward the development of a highly configurable tool, in that a visualization for the semantics of a given piece of information is generated according to user-specified parameters. In Jambalaya, graphical containment is used, by default, to encode the semantics of both sub-classing and instantiation, but users are allowed to modify this behavior by associating whatever property they prefer to the graphical containment drawing primitive. Our approach generalizes the one of Jambalaya one by allowing any kind of semantic structure to be rendered by any kind of graphical structure.

In the context of the W3C's IsaViz visual environment for browsing and authoring RDF documents[1], a language called Graph Stylesheets (GSS) is defined as a way to associate style to node-edge representations of RDF graphs and to offer alternative layouts for some elements. Actually, with respect to our approach, GSS plays three roles at the same time: it resembles representation metaphors because it allows to associate graphical styles to some semantic patterns; it can also be seen as a representation language, since it defines a vocabulary of graphical styles interpreted by a rendering engine; last, it can be classified as an encoding language because it directly feeds a visualization program (the IsaViz tool). Our approach aims at disambiguating this multifold nature by introducing a clean separation of each aspect, and generalizes GSS in that representations are not limited to graph-based drawing primitives.

FRESNEL[2] is a simple vocabulary for specifying which parts of an RDF graph are displayed and how they are styled using existing style languages like CSS. There are analogies between M-FIRE and FRESNEL, but also significant differences. First, the representation paradigm of FRESNEL is centered on *resources*, while the one of M-FIRE is centered on *statements*: this means that in FRESNEL representations are generated for individuals, while in M-FIRE representations are associated to (sets of) RDF triples. The approach based on statements is more general, because the representation of an existing resource X can always be obtained as the representation of the statement X rdf:type rdf:Resource, while representing an arbitrary statement in the resource-based approach requires reification. Moreover, M-FIRE allows the same graphical drawing to be the representation of more than one statement: for instance, a picture may represent both the fact that a person is a soccer player and the fact that he plays in a particular soccer team. Besides, in M-FIRE navigation metaphors are independent from representation, while the two aspects are not well separated in FRESNEL. Finally, FRESNEL comes with a built-in vocabulary for formatting displayed information in a browser-independent way, while M-FIRE, as a pure framework, does not commit to any graphical vocabulary and relies on the existence of a proper encoder capable of translating the produced representation into the chosen format.

3 Visualization

We now provide a simplified definition of an RDF document which is useful for our purpose of detailing how the framework works.

Definition 1 (RDF document). *A* statement *is a triple* $\langle subj, pred, obj \rangle$ *where the* subject $subj$ *is a* resource *identified by a* URI *(Berners-Lee et al., 1998), the* predicate $pred$ *is a* property *identified by a URI too, and the* object obj *is either a* resource *or* literal *(e.g. a string). An* RDF document d *is a set of statements, and its* vocabulary, *denoted by* $Voc(d)$, *is the union of the set of the URIs and literals appearing as the subject, object, or predicate of its statements.*

Visualization is the process of obtaining a representation document in which certain graphical drawings are associated to certain (kinds of) statements belonging to the

---

[1] http://www.w3.org/2001/11/IsaViz/

[2] http://www.w3.org/2005/04/fresnel-info/

source document, according to the directives contained in a visualization metaphor. In other words, disjoint subsets of the source document d_s are defined such that statements in the same subset are represented by instantiating the same type of representation. The problem of classifying statements in d_s raises expressiveness and tractability issues concerning the complexity of queries which can be formulated to select them.

In order to provide a very general solution, visualization in M-FIRE is conceived as a two-step process. Although statement selection is performed through conjunctive queries over RDF triples by relying on a structural pattern matching engine without any reasoning capability (see Subsection 3.2), we allow for a sort of preprocessing step, called *enrichment* and described in Subsection 3.1, during which the source document is augmented with new concept definitions of arbitrary complexity; reasoning w.r.t. such concept definitions allows to infer useful classifications for existing resources in d_s, which are then exploited to formulate expressive statement selections.

Thus, the visualizer module shown in Figure 1 actually consists of two separate modules: the *enricher*, which augments the source document with new classifications and concept definitions for obtaining an *enriched document*, and the *representer*, carrying out the association of particular visual items and graphical styles to certain kinds of statements in the enriched document, in order to produce the representation document (an RDF document describing the drawing that must be presented to the end-user). Both the new concept definitions and the styling instructions come from the metaphor: indeed, parallel to the above separation, visualization metaphors are divided into two components, namely the *enrichment metaphor*, which drives the transformation of the source document into the enriched document, and the *representation metaphor*, which drives the production of a representation document for the enriched document. The vocabulary of the representation document is called the *representation vocabulary* and is not bound to any predefined set of URIs (this will be further discussed in Section 4).

3.1   Enrichment

An enrichment metaphor em is a pair $\langle o_{em}, r_{em} \rangle$, where o_{em} is an OWL document containing concept definitions and r_{em} is a compatible reasoner providing classification services. Ontology o_{em} can only contain concept definitions of the form $A = C$, where A is a concept name and C is a complex concept defined through concept constructors provided by the language that r_{em} supports.[3] The enricher merges o_{em} to the source document and lets r_{em} add new classifications to produce the enriched document d_e.

Example 1. Let d_s be the source document in Figure 2(a), and let o_{em} be the OWL ontology in Figure 2(b). If r_{em} is an OWL-DL reasoner, then the enriched document d_e will include both statements in $(d_s \cup o_{em})$ and $\langle$soccer:ply01 rdf:type soccer: Goalscorer$\rangle$.   □

As previously discussed, visualization is split into two phases because the query language used to select those statements for which a certain representation must be drawn

---

[3] This limitation is necessary to enable query unfolding during navigation, which is out of the scope of this paper.

(a)
soccer:ply01 rdf:type soccer:Player, soccer:ply01 soccer:hasName "Zlatan Ibrahimovic"
soccer:ply01 soccer:playsIn soccer:juve, soccer:juve soccer:hasNation soccer:cty07
soccer:ply01 soccer:hasNation soccer:cty15, soccer:cty15 soccer:hasFlag "Sweden.bmp"
soccer:cty07 soccer:hasFlag "Italy.bmp", soccer:ply01 soccer:hasScored soccer:goal15A4

(b)
soccer:Goalscorer rdf:type owl:Restriction
soccer:Goalscorer owl:onProperty soccer:hasScored
soccer:Goalscorer owl:minCardinality 1

Fig. 2. Sample source document from the soccer domain (a) and enrichment ontology for the same domain (b)

might have limited expressiveness. Our implementation of the representer module is based on SPARQL[4]; as a plain RDF query language, SPARQL does not support any kind of non-trivial reasoning. Should SPARQL interpreters have a built-in support for reasoning with (suppose) OWL-DL vocabulary, enrichment could be unnecessary, as implicit classification could be inferred by the reasoner.

Besides, moving the reasoning step out of the representation process into the enrichment phase enables the support of new languages (or new reasoners) by simply defining different metaphors. Thus, a crisp separation between enrichment and representation gives metaphor designers a better control over the kind of inferences and classifications that are performed, also increasing the flexibility and the modularity of the design.

3.2 Representation

Representation is the process of associating proper graphical structures to certain semantic structures, and is carried out by the representer. More precisely, the representer produces a representation document for the enriched document d_e, where sets of resources in the former represent single statements in the latter, by interpreting the directives contained into the representation metaphor. A representation metaphor is a pair $rm = \langle R, F \rangle$, where R is a set of *representation rules*, and F is a set of *fusion rules*. In order to provide a formal account for the semantics of representation and fusion rules, we need some auxiliary definitions that recall the usage of graph patterns and templates in SPARQL. Due to space limitations, however, we present the syntax for expressing rules through illustrative examples instead of providing the rigorous grammar definition.

Definition 2 (RDF Document Pattern). *A statement pattern is a statement where variable names can appear instead of URIs and literals as the subject, the object, and the predicate. The set of variable names appearing in a statement pattern sp is denoted by $Var(sp)$. An RDF document pattern dp is a set of statement patterns, and we define $Var(dp) = \bigcup_{sp_i \in dp} Var(sp_i)$. Given an RDF document pattern dp and an RDF document d, we say that d matches dp iff there exists at least one $d' \subseteq d$ and a mapping $\beta : Var(dp) \rightarrow Voc(d')$ such that d' is obtained from dp by replacing each variable name $v \in Var(dp)$ with $\beta(v)$. Mapping β is called a binding, and d' is a solution for dp in d.*

Definition 3 (RDF Document Template). *A statement template is a statement pattern where new names used as* resource templates *can appear in place of URIs and variable*

---

[4] http://www.w3.org/TR/rdf-sparql-query/

(a)
REPRESENTATION RULE PlayerInItaly
FOR PATTERN { ?x rdf:type soccer:Player . ?x soccer:playsIn ?y .
?x misc:hasName ?z . }
WITH { #b rdf:type geom:Box . #b geom:hasColor "Blue" . #b geom:hasText ?z . }

(b)
REPRESENTATION RULE Nationality
FOR PATTERN { ?a misc:hasNation ?b . ?b misc:hasFlag ?c . }
?c misc:hasSourceFile ?d . }
WITH { #i rdf:type geom:Img . #i geom:hasSrc ?d . #i geom:nextTo #p . }

Fig. 3. Two sample representation rules for the soccer domain

(a)
geom:b1 rdf:type geom:Box
geom:b1 geom:hasColor "Blue"
geom:b1 geom:hasText "Zlatan Ibrahimovic"

(b)
geom:i1 rdf:type geom:Image
geom:i1 geom:hasSource "Sweden.bmp"
geom:i1 geom:nextTo geom:p1

Fig. 4. Partial representations generated by rules in Figure 3(a) and 3(b) when applied to Example 1

names as the subject and the object only. The set of resource templates appearing in a statement template st is denoted by $Tem(st)$. An RDF document template dt is a set of statement templates, and we define $Tem(dt) = \bigcup_{st_i \in dt} Tem(st_i)$. Given an RDF document template dt, an RDF document d is said to be an instance *of dt iff there exists a mapping $\tau : Tem(dt) \rightarrow U$, where U is the set of URIs contained in $Voc(d)$, such that d is obtained from dt by replacing each resource template $t \in Tem(dt)$ with $\tau(t)$. Mapping τ is called the* instantiation function *from dt to d.*

Intuitively, representation rules in R are used to create one *partial representation document* for each set of statements in d_e matching a particular document pattern, while fusion rules in F properly merge multiple such documents whenever a condition expressed over the sets of statements they represent is satisfied.

Definition 4 (Representation Rule). *A representation rule is a pair $r = \langle ss, rt \rangle$, where ss (statement selector) is a document pattern, and rt (representation template) is an RDF document template, with $Var(rt) \subseteq Var(ss)$.*

Example 2. With reference to the enriched document from Example 1, representation rule PlayerInItaly in Figure 3(a) defines the visualization of soccer players who play in an Italian team, while rule Nationality in Figure 3(b) defines a visualization for the nationality of a person, a team or anything else. The first rule generates, for each graph describing the fact that a soccer player with a certain name plays in an Italian team, an RDF document describing a blue box which contains his name; the second one represents the fact that a person (or a team) belongs to a nation which is symbolized by a flag, and whose picture is stored in a file, by generating a description where the picture of the flag is placed next to the person's representation. □

Clauses FOR PATTERN and WITH in Figure 3 denote, respectively, the statement selector and the representation template for a representation rule. Names beginning with '?' and '#' are, respectively, variables and resource templates.

The semantics of representation rules can be described by illustrating how the representer exploits them for generating partial representation documents. Iteratively, a representation rule r is extracted from R, and the set Z_r of solutions for $r.ss$ in the enriched document d_e is computed. For each solution $z \in Z_r$, there exists exactly one set of statements in d_e that matches $r.ss$. The binding that corresponds to z, say β_z, is then used to transform the representation template $r.rt$ into a matching RDF document template t_z by replacing each variable name $v \in Var(r.rt)$ with $\beta_z(v)$ (with reference to Example 2, statement ⟨#b geom:hasText ?y⟩ becomes ⟨#b geom:hasText "Zlatan Ibrahimovic"⟩). Thus, for every solution z, we obtain an RDF document template t_z. An instance is then created for all such t_z, where the images of the corresponding instantiation functions are pairwise disjoint (thus producing, e.g. geom:123 geom:hasText "Zlatan Ibrahimovic").

The procedure is repeated until all of the representation rules in R have been processed.

Example 3. The partial representation document shown in Figure 4(a) is generated by rule PlayerInItaly in Figure 3(a), and the partial representation document in Figure 4(b) is generated by rule Nationality in Figure 3(b), when applied to the enriched document obtained in Example 1. □

This way, for each representation rule $r \in R$, many partial representation documents are instantiated (one for each set of statements in d_e matching the statement selector of r). Once all $r \in R$ have been processed, fusion rules come into play.

Definition 5 (Fusion Rule). *A fusion rule is a triple $f = \langle S, fp, ft \rangle$, where the* fusion set *S is a multiset containing representation rules in R, fp is an RDF document pattern called the* fusion pattern, *and ft is an RDF document template called the* fusion template. *Variables in the fusion template must also appear in the fusion pattern: formally, $Var(ft) \subseteq Var(fp)$.*

The representer uses fusion rules to link partial representation documents, among those created by representation rules in S, whose represented sets of statements meet the join conditions expressed in the fusion pattern fp. A helpful analogy can be set up with relational algebra, where a join operator merges several tables (and the same table can be included multiple times with different roles in the FROM clause) much like a fusion rule merges the existing partial representation documents generated by a number of representation rules; the difference here is that applying fusion rules leads to the creation of new sets of statements linking the partial representation documents, whereas a join operation in relational algebra produces a mere concatenation of tuples, without new information being created. Representation rules in S thus correspond to the joined tables, and the partial representation documents generated by them correspond to the instances of those tables (tuples).

Fusion pattern fp (corresponding to the join predicate in our analogy with relational algebra) can refer variables used in the statement selectors of any representation rule in S, thus allowing to express a cross-representation condition, involving their represented statements, that must be satisfied in order to instantiate ft; similarly, fusion template ft can refer resource templates used in the representation templates of any representation rule in S, allowing to create a connection among the partial representation documents previously produced (see Example 4 below).

Example 4. The following fusion rule establishes an identity equivalence between the blue box generated by representation rule PlayerInItaly and the graphical placeholder

```
// d_s is the document to represent, vm is the visualization metaphor
// This function returns the final representation document
RDFDocument visualizer(d_s,vm) {
        RDFDocument d_e = enricher(d_s, vm.em);
        RDFDocument r = representer(d_e, vm.rm);
        return r;
}


// d_s is the source document, em is the enrichment metaphor
// This function returns the enriched document
RDFDocument enricher(d_s,em) {
        RDFDocument d_merge = merge(em.o_em, d_s)
        RDFDocument d_e = em.r_em.inferClassifications(d_merge);
        return d_e;
}


// d_e is the enriched document, rm is the representation metaphor
// This function returns the final representation document
RDFDocument representer(d_e,rm) {
        Set A = ∅; // Stores semantic annotations
        for each r ∈ rm.R { // Apply representation rules
                Set Z_r = match(d_e, r.ss); // Stores the matching solutions
                for each z ∈ Z_r { // A solution is a set of represented statements
                        Binding β_z = z.getBinding();
                        RDFDocument repr = β_z.bind(r.rt).instantiate();
                        // Associates a partial representation to the set of statements
                        // it represents, and to the rule it was generated by.
                        Annotation a = new Annotation(repr, z, r); A = A ∪ a;
                }
        }
        for each f ∈ rm.F { // Apply fusion rules
                for each ⟨a_1, ..., a_{|f.S|}⟩ ∈ A^{|f.S|} { // Assume a_i.rule = f.S_i
                        Set Z_f = match(∪_{i=1,...,|f.S|} a_i.solution, f.sp);
                        for each z ∈ Z_r { // Instantiate the fusion template
                                Binding β_z = z.getBinding();
                                RDFDocument repr = β_z.bind(f.ft).instantiate();
                                Annotation a = new Annotation(repr, z, f); A = A ∪ a;
                        }
                }
        }
        RDFDocument repr_final = ∅;
        for each a ∈ A { // Merge the created partial representations
                repr_final = merge(repr_final, a.representation);
        }
        return repr_final;
}
```

Fig. 5. The visualization algorithm

generated by the #p resource template in representation rule Nationality, *whenever their represented set of statements describe, respectively, the fact that a person is a soccer player in an Italian team, and the fact that the same person belongs to a certain nation. As a result, taking into account the semantics of the* owl:sameAs *property, the two graphical objects described by those resources are identified as one – so, practically, they are merged.*

```
FUSION RULE PlayerWithNationality
JOINS PlayerInItaly AS P, Nationality AS N
WHEN { P.?x mfire:sameAs N.?a . }
GENERATES { P.#b owl:sameAs N.#p . }
```

The above fusion rule specifies how to graphically link any two partial representations, generated by rules PlayerInItaly *and* Nationality, *that represent two corresponding sets of statements where the former describes a soccer player and the latter describes his nationality. The statement pattern* P.?x mfire:sameAs N.?x *is intended to ensure that, for two given partial representations obtained by the above representation rules, the fusion template is instantiated only if the resource that was bound to variable* ?x *during the generation of the former actually is the same resource that was bound to variable* ?a *during the generation of the latter. Identifiers* P.#b *and* N.#p *denote the resources that were generated, in the corresponding partial representations, as instances of resource templates* #b *and* #p, *respectively.*   □

In Example 4, clause JOINS denotes the fusion set S, clause WHEN defines the fusion pattern fp, and clause GENERATES defines the fusion template ft. From a high-level perspective, the application of fusion rules does not differ significantly from the application of representation rules: iteratively, a rule f is extraced from F and a corresponding set of $|f.S|$-ples is computed, such that the elements of each tuple are partial representation documents that were generated by rules in $f.S$, and that match the join condition expressed by $f.fp$. For every such tuple, the corresponding set of solutions and related bindings is found, and the RDF document template $f.ft$ is eventually instantiated.

Example 5. With reference to the partial representation documents obtained in Example 3, the application of the fusion rule PlayerWithNationality *in Example 4 yields to the generation of the following partial representation document, consisting of a single RDF statement:*

geom:b1 owl:sameAs geom:p1   □

Finally, after all fusion rules have been processed, partial representation documents created by representation and fusion rules are all merged together in order to obtain the final representation document. Figure 5 summarizes the overall visualization process by means of an illustrative algorithm.

4 Encoding

The encoding process is carried out by the encoder module, that is entitled to translate the representation document into a concrete form, i.e., a document that can be parsed by a proper program to produce a visualization.

In principle, many formats could be used to encode a drawing described in the representation document. Two colored circles connected by a dotted, directed edge could be encoded as both a GraphML[5] document and an SVG[6] document; a table containing names and photos could be encoded as an SVG document as well as an HTML document.

---

[5] http://graphml.graphdrawing.org/
[6] http://www.w3.org/Graphics/SVG/

The choice of the proper encoding can be carried out by considering many criteria, among which user preferences. As users of the Web usually retrieve information by means of a Web browser parsing HTML documents, an HTML encoder could be an option if the drawings described by the representation document can be rendered in HTML. Still, the main decision criterion is, of course, the content of the representation document: if the vocabulary contains instances of a class named geom:DottedArrow (from a fictive geom namespace) which designate edges connecting pairs of objects, it is preferable to drop HTML and to target a visualization program which is able to reproduce graph structures, thus choosing its corresponding encoding format (for instance, GraphML). The encoder selector module solves the aforementioned task: given a set of encoders, it extracts the most suited one according to user preferences, document representation content, and so on.

Formally, an encoder can be defined as a triple $e = \langle p, f, V \rangle$, where p is a program translating the input representation document into the final encoding, f is the target encoding format, and V is the *encoder vocabulary*, i.e. the set of class URIs for which the encoder is able to perform a translation into the target format. Let $E = \{\langle p_i, f_i, V_i \rangle\}_{i=1,...,n}$ be a set of available encoders, and let d_r be a given representation document. Then, a valid decision criterion would be to select the encoder for which the value $|Voc(r) \cap V_i|/|Voc(r)|$ is maximum, to have the broadest representation vocabulary coverage. Other methods could assign different weights to the URIs in the representation vocabulary, so that some drawing primitives are considered more important than others.

A crucial issue involving the encoding process is *semantic annotation*. Semantic annotation traces a mapping between the graphical items that are used to represent a given set of statements and the represented statements themselves. Such mapping is first established at a conceptual level by the representer (see the pseudo-code in Figure 5), by linking each partial representation document to the set of statements it represents. Annotations are then parsed by the encoder, which has the responsibility of embedding them into the encoding document. There, such information can be exploited by the end-user's visualization program to integrate graphical drawings with their semantics. Notably, an HTML encoder would be able to translate representation documents into automatically annotated (pieces of) Web pages.

5   Implementation

The architecture of our framework has been designed in order to maximize flexibility, reusability and extensibility. As to the visualization process, the framework provides an implementation for the enricher and the representer modules, but only defines the interface for the metaphor selector, the encoder and the encoder selector: visualization systems are instantiated by plugging custom implementations of these components into the framework.

We have built the presentation engine (see Figure 1) as a simple Java program taking as input an RDF document and forwarding it to the metaphor selector program. The metaphor selector returns the most suited visualization metaphor for the source

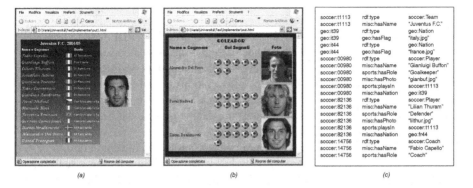

Fig. 6. Rendering of the HTML encoding of two representation documents obtained by applying different visualization metaphors to the same (RDFS) source document containing information about Juventus players, of which an excerpt is shown in (c). In (a), soccer teams are the focus of interest and they are rendered as a list of players (in this case, only Juventus appears); in (b), goalscorers are the relevant information to be highlighted and they are shown together with their score.

document, which is then given as input to the visualizer together with the source document itself. In our prototypical implementation, the metaphor selector does nothing more than presenting the user a list of metaphors, so the decision on which metaphor to apply is actually delegated to the end-user (though, this is neither a desirable nor a realistic behavior). The visualizer is in turn coded as two independent Java programs, implementing the routines listed in Figure 5.

Both the enricher and the representer rely on the Jena[7] library for generic processing of RDF documents; the enricher makes use of Pellet[8] for supporting OWL(-DL and -Lite) reasoning, while the representer module makes additional use of the ARQ[9] SPARQL engine provided by Jena; representation rules are executed by internally translating them into SPARQL queries with a CONSTRUCT clause, which are then parsed by the ARQ interpreter for instantiating the representation templates and generating the partial representation documents.

Since HTML is the standard format used for presenting information across the World Wide Web, we have chosen to implement an HTML encoder. Our HTML encoder is a Java program based on Jena; screenshots in Figure 6(a) and (b) depict the encoding of two representation documents, obtained by applying two different visualization metaphors to the same source document (partly) listed in Figure 6(c).

Since RDF documents can be conceptually understood as graphs, and most tools render them as such, we are currently working on the implementation of a GraphML encoder too.

---

[7] http://jena.sourceforge.net/
[8] http://www.mindswap.org/2003/pellet/
[9] http://jena.sourceforge.net/ARQ/

6   Conclusions

In this paper we presented M-FIRE, an original approach to RDF-based knowledge visualization and navigation where ad-hoc presentations of contents are generated according to different metaphors. We believe that the strength of M-FIRE lies in its ability to deliver expressive, domain-specific presentations to end-users without affecting reusability, which constitutes a significant advance over existing approaches. Navigation primitives are also expressed by metaphors and complete the framework by providing a unified approach to knowledge fruition.

As to the presentation process, we have shown that the architectural design of our framework enjoys a double degree of reusability and flexibility: during visualization, different metaphors could be applied to the same source document (flexibility), and the same metaphor could be applied to two different source documents (reusability); during encoding, different encoders could be used to translate the same representation document (flexibility), and the same encoder could be used to translate two different representation documents (reusability). Figures 6 and 7 provide an illustrative example of this potential.

 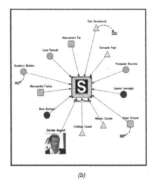 

(a)   (b)   (c)

Fig. 7. Rendering of two encodings, obtained by applying different visualization metaphors to the same (RDFS) source document (c) containing information about a volley team. In (a), the same visualization metaphor and encoder were used as in Figure 6(a). In (b), the applied visualization metaphor produced a representation document describing a graph, which was then processed by a GraphML encoder.

Regarding the creation of metaphors, defining representation and fusion rules is perhaps as difficult as writing a SPARQL query: transformations of source documents into representation documents are expressed by means of a declarative language which recalls the CONSTRUCT form of SPARQL queries. Nonetheless, the same visualization metaphor could be defined by different sets of rules, and the quality of design could have an impact on modularity, reusability, readability, and extendibility of the metaphor. We plan to develop a visual tool aimed at assisting metaphor designers in the definition of rules, as well as in building coherent visualization metaphors.

M-FIRE is a very general environment, aimed at supporting several different classes of applications. Among those, ontology browsing is probably the one which most promises to impact on the deployment of the Semantic Web. A key feature of ontology browsers is that of allowing users to switch between multiple fruition paradigms, either transparently or intentionally; this is accomplished in M-FIRE through metaphors and by plugging different metaphor selectors, that perform either automatic or manual selection of metaphors, into the framework. In case of manual selection, a desirable feature is that of proposing a list of valid metaphors, integrated with legends and previewing functionalities.

Another interesting field of application for M-FIRE, aimed at enhancing the potentiality of current Web technologies, is the support to the development of semantically annotated Web sites. In fact, M-FIRE would allow a domain-dependent translation of RDF documents into HTML encodings to be easily specified. We believe that this would push Web site owners to publish their content by (1) directly implementing knowledge bases on ontology-enabled repositories and (2) translating them into HTML documents whose elements are semantically annotated with the information they represent. Thus, for instance, it would be possible to drag an image from a Web browser and drop it into an ontology editor for exploring the formal description of the resource that image depicts. In general, semantic annotation will allow RDF-aware presentation programs to be integrated with other tools capable of handling the semantics of the underlying information, thus forming a rich environment for knowledge fruition and retrieval.

References

Berners-Lee, T., Fielding, R., Irvine, U., Masinter, L.: Uniform resource identifiers (URI): Generic syntax (1998), http://www.ietf.org/rfc/rfc2396.txt

Domingue, J., Motta, E., Garcia, O.: Knowledge Modelling in WebOnto and OCML: A User Guide. Knowledge Media Institute, Milton Keynes, UK (1999)

Farquhar, A., Fikes, R., Pratt, W., Rice, J.: Collaborative ontology construction for information integration (1995)

Furnas, G.W.: Generalized fisheye views. SIGCHI Bull. 17(4), 16–23 (1986)

Harmelen, F.V., et al.: Ontology-based information visualisation. In: Proc. Workshop on Visualisation of the Semantic Web, pp. 546–554 (2001)

Storey, M. et al.: Jambalaya: Interactive visualization to enhance ontology authoring and knowledge acquisition in Protégé. In: Proc. Workshop on Interactive Tools for Knowledge Capture, Victoria, Canada (2001)

Swartout, B., Patil, R., Knight, K., Russ, T.: Toward distributed use of large-scale ontologies. In: Proc. 10th Knowledge Acquisition Workshop, Banff, Canada (1996)

Volz, R., Oberle, D., Staab, S., Motik, B.: KAON SERVER - a semantic web management system. In: Proc. WWW, Budapest, Hungary (2003)

W3C, Rdf semantics (2004), http://www.w3.org/TR/rdf-mt/

Towards a Data Quality Model for Web Portals

Research in Progress

Angélica Caro[1], Coral Calero[2], Ismael Caballero[2], and Mario Piattini[2]

[1] Universidad del Bio Bio, Departamento de Auditoria e Informática,
La Castilla s/n, Chillán, Chile
mcaro@ubiobio.cl
[2] ALARCOS Research Group
Information Systems and Technologies Department, UCLM-Soluziona Research
and Development Institute
University of Castilla-La Mancha, Paseo de la Universidad, 4 – 13071 Ciudad Real, Spain
{Coral.Calero,Ismael.Caballero,Mario.Piattini}@uclm.es

Abstract. The technological advances and the use of the internet have favoured the appearance of a great diversity of web applications, among them Web Portals. Through them, organizations develop their businesses in a really competitive environment. A decisive factor for this competitiveness is the assurance of data quality. In the last years, several research works on Web Data Quality have been developed. However, there is a lack of specific proposals for web portals data quality. Our aim is to develop a data quality model for web portals focused -oin three aspects: data quality expectations of data consumer, the software functionality of web portals and the web data quality attributes recompiled from a literature review. In this paper, we will present the first version of our model.

Keywords: Data Quality, Information Quality, Web Portals.

1 Introduction

In the last years, a growing interest in the subject of Data Quality (DQ) or Information Quality (IQ) has been generated because of the increase of interconnectivity of data producers and data consumers mainly due to the development of the internet and web technologies. The DQ/IQ is often defined as "fitness for use", i.e., the ability of a data collection to meet user requirements (Strong, Lee et al., 1997; Cappiello, Francalanci et al., 2004). Data Quality is a multi-dimensional concept (Cappiello, Francalanci et al., 2004), and in the DQ/IQ literature several frameworks providing categories and dimensions as a way of facing DQ/IQ problems can be found.

Research on DQ/IQ started in the context of information systems (Strong, Lee et al., 1997; Lee, 2002) and it has been extended to contexts such as cooperative systems (Fugini, Mecella et al., 2002; Marchetti, Mecella et al., 2003; Winkler, 2004), data warehouses (Bouzeghoub and Kedad, 2001; Zhu and Buchmann, 2002) or electronic commerce (Aboelmeged, 2000; Katerattanakul and Siau, 2001), among others.

J. Filipe, J. Cordeiro, and V. Pedrosa (Eds.): WEBIST 2005/2006, LNBIP 1, pp. 228–237, 2007.

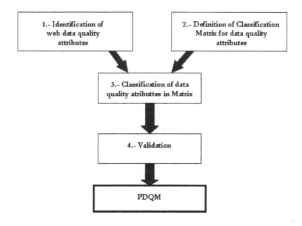

Fig. 1. Stages in the development our model

Due to the characteristics of web applications and their differences from the traditional information systems, the community of researchers has recently started to deal with the subject of DQ/IQ on the web (Gertz, Ozsu et al., 2004). However, there are not works on DQ/IQ specifically developed for web portals. As the literature shows that DQ/IQ is very dependent on the context, we have centred our work on the definition of a Data Quality Model for web portals. To do so, we have used some works developed for different contexts on the web but that can be partially applied or adapted to our particular context. For example, we have used the work of Yang et al., (2004) where a quality framework for web portals is proposed including data quality as a part of it.

As the concept of "fitness for use" is widely adopted in the literature (emphasizing the importance of taking into consideration the consumer viewpoint of quality), we have also considered, for the definition of our model, the data consumer viewpoint.

To produce our model, we defined a four-stage process, as set out in figure 1. In the first of these phases, we recompiled web data quality attributes from the literature and which we believe should therefore be applicable to web portals. In the second stage we built a matrix for the classification of the attributes obtained in stage 1. This matrix reflects two basic aspects considered in our model: the data consumer perspective (by means data quality expectations of data consumers on Internet) and the basic functionalities which a data consumer uses to interact with a Web portal.

Then in our third stage we used the matrix that has been produced, to analyse the applicability of each attribute of Web quality in a Web portal. Finally, in the fourth stage, we will validate our preliminary model, using surveys carried out on the data consumers of a given portal.

In this paper we describe the first version of our model, product of the three first stages of our methodology. The structure of this paper is as follows. In section 2, the components of our model are presented. In section 3, we will deeply describe the first version of our DQ/IQ Web Portal Model. Finally, in section 4 we will conclude with our general remarks and future work.

2 Model Components

Web Portals are emerging Internet-based applications that enable access to different sources (providers) through a single interface (Mahdavi, Shepherd et al., 2004). The primary objective of a portal software solution is to create a working environment where users can easily navigate in order to find the information they specifically need to perform their operational or strategic functions quickly as well as to make decisions (Collins, 2001), being responsibility of web portals' owners the achievement and maintenance of a high information quality state (Kopcso, Pipino et al., 2000).

In this section, we will present the three basic aspects considerate to define our DQ/IQ model for web portals: the DQ/IQ attributes defined in the web context, the data consumer expectations about data quality, and web portals functionalities.

2.1 Data Consumer Expectations

When data management is conceptualized as a production process (Strong, Lee et al., 1997), we can identify three important roles in this process: (1) data producers (who generate data), (2) data custodians (who provide and manage resources for processing and storing data), and (3) data consumers (who access and use data for their tasks).

As in the context of web-based information systems, roles (1) and (2) can be developed by the same entity (Gertz, Ozsu et al., 2004), for web portals context we identify two roles in the data management process: (1) data producers-custodians, and (2) data consumers.

So far, except for few works in DQ/IQ area, like (Wang and Strong, 1996; Strong, Lee et al., 1997; Burgess, Fiddian et al., 2004; Cappiello, Francalanci et al., 2004), most of the works on the subject have looked at quality from the data producer-custodian perspective. The data consumer's perspective of quality differs from this in two important ways (Burgess, Fiddian et al., 2004):

Data consumer has no control over the quality of available data.

The aim of consumers is to find data that match their personal needs, rather than provide data that meet the needs of others.

Our proposal of a DQ/IQ model for web portals considers the data quality expectations of data consumer because, at the end, it is the consumer who will judge whether a data is fitted for use or not (Wang and Strong, 1996).

We will use the quality expectations of the data consumer on the Internet, proposed in (Redman, 2001). These expectations are organized into six categories: Privacy, Content, Quality of values, Presentation, Improvement, and Commitment.

2.2 Web Portal Functionalities

A web portal is a system of data manufacturing where we can distinguish the two roles established in the previous subsection. Web portals present basic software functionalities to data consumer deploying their tasks and under our perspective, the consumer judges data by using the application functionalities. So, we used the web portal software functions that Collins proposes in (Collins, 2001) considering them as basics in our model. These functions are as follows: Data Points and Integration,

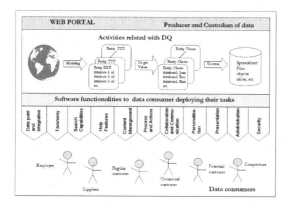

Fig. 2. Roles in web portals

Taxonomy, Search Capabilities, Help Features, Content Management, Process and Action, Collaboration and Communication, Personalization, Presentation, Administration, and Security. Behind these functions, the web portal encapsulates the producer-custodian role. Figure 2 illustrates this fact.

2.3 Web DQ Revision

By using a DQ/IQ framework, organizations are able to define a model for data, to identify relevant quality attributes, to analyze attributes within both current and future contexts, to provide a guide to improve DQ/IQ and to solve data quality problems (Kerr and Norris, 2004). In the literature, we have found some proposals oriented to DQ/IQ on the web.

Among them, we can highlight those showed in table 1. Related to such proposals, we can conclude that there is no agreement concerning either the set of attributes or, in several cases, their meaning. This situation, probably, is a consequence of the different domains and author's focus of the studied works.

However, from this revision we captured several data quality attributes. The most considered are (we present between brackets different terms used for the same concept): Accuracy (Accurate), in 60% of the works; Completeness, in 50% of the works and Timeliness (Timely), in 40% of the works; Concise (Concise representation), Consistent (Consistent representation), Currency (Current), Interpretability, Relevance, Secure (Security), in 30% of the studies. Accessibility (Accessible), Amount of data (Appropriate amount of information), Availability, Credibility, Objectivity, Reputation, Source Reliability, Traceability (Traceable), Value added are stated in 20% of the works.

Finally, Applicable, Clear, Comprehensive, Confidentiality, Content, Convenient, Correct, Customer Support, Degree of Duplicates, Degree of Granularity, Documentation, Understand ability (Ease of understanding), Expiration, Flexibility, Freshness, Importance, Information value, Maintainable, Novelty, Ontology, Pre-decision availability, Price,

Table 1. Summary of web DQ/IQ framework in the literature

Author	Domain	Framework structure
(Katerattanakul and Siau, 1999)	Personal web sites	4 categories and 7 constructors
(Naumann and Rolker, 2000)	Data integration	3 classes and 22 of quality criterion
(Aboelmeged, 2000)	e-commerce	7 stages to modelling DQ problems
(Katerattanakul and Siau, 2001)	e-commerce	4 categories associated with 3 categories of data user requirements.
(Pernici and Scannapieco, 2002)	Web information systems (data evolution)	4 categories, 7 activities of DQ design and architecture to DQ management.
(Fugini, Mecella et al., 2002)	e-service cooperative	8 dimensions
(Graefe, 2003)	Decision making	8 dimensions and 12 aspects related to (providers/consumers)
(Eppler, Algesheimer et al., 2003)	Web sites	4 dimensions and 16 attributes
(Gertz, Ozsu et al., 2004)	DQ on the web	5 dimensions
(Moustakis, Litos et al., 2004)	Web sites	5 categories and 10 sub-categories
(Melkas, 2004)	Organizational networks	6 stages to DQ analysis with several dimensions associated with each one
(Bouzeghoub and Peralta, 2004)	Data integration	2 factors and 4 metrics
(Yang, Cai et al., 2004)	Web information portals	2 dimensions

Reliability, Response time, Layout and design, Uniqueness, Validity, and Verifiability are only studied in 10 % of the works.

Summarizing the above-mentioned attributes, by means of similarity in their names and definitions, we have obtained a set of 28 attributes. Based on these DQ/IQ attributes we will try to identify which ones are applicable to the web portals context by classifying them into the matrix construed by the previous aspects (data consumer expectations x functionalities).

3   Relationships Between the Components of the Model

Based on the previous background, we will determine the relationship between the web portal functionalities and the quality expectations of data consumers. Then, we will present the definition of each function according to (Collins, 2001) and we will show their relationships (see figure 3).

Data Points and Integration. They provide the ability to access information from a wide range of internal and external information sources and display the resulting information at the single point-of-access desktop. The expectations applied to this functionality are: *Content* (Consumers need a description of portal areas covered, use of published data, etc.), *Presentation* (formats, language, and others are very important for easy interpretation) and *Improvement* (users want to participate with their opinions in the portal improvements knowing the result of applying them).

Taxonomy. It provides information context (including the organization-specific categories that reflect and support organization's business), we consider that the expectations of data consumer are: *Content* (consumers need a description of which data are published and how they should be used, easy-to-understand definitions of every important term, etc.), *Presentation* (formats and language in the taxonomy are very important for easy interpretation, users should expect to find instructions when reading the data), and *Improvement* (user should expect to convey his/her comments on data in the taxonomy and know the result of improvements).

Search Capabilities. It provides several services for web portal users and needs searches across the enterprise, World Wide Web, and search engine catalogs and indexes. The expectations applied to this functionality are: *Quality of values* (Data consumer should expect that the result of searches is correct, current and complete), *Presentation* (formats and language are important for consumers, for the search and for easy interpretation of results) and *Improvement* (consumer should expect to convey his/her comments on data in the taxonomy and know the result of improvements).

Help Features. They provide help when using the web portal. The expectations applied to this functionality are: *Presentation* (formats, language, and others are very important for easy interpretation of help texts) and *Commitment* (consumer should be easily able to ask and obtain answer to any question regarding the proper use or meaning of data, update schedules, etc.).

Content Management. This function supports content creation, authorization, and inclusion in (or exclusion from) web portal collections. The expectations applied to this functionality are: *Privacy* (it should exist privacy policy for all consumers to manage, to access sources and to guarantee web portals data), *Content* (consumers need a description of data collections, that all data needed for an intended use are provided, etc.), *Quality of values* (consumer should expect that all data values are correct, current and complete, unless otherwise stated), *Presentation* (formats and language should be appropriate for easy interpretation), *Improvement* (consumer should expect to convey his/her comments on contents and their management and know the result of the improvements) and *Commitment* (consumer should be easily able to ask and have any question regarding the proper use or meaning of data, update schedules, etc. answered).

Process and Action. This function enables the web portal user to initiate and participate in a business process of portal owner. The expectations applied to this functionality are: *Privacy* (Data consumer should expect that there is a privacy policy to manage the data about the business on the portal), *Content* (Consumers should expect to find descriptions about the data published for the processes and actions, appropriate and inappropriate uses, that all data needed for the process and actions are provided, etc.), *Quality of values* (that all data associated to this function are correct, current and complete, unless otherwise stated), *Presentation* (formats, language, and others are very important for properly interpret data), *Improvement* (consumer should expect to convey his/her comments on contents and their management and know the result of improvements) and *Commitment* (consumer should be easily able to ask and to obtain answer to any questions regarding the proper use or meaning of data in a process or action, etc.).

Collaboration and Communication. This function facilitates discussion, locating innovative ideas, and recognizing resourceful solutions. The expectations applied to this functionality are: *Privacy* (consumer should expect privacy policy for all consumers that participate in activities of this function), and *Commitment* (consumer should be easily able to ask and have any questions regarding the proper use or meaning of data for the collaboration and/or communication, etc., answered).

Personalization. This is a critical component to create a working environment that is organized and configured specifically to each user. The expectations applied to this functionality are: *Privacy* (consumer should expect privacy and security about their personalization data, profile, etc.), and *Quality of values* (data about user profile should be correct, current).

Presentation. It provides both the knowledge desktop and the visual experience to the web portal user that encapsulates all of the portal's functionality. The expectations applied to this functionality are: *Content* (the presentation of a web portal should include data about covered areas, appropriate and inappropriate uses, definitions, information about the sources, etc.), *Quality of values* (the data of this function should be correct, current and complete.), *Presentation* (formats, language, and others are very important for easy interpretation and appropriate use of portals data.) and *Improvement* (consumer should expect to convey his/her comments on contents and their management and know the result of the improvements).

Administration. This function provides service for deploying maintenance activities or tasks associated with the web portal system. The expectations applied to this functionality are: *Privacy* (Data consumers need security for data about the portal administration) and *Quality of values* (Data about tasks or activities of administration should be correct and complete).

Security. It provides a description of the levels of access that each user or groups of users are allowed for each portal application and software function included in the web portal. The expectations applied to this functionality are: *Privacy* (consumer need privacy policy about the data of the levels of access of data consumers.), *Quality of values* (data about the levels of access should be correct and current.) and *Presentation* (data about security should be in format and language for easy interpretation).

Fig. 3. Matrix stating the relationships between data consumer expectations and web portal functionalities

Table 2. Web Data Quality attributes applied to web portal functionalities in each category

Category of Data Consumer Expectations	Web portal functionalities related to each category	Web DQ/IQ attributes applying almost one functionality in each category
Privacy	Content management Process and actions Collaboration and Communication Personalization Administration Security	Security
Content	Data Points and Integration Taxonomy Content management Process and actions Presentation	Accessibility, Currency, Amount of data, Understandability, Relevance, Concise Representation, Validity, Traceability, Completeness, Reliability, Credibility, Timeliness, Availability, Documentation, Specialization, Interpretability, Easy to use
Quality of data	Data Points and Integration Search Capabilities Content management Process and actions Personalization Presentation Security	Accessibility, Currency, Amount of data, Credibility, Understandability, Accuracy, Expiration, Novelty, Relevance, Validity, Concise Representation, Completeness, Reliability, Availability, Documentation, Duplicity, Specialization, Interpretability, Objectivity, Relevance, Reputation, Traceability, Utility, Value-added, Easy to use
Presentation	Data Points and Integration Taxonomy Search Capabilities Help Features Content management Process and actions Collaboration and Communication Presentation Administration Security	Amount of data, Completeness, Understandability, Easy to use, Concise Representation, Consistent Representation, Validity, Relevance, Interpretability, User support, Availability, Specialization, Flexibility
Improvement	Data Points and Integration Taxonomy Search Capabilities Content management Process and actions Presentation	Accessibility, Reliability, Credibility, Understandability, User support, Traceability
Commitment	Help Features Content management Process and actions	Accessibility, Reliability, User support,

Concerning the relationships established in the matrix of figure 3, we can remark that Presentation is the category of data consumer expectation with more relations. This perfectly fits with the main goal of any web applications, which is to be useful and user-friendly for any kind of user.

The next step is to fill in each cell of the matrix with Web DQ/IQ attributes obtained from the study presented in 2.3. As a result of this, we have a subset of DQ/IQ attributes that can be used in a web portal to evaluate data quality. In table 2, we will show the most relevant attributes for each category of data consumer expectations.

To validate and complete this assignation we plan to work with portal data consumers through surveys and questionnaires. Once the validation is finished, we will reorganize the attributes obtaining the final version of our model.

4 Conclusions and Future Work

The great majority of works found in the literature show that data quality or information quality is very dependent on the context. The increase of the interest in the development of web applications has implied either the appearance of new proposals of frameworks, methodologies and evaluation methods of DQ/IQ or the adaptation of the already-existing ones from other contexts. However, in the web portal context, data quality frameworks do not exist In this paper, we have presented a proposal that combines three aspects: (1) a set of web data quality attributes resulting from a data quality literature survey that can be applicable and useful for a web portal, (2) the data quality expectations of data consumer on the Internet, and (3) the basic functionalities for a web portal. These aspects have been related by obtaining a first set of data quality attributes for the different data consumer expectations X functionalities.

Our future work, now in progress, consists of validating and refining this model. First of all, it is necessary to check these DQ/IQ attributes with data consumers in a web portal. We plan to make a questionnaire for each web portal functionality.

Then, once we have validated the model, we will define a framework including the necessary elements to evaluate a DQ/IQ in a web portal. Our aim is to obtain a flexible framework where the data consumer can select the attributes used to evaluate the quality of data in a web portal, depending on the existing functionalities and their personal data quality expectations.

Acknowledgements

This research is part of the following projects: CALIPO (TIC2003-07804-C05-03) supported by the Dirección General de Investigación of the Ministerio de Ciencia y Tecnología (Spain) and DIMENSIONS (PBC-05-012-1) supported by FEDER and by the "Consejería de Educación y Ciencia, Junta de Comunidades de Castilla-La Mancha" (Spain).

References

Aboelmeged, M.: A Soft System Perspective on Information Quality in Electronic Commerce. In: Proceeding of the Fifth Conference on Information Quality (2000)

Bouzeghoub, M., Kedad, Z.: Quality in Data Warehousing. In: Piattini, M., Calero, C., Genero, M. (eds.) Information and Database Quality, Kluwer Academic Publishers, Boston, MA (2001)

Bouzeghoub, M., Peralta, V.: A Framework for Analysis of data Freshness. In: International Workshop on Information Quality in Information Systems (IQIS2004), Paris, France, ACM, New York (2004)

Burgess, M., Fiddian, N., et al.: Quality Measures and The Information Consumer. In: IQ2004 (2004)

Cappiello, C., Francalanci, C., et al.: Data quality assessment from the user's perspective. In: International Workshop on Information Quality in Information Systems (IQIS2004), Paris, Francia, ACM, New York (2004)

Collins, H.: Corporate Portal Definition and Features. In: AMACOM (2001)

Eppler, M., Algesheimer, R., et al.: Quality Criteria of Content-Driven Websites and Their Influence on Customer Satisfaction and Loyalty: An Empirical Test of an Information Quality Framework. In: Proceeding of the Eighth International Conference on Information Quality (2003)

Fugini, M., Mecella, M., et al.: Data Quality in Cooperative Web Information Systems (2002)

Gertz, M., Ozsu, T., et al.: Report on the Dagstuhl Seminar "Data Quality on the Web". SIGMOD Record 33(1), 127–132 (2004)

Graefe, G.: Incredible Information on the Internet: Biased Information Provision and a Lack of Credibility as a Cause of Insufficient Information Quality. In: Proceeding of the Eighth International Conference on Information Quality (2003)

Katerattanakul, P., Siau, K.: Measuring Information Quality of Web Sites: Development of an Instrument. In: Proceeding of the 20th International Conference on Information System (1999)

Katerattanakul, P., Siau, K.: Information quality in internet commerce desing. In: Piattini, M., Calero, C., Genero, M. (eds.) Information and Database Quality, Kluwer Academic Publishers, Dordrecht (2001)

Kerr, K., Norris, T.: The Development of a Healthcare Data Quality Framework and Strategy. In: IQ2004 (2004)

Kopcso, D., Pipino, L., et al.: The Assesment of Web Site Quality. In: Proceeding of the Fifth International Conference on Information Quality (2000)

Lee, Y.: AIMQ: a methodology for information quality assessment. In: Information and Management, pp. 133–146. Elsevier Science, North-Holland, Amsterdam (2002)

Mahdavi, M., Shepherd, J., et al.: A Collaborative Approach for Caching Dynamic Data in Portal Applications. In: Proceedings of the fifteenth conference on Australian database (2004)

Marchetti, C., Mecella, M., et al.: Enabling Data Quality Notification in Cooperative Information Systems through a Web-service based Architecture. In: Proceeding of the Fourth International Conference on Web Information Systems Engineering (2003)

Melkas, H.: Analyzing Information Quality in Virtual service Networks with Qualitative Interview Data. In: Proceeding of the Ninth International Conference on Information Quality (2004)

Moustakis, V., Litos, C., et al.: Website Quality Assesment Criteria. In: Proceeding of the Ninth International Conference on Information Quality (2004)

Naumann, F., Rolker, C.: Assesment Methods for Information Quality Criteria. In: Proceeding of the Fifth International Conference on Information Quality (2000)

Pernici, B., Scannapieco, M.: Data Quality in Web Information Systems. In: Proceeding of the 21st International Conference on Conceptual Modeling (2002)

Redman, T.: Data Quality: The Field Guide. Digital Press (2001)

Strong, D., Lee, Y., et al.: Data Quality in Context. Communications of the ACM 40(5), 103–110 (1997)

Wang, R., Strong, D.: Beyond Accuracy: What Data Quality Means to Data Consumer. Journal of Management Information Systems 12(4), 5–33 (1996)

Winkler, W.: Methods for evaluating and creating data quality. Information Systems 29, 531–550 (2004)

Yang, Z., Cai, S., et al.: Development and validation of an instrument to measure user perceived service quality of information presenting Web portals. In: Information and Management, vol. 42, pp. 575–589. Elsevier Science, North-Holland, Amsterdam (2004)

Zhu, Y., Buchmann, A.: Evaluating and Selecting Web Sources as external Information Resources of a Data Warehouse. In: Proceeding of the 3rd International Conference on Web Information Systems Engineering (2002)

Domain Ontologies: A Database-Oriented Analysis

Stéphane Jean, Guy Pierra, and Yamine Ait-Ameur

Laboratory of Applied Computer Science (LISI)
National Engineering School for Mechanics and Aerotechnics (ENSMA) - Poitiers
86960 Futuroscope Cedex, France
{jean,pierra,yamine}@ensma.fr

Abstract. If the word ontology is more and more used in a number of domain, the capabilities and benefits of ontology for Information Systems management are still unclear. Therefore, the usage of ontology-based Information Systems in industry and services is not widespread. This paper analyses the concept of a domain ontology from a database perspective. As a result, firstly, we provide three criteria that distinguish domain ontology from other existing domain modeling approach which lead us to propose a new definition of domain ontologies. Secondly, based on the various approaches of ontology modeling followed by different communities, we propose a taxonomy of domain ontology. We show how they may be organized into a layered model, called the onion model, allowing to design and to use the capabilities of each category of ontology in an integrated environment. Finally, this paper presents several information systems based on ontology technologies and describe the kinds of services that should be provided to allow a powerful usage of ontology in data management.

Keywords: Ontology, Semantic Web, Ontology Based Information Systems, Semantic Integration, Data Exchange, PLIB.

1 Introduction

Defined by T. Gruber (Gruber, 1993) as an explicit specification of a conceptualization, an ontology may be considered as a quite new and exciting artefact in computer science allowing to represent explicitly meaning. Nowadays, the word ontology is used in a lot of diverse research fields including natural language processing, information retrieval, electronic commerce, Web Semantic, software component specification and information systems integration. In this context, several proposals for ontology models and languages and corresponding operational systems have been developed in the last decade. The growth of both the number and the diversity of such models for ontologies leads to some difficulties encountered by engineers when they need to identify the right ontology(ies) and the right ontology model(s) to use or to apply in practical engineering areas.

Due to the wide domain of usage, the meaning of the word ontology is of course context-dependent. Borrowed from philosophy, where it stand for "a systematic account of existence"[1], the term ontology got a quite new meaning in technical and

---

[1] FOLDOC: http://foldoc.org

J. Filipe, J. Cordeiro, and V. Pedrosa (Eds.): WEBIST 2005/2006, LNBIP 1, pp. 238–254, 2007.

computer science fields. In this new context, one may distinguish *upper-level* or *foundation ontologies*, the goal of which is to provide definition for general-purpose concepts, such that process, object or event, and to act as foundation for more specific domain ontologies (Niles and Pease, 2001; Gangemi et al., 2003), and *domain ontologies* that are tied to a specific universe of discourse and model the corresponding domain knowledge.

The goal of this paper is to analyse the concept of a domain ontology in a database perspective. Most of the usual definitions, such that the one of the Free On-line Dictionary of Computing "an explicit formal specification of how to represent the objects, concepts and other entities that are assumed to exist in some area of interest and the relationships that hold among them" are so broad that they covers most of the previous information modelling artefacts such that conceptual models, knowledge model or specification of information exchange formats. As a result the high potential of ontologies for semantic integration is hidden, and a number of engineers consider ontology as a buzzword.

In this paper, we suggest that the above definition should be refined and we propose three criteria to distinguish domain ontologies from other information modelling artefacts. Such domain ontologies introduce a new modelling level in the database field and we propose a taxonomy of the various possible domain ontologies together with integration scenarios that show how this taxonomy may be helpful for addressing various data management issues. Then we discuss what kind of tools, called Ontology-based Data Management System (OBDMS) would be useful for promoting ontology usage in the data processing community. It is expected that this analysis will promote the development of new OBDMS and help engineers and practitioners to choose relevant OBDMS in order to solve their business problems. Our work is different from previous related work (Cullot et al., 2003; Meersman, 2001) aiming at clarifying the differences between ontology and database technologies. The main contribution of this paper are the following:

- a proposal for criteria that distinguish domain ontologies from other domain modeling approaches;
- a new definition of domain ontology;
- a taxonomy of domain ontology and a layered model (the onion model) that shows how these different kinds of ontology may cooperate for solving data processing issues.

This paper is organized as follows. Next section presents the concept of an ontology by focussing on three criteria that distinguish ontology from other existing modeling approach. This suggest a new definition of domain ontologies. Section 3 describes the various possible usages of ontologies in data management. A database-oriented taxonomy of ontologies is proposed in section 4 and section 5 proposes an integrated view of these different kinds of domain ontology for addressing various data processing problems. Finally, section 6 describes several OBDMS and compares their capabilities.

2   Specificity of Domain Ontology as Domain Models

We propose in this section three criteria that characterize domain ontologies. These criteria suggest a new definition of domain ontology. Finally, we discuss the difference between domain ontologies and conceptual models.

2.1   Ontology Criteria

From our point of view, a domain ontology is a domain conceptualization obeying to the three following criteria.

1. **Formal.** An ontology is a conceptualization based on a formal theory which allows to check some level of consistency and to perform some level of automatic reasoning over the ontology-defined concepts and individuals. We note that this criterion excludes most meta-models that do not provide automatic reasoning capabilities.
2. **Consensual.** An ontology is a conceptualization agreed upon by a community larger than the members involved in one particular application development. For instance, The Gene Ontology (GO) project[2] is a collaborative effort between more than 10 organisms to address the need for consistent descriptions of gene products. Moreover, users are invited to submit suggestions for improving the GO ontologies. ISO 13584-compliant (PLIB) product ontologies follow a formal standardization process and are published as ISO or IEC international standards. We note that this criterion excludes most database, conceptual models which are just tailored for a particular database application.
3. **Capability to be referenced.** Each ontology-defined concept is associated with an identifier allowing to refer to this concept from any environment, independently of the particular ontology model where this concept was defined. We note that this criterion exclude, in particular, all specification of information exchange formats, such that STEP (Standard for the Exchange of Product Model Data) Application Protocols (ISO10303, 1994), where entities and attributes may only be referenced from the specified exchange structure.

2.2   A Proposed Definition for Domain Ontology

These three criteria lead us to propose a new definition for domain ontology. For us, a domain ontology is a *formal and consensual dictionary of categories and properties of entities of a domain and the relationships that hold among them.* By entity we mean being, i.e, anything that can be said to be in the domain. The term dictionary emphasizes that any entity of the ontology and any kind of domain relationship described in the domain ontology may be referenced directly, for any purpose and from any context, independently of other entities or relationships, by a symbol. This identification symbol may be either a language independent identifier, or a language-specific set of words. But, whatever be the symbol, and unlike in linguistic dictionary, this symbol denotes directly a domain entity or relationship, the *description* of which is formally *stated* providing for automatic reasoning and consistency checking.

---

[2] http://www.geneontology.org/

We show in the next section that the criteria used for characterizing domain ontologies allow to distinguish them with previous kind of concept modeling like conceptual models and knowledge models.

2.3   Ontologies vs. Conceptual Models

As both an ontology and a conceptual model define a conceptualization of a part of the world, an ontology seems similar to a conceptual model. Conceptual models respect the *formal* criterion. Indeed, a conceptual model is based on a rigorously formalized logical theory and reasoning is provided by view mechanisms. However, a conceptual model is application requirement driven: it *prescribes* and *imposes* which information will be represented in a particular application (logical model). Two different application systems having always at least slightly different application requirements, conceptual models are always different from systems to systems. Thus, conceptual models do not fulfill the *consensual* criterion. Moreover, an identifier of a conceptual model defined concept is a name that can only be referenced unambiguously inside the context of an information system based on this particular conceptual model. Thus, conceptual models also do not fulfill the *capability to be referenced* criterion.

In the same manner, a conceptualization defined in Knowledge Representation and Artificial Intelligence using logic constructors are not, in general, an ontology. Such conceptualizations satisfy the *formal* criterion. Indeed, logic is equipped with formal semantics that enables automatic reasoning. However, in such knowledge models, the main goals are the inference capabilities of the models. Before that the notion of an ontology emerged, neither mechanisms for referencing each particular concept of a knowledge model, nor processes for ensuring a consensus on the concepts were considered. Therefore, like conceptual models, such usual knowledge models do not fulfill the *consensual* and the *capability to be referenced* criterion.

However, data model constructs issued from database design and logic are suitable for ontology models definitions. Indeed, several ontology models, like OWL (Bechhofer et al., 2004), RDFS (Brickley and Guha, 2004) and KAON (Bozsak et al., 2002) for description logic and PLIB (Pierra, 2003), DOGMA (Jarrar and Meersman, 2002) and MADS (Parent et al., 1999) for database design, are based on constructors provided either by database conceptual models or by artificial intelligence knowledge base models. These models add other constructors that enable to satisfy the *consensual* criterion (context definition, multi instantiation, separation between concept definition and data structure prescription) and *the capability to be referenced* criterion (URI, GUI).

On the basis of this distinction between ontology and other concepts models, we study in next section what ontologies are good for.

3   What Are Ontologies Good For?

As stated in the introduction, ontology technologies is widespread in a lot of diverse application domains and it may be used in various engineering steps like specification, data exchange, data integration and search.

3.1   Specification

Two usages of ontologies as specification are reported.

The usage of a conceptualization as a specification is the basis of the Model-Driven Architecture (MDA). A model of the application is first defined. This model is then used to generate the code of the application. The existing formal link between the specification and the software enables to evolve the code when the specification evolves. Currently, several softwares addressing similar problems on the same domain are defined using different conceptualizations. This makes difficult interoperation between these softwares. Ontology usage is a solution to this problem. Because ontologies satisfy the *consensual* criterion, the various conceptualization corresponding to various domain softwares may be connected to a domain ontology. Then, softwares can interoperate using accessors provided by this ontology. This approach is called ontology-driven software engineering (Tetlow et al., 2005).

The same approach can be followed in database design. The proposition of Ontology-Based Database approach (Pierra et al., 2005) is to use an ontology as a first level of database concepts specification. This ontology is then specialized to define a conceptual model. Because all particular systems have particular requirements, different conceptual models may be built on the same consensual ontology. The link between ontologies, conceptual and logical models is kept inside a database. This architecture enables the evolution of both the conceptual model and of the ontology and provides a common access to information through the ontology. The advantage of this approach is to make clear what is common between two systems, and what is different.

3.2   Data Exchange

A consensual domain conceptualization that can be referenced may easily be used as an interchange format for data over this domain (ISO13584-42, 1998; Chawathe et al., 1994). Unlike usual exchange format that specify the complete structure of the exchanged data and where the meaning of each piece of data results from its place in the *global* structure, ontology-based exchange are very flexible. In such an exchange, the meaning of each piece of data may be defined *locally*, by referencing ontology identifiers. This allow quite different exchange structures to be soundly interpreted by the same receiving system.

3.3   Data Integration

Domain ontologies is the only artefact that allows to reconcile, at the semantics level, heterogenous data source models. When domain ontologies are explicitly represented in databases, the integration may be fully automated even when each source specializes locally the shared ontology (Bellatreche et al., 2004). In the Semantic Web approaches, the link between source and ontology is usually supported by metadata. The integration is often automatic because the ontologies used in this process capture and identify concepts in a formal and unique way.

In natural language processing, the link between sources and an ontology consists of the words contained in the documents. Most of the words having context-dependent meaning, the integration process is often user-assisted to provide meaningful results.

3.4 Data Access and Search

An ontology provides an access to data that reference the concepts it defines. Depending on the expressive power of the ontology model, data may be browsed using the is-a concept hierarchy, queried using keyword or with more sophisticated query languages.

Ontologies are also used to query databases. The approach consists in enriching the queries on the logical model by expressions involving ontology-defined concepts and expressions (Das et al., 2004).

To sum up, ontology applications are widespread. For a complete survey describing various usages of ontology, the interested reader can refer to (Uschold and Jasper, 1999). However all ontologies are not similar. Next section proposes a taxonomy of ontologies to highlight their differences and the consequences on their usage for the various application domains seen previously.

4 A Taxonomy of Domain Ontologies

Several orthogonal criteria need to be used to classify ontologies. The first major criterion is the manner of conceptualizing a domain. Indeed, a domain can be conceptualized as a set of words or as a set of concepts. This conceptualization way leads to the distinction between linguistic (taxonomic) ontologies and conceptual (descriptive) ontologies (Cullot et al., 2003; Pierra, 2003). Following (Pierra, 2003), we call Linguistic Ontologies (LO) those ontologies whose scope is the representation of the meaning of the words used in a particular Universe of Discourse, in a particular language. On the other hand, Conceptual Ontologies (CO) are those whose goal is the representation of the categories of objects and of the properties of objects available in some part of the world.

As these two kinds of ontology address quite different problems and fields, it is fundamental to clarify which kind of ontology is suited in each particular business context. Before presenting our taxonomy, let us review some fundamentals of ontologies.

4.1 Fundamentals of Ontologies

Concepts defined in a conceptual ontology can be classified in two categories.

- _Primitive concepts_ are those concepts "for which we are not able to give a complete axiomatic definition" (Gruber, 1993). Here, the definition relies on a textual documentation and a knowledge background shared between the readers. The set of primitive concepts define the border of the domain conceptualized by an ontology. Primitive concepts are the ground on which all other ontology concepts will be built. The definition of primitive concepts being always, at least partially, informal, the only quality criteria, one has for such definitions, is that they represent a consensus over some community. Without such a consensus one cannot asset the usability of an ontology.
- Besides primitive concepts, a number of ontology models focus on the capability to create conservative definitions (Gruber, 1993), i.e, to associate a new term or a new concept to something that is already defined by another mean in the ontology under design. This characteristic is the basis of inference mechanisms like automatic

classification. *Defined concepts* are those concepts for which the ontology provides a complete axiomatic definition by means of necessary and sufficient conditions expressed in terms of other concepts (either primitive concepts or other defined concepts).

When defined concepts are introduced, *concept equivalence* relation needs to be defined in order to be able to compare, classify or relate defined and/or primitive concepts.

Concept equivalence can be defined at the class level. This is the approach followed by models based on Description Logics (DL) like OWL (Bechhofer et al., 2004) or on the Carin language used in the PICSEL project (Rousset et al., 2002). For example, in PICSEL the concept of Hotel is defined as a specialization of the primitive concept HousingPlace. A HousingPlace is defined as a place having associated buildings, rooms and meal services. A hotel is then fully defined as those Housing Places which have more than five rooms and have only CollectiveBuilding.

Concept equivalence can also be expressed at the property level. This is the case in models where derivation functions can be defined. F-Logic (Kifer et al., 1995) is one of the models supporting this capability. For example, the property "boss" relating an employee to another employee can be derived from the properties "belong to" and "chair".

Thanks to the distinction between primitive concepts and defined concepts, we are now able to propose our database-oriented taxonomy of ontologies.

4.2   Canonical Conceptual Ontology (CCO)

In database design, when conceptual model is defined, ambiguity or possible multi-representation of the same fact is forbidden. The same approach is followed for performing exchanges between two different databases. It consists in defining a canonical vocabulary in which each information in the target domain is captured in an unique way without defining any synonymous constructs. For example, in the STEP project, exchange models are defined in the EXPRESS language as a STEP Application Protocol (AP). These canonic exchange models are used by industrial users to exchange product descriptions between different organizations.

Ontologies whose definitions follow this approach are called *Canonical Conceptual Ontologies*. In CCOs, each domain concept is described in a single way, using a single description that may include necessary condition. As a consequence, CCOs include *primitive concepts* only.

Defining CCOs is the main goal of the ontology model defined in the PLIB (Part Library) standard (ISO13584-42, 1998) with a first focus on representing and exchanging formal ontologies of technical domains. Such CCOs use a property-based characterization of the involved concepts. This means that a class is only created when it proves necessary for defining the domain of some properties. Therefore, in PLIB, the generalization/specialization concept hierarchies are rather "flat". An example of such an ontology for electronic components can be found in (IEC61360-4, 1999).

These examples show that usage of CCOs in the context of data exchange is fruitful. More arguments are given latter in this paper by studying an exchange scenario.

4.3   Non Canonical Conceptual Ontology (NCCO)

In database design, concept equivalence plays an important (but second-order) role. Each database addresses a particular domain and defines a canonic way of representing any fact about this domain. Then, in order to achieve a degree of independence with respect to the choice of the concepts offered to users, a database designer provides *views*. These *defined concepts* are specified using the CREATE VIEW operator on the basis of the primitive concepts that constitute the database schema. In deductive database this functionality also exists, provided with derived entities.

So, whatever the construct offered to express concept equivalence, we call *Non Canonical Conceptual Ontologies* those ontologies which contain not only primitives concepts but also defined concepts.

NCCOs are particulary useful when they are used as global query schemas. For example, in the PICSEL project mentioned earlier, primitive concepts of local CCOs are expressed as defined concepts for the primitive concepts of a global ontology used as global query schema. In the global ontology, concept expressions and rules expressed on basic concepts of the tourism domain (*HousingPlace, Flight . . .*) define a wide range of terms (*Hotel, Bed&Breakfast . . .*) useful for users to formulate a query on data referenced by local CCOs.

NCCO constructors are also very useful to define mappings between different ontologies. For example, figure 1 presents two CCOs of the domain of wines. The CCO (A) is property oriented while the CCO (B) is entity oriented.

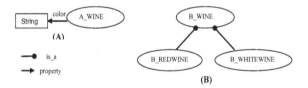

Fig. 1. Local Wine CCO

Applying some NCCO operators, issued from a DL syntax, we can write that:

$$B\_REDWINE \equiv A\_WINE \sqcap color : red$$

This axiom states that the concept of B_REDWINE defined in CCO (B) is equivalent to the concept A_WINE defined in CCO (A) restricted by the value of the color attribute. These primitives have formal semantics which enables a powerful reasoning mechanism implementation in tools named reasoners (e.g, RACER (Haarslev and Möller, 2001)). These tools support mechanisms for concepts and instances classification. As a result, the two local CCOs can be automatically merged into the NCCO of figure 2. This NCCO provides a global access to data of the two CCOs.

In this example, the reasoner has inferred that all instances of $B\_REDWINE$ are instances of A_WINE having the value *red* for the property *color*. When these facts are materialized, as it is proposed in OntoMerge (Dou et al., 2003), it become possible to split the merged ontology into the CCO (A) and the CCO (B) with the new inferred instances. This process shows that NCCO constructors are useful for integration tasks.

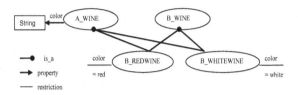

Fig. 2. Integrated Wine NCCO

4.4   Linguistic Ontologies

In other application domains like information retrieval or natural language processing, human languages play a key role. Even in database, natural languages are used in various places. Indeed, table and attribute names are chosen to reflect their meaning. Moreover, conceptual model documentation is largely, and in a number of cases completely, expressed in natural language.

We call Linguistic Ontology (LO) those ontologies that define words or contextual usages of words. In this kind of ontology only words relationships (synonym, hyponym, . . .) are available. Words relationships being highly contextual, machine inference in general needs expert supervision. Moreover, approximate relationships may be defined.

Wordnet (http://www.cogsci.princeton.edu/wn) is the most well-known representative of this category of ontologies. It provides with textual definitions, synonymous terms and representations for the various concepts that can be denoted by a term. They are intended to be used as a sophisticated thesauri.

LOs help to recognize conceptual similarities between sentences even if different terms are used. Since word meanings are contextual and their relationships are approximative, wrong similarities may be produced and results can never be considered as reliable. An example of LOs usage is given in (Das et al., 2004). A LO on types of cooking is used to retrieve more meaningful results on the food served in a restaurant. Thus, querying the 'latin american' served food retrieves tuples having 'american' or 'mexican' as value of type of cooking. A number of semi-automatic database integration approaches, e.g., (Visser et al., 1999), use such linguistic ontologies.

4.5   Discipline Specific View of Domain Ontology

Currently, the three categories of ontology mainly correspond to three different disciplines of computer science and have few connexions. Ontology models focus either on CCO, NCCO or LO design.

CCO are mainly considered in the data processing community. In CCOs, ontology descriptions focus on primitives concepts characterization and identification.

- They include precise and complex descriptions of the primitive concepts. These descriptions are provided using CCO oriented model constructs. For example, the DOGMA formalism (Jarrar and Meersman, 2002), a database inspired ontology model, provides contextual identification of concepts. In the PLIB model, primitive concepts can be associated with reference to real documents, pictures, usage restrictions .... This model also distinguishes the rigid properties

(Guarino and Welty, 2002), i.e., properties essential for any instance of a class from those that may or not hold or exist according to the role in which an entity is involved.
- They don't contain model mappings. Consequently, the encoding of such conversions is achieved in an application.

NCCO models were developed by artificial intelligence community. Therefore, they focus on inference and concept equivalence.

- NCCOs contains conservative definition of defined concepts using useful operators like boolean operators (union of classes ...).
- As a rule, they include less precise descriptions for the primitive concepts. For example, in OWL, a primitive concept description is limited to a label, a comment and the properties (roles) that can apply to its instances.

LOs were designed for computational linguistic. In LOs (e.g Wordnet), each word is associated with several synsets (sets of synonymous) that reflects its various meanings. The imprecision of the conceptualization is due to the following facts:

- words meaning depends upon a context;
- words relationships (e.g synonymy) have no formal definition whereas concepts relationships (e.g subsumption) have.

5   Relationship Between Ontology Categories and Proposal for a Layered Model

The previous observations lead us to identify some relationships between CCOs, NCCOs and LOs.

- Mappings between CCO might also be defined as equivalence operators of some NCCO;
- NCCO models can use powerful CCO-oriented model constructs to define their own primitive concepts;
- LOs might define the various meaning of each word of a particular language by reference to a NCCO. This reference would provide a basis for formal and exact reasoning and automatic translation of context-specific terms.

As a further step towards this observation, we first propose a layered model for domain ontology design. Then, we present an example of usage of this layered model.

5.1   A Layered Model for Ontology Design

An often used guide (Noy and McGuinness, 2001) proposes a seven steps approach for NCCO development.

1. Determine the domain and scope of the ontology to be developed.
2. Consider reusing existing available ontologies that someone else has developed.

3. List the important terms in the ontology without considering the possible concepts overlaps they may lead to.
4. Define the classes and the associated class hierarchy. From the list created in step 3, select the terms that describe objects having independent existence. These terms will be classes in the ontology and will become anchors in the class hierarchy.
5. Define the properties associated to classes. Indeed, most of the remaining terms are likely to be properties of these classes.
6. Define the constraints (cardinality, domain and range restrictions) that hold on properties.
7. Create instances of classes in the hierarchy.

This approach exploits the NCCO capability to define equivalent concepts and thus to integrate several ontologies addressing the same domain. Since we claim that NCCOs can benefit from being articulated with CCOs, we propose an alternative approach for the development of a NCCO starting from a CCO.

1. The first step of the design of an ontology should be to agree within a community on a CCO. To reach this agreement, it is required to:
   _ define clearly what is the domain covered by the ontology;
   _ choose a powerful model to define precisely the primitive concepts existing in the domain and allow to explicate the evaluation context of a property value (Pierra, 2003);
   _ provide a common understanding of a canonic set of concepts covering the domain. This conceptualization must accommodate a wide and diverse range of technical and business requirements shared by the members of the community. It must reach a wide recognition and acceptance.
2. Within the community of users and/or developers, on the basis of the defined CCO, a NCCO may be built for use by members of this community either to build their own view of the domain or to model formally all the concepts existing in the target domain that are associated with a usual linguistic denotation (word or sequence of words). Proceeding this way ensures the preservation of the capability to share and exchange information expressed in terms of the CCO.
3. In order to allow the use of the defined NCCO for linguistic inference and/or to provide an end-user friendly user interface in various languages, a list of language-specific terms needs to be defined and associated to each concept in the NCCO.

According to this alternative approach, figure 3 illustrates a layered model, called the onion model, of the resulting domain ontology. A CCO provides a formal basis to model and to exchange efficiently the knowledge of a domain. A NCCO provides mechanisms to relate different conceptualizations made on this domain. Finally, LO provides natural language representation of the concepts of this domain, possibly in the various languages where these concepts are meaningful.

5.2   An Exchange Scenario Based on Layered Domain Ontology

In database universe, each database uses a canonical vocabulary. Usually, each database uses a different canonical vocabulary. Instead of defining a NCCO covering all the

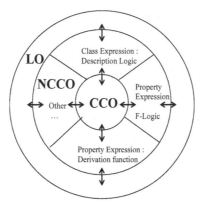

Fig. 3. The onion model of domain ontology

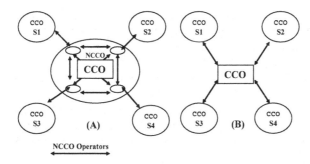

Fig. 4. Use of ontologies for canonic data exchange

terms of all the sources (see fig 4 (A)), the onion model suggests that all exchanges are performed using a consensual CCO. Each source just contains the descriptions of its own concepts in terms of the (primitive) concepts of the canonical conceptual ontology (see fig 4 (B)). This approach has been put into practice for databases integration in (Bellatreche et al., 2004). Notice that if each concept is represented differently in the n participating sources, and if there exists in each source a mean value of p concepts, solution (A) needs to implement $n * p$ mappings in each source, when solution (B) requires only p mappings in each source. Moreover, this approach also applies to virtual exchange, i.e, mediator (Wiederhold, 1991).

This clause, and the above show the interest of articulating the three categories of ontologies according to our onion model across the whole life cycle of domain ontologies.

- CCOs provide canonical and accurate descriptions of each concept of a given domain. It provides sound basis for exchange between different sources.
- NCCO operators are used to interact with other applications or sources that have already their own particular ontologies.
- LOs provide linguistic capabilities over primitive and defined concepts.

Next section discusses the various tools that would be useful to facilitate the use of ontologies in data management activity and compare with those currently existing.

6   Ontology Based Data Management System (OBDMS)

An OBDMS is a suite of tools providing support for using ontologies and ontology instances data. In data management, many different functionalities may be expected from an OBDMS. In this section we list a set of such functionalities and relate them to our taxonomy.

6.1   OBDMS Functionalities

An OBDMS may provide the following functionalities.

F1. Respect of standard. If a formal semantics is defined for some supported ontology model standard, this semantics shall be respected by the defined OBDMS.

F2. Handling of exchange format. When an exchange format is provided with an ontology model, import/export ontologies and ontologies instance data in this format are needed.

F3. Data manipulation. An OBDMS should provide support to insert, update or delete ontology concepts and instance data (support of CCO).

F4. Linguistic support. An OBDMS should support and exploit linguistic-oriented naming and description of concepts in various languages (support of LO).

F5. Data querying. An efficient way should be available for querying both ontologies and ontologies data.

F6. Ontology Mapping. An OBDMS should provide mapping functionalities to integrate different ontologies (support of NCCO operators).

F7. Ontology as a specification. An OBDMS should provide the possibility to extract from an ontology a specification of a software or of a database schema.

6.2   Comparison of Some OBDMS Implementations

The description of various useful capabilities needed to facilitate the use of ontologies in data management being completed, this section reviews three OBDMS according to the functionalities they offer.

6.2.1   RDF Tools

RDF Suite and Sesame are two suites of tools for RDFS storage and querying. A database is used for the persistence of the data. These two tools add constraints on the RDFS standard. They propose import/export module to manage data described in an RDF syntax. Third-party tools can be associated to this suite by using this module. Thus, an ontology editor (e.g. Protege) can be associated to these tools. However, this editor will not be synchronized with the storage system. Querying data in Sesame and

RDF Suite is performed through the RQL language. There is no support provided by these tools to integrate different ontologies or to use them as a specification.

6.2.2 PLIB Suite

PLIB Suite (http://www.plib.ensma.fr) is a set of tools for PLIB ontologies storage, edition, querying and integration. The exchange format of PLIB ontologies is EXPRESS physical file. PLIB Suite include full support of this format. Currently, ontologies storage rely on the OntoDB prototype. This prototype is an implementation of the notion of Ontology Based Database presented in section 3. Thus, it stores ontologies, data and logical models of data defined by extraction and/or specialization from ontologies. It respects full definition of the PLIB standard and its architecture is flexible enough to manage the evolution of this standard. This prototype is directly linked to the PLIB Editor software that can be used to visualize and manage ontologies and data. Each concept is associated to a name in different natural languages with synonymous names. PLIB Editor exploits this natural language capability to provide a multilingual interface. However, there is no linguistic inference using synonymous names. PLIB Editor provides a query module that enables to build visually a query on data from the ontologies. This module relies on the OntoQL query language allowing to manage and to query both ontologies and data. Integration of PLIB ontologies is enabled when subsumption links are defined between different ontologies.

6.2.3 RacerPro

RacerPro is an in-memory OWL reasoning system. RacerPro supports OWL DL almost completely and includes a graphical user interface to manipulate ontologies and data. These data are directly persisted in an OWL file. Querying these data is possible through the query language nRQL. However, memory demands, concurrency control and scalability of this implementation are still open issues. As a payoff, RacerPro offers a full reasoning system that enables automatic classification of concepts and of data. As we have seen in section 4.3, this functionality is very useful for integration.

Table 1 summarizes the previous study.

Table 1. Fulfilled functionalities by existing OBDMS

	RDF Tools	Racer Pro	PLIB Suite
F1	partial	yes	yes
F2	yes	yes	yes
F3	partial	yes	CCO
F4	no	no	partial
F5	yes	partial	yes
F6	no	NCCO	partial
F7	no	no	yes

It appears that none of the existing tools covers the complete set of functionalities required to implement the scenario proposed in section 5.2. Therefore, next section proposes an architecture using existing OBDMS to solve this problem.

6.3   An Integrated Architecture to Implement Our Data Exchange Scenario

Our exchange scenario requires one consensual CCO managed in an OBDMS providing the possibility to map NCCOs (F6). Since Racer is the only existing OBDMS providing this functionality we propose to use it for this purpose.

Each source defines its own CCO and manages its instances. We propose to use PLIB Suite for each particular source. The use of PLIB Suite for this purpose ensure that a precise description of the concepts will be available (F3). Moreover it provides a scalable repository to store all the data (F5). For linguistic support (F4), it provides the necessary resources to reference a LO such as Wordnet.

The exchange of data requires the following steps:

1. A source exports its primitive concepts to Racer (F2). They become the consensual CCO. Notice that this step requires that PLIB Suite can export data in OWL format.
2. Other sources may use Racer editor to define mapping between their concepts and the defined consensual CCO.
3. Using the Racer reasoning system, a *classification of all the concepts* is done. Thus, the consensual CCO become a NCCO.
4. Data instances to be exchanged between the defined sources are imported into Racer.
5. Using the Racer reasoning system, a *classification of these instances* is performed.
6. For concepts of a given source under which instances have been classified, an export of these instances to this source is achieved. This step requires to keep track of the origin of each concept.

Other propositions like (Pan and Heflin, 2003) are made to associate a reasoner with a database. However the aims of these propositions is to provide a full reasoning system using a database. Yet, OWL reasoning is not fully supported by these systems.

7   Conclusion

This paper has investigated the concept of domain ontology in a database perspective. Ontology becoming a buzzword, often used as a new term for already existing models, we have first proposed three criteria to characterize ontology. A domain ontology must be formal, i.e, allowing some automatic reasoning and consistency checking capability, consensual in some community and able to be referenced from any environment. These three criteria characterize domain ontology as a new kind of model in computer science and lead us to propose a new definition of domain ontology as a formal and consensual dictionary of categories and properties of entities of a domain and the relationships that hold among them.

Domain ontology models being mainly developed by three communities, we have proposed a taxonomy of domain ontology into CCO, NCCO and LO. After review-ing the partial domain coverage of these various models, we have proposed a layered model, called the onion model of domain ontology, allowing to design and to use the capabilities of each category of ontology in an integrated environment. We have also discussed under the name of OBDMS what kinds of services should be provided to allow a powerful usage of ontology in data management.

Currently there exist neither exchange format nor OBDMS able to represent and to manage domain ontologies corresponding to the complete onion model. First, we are developing an XML schema that will integrate both OWL and PLIB capabilities. Second, we are extending the PLIB Suite to support OWL class expression constructs using both a connexion with an OWL reasoner and a representation by SQL views. Finally, we are working on a query language, called OntoQL, allowing to query the three layers of the onion model.

Acknowledgements

The authors would like to thank the anonymous referees of this paper. Their relevant comments and suggestions were very helpful to improve the quality of this paper.

References

Bechhofer, S., van Harmelen, F., Hendler, J., Horrocks, I., McGuinness, D.L., Patel-Schneider, P.F., Stein, L.A.: OWL Web Ontology Language Reference. World Wide Web Consortium (2004)

Bellatreche, L., Pierra, G., Xuan, D.N., Hondjack, D., Ait-Ameur, Y.: An a priori approach for automatic integration of heterogeneous and autonomous databases. In: Galindo, F., Takizawa, M., Traunmüller, R. (eds.) DEXA 2004. LNCS, vol. 3180, pp. 475–485. Springer, Heidelberg (2004)

Bozsak, E., Ehrig, M., Handschuh, S., Hotho, A., Maedche, A., Motik, B., Oberle, D., Schmitz, C., Staab, S., Stojanovic, L., Stojanovic, N., Studer, R., Stumme, G., Sure, Y., Tane, J., Volz, R., Zacharias, V.: Kaon - towards a large scale semantic web. In: Bauknecht, K., Tjoa, A.M., Quirchmayr, G. (eds.) EC-Web 2002. LNCS, pp. 304–313. Springer, Heidelberg (2002)

Brickley, D., Guha, R.: RDF Vocabulary Description Language 1.0: RDF Schema. World Wide Web Consortium (2004)

Chawathe, S.S., Garcia-Molina, H., Hammer, J., Ireland, K., Papakonstantinou, Y., Ullman, J.D., Widom, J.: The tsimmis project: Integration of heterogeneous information sources. In: IPSJ, pp. 7–18 (1994)

Cullot, N., Parent, C., Spaccapietra, S., Vangenot, C.: Ontologies: A contribution to the dl/db debate. In: Bussler, C.J., Tannen, V., Fundulaki, I. (eds.) SWDB 2004. LNCS, vol. 3372, pp. 109–129. Springer, Heidelberg (2005)

Das, S., Chong, E.I., Eadon, G., Srinivasan, J.: Supporting ontology-based semantic matching in rdbms. In: Aberer, K., Koubarakis, M., Kalogeraki, V. (eds.) Databases, Information Systems, and Peer-to-Peer Computing. LNCS, vol. 2944, pp. 1054–1065. Springer, Heidelberg (2004)

Dou, D., McDermott, D., Qi, P.: Ontology translation on the semantic web. In: Proceeding of the 2nd International Conference on Ontologies, Databases and Applications of Semantics (ODBASE'2003), pp. 952–969 (2003)

Gangemi, A., Guarino, N., Masolo, C., Oltramari, A.: Sweetening wordnet with dolce. AI Magazine 24(3), 13–24 (2003)

Gruber, T.R.: A translation approach to portable ontology specifications. Knowl. Acquis. 5(2), 199–220 (1993)

Guarino, N., Welty, C.: Evaluating ontological decisions with ontoclean. Commun. ACM 45(2), 61–65 (2002)

Haarslev, V., Möller, R.: Racer system description. In: Goré, R.P., Leitsch, A., Nipkow, T. (eds.) IJCAR 2001. LNCS (LNAI), vol. 2083, pp. 701–706. Springer, Heidelberg (2001)

IEC61360-4. Standard data element types with associated classification scheme for electric components - part 4 : Iec reference collection of standard data element types, component classes and terms. Technical report, International Standards Organization (1999)

ISO10303. Initial release of international standard(is) 10303. Technical report is 10303, International Standards Organization (1994)

ISO13584-42. Industrial automation systems and integration parts library part 42 : Description methodology : Methodology for structuring parts families. Technical report, International Standards Organization (1998)

Jarrar, M., Meersman, R.: Formal ontology engineering in the dogma approach. In: Meersman, R., Tari, Z., et al. (eds.) CoopIS 2002, DOA 2002, and ODBASE 2002. LNCS, vol. 2519, pp. 1238–1254. Springer, Heidelberg (2002)

Kifer, M., Lausen, G., Wu, J.: Logical foundations of object-oriented and frame-based languages. J. ACM 42(4), 741–843 (1995)

Meersman, R.: Ontologies and databases: More than a fleeting resemblance. In: OES/SEO Workshop Rome (2001)

Niles, I., Pease, A.: Towards a standard upper ontology. In: Proceedings of the 2nd International Conference on Formal Ontology in Information Systems (FOIS-2001), pp. 2–9 (2001)

Noy, N.F., McGuinness, D.L.: Ontology development 101: A guide to creating your first ontology. Technical report ksl-01-05 and stanford medical informatics technical report smi-2001-0880, Stanford Knowledge Systems Laboratory (2001)

Pan, Z., Heflin, J.: Dldb: Extending relational databases to support semantic web queries. In: PSSS (2003)

Parent, C., Spaccapietra, S., Zimanyi, E.: Spatio-temporal conceptual models: data structures + space + time. In: GIS '99: Proceedings of the 7th ACM international symposium on Advances in geographic information systems, pp. 26–33. ACM Press, New York (1999)

Pierra, G.: Context-explication in conceptual ontologies: The plib approach. In: Jardim-Goncalves, R., Cha, J., Steiger-Garcao, A. (eds.) Proceedings of the 10th ISPE International Conference on Concurrent Engineering (CE 2003), pp. 243–254 (2003)

Pierra, G., Dehainsala, H., Aït-Ameur, Y., Bellatreche, L.: Base de données à base ontologique: principes et mise en œuvre. Ingénierie des Systèmes d'Information 10(2), 91–115 (2005)

Rousset, M.-C., Bidault, A., Froidevaux, C., Gagliardi, H., Goasdou, F., Reynaud, C., Safar, B.: Construction de médiateurs pour intégrer des sources d'information multiples et hétérogènes: Picsel. revue I3 2(1), 9–59 (2002)

Tetlow, P., Pan, J., Oberle, D., Wallace, E., Uschold, M., Kendall, E.: Ontology Driven Architectures and Potential Uses of the Semantic Web in Systems and Software Engineering. World Wide Web Consortium (2005)

Uschold, M., Jasper, R.: A framework for understanding and classifying ontology applications. In: Proceedings of the IJCAI99 Workshop on Ontologies and Problem-Solving Methods(KRR5), Stockholm, Sweden (August 1999)

Visser, P.R.S., Beer, M.D., Bench-Capon, T.J.M., Diaz, B.M., Shave, M.J.R.: Resolving ontological heterogeneity in the kraft project. In: Bench-Capon, T.J.M., Soda, G., Tjoa, A.M. (eds.) DEXA 1999. LNCS, vol. 1677, pp. 668–677. Springer, Heidelberg (1999)

Wiederhold, G.: Obtaining information from heterogeneous systems. In: Proceedings of the First Workshop on Information Technologies and Systems (WITS'91), pp. 1–8. Cambridge MA, MIT Sloan School of Management (1991)

Real-Time Discovery of Currently and Heavily Viewed Web Pages

Kazutaka Maruyama[1], Kiyotaka Takasuka[2], Yuta Yagihara[2], Satoshi Machida[2],
Yuichiro Shirai[2], and Minoru Terada[2]

[1] Information Processing Center, The University of Electro-Communications
Chofugaoka 1-5-1, Chofu, Tokyo, 182-8585, Japan
kazutaka@acm.org
[2] Dept. of Information and Communication Engineering, The University of
Electro-Communications
Chofugaoka 1-5-1, Chofu, Tokyo, 182-8585, Japan
{takasuka,yagihara,machida,gechena,terada}@ice.uec.ac.jp

Abstract. The amount of information on web increases explosively, so it is difficult for web users to find web pages they want. There are some approaches to resolve this problem, such as semantic web which make web information systematic, the improvement of search engines' algorithm, and so on. Dealing with web as a huge database, these technologies works well, however, they cannot provide any useful solutions to get hot news which expands quickly to the world because of their time lag.

In this paper, we propose a system whose users can know currently and heavily viewed web pages. The key features of this system are as follows: (1) to find hot news in web, (2) to provide recommendations to users without any content analysis, and (3) to apply the system to other communication tools like IM as their infrastructure to find appropriate contact targets. We describe our policy of the system implementation and show the result of a pilot experiment with a pilot implementation.

Keywords: Peer-to-peer, clustering, web browsing, browser extension.

1 Introduction

In the recent web, the amount of information on web increases explosively, for example consumer generated media like blog, and the pace seems to be accelerated much more in future. Users know that web pages they want to find exist somewhere in web world, but they can find only part of the target pages and always worry about the lack of useful ones.

Two major approaches to this problem are semantic web and the improvement of search engines. Web contents with rich meta data and search engine algorithms such as PageRank can produce more appropriate answers to users' queries. However these solutions have three problems. First, it is considerably difficult to add appropriate and sufficient meta data to all existing web contents, and also probably all ones generated in future. Second, the intervals of crawling by search engine robots and of updating the

J. Filipe, J. Cordeiro, and V. Pedrosa (Eds.): WEBIST 2005/2006, LNBIP 1, pp. 255–266, 2007.

indexes do not become much shorter and are not in real-time. Third, the solution cannot create any clusters of the users, not the contents. We call them *communities*. In real life, communities exist everywhere such as in schools, offices, web bulletin boards, and so on. We can always talk with each other about various hot topics in such communities. For instance, a person who knows music scene thoroughly may tell us about not only recent trends of CD charts, but also a rumor about unpublished next iPod. Search engines provide results only to explicitly given terms by users, but we cannot find other topics which implicitly relate to the terms because they have no user communities.

We propose an infrastructure to find currently and heavily viewed web pages in real-time by exchanging viewed URLs at the client side. Three advantages of this architecture are as follows.

1. We can quickly discover web pages which are attracting considerable attention, such as a new beta service of Google disclosed tonight.
2. We can know web pages which most of *friendly* users view. The term of friendly users means ones who usually view the same web pages as we have viewed.
3. Communication tool developers or researchers can use our system as an infrastructure of new tools they are developing, such as IM, because it creates communities of users who usually view the same web pages, and probably have the same preferences.

Since our system does not need any meta data, all the existing web contents in the world are available and the content providers and consumers can use the system without any special actions (the first problem above is solved). The system provides currently and heavily viewed web pages mostly in real-time, because exchanging URLs need not crawl or index any web pages (the second is solved). In addition, it can very easily introduce the mechanism correspondent to mouth-to-mouth advertising in real life by creating user communities with only usual actions of web users, that is to view web pages in their browsers (the third is solved).

The remainder of this paper is organized as follows. Section 2 shows the features of our proposal with an use case scenario. In section 3, we discuss the losses against gains of the implementation strategies of the client and server side subsystems, and describe the implementation of our currently developing system. Section 4 shows the result of a pilot experiment with a pilot system. Other applications of our system are described in section 5 and the related works are discussed in section 6. Section 7 and 8 describe conclusion and future works respectively.

2   Features of Our System

In this section, we show the features of our proposal in the view point of users and the current user interface through an use case scenario.

2.1   An Use Case Scenario

Alice is a very common user of web, every day crawls her favorite news sites and blogs, and looks for a reputation of a restaurant which she found on her way home by using search engines. She changed her jobs recently and was not satisfied because she could not find interesting topics in web well, which a well-informed colleague in the former office told her, through news sites, blogs or search engines. She could not find news sites or blogs just suitable for her interests and was tired of reading so many RSS feeds. Search engines are very powerful tools when she is looking for topics with explicit purpose, but they do not help her to look for recently popular topics or somehow nice events.

One day, she began to use a system mentioned in a certain blog. It was said that users of the system exchange URLs they are just viewing. The information exchanged is only URL, so she did not have to take care of copyright violation in contrast to file sharing. Following the instruction of the official site of the system, she installed a tiny extension for Mozilla Firefox, an add-on program for the web browser, to her own Firefox. She clicked an icon added by the extension at the lower right of Firefox, then a pop-up menu appeared there. It controls the appearance of the sidebar described below, and enables or disables the mechanism of sending out URLs she is viewing. Turning on the sidebar, she saw the appearance of her Firefox such as figure 1. The sidebar lying on the left side of the window has a few buttons to list the correspondent rankings, and clicking these buttons causes switches of the list displayed in the pane. Entries of blogs or diaries in social network services viewed heavily were listed at the top of the lists. Alice attempted to participate in the project of exchanging URLs and enabled the mechanism of sending out URLs by the menu of the lower right icon. Therefore URLs she is viewing became to be shared in the world.

One week after, URLs listed in the sidebar became suitable for Alice's preference. The project web page said that the system connects users to each other with fewer hops, who tend to view the same web pages, and consequently provides more appropriate rankings. She viewed web pages in the same way as before, but she became to know some cool products which she had never known or some recipes of healthy diets. Using the new way of retrieving information different from news sites, blogs or search engines, she became to use web more efficiently and had fun with various hot topics.

2.2 Summary of Features

We described a basic use case of our proposal through Alice's experience. The summary of the features is as follows.

- A quite new channel for information retrieval is established. In real life, for instance, a crowd on a street shows that there is something interesting such as a street performer. While the same method of information retrieval did not exist so far, it is introduced into the world of web.
- The proposed system provides real-time information. Users need not to wait for a blog entry to be submitted by the owner who saw a news source. For example, we can reach an entry of Slashdot, to which comments are increasing.
- Communities are created. The server side system connects friendly users to each other with fewer hops by using URLs they have viewed. In other words, unfriendly users are kept away from each other and S/N ratio of the provided rankings would be improved.

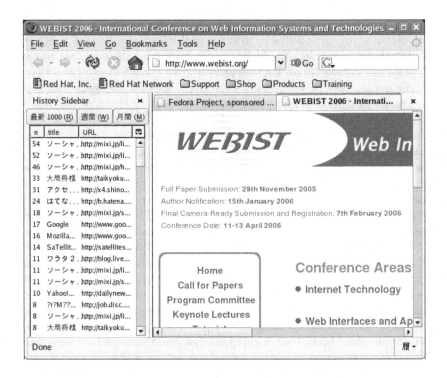

Fig. 1. Alice's Firefox with our extension

- All users have to do is an installation of a single extension once, in contrast to social bookmarkings which need their users to continue submitting each entry for exchanging URLs. The users of our system can provide useful information of web pages only by viewing web pages in their usual way and can get useful URLs from others in the world.

The use case described in this section includes the functions which are not implemented yet, but shows the user experience through our proposal. Another aspect of the system, an infrastructure of communication tools, is described in section 5.

3   System Structure

In this section, we describe the implementation strategies of the client side and the server side subsystems, discuss the losses against gains of the strategies, and describe the current system implementation.

3.1   Extension vs. Proxy

One of the important behavior is to capture URLs an user is viewing in real-time without any interferences. There are two implementation choices: (1) add-on program for web browsers such as extension or toolbar, and (2) web proxy server.

Fig. 2. Three buttons of the sidebar

Fig. 3. Pop-up menu

The best way for users is web proxy. All users have to do is to set up their browsers so that the proxy is used, then all the web behavior of the users is captured by the proxy in real-time. The proxy would be placed at school or office, or be installed as a quite small Java program without cache facility into each user's PC. The greatest benefit of this choice is that the installation procedure of users is the minimum. When a proxy is used by many users, for example for all students in a college, the single client side subsystem can capture so many users' web behavior. However, this solution has a disadvantage of collecting too many meaningless URLs. When an user clicks a certain link, his browser, and the proxy of course, must retrieve many resources in the clicked document, such as images, style sheets, flash applications including advertisements. The ranking of captured URLs will place the Google logo image at the top of the list. Of course such a result is not expected. Using Referer fields in HTTP or analyzing transferred HTML, clicked images may be distinguished from ones included clicked web pages. But the analysis makes the system complex and the performance down, consequently, the users must become irritated.

Another implementation choice is extension or toolbar, which have the opposite features. These add-on programs work as a part of a web browser and can capture explicitly clicked URLs only. This feature is an obvious advantage against the proxy. On the other hand, the extension has a few disadvantages. First, users have to install the extension or toolbar, even if it is a very small program and only two or three clicks finish the installation. Second, at least two implementations for Firefox and Internet Explorer are required in order to support over 90% of web browsers in the world. Since a Firefox extension works on all platforms supported by Firefox, such as Windows, Linux, Mac OS X and so on, a toolbar for Windows IE and the extension can cover almost all the client environment.

As described in section 2, we chose the extension/toolbar implementation, but the toolbar for IE is not implemented yet. The appearance of Firefox with the extension is shown in figure 1. In the current version, the sidebar on the left of the window has three buttons (figure 2), and three rankings appear by the correspondent buttons, i.e. recent top 1000, weekly chart and monthly chart. An additional ranking of URLs to which accesses increase suddenly would be added. Figure 3 shows the pop-up menu from the icon at the lower right of the window. Sending URLs is disabled in the default setting.

3.2 Server Centric vs. Peer-to-Peer

The extension is the client side half of our system. The server side one collects URLs sent from the client side. There are also two choices: (1) server centric and (2) peer-to-peer.

Obviously, the server centric approach is simpler. Powerful servers with high speed CPUs and large disks in a data center could deal with URLs sent from all users in the world. For example, Google and Yahoo! start their services which save the search histories of each user. They must use such many servers and disks. In this approach, it is easier to exchange users' web behavior and to analyze relevance among users. On the other hand, the disadvantage is that the large system of many servers is too expensive and requires a large amount cost for maintenance.

Another approach is P2P. The users install a tiny program running on background written in Java into their PC and the program works as a node of the P2P system. The client side programs, extensions or proxy servers, send URLs to and receive rankings from the node. The large system need not be constructed. However, a simple and flat P2P network such as Gnutella cannot deal with so many URLs from so many users in the world and cannot connect friendly users to each other. Clustering P2P nodes and a layered architecture, such as Skype(Skype - The whole world can talk for free, nd) or Winny(Kaneko, 2005), could resolve this problem.

At present, we choose the server centric approach because of the ease of development. The server consists of some CGI programs, the extension sends URLs to it as POST data of HTTP and receives the rankings from it by GET method of HTTP. Note that there is an explicit interface between the client side subsystem and the server side one. The interface is defined as URLs and CGI parameters over HTTP. When we replace the server with P2P based subsystem, if the interface between the extension and the server is preserved, no changes are required for the extension. In addition, the interface of HTTP is extremely suitable for web browser extensions.

3.3 Current System Structure

The current system structure is shown in figure 4. The client side subsystem consists of Firefox web browser and the extension and the server side subsystem consists of Apache web server and some CGI programs written in Perl. The extension sends clicked URLs to the server by POST method and the server stores them into disks. When the user clicks a button of the sidebar shown in figure 2, the extension sends a GET requests to the CGI program correspondent to the clicked button, then receives the list of the ranking.

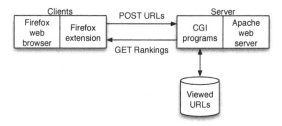

Fig. 4. Current system structure

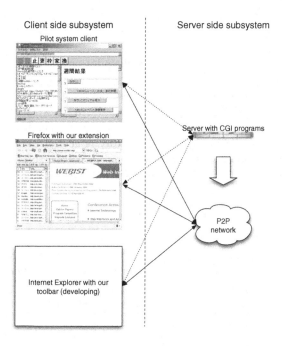

Fig. 5. Three kinds of clients and two of servers

The system produces any explicit recommendations of web pages, because the ranking of the recent top 1000 shows the recommendations from users of the system. The weekly and monthly charts show the recommendations from them in the week and the month respectively. The ranking of URLs to which accesses increase suddenly, which is still developing, shows the recommendation at the moment.

Prior to developing the extension, we developed a pilot implementation of the client side subsystem, the top in figure 5 (Takasuka et al., 2005). In fact, the server side subsystem was developed for the pilot client. The current client, the middle in figure 5, preserves the interface between the pilot client and the server, and replaces the pilot one without any changes of the CGI programs. The coming toolbar of IE shown in figure 5 would work together these existing clients.

Clustering users are not introduced yet into our system. First, users of our system are still around ten. Because the extension has some problems, our system is not released yet to the outside of our laboratory. Second, the clustering is relevant to the identification of URLs. This point is described in section 8.

4   Pilot Experiment

In order to examine the usefulness of our proposal, we implemented a pilot system to do a pilot experiment. In the pilot system, a client side subsystem is a simple and tiny web browser written in C# with IE component on Windows (shown in figure 5), and a server side subsystem consists of the CGI programs described above. The simple browser has forward/backward buttons, a simple bookmarklet and a facility of sending URLs to the server side subsystem.

In this experiment, nine student users used the pilot system for four days. The total accesses from the browser to web pages were 448 times. 70 accesses in them were from the rankings of the simple browser. Table 1 shows the result of the questionnaire. Each item is rated in one to five, one means the best and five the worst. The usefulness of the system we propose is evaluated comparatively highly. In addition, note that the rate of the psychological barrier in sharing web history is neutral. While the experiment is really small, the proposed system was accepted favorably, and the increase of the number of users would make the benefit more and the barrier lower.

Table 1. Evaluation of the pilot system

Questions (1:good, 5:bad)	Av.
Serviceability of the browser	3.1
Usefulness of sharing web history	2.0
To watch URLs others view is helpful	1.7
There is no psychological barrier in sharing web history	2.8

5   Other Applications of Our System

While we do not implement the facility to connect friendly users yet, once the facility is introduced, it could be used as an infrastructure of communication tools. Two application examples are described below.

The first is a chat among the users who are viewing the same web page. In contrast to Instant Messenger, of which the users designate their partners to talk to in advance, the chat we propose connects users who are viewing or have been viewing the same web page and helps them to talk to each other about the web page or some topics about it. In web bulletin boards such as Slashdot, the users who have never met before can talk to each other, but the place for the discussion must exist already and they cannot know whether the user who wrote a certain comment is viewing the page now. Our proposal provides the interchange between the web users through ordinary web pages. The users need not look for a thread, in which they are interested, and can talk to friendly users

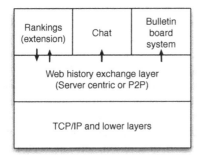

Fig. 6. Web history exchange network as a basis of communication tools

only by viewing their favorite web pages usually. Improving the chat system, as IM users can know that their friends have logged in, the users could know the others are viewing a certain web page. The improvement makes web pages rendezvouz.

The second is a P2P based bulletin board system. It is difficult for P2P based BBSs to gather friendly users in the same thread because of the structure of P2P. However, using our system as its infrastructure, the P2P based BBS could gather many users, who tend to view the same web pages and may have the similar preferences.

The core application is the rankings extension described in section 3, which sends data to web history exchange layer in order to connect friendly users to each other and receives the rankings from the layer (figure 6). The other two applications described in this section only receive location information of friendly users from the layer.

Other projects of communication tools would use the layer as their infrastructure. Whenever a quite new network service starts, there are two problems, the scalability of the server and the gathering of the sufficient initial users. Our system is useful for new network services or communication tools. Singh et al.(Singh et al., 2001) said that P2P networks can provide a substrate for community-based service location. The system we propose just can be applicable to it.

6   Related Works

Webmemex(Alaniz et al., 2003) provides the web page recommendations based on sharing web behaviors among the well-known users. They register each other in their contact list of Yahoo! Messenger, probably also well-known in real life. The proxy server gathers the viewed URLs and the back end system computes the relevance among the web pages by HTML analysis. When an user clicks a certain link, the system recommends some web pages which are related to the clicked web page and are viewed by other users of the group. It is similar to our proposal, but there are some essential differences.

- Our system deals with only URL strings, not the contents of the web page. The vocabulary in the web world is changing very quickly, so it is too difficult for such the analysis based system to continue following the changes, especially in some languages which do not place a space between the words such as Japanese. Since the data format used in the web world is also changing quickly, it seems not to be realistic to analyze the various contents of the web pages in the various areas.

- We aim for the discovery of the web pages which are attracting considerable attention with little time lag. The computation of the relevance of the contents among the web pages causes the opposite result to the purpose and it is suitable for post-processing. It should be dealt with as a different challenge.
- Our system does not limit the range of exchanging URLs. Limiting the range to the well-known users leads to the consequence of losing chance of coming across information in different areas. In addition, since the well-known users strongly connect to each other both in real and virtual life, their psychological barriers avoid exchanging URLs.

Social bookmarking services such as del.icio.us(del.icio.us, nd) aim for the similar goal. When an user finds others who bookmarks some web pages in which the person are also interested, the person implicitly gets their recommendations of hot topics or good web pages through their bookmarks. The first disadvantage is that the social bookmarking users have to explicitly go into action to add the URLs they prefer. The second is that the users looking for hot topics or good web pages have to look for friendly users too.

Fast el al.(Fast et al., 2005) introduce a social networking in order to cluster the nodes of P2P file sharing based on the downloaded music file categories of the P2P users. In comparison between P2P file sharing and P2P URL sharing, search queries in file sharing correspond to advertising of URLs in URL sharing, and downloaded files correspond to really viewed URLs by the users who receive the others' advertisements. The number and frequency of the transmission between the queries and the advertisements seem to be considerably different, and URL sharing mostly deals with statistical information, for instance many users are viewing a certain URL, in contrast to file sharing which finds the real entities, music files. The different knowledge from the paper about P2P clustering would be found.

Winny(Kaneko, 2005), a P2P file sharing software with over 200,000 users in Japan, uses three keywords for a background file downloading process. The keywords are also used for P2P clustering, but the users have to set the keywords in advance. In the Winny network, the files opened to be shared by a certain node is cached at the other nodes, such as Freenet(Clarke et al., 2002), and the network load is heavy. Therefore, in order to realize more efficient file sharing, Winny constructs the layered P2P network based on each node's connection speed, for example, up to 64kbps, xDSL or fiber. The P2P URL sharing distributes much smaller data such as URLs, so it have to make much of whether the reboot intervals of the nodes are long or whether the nodes have a fixed global IP address, rather than the connection speed.

7   Conclusion

Exchanging URLs which users are viewing in real-time brings hot topics, which are attracting considerable attention, without any keywords explicitly designated. The effective way to realize it is that the client side subsystem should be implemented as an add-on program for web browsers, and the server side as P2P. In the current version of our system, the server side is implemented as the server centric CGI programs, but the P2P could take the place of it by preserving the interface, which consists of HTTP and CGI, between the server side and the client side. The pilot experiment showed the usefulness of our proposal. In addition, the system for exchanging URLs could be applied to other communication tools as their infrastructure.

8 Future Works

The top pages of portal sites tend to be placed at the higher rank. This problem could be resolved through the user interface of the extension. The users disable the appearance of such entries in the rankings, for example by a right click on a target entry, and exchange the *disabled* portal sites via the server side subsystem.

The strategy of clustering users is quite important and difficult. Creating clusters is an effective way to reduce the number of connections, the traffic on P2P network, and the computation of the similarity of users. The separation of clusters, however, may make users lose opportunity to be offered interesting web pages(Linden et al., 2003). In ordinal recommendation systems such as e-commerce marketing systems, each user's purchases in a day may be usually less than ten items, even if they are heavy users of the system. But web pages each user views in a day are at least ten pages, and heavy web users view more than 100 pages. In addition, there are web users obviously more than e-commerce site users. Reduction by clusters must be introduced for effective exchange of web histories. Parameters for establishing clusters, such as the number of connections of each node, the limit of hops of web history transfer, and so on, could be found through simulation by using huge amount of proxy logs of our university.

The identity of URLs is also important. While CMSs generate different URLs to each blog entry, known as *permalink*, visitors can read the entries not only in their permalinks but also in the summary pages of recent entries, of the day, of the month and so on. Consequently, a certain entry has many URLs where it can be read. It is desirable that these URLs are dealt with as the same. This problem could be resolved by the introduction of scores between similar URLs. The URLs which indicate the same entry are similar, because most CMSs add the date of the entry to its permalink. In addition, the similarities between URLs would help us to cluster users. Users who often see different entries of the same blog should be placed in the same cluster.

In the view of the privacy, it is important not to send URLs which should not be shared. Our extension does not send any URLs in the default setting and explicitly shows its setting, whether sending URLs is turned on or off, by the correspondent icons. On the other hands, the web pages without appropriate access controls, such as password authentications or Limit directives of web servers, must be seen by outsiders. It is equivalent to being opened even if the URLs are not opened. This problem is known as "Google hacking" among security experts. Appropriate settings of access controls would make the problem trivial.

Spammers may attack this system by sending URLs which they want to advertise. This problem is known as "shilling attacks". However, since the information for clustering is URLs themselves, the spammers may be classified to a spammers' cluster and cannot influence the ordinal users. The clustering of spammers would be inspected through simulation.

References

Alaniz, A., Truong, K.N., Antonio, J.: Automatically Sharing Web Experiences through a Hyperdocument Recommender System. In: Proceedings of the 14th ACM Conference on Hypertext and Hypermedia, pp. 48–56 (2003)

Clarke, I., Miller, S.G., Hong, T.W., Sandberg, O., Wiley, B.: Protecting free expression online with Freenet. IEEE Internet Computing 6(1), 40–49 (2002)

del.icio.us (n.d.) http://del.icio.us/

Fast, A., Jensen, D., Levine, B.N.: Creating Social Networks to Improve Peer-to-Peer Networking. In: Proceedings of the 11th ACM SIGKDD International Conference on Knowledge Discovery in Data Mining, pp. 568–573 (2005)

Kaneko, I.: Technology of Winny (In Japanese) Ascii Publishing (2005)

Linden, G., Smith, B., York, J.: Amazon.com Recommendations: Item-to-Item Collaborative Filtering. IEEE Internet Computing 7(1), 76–80 (2003)

Singh, M.P., Yu, B., Venkatraman, M.: Community-based Service Location. Communications of the ACM 44(4), 49–54 (2001)

Skype - The whole world can talk for free (n.d.) http://www.skype.com/

Takasuka, K., Shirai, Y., Maruyama, K., Terada, M.: A web browser that shares browsing histories. In: FIT2005 (In Japanese), pp. 355–356 (2005)

Metamodeling the Requirements of Web Systems

María José Escalona[1] and Nora Koch[2,3]

[1] Universidad de Sevilla
[2] Ludwig-Maximilians-Universität München
[3] FAST GmbH
`mjescalona@us.es`, `kochn@pst.ifi.lmu.de`

Abstract. A detailed requirements analysis is best practice in the development of traditional software. Conversely, the importance of requirements engineering for Web systems is still underestimated. Only few Web methodologies provide an approach for the elicitation of requirements and techniques for their specification. This paper focuses on specification through requirements models of Web systems. We present a metamodel, which contains the key concepts needed for the requirements specification of Web systems. The benefit of such a metamodel is twofold: (1) The key concepts are used for the definition of a common modeling language: a UML profile for Web requirements. (2) The elements of the metamodel are mapped to the modeling constructs of the different Web methodologies. In this way the prerequisite for model-to-model transformations is given, which allows to build different views of the requirements of a Web system using different Web methodologies.

Keywords: Web Engineering, Metamodel, UML Profile, Web Requirements.

1 Introduction

Web Engineering is a new area of Software Engineering, which focuses on the development of Web Systems (Kappel et al., 2003). In the last years, several approaches have been proposed for the Web environment. These methods provide specific modeling elements for the analysis and design and most of them define a proprietary notation used for the graphical representation of the elements. Almost all methods propose specific processes to support the systematic or semi-automatic development of Web applications. However, only few of the existing Web methodologies start the development cycle with a detailed requirements analysis (Escalona & Koch, 2004).

Conversely, the requirements analysis is considered by all software engineering approaches to be a key step in the development of successful software systems (Lowe & Ecklund, 2002). Empirical data demonstrate that efforts invested in a detailed requirements analysis considerably reduce drawbacks in later phases of the development (Sommerville & Ransom, 2005).

In this work we present an approach which aims to improve the development of Web applications reinforcing the requirements engineering aspects of the methods. We start with an analysis of the requirements of *requirements specification* of Web systems. We take into account both general characteristics of Web applications and

J. Filipe, J. Cordeiro, and V. Pedrosa (Eds.): WEBIST 2005/2006, LNBIP 1, pp. 267–280, 2007.

how Web engineering deals with requirements. We restrict the analysis to those methodologies that support requirements engineering by a process, a notation and/or tool support. The most relevant methods fulfilling these restrictions are NDT (Escalona, 2004), OOHDM (Rossi & Schwabe, 1998), UWE (Koch & Kraus, 2002) and W2000 (Baresi et al., 2003).

The key concepts related to the requirements engineering of Web systems and their relationships were identified through the analysis of these different Web engineering approaches and the review of literature. We have developed a common *metamodel* for the representation of concepts and relationships of Web requirements engineering (WebRE). The metamodel is visualized with a UML class diagram and constitutes the basis for the definition of a so called *UML profile for Web requirements* and tool support. Such a UML profile contains a set of modeling elements for which a specific graphical notation can be defined.

The advantage of the metamodel and its associated profile is twofold: On the one hand it offers a common modeling language of requirements engineering. This common modeling language provides NDT with a graphical notation and extends current methodologies as UWE and W2000 with additional modeling elements. And it provides OOHDM with a standard notation for User Interaction Diagrams (UIDs) as an alternative to its proprietary notation. On the other hand the mapping of methods to the metamodel is the basis for the definition of model transformations (PIM to PIM transformations) from models specified with one method, e.g. in NDT, to models of another method, e.g. UWE.

The vision is to integrate the requirements model in the model-driven process, more precisely, to start the model-driven process with a requirements model.

The remainder of this paper is structured as follows: Section 2 gives an overview of the state of the art of requirements analysis in Web engineering. Section 3 presents the metamodel that comprises the elements needed to model requirements of Web applications. Building on the metamodel a UML profile is defined in Section 4. Finally, in Section 5 a set of conclusions and future work are outlined.

2 Requirements in Web Engineering

The aim of a requirements engineering phase is always to obtain a stable set of requirements, which serves as basis for the further steps in the development process. Three activities are used to achieve this goal: elicitation, specification, and validation of requirements (Lowe & Hall, 1999).

The *elicitation of requirements* is the activity by means of which the functionalities of the system to be built are collected from any available source. The overall requirements elicitation objectives for software engineering remain unchanged when applied to Web systems. However, the specific objectives for Web systems become: (1) the identification of content requirements, (2) the identification of the functional requirements in terms of navigation needs and businesses processes, and (3) the definition of interaction scenarios for different groups of Web users.

Requirements specification consists of producing a description of the requirements. Different techniques can be used for the specification: from informal textual description to formal specification in languages like Z (Kappel et al., 2003; Escalona & Koch, 2004).

Finally, *requirements validation* consists of checking the requirements specification in order to establish whether the Web application user's needs are fulfilled.

This work focuses on requirements specification.

2.1 An Overview of Requirements Specification for Web Systems

Requirements specification can be focused on the description of the problems or the solutions (Wieringa, 2004). Problem description is goal-oriented; in contrast solution description is pattern-oriented. In both cases, it is important to write specifications or build models that are understandable for managers, provide sufficient information for developers, and allow validation of the models by final users. The development in the Web domain is influenced by a higher reliability of the user interface, volatility of user requirements and the business model, an unpredictable publishing environment and fine-grained evolution and maintenance.

Requirements specifications need to be described in documents in the degree of detail and formality that is appropriate for the corresponding project. The appropriateness of the specification technique is mainly established by the project risk and complexity of the Web application to be built. The techniques that can be used to produce the resulting description are natural language, templates, use cases, formal languages or prototypes. For a detailed analysis of such techniques for the Web development see Escalona & Koch (2004). Informal descriptions such as user stories, and semi-formal descriptions like templates and use cases, are particularly suited to describe how users intend to perceive their interaction with a Web system.

Use cases are further refined using for this purpose formatted specifications or workflows. Both representations usually include actors, pre- und post-conditions, workflow descriptions, exceptions and error situations, variations, information sources needed, produced results, references to other documents, and interdependencies with other models. In particular, in the development of Web systems the informational, navigational and process goals have to be gathered and specified. Informational goals indicate the need of content to be provided to the Web system user. Navigational goals point toward the kind of access to this content. Process goals specify the ability of the user to perform some tasks within the Web system (Pressman, 2005).

2.2 Comparing Current Approaches

Our preliminary survey (Escalona & Koch, 2004) gives an overview about techniques and notations for Web requirements provided by Web methodologies. This comparative study shows that NDT (Escalona, 2004), OOHDM (Rossi & Schwabe, 1998), UWE (Koch& Kraus, 2002) and W2000 (Baresi et al., 2003) are the Web methodologies that pay special attention to requirements. Other approaches analyzed in the survey either propose the use of classical techniques to deal with Web requirements or ignore this phase of the development process.

The selected approaches recognize the relevance of the separation of concerns in the early requirements phase. In order to illustrate the characteristics, similarities and differences of these methods, we model the requirements of the same example Web system with each of the four methodologies.

The running example is a simplified CD e-shop, whose functionality is restricted to (1) the registration of users at the CD e-shop, (2) login, (3) search of CDs, (4) add to the shopping cart, and (5) checkout for buying the CDs. The approaches NDT, OOHDM, UWE and W2000 start the modeling process by identifying actors and use cases, and build in the next step a use case model with them. Fig. 1 depicts the use case model for the simplified e-shop example.

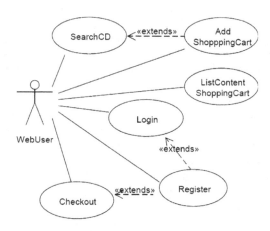

Fig. 1. UML use case diagram for the *CD e-shop*

Further modeling results produced in the requirements phase by these methodologies differ from each other and are shown in the following.

Navigational Development Techniques (NDT) is a methodology that mainly focuses on requirements and on the analysis phase. NDT (Escalona, 2004) uses several techniques to deal with requirements; basically, it proposes to use uses cases and provides formatted templates to describe requirements.

NDT classifies requirements in *storage information, actor, functional, interaction* and *non-functional requirements.* For each type, NDT defines a special template, i.e. a table with specific fields that are completed by the development team during the phase of requirements elicitation. Each template is assigned an identifier. The structured requirements specification performed by NDT allows the generation of the analysis models of the Web system from this specification. In this sense, NDT is a model-driven proposal. The complete life cycle of NDT is supported by its associated tool, named NDT-Tool (Escalona at al., 2003).

Concretely, for the CD e-shop example, NDT specifies several storage information requirements. A storage information requirement expresses all the information that has to be stored for a concrete application concept. For instance, a template for the registered user's information is identified by SR-01, another for the CD information by SR-02, etc. Table 1 shows the most relevant fields of the template for the requirements SR-01.

Each use case is also described by a functional template in NDT. Table 2 shows an example of such a template for the use case *Login.*

Table 1. Template for storage of information requirements (NDT)

SR-01	WebUser	
Description	The system manages information about users	
Specific data	Name & description	Nature
	name: contains *user's name*	String
	address: this field stores the user's postal address	String
	userID: is the user's identification to access the e-shop	String
	password: is the user's password to access the e-shop	String

The process starts when the system asks for the userID and the password, and for the "remember field". Remember has the value "true" if the application should remember the user identification and the password of the user, otherwise it has the value "false". In addition, NDT provides a template for actors, i.e. a template to describe the role the Web system user will play. Such a template is identified by e.g. identifier AC-01.

Finally, NDT also designs specific templates for interaction requirements. In this example, an interaction requirement for the CD information will be developed.

Table 2. Template for functional requirements (NDT)

FR-01	Login	
Description	Authentication to allow access to the checkout process	
Actors	**Use case actor**	
	AC-01. *WebUser*	
Normal sequence	**Step**	**Action**
	1	The system asks for the *userID* and *password* and the option to *remember* both *userID* and *password*
	2	The user puts the *userID* and the *password*
	3	The *userID* and the *password* *are checked*
	4	The *userID* and the *password* is stored if the field *remember* is true
	5	Access to checkout is allowed
Exceptions	**Step**	**Action**
	4	The user is not registered, so the user executes FR-02
	4	The *userID* or the *password* are not valid, continue with step 1

Object-Oriented Hypermedia Design Method (OOHDM) supports separation of concerns by developing separated conceptual, navigational and abstract interface models of Web systems. The navigation model is built with a variety of concepts, among others the powerful *navigation context*. The first versions of OOHDM (Schwabe & Rossi, 1998) did not cover the requirements phase focusing instead on design and implementation.

OOHDM was extended afterwards with use cases and a special technique to deal with user interaction in the requirements phase. The technique used is called *User Interaction Diagram* (UID) (Vilain et al., 2000). A UID is built for each special interaction of the Web user with the Web system.

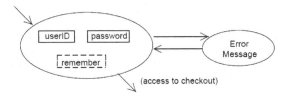

Fig. 2. UID for the *Login* use case (OOHDM)

A UID models interactions, information that require input from the user, and choices that allow changes between interactions. Each choice can be a single one or provoke the execution of a special operation. UIDs have a special notation, not based on standards. In Fig. 2, the UID for the use case *Login* is presented. The use case starts with the initial interaction where the userID and the password have to be entered by the user. In contrast Remember data is optional. After the user has entered the data, either the user will be able to checkout or (if userID or password is not correct) a new interaction will occur. In our example an error message is presented.

UML-based Web Engineering (UWE) is a model-driven software engineering approach for the Web domain. UWE provides a UML-based notation, a methodology and a tool environment for the systematic development of Web applications (Koch & Kraus, 2002). The systematic design follows the principle of separation of concerns, which is the intrinsic characteristic of the Web domain. Thus, UWE models a Web application from different points of view: the content, the navigation structure, the business processes, the presentation and the adaptive aspects. UWE provides semi-automatic transformations, for example from content to navigation structure models.

The UML compliance of UWE allows for the use of all CASE tools, which support the Unified Modeling Language. In addition, an open source plug-in – called ArgoUWE – for the open source tool ArgoUML (www.argouml.org) has been implemented supporting the systematic transformation techniques of UWE.

UWE models requirements with UML use case diagrams and UML activity diagrams. Use case diagrams are used to represent an overview of the functional requirements while activity diagrams provide a more detailed view. In UWE, the requirements process starts with the modeling of use cases using a stereotype for navigational use cases. After that, UWE recommends to develop an activity diagram for each process use case. In Fig. 3, the activity diagram for the *Login* use case is presented.

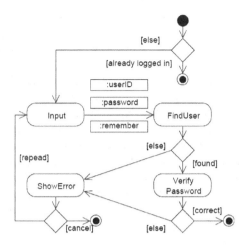

Fig. 3. Activity diagram for the *Login* use case (UWE)

Finally, **W2000** is an object-oriented approach derived from HDM (Baresi et al., 2001) that supports separation of concerns during the development process. W2000 extends the UML notation to model hypermedia applications. The requirements analysis in W2000 is divided into two sub-activities: functional and navigational requirements analysis. Every actor identified during the requirements elicitation phase has his own navigation and functional requirements model. W2000 thus proposes to develop two different types of use case diagrams. The first one includes the functional use cases. In our running example these use cases are Login, Register, AddToShoppingCart and Checkout. The second one, named the *navigation use case diagram*, represents the navigation possibilities of each actor. These are the use cases SearchCD and ListContentShoppingCart for the e-shop example.

3 Metamodel for Web Requirements

After consideration of the different proposals we concluded that they address many similar concepts, however not always using the same terminology. Each methodology has also its strengths and weaknesses. NDT proposes a detailed specification of requirements from the outset of a project but the templates are not easy to complete as they require intensive interviews. Conversely, visual representations like those proposed by UWE, W2000 or OOHDM are more intuitive for a first blueprint. But graphical notations are usually too abstract for the next phases (Insfrán et al., 2002). Modeling with UIDs faces the additional difficulty that CASE tools cannot be used due to the UIDs proprietary notation.

The modeling concepts we present for the Web requirements specification are defined based on the similarities of the methods that were analyzed. They are represented as UML metaclasses and constitute our metamodel for Web requirements engineering (WebRE), which is depicted in Fig. 4. The metaclasses represent the concepts without any information about its representation. They are grouped in two packages, following the structure of the UML metamodel: the WebRE structure and the WebRE behavior package.

The **behavior** package consists of the metaclasses Navigation, WebProcess, WebUser, Browse, Search and UserTransaction. Functionality of a Web system is modeled by a set of instances of two kinds of specific use cases: navigation and process use cases and specific activities, such as browse, search and user transactions. A **Navigation** use case comprises a set of browse activities that the WebUser will perform to reach a target node. A browse activity is the action of following a link and is represented by the metaclass **Browse**. A browse activity can be enriched by search actions, which is represented by a **Search** metaclass. A Search has a set of parameters, which let define queries on the content. The results are shown in the target node.

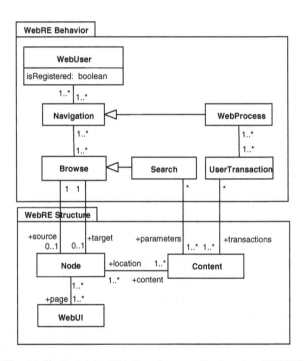

Fig. 4. Metamodel for Web Requirements Engineering (WebRE)

More complex activities are expressed in terms of transactions initiated by the user, like checkout in an e-shop or an online reservation. Such actions, which imply a transaction operation, are modeled by a metaclass **UserTransaction** in the behavior package. The second kind of use case is the **WebProcess,** which is refined by activities of type browse, search, and at least one user transaction.

A **WebUser** is any user who interacts with a Web System. Examples of instances of WebUser are RegisteredUser, Non-Registered User and System Administrator.

The second package of the metamodel is the **structure** package, which contains the metaclasses used to describe the structural elements of a Web system: content, node and Web user interface.

A **Node** is a point of the navigation where the user finds information. Each instance of a browse activity starts in a node (source) and finishes in another one (target). Nodes are presented to the user as pages. Note that a node can be associated to one or more pages, and a page may be associated to one or more nodes (e.g. asynchronous communication). The concept of page is represented by the **WebUI** metaclass. Besides, each node can show different pieces of information. Each piece of information of a Web system is represented as a metaclass **Content**.

The metamodel can be specified in more detail including invariants. For instance, a search activity has associated a node as source, which is the location of the parameters that will be used for the query of the search. Such an invariant can be formally expressed as an OCL constraint as follows:

```
context Browse
inv: self.oclIsKindOf(Search) implies
     self.parameters -> forAll
     (p | p.location -> includes(self.source))
```

Table 3 shows the mappings from the metaclasses of both packages WebRE Behavior and WebRE Structure to the modeling elements of the methods NDT, OOHDM, UWE and W2000. The shadowed cells express that the method of the corresponding row does not provide a modeling element that supports the metamodel concept of the first column.

Table 3. Mapping metamodel concepts to elements of Web methodologies

WebRE Concept		NDT	OOHDM	UWE	W2000
Behavior	WebUser	Actor	Actor	Actor	Actor
	Navitation	Visualization prototype	Use case	Navigation use case	Browse use case
	WebProcess	Use case	Use case	Use case	Use case
	Browse	Visualization prototype	Single choice	Activity	
	Search	Phrase	Optional data entry	Activity	
	UserTransaction	Functional requirement	Application processing	Activity	
Structure	Node	Visualization prototype			
	Content	Storage requirement	Data entry	Class	
	WebUI		Interaction		

In NDT, WebUsers are defined with the template AC used to define actors of a Web system. The concepts of Navigation, Browse and Node are modeled as interaction requirements in a template named visualization prototypes (VP). A Search action is modeled with phrases, which are written in BNL (bounded natural language) in order to select a set of content instances to be presented to a WebUser. WebProcesses are treated with use cases and the UserTransaction activities are modeled with the functional requirements template (FR). Finally, the Content concept is described by the storage information requirement (SR). NDT does not contain any modeling element that covers WebUIs from the metamodel.

OOHDM uses use cases and actors to represent WebUser, Navigation and Web-Process. In addition, OOHDM provides UID elements to model in the requirements phase activities and structural elements with exception of Node. The Browse activities are represented in OOHDM with single choices, the Search activities with optional data entries and UserTransaction activities with application processing. Content is represented by data entries and WebUI with interactions.

UWE uses the UML behavioral elements use case and activity and the structural element class to model the concepts defined in the Web requirements metamodel. From the structural elements UWE only supports the content concept in requirements modeling. UWE extends the UML using the extension mechanism provided by the UML to define the modeling element Navigation use case, which is defined to represent the typical browsing interaction of Web users with Web systems. For the more detailed description of the Web user-Web system interactions activity diagrams are used without specific modeling elements that distinguish between Browse, Search and UserTransaction activities. Finally, classes in object flows associated to the activity diagrams model Content.

W2000 restricts the support to modeling elements actor and both types of use cases. In fact, it only provides elements for modeling in the large, i.e. building a UML use case model. The use case model contains actors, general use cases and specific browse use cases. W2000 recommends depicting two separated use case diagrams: one for general use cases and another for use cases of type browse, thus separating the navigation and process concerns.

4   Towards a Common Notation

A metamodel provides a basis for the definition of a notation and the development of tools.

The objective is to define on the one hand a notation for the concepts included in the metamodel for Web requirements that allow for intuitive and expressive specification of the requirements of Web applications.

On the other hand a domain specific modeling language requires tool support for their use in the development of Web systems. Limited impact can be achieved by proprietary notation and prototypes. Instead wide dissemination is achieved by providing plug-ins or extensions of already in use CASE tools, such as those for the UML. Therefore we define the modeling language for Web requirements as an extension of UML using the extensions mechanisms provided by the UML – a so-called UML profile.

The UML profile for Web requirements engineering specifies how the concepts of the WebRE metamodel relate to and are represented in standard UML using stereotypes and constraints.

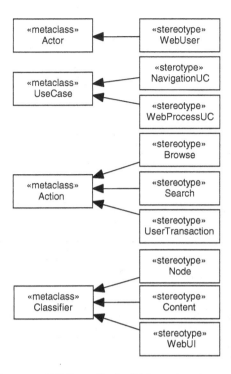

Fig. 5. Modeling elements of UML profile for Web requirements engineering (WebRE)

Table 4. Icons for stereotypes of the WebRE profile

WebRE Behavior	Navigation	☐
	WebProcess	Σ
	Browse	⇒
	Search	?
	UserTransaction	⇔
WebRE Structure	Node	☐
	Content	O
	WebUI	▣

Fig. 5 shows the graphical representation of the UML profile showing how the stereotypes defined for each class of the metamodel extend a UML metaclass (OMG-UML 2.0, 2005). Table 4 shows the icons proposed for stereotypes of the WebRE profile. We use the common language provided by the profile to depict the use case diagram of the CD e-shop example presented in Sect. 2 (Fig. 6a). The model of the Checkout process is shown in Fig. 6b.

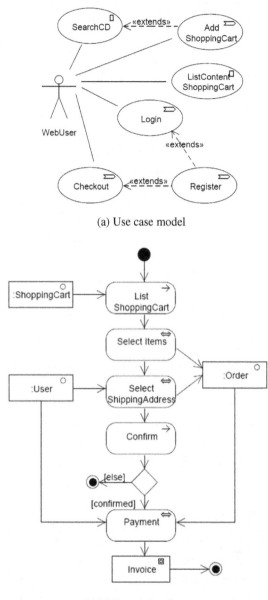

(a) Use case model

(b) UML activity diagram

Fig. 6. CD e-shop example using the UML Profile notation for Web requirements

5   Conclusions and Future Work

In order to reinforce requirements engineering in Web methodologies we present a metamodel for Web requirements (WebRE). The metamodel provides key concepts for the requirements specification in the Web domain, such as specific use cases: navigation use case and Web process use case; specific activities such as browse, search and user transaction; and structural elements such as content, node and user interface of Web systems. We define a common modeling language – a so-called UML profile – to express these Web requirements concepts. A modeling language with Web specific constructs has the advantage of producing compact but semantically rich domain specific models. The additional advantage of a UML profile is the tool support given by UML generic CASE tools.

The disadvantage of such a common modeling language is the high probability that Web methodologies that already cover requirements engineering tasks will not replace the own notation and techniques in use by now. In contrast, methods that do not address requirements specification, can easily integrate the presented approach. However, we show that a mapping between elements of the metamodel and the modeling elements of the methodologies of the first group is possible.

A consensus would offer therefore the application of model transformations based on the model-driven development (MDD) principles. For example, the development of a Web system could be started using a graphical notation like activity diagrams proposed by UWE or UIDs of OOHDM, which are more intuitive to provide an overview of the Web system to be built. Afterwards, the visual models are transformed into a set of NDT formatted specifications, in order, for instance, to allow further modeling of details needed in next phase of the development process.

Subject to future work will be the specification of relations and transformations among the elements of the metamodel of Web requirements and the modeling elements of the different methodologies. For the specification we will use QVT (OMG-QVT, 2005), which is an OMG standard for model-to-model transformations.

For tool support, we plan to integrate transformation facilities among NDT and UWE or NDT and the modeling language defined in this paper for Web requirements (WebRE) into the NDT-Tool.

References

Baresi L., Garzotto F., Paolini P.: Extending UML for Modelling Web Applications. In: Annual Hawaii Int. Conf. on System Sciences, pp. 1285–1294. Miami, USA (2001)

Escalona, M.J., Torres, J., Mejías, M., Reina, A.M.: NDT-Tool: A CASE Tool to deal with Requirements in Web Information Systems. In: Lovelle, J.M.C., Rodríguez, B.M.G., Gayo, J.E.L., Ruiz, M.d.P.P., Aguilar, L.J. (eds.) ICWE 2003. LNCS, vol. 2722, pp. 212–213. Springer, Heidelberg (2003)

Escalona, M.J.: Modelos y Técnicas para la Especificación y el Análisis de la Navegación en Sistemas Software. Ph. Thesis University of Seville (2004)

Escalona, M.J., Koch, N.: Requirements Engineering for Web Applications: A Comparative Study. Journal on Web Engineering 2(3), 193–212 (2004)

Insfrán, E., Pastor, O., Wieringa, R.: Requirements Engineering-Based Conceptual Modelling. Requirements Engineering Journal 7(1) (2002)

Kappel, G., Pröll, B., Reich, S., Retschizegger, W.: Web Engineering, dpunkt Verlag (2003)

Koch, N., Kraus, A.: The expressive Power of UML-based Web Engineering. In: Second Int. Workshop on Web-oriented Software Technology (IWWOST02), pp. 105–119. Málaga, Spain (2002)

Lowe D., Eklund J. Client Needs and the Design Process in Web Projects. Journal on Web Engineering 1(1), 23–36 (2002)

Lowe, D., Hall, W.: Hypermedia and the Web. An Engineering Approach. John Wiley & Son, Chichester (1999)

OMG, MOF 2.0 Query/Views/ Transformations Final Adopted Specification, Object Management Group (2005), http://www.omg.org/cgi-bin/apps/doc?ad/05-11-01.pdf

Pressman, R.: Software Engineering: A Practitioner's Approach. McGraw Hill, New York (2005)

Schwabe, D., Rossi, G.: An Object Oriented Approach to Web-Based Application Design. In: Theory and Practice of Object Systems, vol. 4(4), Wiley and Sons, New York, USA (1998)

Sommerville, I., Ransom, J.: An Empirical Study of Industrial Requirements Engineering Process Assessment and Improvement. ACM TOSEM 14(1), 85–117 (2005)

Vilain, P., Schwabe, D., Sieckenius de Souza, C.: A diagrammatic Tool for Representing User Interaction. In: Evans, A., Kent, S., Selic, B. (eds.) UML 2000. LNCS, vol. 1939, pp. 133–147. Springer, Heidelberg (2000)

Wieringa, R.: Requirement Engineering: Problem Analysis and Solution Specification. In: Koch, N., Fraternali, P., Wirsing, M. (eds.) ICWE 2004. LNCS, vol. 3140, pp. 13–16. Springer, Heidelberg (2004)

Part III

Society, e-Business and e-Government

Efficient Management of Multi-version XML Documents for e-Government Applications*

Federica Mandreoli[1], Riccardo Martoglia[1], Fabio Grandi[2], and Maria Rita Scalas[2]

[1] Dip. di Ingegneria dell'Informazione, Università di Modena e Reggio Emilia
Via Vignolese 905/b, I-41100, Modena, Italy
{mandreoli.federica,martoglia.riccardo}@unimo.it
[2] Dip. di Elettronica, Informatica e Sistemistica, Alma Mater Studiorum - Università di Bologna
Viale Risorgimento 2, I-40136, Bologna, Italy
{fgrandi,mrscalas}@deis.unibo.it

Abstract. This paper describes our research activities in developing efficient systems for the management of multi-version XML documents in an e-Government scenario. The application aim is to enable citizens to access personalized versions of resources, like norm texts and information made available on the Web by public administrations. In the first system developed, four temporal dimensions (publication, validity, efficacy and transaction times) were used to represent the evolution of norms in time and their resulting versioning and a stratum approach was used for its implementation on top of a relational DBMS. Recently, the multi-version management system has migrated to a different architecture ("native" approach) based on a multi-version XML query processor developed on purpose. Moreover, a new semantic dimension has been added to the versioning mechanism, in order to represent applicability of norms to different classes of citizens according to their digital identity. Classification of citizens is based on the management of an ontology with the deployment of semantic Web techniques. Preliminary experiments showed an encouraging performance improvement with respect to the stratum approach and a good scalability behaviour. Current work includes a more accurate modeling of the citizen's ontology, which could also require a redesign of the document storage scheme, and the development of a complete infrastructure for the management of the citizen's digital identity.

Keywords: e-Government, XML, document retrieval, temporal database, semantic Web.

1 Introduction

In this paper we present our research activities concerning the implementation of Web information systems for e-Government applications (EC E-Gov, 2004; US E-Gov, 2004). More precisely, our work makes use of temporal database and semantic Web techniques to provide *personalized* access to multi-version resources and services provided by the

---

* This work has been supported by the MIUR-PRIN Project: "The European citizen in e-Governance: philosophical-juridical, legal, information and economic profiles".

J. Filipe, J. Cordeiro, and V. Pedrosa (Eds.): WEBIST 2005/2006, LNBIP 1, pp. 283–294, 2007.
© Springer-Verlag Berlin Heidelberg 2007

Public Administration (PA). The offering of personalized versions is aimed at improving and optimizing the involvement of citizens in the e-Governance process. In particular, we consider the selective access to norm texts and documents made available on Web repositories in XML format (XML, 2004).

First of all, the fast dynamics involved in normative systems implies the coexistence of *multiple versions* of the norm texts stored in a repository, since laws are continually subject to amendments and modifications. In fact, it is crucial to reconstruct the *consolidated version* of a norm as produced by the application of all the modifications it underwent so far, that is the form in which it currently belongs to the regulations and must be enforced today. However, also past versions are still important, not only for historical reasons: for example, if a Court has to pass judgment today on some fact committed in the past, the version of norms which must be applied to the case is the one that was in force then.

In other words, temporal concerns are widespread in the e-Government domain and a legal information system should be able to retrieve or reconstruct on demand any version of a given document to meet common application requirements. Moreover, another kind of versioning plays an important role, because some norms or some of their parts have or acquire a limited applicability. For example, a given norm (e.g. defining tax treatment) may contain some articles which are applicable to different classes of citizens: one article is applicable to unemployed persons, one article to self-employed persons, one article to public servants only and so on. Hence, a citizen accessing the retrieval service may be interested in finding a *personalized version* of the norm, that is a version only containing articles which are applicable to his/her personal case. Finally, notice that temporal and limited applicability aspects, though orthogonal, may also interplay in the production and management of versions. For instance, a new norm might state a modification to a preexisting norm, such as the modified norm becomes applicable to a limited category of citizens only (e.g. retired persons), whereas the rest of the citizens remain subject to the unmodified norm.

In this context, we defined data models for multi-version XML documents and built prototype systems for their efficient management in a Web-based e-Government application scenario. In particular, in this work we will describe and compare two management systems, meeting different application requirements, that we recently developed using different architectures and implementation techniques.

The first system is based on multi-dimensional temporal versioning, where temporal aspects are captured by adding timestamping attributes to the XML markup. The prototype was implemented using a "stratum" approach on top of a commercial DBMS and will be briefly described in Section 2 (a more detailed description and evaluation has also been published before as (Grandi et al., 2003a; Grandi et al., 2003b; Grandi et al., 2005)).

The second system is the current outcome of an ongoing research, which is introduced in (Grandi et al., 2004), and represents the original contribution of the present work. The XML data model on which it is based includes semantic annotations in the multi-versioning mechanism, in order to capture limited applicability and to support personalized access, and will be described in Section 3. The prototype is implemented following a "native" approach, which will be presented in Section 4 and is currently under evaluation.

Developments and extensions of the system which are planned for the near future will be described in Section 5. These include an improvement in the ontological modeling of citizens to meet more advanced application requirements and a completion of the technological infrastructure needed to make our system fully operational in a real e-Government environment.

Conclusions will finally be found in Section 6.

2   Temporal Versioning in the "Stratum" Approach

In a first phase of the research we focused on temporal aspects and on the effective and efficient management of time-varying norm texts. To this purpose, we developed a temporal XML data model which uses four time dimensions to correctly represent the evolution of norms in time and their resulting versioning. The considered dimensions are:

Publication time. It is the time of publication of the norm on the Official Journal. It has the same semantics as event time (and availability time, as the two time dimensions, in such a context, coincide). It is a global and unchangeable property for the whole norm contents and, thus, it is not used as a versioning dimension inside text.

Validity time. It is the time the norm is in force. It has the same semantics of valid time as in temporal databases (Jensen et al., 1998), since it represents the time the norm actually belongs to the regulations in the real world.

Efficacy time. It is the time the norm can be applied to a concrete case. It usually corresponds to the validity of norms, but it can be the case that an abrogated norm continues to be applicable to a limited number of cases. Until such cases cease to exist, the norm continues its efficacy though no longer in force.

Transaction time. It is the time (some part of) the norm is stored in a computer system. It has the same semantics of transaction time as in temporal databases (Jensen et al., 1998).

The data model was defined via an XML Schema (XMLSchema, 2004), where the structure of norms is defined by means of a contents-section-article-paragraph hierarchy and multiple content versions can be defined at each level of the hierarchy. Each version is characterized by timestamp attributes defining its temporal pertinence with respect to each of the validity, efficacy and transaction time dimensions.

The model is also equipped with two basic operators for the management of norm modifications: one is devoted to change the textual content of a norm portion and the other allows modifications to the temporal pertinence of a given version. The former can be used for deletion of (a part of) the norm (abrogation), or the introduction of a new part of the norm (integration), or the replacement of (a part of) the norm (substitution). The latter can be used to deal with the time extension or the suspension of (part of) the norm.

```
FOR $a IN path
WHERE constraints on $a
RETURN const-tree(document($a),
                  temporal specs)
```

Fig. 1. An XQuery-equivalent query executable on our first system

Legal text repositories are usually managed by traditional information retrieval systems where users are allowed to access their contents by means of keyword-based queries expressing the subjects they are interested in. We extended such a framework by offering to users the possibility of expressing temporal specifications for the reconstruction of a consistent version of the retrieved normative acts (consolidated act). More precisely, the system is able to answer queries having the XQuery (XQuery, 2004) form as in Fig. 1.

The statement following the standard XQuery FLWR syntax allows users to express selection constraints on the variable $a iterating over the nodes returned by the path expression path. Search keywords can be specified by means of the function contains in the WHERE clause (e.g. contains($a,'sea')). In the RETURN clause, the operator const-tree is devoted to the reconstruction of the temporally consistent versions of the XML documents containing the selected nodes (*consolidated norms*). The temporal specs expression is the conjunction of temporal selection predicates on the four supported temporal dimensions.

Our approach is the first to provide full search and reconstruction functionalities with respect to all time dimensions, whereas previous approaches only provided a limited support. For example, the temporal XML markup adopted in the Norma-System described in (Palmirani and Brighi, 2002) includes publication, validity and efficacy time but reconstruction of consolidated versions is made with respect to validity only (other time dimensions can be used as additional search fields in full-text search).

Our temporal data model with the modification and query operators was implemented in a prototype system for the management and maintenance of a collection of time-varying norms. The system is able to store norms encoded as XML documents and efficiently access them by answering queries which can involve both temporal constraints and search keywords.

The system architecture is based on two different components: the former consists of the XML document management facilities offered by Oracle 9i (Oracle, 2004) to handle structural and textual constraints, the latter is a software stratum that we built on top of the former to handle the temporal aspects. Extensive experimental results on the system behaviour show good performance and the ability to manage large collections of XML multi-version documents. A discussion of such architectural solution, named the "stratum" approach, in comparison with our new implementation solution, named the "native" approach, is carried out in Section 4.

A detailed description of the stratum approach and an account of its evaluation can be found in (Grandi et al., 2003b; Grandi et al., 2005).

3   Introduction of the Semantic Versioning

In a second phase of the research, the multi-version model based on temporal dimensions was extended to include a semantic versioning dimension in order to provide personalized access to norm texts. In general, machine-understanding of the information available on the Semantic Web requires a semantic markup of the contents and the availability of automated reasoning tools. In order to let information and its interpretation be shared by several agents including automatic tools, the introduction of common reference *ontologies* becomes necessary (Guarino, 1998; WebOnt, 2004). In our case, we defined a *civic ontology*, which corresponds to a classification of citizens based on the distinctions introduced by successive norms (*founding acts*) that imply some limitation, total or partial, in their applicability. Hence, in our extended model, the new versioning dimension encodes information about the applicability of different parts of a norm text to the relevant classes of the civic ontology.

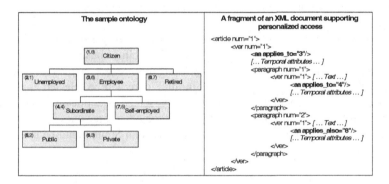

Fig. 2. An example of civic ontology, where each class has a name and is associated to a (pre,post) pair, and a fragment of a XML norm containing applicability annotations

Consider, for instance, Fig. 2. The left part of the figure depicts a simple civic ontology built from a small corpus of norms ruling the status of citizens with respect to their work position. The right part of the figure shows a fragment of a multi-version XML norm text supporting personalized access with respect to this ontology. Notice that, at this stage of the project, we manage "tree-like" ontologies defined as class taxonomies induced by the IS-A relationship. This allows us to exploit the pre-order and post-order properties of trees in order to enumerate the nodes and check ancestor-descendant relationships between the classes; such codes are displayed in the upper left corner of the ontology classes in the Figure, in the form: (pre-order,post-order). For instance, the class "Employee" has pre-order "3" which is also its identifier, whereas its post order is "6". The article in the XML fragment on the right of Fig. 2 is composed of two paragraphs and contains applicability annotations (*aa*). Notice that applicability is inherited by descendant nodes unless locally redefined. Hence, by means of redefinitions we can also introduce, for each part of a document, complex applicability properties including extensions or restrictions with respect to ancestors. For instance, the whole article in the

```
FOR      $a IN norm
WHERE    textConstr ($a//paragraph//text(), 'health AND care')
AND      tempConstr ('vTime OVERLAPS PERIOD('2002-01-01','2004-12-31')')
AND      tempConstr ('eTime OVERLAPS PERIOD('2002-01-01','2004-12-31')')
AND      applConstr ('class_7')
RETURN   $a
```

Fig. 3. An XQuery-equivalent query executable on our second system

Figure is applicable to civic class "3" (*applies_to*) and by default to all its descendants. However, its first paragraph is applicable to class "4", which is a restriction, whereas the second one is also applicable to class "8" (*applies_also*), which is an extension. The reconstruction of pertinent versions of the norm based on its applicability annotations is very important in an e-Government scenario. The representation of extensions and restrictions gives rise to high expressiveness and flexibility in such a context.

As to the queries that can be submitted by a user in the new system, they can contain four types of constraints: temporal, structural, textual and applicability. Such constraints are completely orthogonal and allow him/her to perform very accurate searches in the XML norm repository. Let us focus first on the applicability constraint. Consider again the ontology and norm fragment in Fig. 2: for John Smith, a "self-employed" citizen (i.e. belonging to class "7"), the sample article in the Figure will be selected as pertinent, but only the second paragraph will be actually presented as applicable. Furthermore, the applicability constraint can be combined with the other three ones in order to fully support a multi-dimensional retrieval. For instance, John Smith could be interested in all the norms ...

- ... which contain paragraphs (*structural constraint*) dealing with health care (*textual constraint*), ...
- ... which were valid and in effect between 2002 and 2004 (*temporal constraint*), ...
- ... and which are applicable to his class (*applicability constraint*).

Such a query can be issued to our system using the standard XQuery FLWR syntax in Fig. 3, where `textConstr`, `tempConstr`, and `applConstr` are suitable functions allowing the specification of the textual, temporal and applicability constraints, respectively (the structural constraint is implicit in the XPath expressions used in the XQuery query). Notice that the temporal constraints can involve all the four available time dimensions (publication, validity, efficacy and transaction), allowing high flexibility in satisfying the information needs of citizens in the e-Government scenario. In particular, by means of validity and efficacy time constraints, a user is able to extract consolidated current versions from the multi-version corpora, or to access past versions of particular norm texts, all consistently reconstructed by the system on the basis of its needs and personalized on the basis of his/her identity.

4   The "Native" Approach

All the multi-version and personalized-access XML norm querying features have been implemented in our second prototype system. The system architecture is shown on the

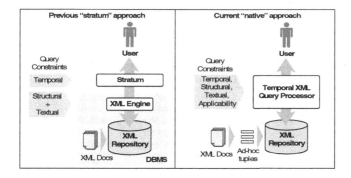

Fig. 4. First ("stratum") versus second ("native") system architecture

right part of Fig. 4 and is based on an "XML-native" approach, since it is composed of a Temporal XML Query Processor designed on purpose, which is able to manage the XML data repository and to provide all the temporal, structural, textual and applicability query facilities in a single component. The prototype is implemented in Java JDK 1.5 and exploits ad-hoc data structures (relying on embedded "light" DBMS libraries) and algorithms which allows users to store and reconstruct on-the-fly XML norm texts satisfying the four types of constraints. Differently from the stratum approach we used in our previous prototype (see the left part of Fig. 4), where temporal constraints were processed separately, all the structural, textual and temporal constraints are simultaneously handled by the Temporal XML Query Processor. Such a component stores the XML norms not as entire documents but by converting them into a collection of ad-hoc temporal tuples, representing each of its multi-version parts (i.e., paragraphs, articles, and so on); these data structures are then exploited to efficiently perform structural join algorithms (Al-Khalifa et al., 2002) we specifically devised and tuned for the temporal/semantic multi-version context. Textual constraints, like in the stratum approach, are handled by means of an inverted index. Furthermore, the current architecture also provides support to personalized access by handling the new applicability constraints as required by the reference e-Government application scenario. The benefits of our native approach over the stratum one are manifold:

- by querying ad-hoc and temporally-enhanced structures (which have a finer granularity than the entire documents managed by standard XML engines), the native approach is able to access and retrieve only the strictly necessary data;
- only the parts which are required and which satisfy the temporal constraints are used for the reconstruction of the retrieved documents;
- there is no need to retrieve whole XML documents and build space-consuming structures such as DOM trees, as required in the stratum approach.

As a consequence, we expect the query processing efficiency could greatly be enhanced and the memory requirements dramatically reduced. In order to evaluate the effectiveness of the "native" approach, we compared its performance with our previous "stratum" implementation on a common query benchmark and also conducted a number of exploratory experiments to analyse its behaviour in performing personalized access

Table 1. Features of the test queries and query execution time of the "stratum" and "native" approaches (time in milliseconds, collection C1)

Query	Constraints				Selectivity	Performance (msec)	
	Tm	St	Tx	Ap		Stratum	Native
Q1	-	✓	✓	-	0.6%	2891	1046
Q2	-	✓	✓	-	4.02%	43240	2970
Q3	✓	✓	-	-	2.9%	47638	6523
Q4	✓	✓	✓	-	0.68%	2151	1015
Q5	✓	✓	✓	-	1.46%	3130	2550
Q1-A	-	✓	✓	✓	0.23%	n/a	1095
Q2-A	-	✓	✓	✓	1.65%	n/a	3004
Q3-A	✓	✓	-	✓	1.3%	n/a	6760
Q4-A	✓	✓	✓	✓	0.31%	n/a	1020
Q5-A	✓	✓	✓	✓	0.77%	n/a	2602

through applicability constraints. The experiments have been effected on a Pentium 4 2.5Ghz Windows XP Professional workstation, equipped with 512MB RAM and a RAID0 cluster of 2 80GB EIDE disks with NT file system (NTFS). We performed the tests on three XML document sets of increasing size: collection C1 (5,000 XML norm text documents), C2 (10,000 documents) and C3 (20,000 documents). In this paper, due to space requirements, we will present in detail the results obtained on the collection C1, then we will briefly describe the scalability performance shown on the other two collections. The total size of the collections is 120MB, 240MB, and 480MB, respectively. In all collections the documents were synthetically generated by means of an ad-hoc XML generator we developed, which is able to produce different documents compliant to our multi-version and personalized access model. For each collection the average, minimum and maximum document sizes are 24KB, 2KB and 125KB, respectively.

Experiments were conducted by submitting queries of five different types (Q1-Q5). Table 1 presents the features of the test queries and the query execution time for both the "stratum" and the "native" architectures. All the queries require structural support (St constraint); types Q1 and Q2 also involve textual searches by keywords (Tx constraint), with different selectivities; type Q3 contains temporal conditions (Tm constraint) on three time dimensions: transaction, valid and publication time; types Q4 and Q5 mix the previous ones since they contain both keyword searches and temporal conditions. For each of those query types, we also present a personalized access variant involving an additional applicability constraint (denoted as Qx-A in Table 1).

Let us first focus on the upper part of the table, and in particular on the comparison of the performances offered by the two approaches. The native approach shows to be faster in every context, providing a shorter response time (including query analysis, retrieval of the qualifying norm parts and reconstruction of the result) of approximately one or two seconds for most of the queries. Notice that, while the response time of the stratum approach is not too different for query types Q1, Q4, Q5, for the other query types the performance gap is quite important (for instance, query Q2 is answered approximately 15 times slower in the stratum approach). The reason is that the selectivity of the query predicates strongly influences the performance of the stratum approach, seriously impairing its performance when large amounts of documents containing some (typically small) relevant portions have to be retrieved, as it happens for queries Q2 and Q3. On the other hand, the native approach is able to deliver a faster and more reliable performance in all cases, since it practically avoids the retrieval of useless document parts. Further, consider that, for the same reasons, the main memory requirements of the Temporal XML Query Processor embedded in the native approach are, on average, 5% or less of the stratum approach. This property is also very promising towards future extensions to cope with concurrent multi-user query processing.

The lower part of the table presents the performance of our second system with respect to the queries involving additional applicability constraints, enabling personalized access. Thanks to the properties of the adopted pre-order and post-order encoding of the civic classes, the system is able to solve personalization problems by means of simple comparisons involving such encodings and, thus, with a very high efficiency. The time needed to answer the personalized access versions of the Q1–Q5 queries is approximately 0.5-1% more than for the original versions. Moreover, since the applicability annotations of each part of an XML document are stored as simple integers, also the size of the applicability annotated tuples, as stored in the system, is practically unchanged (only a 3-4% storage space overhead is required with respect to documents without semantic versioning), even with quite complex annotations involving several applicability extensions and restrictions.

Finally, we only report a comment about the performance of our current prototype in querying the other two collections C2 and C3 and, therefore, concerning the the scalability of the system. We ran the same queries of the previous tests on the larger collections and saw that the computing time always grew sub-linearly with the number of documents. For instance, query Q1 executed on the 10,000 documents of collection C2 (which is as double as C1) took 1,366 msec (i.e. the system was only 30% slower); similarly, on the 20,000 documents of collection C3, the average response time was 1,741 msec (i.e. the system was less than 30% slower than with C2). Also with the other queries the measured trend was the same, thus showing the good scalability of the system in every type of query context.

5 Future Developments

Our current research work is devoted to the extensions of the current framework and to the development of a complete technological infrastructure to enable our approach to be self-contained and usable in a large Web-based e-Government scenario, as envisioned in (Grandi et al., 2004).

The adoption of a tree-like civic ontology –that is based on a taxonomy induced by the IS-A relationship– is sufficient to satisfy basic application requirements as far as applicability constraints and personalization services are concerned. However, more advanced application requirements may include a more sophisticated ontology definition. As a matter of fact, real-world norm corpora, if analyzed in full detail, can lead to the formalization of complex relationships between civic subclasses giving rise to ontologies structured, in general, as a graph. Hence, extensions to the framework are required in order to overcome the limitations of dealing with a tree-like civic ontology in our current approach: the XML storage organization and the query processing algorithm must be revisited, since the solutions adopted so far rely both on the ontology and document tree structure (e.g. decomposition in temporal tuples and exploitation of pre- and post-order numbering).

On the other hand, the development of a complete infrastructure is needed to make our approach self-contained and fully operational in a real-world e-Government environment. In fact, in addition to the availability on the Web of the query answering system and of the civic ontology, several other components are needed for a full operativeness of the whole system, including administration and maintenance facilities.

First of all, the citizen's digital identity is defined as the total amount of information concerning him/her, which is necessary for the sake of classification with respect to the ontology. All such information must be retrievable in an automatic way from the PA databases. To this purpose, facilities for querying PA databases must be provided and implemented through standardized access services. In order to supply the desired services, the digital identity is to be modelled and represented within the system in a form such that it can be translated into the same language used for the ontology (e.g. a Description Logic (Baader et al., 2002)). In this way, during the classification procedure, the matching between the civic ontology classes and the citizen's digital identity can be reduced to a standard reasoning task (e.g. ontology entailment for the underlying Description Logic). The reconstruction and the classification operations will be encapsulated into suitable Web services.

Moreover, each time a new founding act is enforced, the civic ontology needs to be updated and its consistency re-checked. Actually, the ontology update process cannot be fully automated, since it is a delicate task which needs advice by human experts and "official validation" of the outcomes. However, computer tools and graphic environments (e.g. based on the Protégé platform (Protégé, 2004)) could be provided to assist the human experts to perform this task. Moreover, the introduction of a new founding act must also trigger the specification of a new Web service aimed at retrieving from the network the information necessary to verify the position of a citizen with respect to the distinguishing features newly introduced by the founding act. For example, if the new law states some benefit for former public servants retired since 2001, the ontology must be enriched with a new subclass corresponding to such a description, the norm will be annotated with a reference to the new subclass and, at the same time, a new Web service must be specified in order to verify whether a citizen belongs to the new subclass by querying the database of the public body paying out pensions. The specification of such services could be completely automated or, more likely, should be effected through a semi-automated process involving a human expert by means of an "intelligent" interactive editor, to be used for the recording of the new laws in legal databases. Once formally specified (and "officially" validated), such services will anyway allow a completely automated verification, by effectively and efficiently supplying the fragment of the citizen's digital identity which can be used for the desired high-level services.

For the specification of reconstruction, classification and identification services, we intend to adopt a standard declarative formalism (e.g. based on XML/SOAP

(SOAP, 2004), like WSDL, DAML-S, BPEL4WS). The study of services and of the mechanisms necessary to their semi-automatic specification will be dealt with in future research.

6 Conclusion

In this paper we presented our research work concerning the design and implementation of efficient Web-based information systems for e-Government applications. Recent activities include the development of a platform ("stratum" approach) for temporal management of multi-version norm texts on top of a commercial DBMS and the migration of such a system towards a more efficient platform ("native" approach) for which a specialized Temporal XML Query Processor has been designed. The new system also offers advanced functionalities, as it provides a personalized access to resources on the basis of the digital identity of citizens. While the first system employs temporal database techniques for the management and maintenance of multi-version XML data, the second system also employs Semantic Web techniques, including the adoption of an ontology, for the management of applicability constraints and personalized access.

Preliminary experimental work on query performance, with repositories of syntectic XML documents, showed encouraging results. In particular, the native approach proved to be very efficient in a large set of experimental situations and showed excellent scale-up figures with varying load configurations.

Future work will consider the improvement of the approach to cope with more advanced application requirements and the completion of the technological infrastructure required with the implementation of auxiliary services. Further work will also include the assessment of our developed systems in a concrete working environment, with real users and in the presence of a large repository of real legal documents.

References

Al-Khalifa, S., Jagadish, H., Patel, J.M., Wu, Y., Koudas, N., Srivastava, D.: Structural joins: A primitive for efficient xml query pattern matching. In: Proc. of 18th International Conference on Data Engineering (ICDE 2002). San Jose, CA, pp. 141–154 (2002)

Baader, F., Horrocks, I., Sattler, U.: Description logics for the semantic web. Künstliche Intelligenz 16(4), 57–59 (2002)

EC E-Gov. European commission e-government home page: (2004) http://europa.eu.int/information_society/eeurope/2005/all_about/egovernment/index_en.htm

Grandi, F., Mandreoli, F., Scalas, M.R., Tiberio, P.: Management of the citizen's digital identity and access to multi-version norm texts on the semantic web. In: Proc. of the Intl' Symposium on Challenges in the Internet and Interdisciplinary (IPSI 2004), Pescara, Italy (2004)

Grandi, F., Mandreoli, F., Tiberio, P.: Temporal modelling and management of normative documents in xml format. Data & Knowledge Engineering. vol. 47 (in press 2005)

Grandi, F., Mandreoli, F., Tiberio, P., Bergonzini, M.: A temporal data model and management system for normative texts in xml format. In: Proc. of the 15th ACM Intl' Workshop on Web Information and Data Management (WIDM), New Orleans, LA, pp. 29–36 (2003)

Grandi, F., Mandreoli, F., Tiberio, P., Bergonzini, M.: A temporal data model and system architecture for the management of normative texts. In: Proc. of the 11th Natlional Conf. on Advanced Database Systems (SEBD), Cetraro, Italy, pp. 169–178 (2003)

Guarino, N. (ed.): Formal Ontology in Information Systems. IOS Press, Amsterdam (1998)

Jensen, C.S., Dyreson, C.E., et al.: The Consensus Glossary of Temporal Database Concepts - February 1998 Version. In: Etzion, O., Jajodia, S., Sripada, S. (eds.) Temporal Databases: Research and Practice. LNCS, vol. 1399, pp. 367–405. Springer, Heidelberg (1998)

Oracle. The Oracle 9i database home page. Oracle corporation (2004), http://www.oracle.com/technology/products/oracle9i/

Palmirani, M., Brighi, R.: Norma-system: A legal document system for managing consolidated acts. In: Hameurlain, A., Cicchetti, R., Traunmüller, R. (eds.) DEXA 2002. LNCS, vol. 2453, pp. 310–320. Springer, Heidelberg (2002)

Protégé. The OWL plugin for Protégé home page: Stanford University (2004) http://protege.stanford.edu/plugins/owl/

SOAP. The web services activity home page: W3C Consortium (2004), http://www.w3.org/2000/xp/Group/

US E-Gov. U.S. president's e-government initiatives (2004), http://www.whitehouse.gov/omb/egov/

WebOnt. The web ontology group home page, W3C Consortium (2004), http://www.w3.org/2001/sw/WebOnt/

XML. The extensible markup language home page, W3C Consortium (2004), http://www.w3c.org/XML/

XMLSchema. The xml schema home page, W3C Consortium (2004), http://www.w3c.org/XML/Schema/

XQuery. The xml query home page, W3C Consortium (2004), http://www.w3c.org/XML/Query

E-namoSupport: A Web-Based Helpdesk Support Environment for Senior Citizens

Wei Zhou, Takami Yasuda, and Shigeki Yokoi

Graduate School of Information Science, Nagoya University, Japan
zhou@mdg.human.nagoya-u.ac.jp
yasuda@is.nagoya-u.ac.jp
yokoi@is.nagoya-u.ac.jp

Abstract. This study aims to track the development of a helpdesk support environment – E-namoSupport – to solve digital divide between seniors and other generations. This is one part of the E-namokun project, an information promotion project started in Nagoya city, Japan. E-namoSupport is a helpdesk system that has the following characteristics: (1) unlike general helpdesk systems, which generally only cover one organization, E-namoSupport has been developed through joint government, university, and NPO cooperation; (2) users are senior citizens with little or no PC experience; (3) its aim is not only to solve problems or answer questions, but also helping senior citizens learn more computer knowledge and further their computer skills. In the E-namoSupport environment we have developed four subsystems: a case trace system (CTS); a consultation management system (CMS); an FAQ System (FAQS); and an FAQ analysis system (FAQAS). We propose an information cycle model that efficiently manages information flow in the four subsystems as well as in organizations. We take senior citizens' attributes into account using a set of quizzes that help operators describe enquiry cases and make conversation flow more smoothly. We also design an easy-to-use interface and functions that help users access FAQS. Moreover, we develop E-namoSupport as a learning environment, providing suitable learning contents by analysing users' interests and needs, which helps users to improve their IT abilities of and enjoy life in the information age.

Keywords: Helpdesk, Lifelong learning, Frequently Asked Questions, Information Cycle Model.

1 Introduction

Although the availability of personal computers to senior citizens has increased, this availability is lower than for other generations. A recent survey (MPHPT, 2003) revealed that in Japan, over 90% of those aged between 13 to 39 years use the Internet, the percentage of use by those aged over 65 years old is extremely low, at less than 15%. This remarkable gap has been a cause for considerable concern. To combat this digital divide, in 2004, the easy-to-use E-namokun project, which aims at bringing more people, especially senior citizens, in touch with the information age by providing

J. Filipe, J. Cordeiro, and V. Pedrosa (Eds.): WEBIST 2005/2006, LNBIP 1, pp. 295–306, 2007.

simple Internet (Masato, 2005) and email (Kiichirou, 2005) tools, was been started in Nagoya city. The project was developed through joint government, university, and NPO cooperation, which is a national first.

In order to encourage more senior citizens to enjoy the project, several help and support methods have been planned and implemented. Courses on the use of E-namokun software were held at each ward's Lifelong Learning Center; special consultation rooms have been set up in two wards' Lifelong Learning Centers, providing face-to-face consultation for those using computers or the E-namokun software. Furthermore, a call center was set up to provide installation, utilization, and certification support, and other help for E-namokun software users. Such supports are viewed as key processes because the level of user satisfaction has a significant impact on whether they will maintain their interest in using computers.

As the importance of customer support is widely recognized, helpdesk systems are becoming more popular. In this context, we developed an enhanced web-based help-desk-support environment called E-namoSupport, which has four subsystems including a Case Trace System (CTS) for call center, a Consultation Management System (CMS) for consultation rooms, an FAQ System (FAQS) for users, and an FAQ Analysis System (FAQAS). Together, these provide an integrated and extensible platform that transforms the user service support into an effective and efficient service that meets senior citizens' requirements and offers them satisfaction.

The rest of the paper is organized as follows. In section 2 we discuss related work; section 3 describes E-namoSupport features; section 4 describes the architecture and information cycle model; and section 5 shows the four subsystems. In section 6 and 7 we offer some conclusions and discuss both our present and future works.

2 Related Work

Currently there is no hard and fast definition of the term 'help desk,' however its name implies a basic function of being a source of information or action on demand, to aid the caller in carrying out a given task. The Gartner group's definition of the help desk's mission (R.C.Marcella, 1996) is to provide a single point of contact and responsibility for rapid closure of end-user's problems.

With the advent of web technology that can provide dynamic, interactive, platform independent, and distributed services, operators and supporters can access online knowledge databases to track cases and provide answers; users can ask a question and get suitable solutions via any web browser. Web-based help desk systems provide several key functions that organize helpdesk activities into single web-based applications that can be accessed and maintained through a web browser. A number of web-based helpdesk products are popularly used in enterprises. For example, WebHotLine (S Foo, 2002) is designed and developed as an intelligent helpdesk environment in a large multinational corporation with major functions including fault information retrieval, online multilingual translation capability, different operating modes of video-conferencing, and direct intelligent fault diagnosis. NTT Inc (Kuwata, 1998) suggested an automated follow-up service for help desk customers, which identifies customer interests from their queries and automatically sends related Q&A information back to the customers.

In the field of education, some universities create their own help desks based on the FAQ style. For example, the State University of New York (Sandra, 1992) has an automated help desk system to answer student questions. FAQ share systems (Huu Le Van, 2002) aim to optimize the student-teacher interaction and evaluate learning effectiveness. These cases have been used in educational environments.

Currently, there are some commercial FAQs available for senior users, visually handicapped people, and novices, such as IBM and Fujitsu, which adopt easily accessed interfaces that take into consideration the difficulties users face when using computers.

Also, there are several relevant studies that examine the use of help desks. For example, Christine evaluates how shifts in management, organizational structure, incentives, software technologies, and other factors affect the development of help desk systems in a large organization (Christine, 2004).

3 The Features of E-namoSupport System

All of the above mentioned help desk systems have two major goals – to make the best use of the customer information gathered and to provide the best service quality. Our goals are as the same as these; moreover, because E-namokun project's organizations and users differs from general systems, the E-namoSupport helpdesk support system has some additional features, which are listed below:

(1) Information cycle in multiple organizations.
The E-namokun project was developed through joint government, university, and NPO cooperation, which was a first for Japan. Therefore, unlike general helpdesk systems that assist only one organization, the E-namoSupport system is used by multiple organizations. Our main tasks have been related to how to gather information from different parts and how to retrieve, reuse, and retain information. We proposed an information cycle model that processes information gathering, information publishing and information analysis among these organizations.

(2) Design for senior citizens.
Our users are mainly senior citizens and almost all of them are computer novices. When these users encounter a problem and call the operator, most of them cannot describe the problem in detail. In order to help operators describe enquiry cases correctly and in detail, we designed a set of case items to make conversations between the operator and the user run more smoothly. Further, in consideration of senior citizens' age-related attributes, we designed an easy-to-use interface with enlarged characters, buttons, and pointers, simplifying the operations, providing easily understood contents, and avoiding the use of technical terms.

(3) Learning content provisions.
Our aim is not only to answer questions and provide solutions to problems; we also aim to help senior citizens learn more computer knowledge and improve their IT abilities, helping them enjoy their lives in the information age. By analyzing the FAQ accessing status, we can understand senior citizens' learning needs and interests; based on this information, we can provide suitable learning content.

4   Overview of the E-namoSupport System

4.1   Structure of the E-namoSupport Environment

Before showing our system, we should first describe the duties and relationships of organizations in the E-namoSupport environment. As shown in figure 1, there are three types of organizations: a local government, two universities, and an NPO. Their duties are listed below:

- (Government) Local Lifelong Learning Center:

Local lifelong learning center in Nagoya city sets up special consultation rooms in ward lifelong learning centers to provide face-to-face consulting services for senior citizens. Consultants exchange information with each other, cooperate with the call center to get case solutions if they cannot resolve them alone, and give advice to help the call center create FAQ contents.

- (University) Technical support group:

The technical support group at Nagoya University and Chukyo University takes charge of technical and system support, including E-namoSupport maintenance and solving technical problems coming from the call center.

- (NPO) IT promotion organization:

The IT promotion Agency of the eco-cycle NPO, short for IT promotion organization, establishes the call center to provide support service through telephone and email, 8 hours a day, 5 days a week, as well as developing the FAQ system that users can access anytime via the Web. It manages user personal data, traces enquiry cases, answers and solves problems, asks for technical help from technical support group,

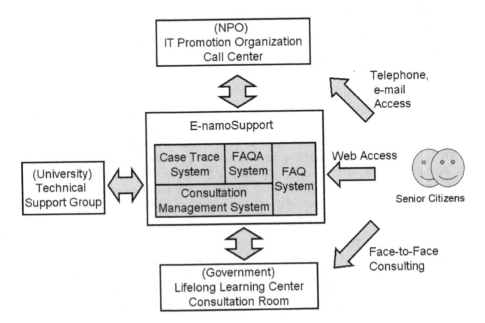

Fig. 1. Overview of E-namoSupport Environment

gathers enquiry cases from the consultation rooms, creates the FAQ documents and publishes them, analyzes the FAQ accessing status, and so on.

We developed four subsystems, including the consultation management system (CMS) for consultation rooms, the case trace system (CTS), the FAQ system (FAQS), and the FAQ analysis system (FAQAS) for the call center.

The E-namoSupport environment offers total support to users: telephone and mail support from the call center, face-to-face support from the consultation room and problem solving by the users themselves using the FAQs on the Web.

4.2 Information Cycle Model

We built an integrated information cycle flow that not only covers the organizations but also uses information gathered during the fulfillment of a problem, resolving to improve effectiveness and efficiency. The representation of the subsystems' relationships and the information processes are described in the information cycle model shown in figure 2, which stresses the importance of an interconnected and integrated flow of information.

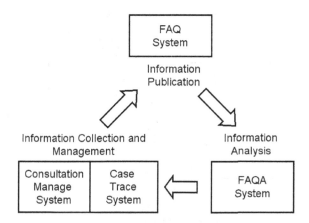

Fig. 2. Information Cycle Model

First, enquiry case information is gathered and managed by CTS and CMS. The call center's operators turn the well-organized case information into FAQs and then publish them. FAQAS monitors and collects users' FAQ access information and analyzes and reports the results. Based on these analysis data, operators adjust the case information, add necessary case, and modify the FAQ contents to meet and reflect users' needs and interests.

5 System Configurations

There are 4 subsystems in E-namoSupport environment. In this chapter we describe their functions and characteristics in detail.

5.1 Case Trace System (CTS)

The case trace system (CTS) used by the call center allows operators to input, retrieve, search, and deal with enquiry case information accessed by telephone or email. In order to process cases efficiently, we set five-status marks to each case: new, confirming, answer-waiting, calling back, and closed, as shown in figure 3.

When operators add a new case, the case's status is "new". After they finish dealing with the case, its status is changed to "closed". When the operators are in the process of solving the case, the case's status is "confirming". If the operators cannot answer the case and they dispatch it to the technical support group, the case status is set to "answer-waiting". After they receive an answer from technical support group, the operators then call back to the user. If the user cannot be contacted, the case status is set to "calling back".

Every case is marked as being one of five statuses, so it can be easily located and managed. Each operator can retrieve, trace, and deal with other operators' cases, so that each case can be dealt with in a smooth and timely manner.

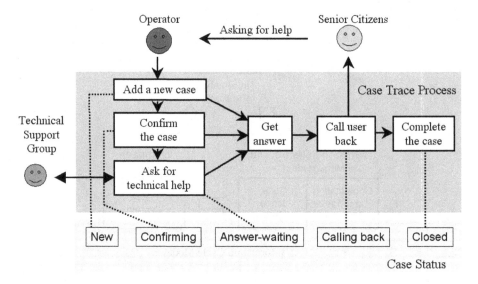

Fig. 3. Case Process Flow and Five Statuses

Table 1. Quizzes and Case Items

Quizzes	Items
Can you tell me what current interface you are using?	Category, Inquiry Info
Can you move your mouse and see your pointer moving on screen?	Inquiry Info
Is there any error message showing on the screen?	ErrMessage
What did you do after the problem occurred?	ErrMessagedo
Can you tell me PC's maker, software version or other information? If you do not know how to find them, I can tell you…	OSVer, E-namoVer, Hardware, Maker
When do you want us to call you back and what is your contact phone number?	Emergency, UserInfo, Contact Info

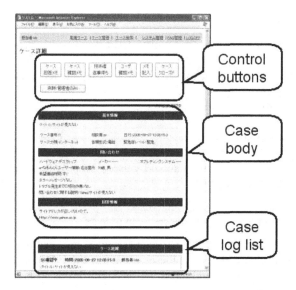

Fig. 4. Case Process Interface

Our users are mostly computer novices, who do not know even basic technical terms. When they encounter a problem and call the operator, it is difficult for them to describe the problem in detail; usually they can only say "It does not work", "It turns dark", "A strange window appears" and so on. In order to help operators describe a case correctly and in detail, we designed a set of case items and quizzes to make the conversation between operator and user run smoothly. The relationship between the quizzes and items are shown in table 1. Talking with users while using these quizzes, the operator can easily get useful information then input the case item.

Figure 4 shows the case process interface. The top of the interface is a set of buttons to let operators change the case's status; the bottom of the interface is the log list, which records the change process of the case. The middle of interface shows details of the case.

5.2 Consultation Management System (CMS)

Two lifelong learning centers at a ward level have established special consultation rooms to provide a face-to-face consulting service for E-namokun users. Consultants are not full-time staff but rather volunteers who work in their spare time. In order to exchange and utilize consultation case information among the consultants to improve their consulting abilities, we developed the consultation management system (CMS).

Similar to the enquiry case, the consultation case has 4-status marks: new, answer-collecting, commenting, and closed. Through CMS, consultants can exchange their opinions; comment and offer feedback to others, and ask for solutions. The system can enrich consultants' knowledge and strengthen their problem solving skills.

5.3 FAQ System (FAQS)

By providing FAQs on the Web, we aim to train users and improve their problem solving abilities. We developed the FAQ system not only as a support method, but also as a learning platform. We choose suitable learning content that will satisfy user needs. We also designed the interface and functions taking into consideration those physical attributes affected by the aging process.

5.3.1 Learning Content

The FAQs come from cases produced by CTS and CMS. All are "closed" status cases that relate to issues frequently asked about by users. To provide suitable contents, we consider two content select criteria:

(1) Content should satisfy users' interests.
(2) Content should satisfy what users want to learn.

From FAQAS, we can get the statistics and analysis information required to grasp users' interests and needs. Based on these, we adjust the FAQs by adding contents, modifying content categories, and adjusting difficulty levels to provide highly relevant knowledge for users.

5.3.2 Interface and Function Design

Current websites are twice as hard for seniors to use as they are for younger users (Coyne P. K., 2003). In relation to the attributes of the aging process, "eyesight," "precision of movement," and "memory and understanding" typically deteriorate (Coyne P. K., 2003). If we don't consider these attributes when designing guidelines for seniors, they will not use the system. We follow the design guidelines (Mari Fujiwara, 2005) listed below in order to make websites easier to use for seniors:

(1) Visibility improvement
We enlarged the size of the characters, buttons, and pointer, and set the color of character and background to be easily distinguished. Moreover, the color changes when the user clicks a button, so users can confirm the operation immediately.

(2) Operation improvement
To avoid missing an operation, we put more intervals between the buttons, and scroll-movement is replaced by button-click. Complex and multi operations are simplified by a single click. To avoid a situation where the user misses the focus, we don't use pop-up windows.

(3) Consideration of Cognitive Factors
We aimed for a simple interface including only the necessary minimum functions and limited the quantity of buttons to 8, the hierarchy of depth to 4, and the result list to 10. Moreover, the "Topic Path" is always shown on the top of the main body so that the user will not lose their way while browsing. In addition, we replace technical terms for familiar expressions.

To access FAQ easily we define a button named "when in trouble" embedded in the E-namokun software. When the button is clicked, the FAQ site appears. The FAQ interface is shown in figure 5. The left one is the top of the FAQ pages and the right one is the FAQ list result searched by users.

Fig. 5. FAQ Interface

5.4 FAQ Analysis System (FAQAS)

The main aim of FAQAS is to determine senior citizens' information needs:

(1) Identify the types of information which are of most interest to senior citizens.
In the FAQ system, we set a counter when accessing each page, so we can see which content is more popular and which functions are used most frequently. FAQAS analyses this counter data and reports it in a graph or table (see Figure 6).

(2) Investigate the willingness of senior citizens to learn.
In the FAQ system there is a search function by which users can enter words to find information they want. We analyze the inputted words and record each word's frequency. If the inputted word doesn't appear on the result list and the inputted word's frequency exceeds the normal value defined beforehand, FAQAS will notice it and create a users' learning needs report, which can help to find holes in the FAQ content.

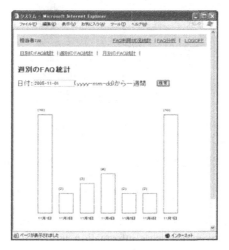

Fig. 6. FAQ Access Statistics Interface

6 Current Work and Evaluation

The E-namoSupport is a part of the E-namokun project, which is an information promotion project to help bridge the digital divide for senior citizens. In order to allow more senior citizens enjoy the project, other than the use of the E-namoSupport environment, other support methods such as short courses, text support, and hardware support, providing recycled PCs for free have been implemented.

E-namokun short courses began running in the local lifelong learning centers of wards in Nagoya city from September 2005 and will be held until March 2006. These courses were publicized to senior citizens throughout Nagoya City through public brochures, and also received coverage in the newspaper and on television. As a result, more than 2,000 seniors applied to join the courses, although the capacity was only 600 places. The teaching scene in the E-namokun course is shown in figure 7. This highlights the level of demand from senior citizens. This also highlights demand and the need to increase the availability of computer education and support for senior citizens.

Fig. 7. E-namokun Course Scene

Fig. 8. Scene depicting use of E-namoSupport System by call center operator

We are now implementing the E-namoSupport system beginning from November 2005. A scene depicting the use of the E-namoSupport system by a call center operator is shown in figure 8. Call center operators are using the CTS for their daily case process work and about 10-20 cases are managed every day. We have obtained operators' comments. They expressed that the system is an effective system to input, retrieve, search, deal with enquiry case information and easily turn the case into FAQ.

We are collecting the evaluation results, which we get in two ways: (1) questionnaires about satisfaction levels related to the interface, function and content provided by call center operators, consultants from the consultation room and end users; (2) FAQAS analysis data, from which we get access frequency, interest levels and learning needs. In the future we plan to improve our system based on the experiment results and extend system functions by increasing the support service's range.

7 Conclusion

In this paper, we described a helpdesk support environment – the E-namoSupport – for computer beginner with a special emphasis on senior citizens. Unlike general helpdesk systems, E-namoSupport proposes an information cycle model, which integrates information among three types of organizations and four subsystems: the case trace system (CTS) for call centers, the consultation management system (CMS) for consultation rooms, the FAQ system (FAQS) for users, and the FAQ analysis system (FAQAS). E-namoSupport considers users with little or no computer experience by using a set of quizzes to help describe enquiry cases. Seniors' attributes were taken into consideration when designing the easy-to-use interface and functions. Moreover, E-namoSupport is not only a support environment but also a learning environment that provides suitable learning contents by analyzing users' interests and needs.

Acknowledgements

We thank Li Yi, who has a lot of practical experience in working as helpdesk operator in a large international enterprise and who gives us useful advice in the design of the E-namoSupport system.

We would like to thank all people connected to the E-namokun project, especially Nagoya City, the Nagoya Urban Industries Promotion Corporation, and the IT promotion Agency of the eco-cycle NPO.

This research was partially funded by Nagoya Urban Industries Promotion Corporation Joint Research, and Grants-in-Aid for Scientific Research – 21st century COE program "Intellectual integration (IMI) of the voice images for the social information base" of the Ministry of Education, Culture, Sports, Science and Technology, Japan.

References

MPHPT Survey (Ministry of Public Management, Home Affairs, Posts and Telecommunications, Japan) Communications usage trend survey. (2003) Retrieved August 10, 2005 from http://www.soumu.go.jp/s- news/2004/pdf/040414_1_a.pdf

Goto, M., Endo, M., Yasuda, T., Yokoi, S.: Web Search System and Learning Environment for Senior Citizens. Digital Learning, CSDMS India 1(1), 24–26 (2005)

Sasaki, K., Iribe, Y., Goto, M., Endo, M., Yasuda, T., Yokoi, S.: Simple Web Mail System That Makes the Best Use of the Senior Citizens Social Experience. In: Khosla, R., Howlett, R.J., Jain, L.C. (eds.) KES 2005. LNCS (LNAI), vol. 3684, pp. 1274–1280. Springer, Heidelberg (2005)

Marcella, R.C., Middleton, I.: Key factors in help desk success. BLR+DD Report No.6247, from British Library (1996)

Foo, S., Hui, S.C., Leong, P.C.: Web-based intelligent helpdesk-support environment. International Journal of Systems Science 33(6), 389–402 (2002)

Yoshitaka, K., Masashi, Y., Nobuo, K.: An Automated Follow-up Service for Technical Support Help Desks. IPSJ technical reports 1998(080), 43–48 (1998)

Peters, S.L.: Setting up and automating a help desk: the first year of operation. ACM SIGUCCS, pp. 187–191 (1992)

Le Van, H., Trentini, A.: FAQshare: a frequently asked questions voting system as a collaboration and evaluation tool in teaching activities. SEKE 2002, pp. 557–560 (2002)

IBM Accessibility Center Retrieved August 18, 2005 from https://www-06.ibm.com/jp/accessibility/main

Fujitsu, Rakuraku product support.

Retrieved August 18, 2005 from http://www.personal.fujitsu.com/products/support

Halverson, C.A., Erickson, T., Ackerman, M.S.: Behind the help desk: evolution of a knowledge management system in a large organization. CSCW'04, pp. 304–313 (November 2004)

Coyne, P.K., Nielsen, J.: Web Usability for Senior Citizens: Design Guidelines Based on Usability Studies with People Age 65 and Older. Nielsen Norman Group Report (2003)

Fujiwara, M., Yasuda, T., Yokoi, S.: Usability Design of Introductory Web Browsing System for Senior. Master's thesis, Nagoya university, Japan (2005)

Analysis of Weblog Link Structure – A Community Perspective

Ying Zhou and Joseph Davis

School of Information Technologie, The University of Sydney, Australia
{zhouy,jdavis}@it.usyd.edu.au

Abstract. In this paper, we report a two level study on weblog link structures. At the micro level, we carried out an in-depth investigation of individual weblogs. Our goal was to obtain some preliminary understanding of the different types of links that might indicate underlying communities of bloggers. Complete and detailed link data was collected from eight weblogs followed by a variety of analyses. The result shows that both incoming and outgoings follow Zipf like distribution in terms of the sources of those links. These suggest clustering patterns (communities) within the whole blogspace. We also examine the temporal aspects of weblogs. The average life span of a weblog entry is fairly long in most of our sample cases. In addition, analysis on individual comment authors shows that in average, active comment authors maintain a rather long relationship with a certain weblog. It provides evidence that historical data may be useful in understanding weblog communities. On a larger scale, we developed a program to collect complete link data from large number of interconnected weblogs and performed cluster analysis on it. Communities with common topics are successfully extracted using those link data.

Keywords: Weblog, community, social network, social tie.

1 Introduction

Weblogs are web pages with several dated entries usually arranged in reverse chronological order (Kuma et al. 2004). This new form of online diary has become an influential web application, with thousands of blogs added on the web everyday. In general, blog sites cover a wide range of topics. Sites devoted to politics or technology-related topics usually receive thousands of hits per day.

Blogs usually contain a large number of links to other pages (Barabasi et al. 2001). This could be links to regular webpages or links to other blog entries. Each entry of a blog has its own *"permalink"* (permanent link). It could be an individual webpage or a section in a webpage. Blogs with similar topic are usually interwoven into a network of communities referred to as blogspace (Searls & Sifry 2003). Within a blogspace, bloggers list blogs they read and other links on the sidebar, sometimes referred to as *blogrolls*. They comment on each other's postings, generating periods of bursty activities around interesting topics. Such bursty activities are usually exemplified by heavy linkage amongst the blogs involved with in a time interval (Kumar et al. 2003).

J. Filipe, J. Cordeiro, and V. Pedrosa (Eds.): WEBIST 2005/2006, LNBIP 1, pp. 307–320, 2007.

Blogs have evolved into both link magnets and sources of links on Internet. The result, as illustrated by Searls and Sifry (2003), is both striking and to be expected, They state "name a topic with a community of interest around it. Now go to Google and look it up. There is a good chance one or more of the top results will include somebody's weblog (aka blog)". The example given by them are: 802.11b, Segway and webblog. For each search term, Google listed a weblog among the top three results, which still holds at the time of writing of this paper. There are also reports that people prefer to have the latest news or development trends through blogs rather than through traditional media.

Blogspace represents a new form of online community as well as a new form of online knowledge repository connected by hyperlinks. Yet it is not an easy task for a newcomer to discover the virtual communities if they are interested in tracking particular community discussions. Google recently released a beta version of blog search services (http://blogsearch.google.com/). It indexes a huge collection of blog and news feeds. This search service is based on the feed data. Most query results point to individual entry of a weblog, with a few highlighted matched entire weblogs appear on the top. Beside the latest Google blog search, a few specialized blog/news search engine has also emerged, including bloglines.com, daypop.com and blogdex.com. Each has its own copy of a collection of weblogs and can perform content related search for weblogs and news. Most of them are focused on page-level search rather than community oriented search. Hence the results are usually a mixture of regular news pages and some blog pages based on conventional static page rank algorithm. Weblogs, compared the regular webpages are more dynamic and evolves very quickly. Besies, People typically search search weblogs for a different purpose. Most of the time, they are trying to find a weblog that they can keep reading regularly. A desirable weblog search and ranking service requires different methods to model and organize the whole blog space. Understanding of individual blogs as well as the structure of linkage interaction among weblogs is important in the design of a weblog search service.

We carried out a two level study on weblog search. We first conduct a case study on a number of weblogs and investigated the feature of link component within each of them. This case study tries addresses the following questions: what kind of data should we collect to study the community of weblogs? what is the average life span of a weblog entry? what are the general interaction patterns of a weblog with other weblogs? Based on the findings of the case study we conducted a larger scale experiment to extract weblog communities by exploiting their link structure.

2 Related Works

At a macro scale there are Gruhl et al. (2004)'s information diffusion study and Kumar et al. (2003)'s bursty evolution study. Both studies draw on a large collection of weblogs over time. Gruhl et al. (2004) utilizes the epidemic model of disease-propagation to investigate the dynamics of information propagation through networks of bloggers. Their work can help to identify the hottest topics and predict the diffusion of certain piece of information in the community of bloggers. Kumar et al. adopted the notion of time graph and use that as a basis to extract temporal communities and studied bursty behavior. They argued that blog communities have striking temporal characteristis; in particular, communities only formed when an interesting topic arose and it faded away after a certain period.

On a micro scale, Judit Bar-llan (2004) monitored 15 sample weblogs for 2 months and generated statistics related to the blogs and posts such as, average postings per day, number of posting day in a period of time, average links per post and so on. The majority of her sample weblogs are technology or research oriented. Her results show that the topics of most postings in the blogs were typically closely related to the declared topics. Since the data collected by Bar-llan were over a two- month period, it cannot give a complete picture of long running blogs and their evolution.

3   Blog Communities

We define a blog community as a network of weblogs with similar topics connected through hyperlinks. Within the community, bloggers may read, write and comment on other bloggers' entries. These are reflected by the three types of links indicating certain interactions between two weblogs. They are candidate links we need to consider for discovering and constructing the blogspace.

Many bloggers list a few other blogs they read on the siderbar. The list is called a blogroll. The blogroll links indicate a *read* relationship between this blogger and others.

It is very common for a blogger to cite or reference another blogger's writing on his/her own post. This indicates a response relationship between the two bloggers.

Bloggers may respond to one another's writing through other channels. They may leave a comment on the posting site. Sometimes, a commenter identifies self by a link to his or her own weblog in the comment body. This enables a crawler to build the connection between the two weblogs. In addition, some blog authoring tools provide "trackback" feature. This is a protocol that a responder can use to notify the author that he(she) has cited a particular article of the author in his(her) own blog. The notification is achieved by sending a ping message to the original blog entry, which will then update its trackback list to include the senders's URL. Trackback links make it very easy to get all incoming links of a particular blog entry. However, this feature is not used extensively at present.

4   Methodology

In this study, we first take a micro scale approach and closely investigated links in a few individual weblogs and the three different types of associations between blogs. The micro level is more appropriate here since we are not going to study the general structure of the whole blogspace. Rather, we are more interested in the individual weblogs, and their communication pattern with other weblogs.

The sample we traced consists of eight Weblogs. The main criterion we use to choose the sample cases is that the weblogs should have been running actively for some time to make sure there are enough data. In addition, the sample weblog should have extensive comments to ensure the activeness of the interactions. The cases chosen include two cooperate weblogs, four pure technology weblogs and two weblogs on personal opinions. These are:

1. MSN Search's Weblog (http:// blogs.msdn. com/msnsearch/): an official weblog on MSN's search related products and discussion since November 2004.
2. Yahoo! search weblog (http://ysearchblog. com): a weblog written by Yahoo! staff on Yahoo! search product since August 2004.
3. Fabulous Adventures In Coding (http:// blogs.msdn.com/ericlippert/): a weblog written by Eric Lippert discussing all sorts of coding issues, .NET technology and a few other things. It is started on September, 2003.
4. Sorting it all out (http://blogs.msdn.com/ michkap/): a weblog written by Michael Kaplan mainly about locales, keyboards, Unicode and other language related techniques. It is started on November 2004.
5. Micro persuasion (http://www. micropersuasion.com/): a weblog written by Steve Rubel on "how new technologies are transforming marketing, media and public relations". The weblog started since since April 2004. There are many articles regarding blogging news, practices and systems in micropersuasion.
6. Schneier on Security (http://www.schneier. com/blog/) : Bruce Schneier's weblog on security and security technology since October, 2004.
7. BuzzMachine(http://www.buzzmachine.com/):   started   since   July   2005, buzzmachine is a weblog written by Jeff Jarvis, currently the president and creative director of Advance.net. Jeff Jarvis is a high profile media people and long time supporter of weblogs. Buzzmachine has a wide coverage on many topics including weblogs, newspapers, open source and politics.
8. Hot Points with BOB Parsons (http:// www.bobparsons.com/): a weblog written by Bob Parsons, the president and founder of GoDaddy.com, a company that provide Internet domain name registration, web hosting, email accounting and lots of other Internet related services. The weblog contains his thoughts and opinions on Internet innovations and lots of other things. It is started on December 2004.

All the chosen weblogs have different layouts. A few specialized web crawlers were developed to extract and collect the required information from them. The customized crawlers can accurately extract specified information, which is different from the simple heuristic based crawling algorithm used in Kumar et al. (2003) study. Information collected include blogroll links, links appeared in each entry, and comments made on each entry. Each entry's publishing date and time as well each comment's publishing date and time are also collected. The links referenced in entries are placed in two broad categories: *blog* link and *other* link. *Blog* link points to another webblog or webblog entry. We use the algorithm proposed by Ceglowski (2003) to judge if a link point to a blog entry. The data collection was carried out in October 2005. All data were current up to that month.

5 Results

5.1 Basic Demographic Information

Table 1 gives a summary of the basic information based on the target weblogs. For all weblogs except Schneier, we collected all data from the very first posting. The number of occurrences for each type of interactions is given to provide an overall picture of the intensity of the communication coming in and going out of a particular weblog. All of our target weblogs have significant levels of communication with other sites or weblogs. They referenced many web pages and also attracted lots of discussions on their own sites.

Table 1. Basic demographic information

	Blogroll Link.	No. of Entries	Entry Link	Comments
MSN Search	9	77	468 (6)**	1545 (20)
YSearchblog	21	55	320 (5.9)	634 (11.7)
MichKap	0	887	4398 (4.9)	4272 (4.8)
EricLippert	12	605	889 (1.5)	4995 (8.3)
Micropersuasion	0	2548	7252 (2.8)	4672 (1.8)
Schneier*	0	86	200 (2.3)	3354 (39)
buzzmachine	1	580	4211 (7.3)	8485 (14.6)
BobParsons	0	68	197 (2.9)	5924 (87)

* Only 3 months data of this weblog is collected
** Average number

5.2 Tie Strength Distribution

The blog community can be viewed as a special type of social network. A social network is a set of people or groups connected with each other under a particular relationship (Wasserman & Faust 1994). Examples of typical social networks include the friendship network of high school students, email network of employees, and scientific co-authorship network of academics (c.f. Barabasi et al. 2001, Newman 2001). In social network terminology, the people or groups are called "actors" and the connections are called "ties". In a blog community context, the bloggers who write weblogs are the actors and the hyperlinks between weblogs are the ties between two bloggers. If we consider each link as a communication instance between two bloggers, we can measure the strength of the tie according to the number of links between two particular weblogs. In this section, we will use links appearing in blog entries and links created by comment authors to study the distribution of tie strength for each particular weblog.

Figure 1 shows the tie strength distribution for the outgoing links found in weblog entry. The x-axis represents the number of times a weblog has been referenced (strength score of tie) and the y-axis represents the number of weblogs that have been

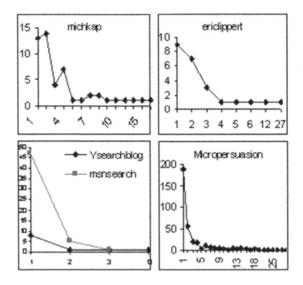

Fig. 1. Outgoing tie strength distribution

references for a particular number of times (number of ties with a certain strength score). For instance, in Michkap weblog, we have 15 other weblogs being referenced by Michkap once (15 weak ties), 1 weblogs being referenced by MichKap 10 times (1 strong tie with strength score 10) and so on.

All links appearing in the blog entry of *blog* type are extracted. Those links usually point to a blog entry of another weblog. To construct the tie between two weblogs, we need to find weblog home page URL of those links. This is achieved through the RSS or ATOM feed of a weblog. The <link> value of the <channel> element in RSS usually gives the homepage of a weblog. By replacing the actual links with its home page URL we can easily count the number of links between two weblogs and discover how many strong and weak ties exist for a weblog.

Five weblogs are included in the diagram. The rest do not have enough links pointing to other blog entries. The chart on the bottom left panel contains data for two weblogs. The data from all five weblogs follows Zipf-like distribution. From the social network point of view, the observation can be interpreted as a weblog has many weak ties (being referred once or twice), and only a few strong ties (being referred many times) to other weblogs.

Similar procedures are performed on the incoming ties reconstructed from the comment section of each weblog entries. Each unique comment author is considered as an agent in a social network and one comment is considered as a communication instance between the comment author (usually a blogger) and the blogger. We use the number of comments left by the same author to measure the strength of the tie between comment author and blogger. Figure 2 shows the tie strength distribution for the incoming ties. The x-axis represents the number of comments a reader left (strength score of tie) and the y-axis represents the number of readers that have left a particular number of comments (number of ties with a certain strength score). All

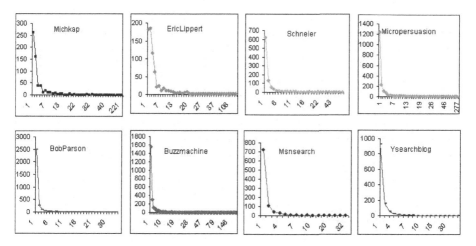

Fig. 2. Incoming tie strength distribution

weblogs show clear Zipf-like distributions. All weblogs have large number of occasional visitors who only made one or two comments and a few frequent visitors who made lots of comments.

The Zipf like distribution of the tie strength is consistent with Granovetter (1983) view of social world. In his description, social world is structured with highly connected clusters (strong ties) with many external weak tie connecting these clusters. The observation implies the existence of clusters consisting of weblogs with strong ties to each other in the blogspace. These clusters are actually weblog communities of interest. It also indicates that we can discover these blog communities by measuring the link strength between weblogs.

5.3 Blog Entry Life Span

The study of weblog community would involve both spatial and temporal dimensions. In the previous section, we investigate the dynamics of weblog interactions and discovered that around each weblog, there is a small circle with highly frequent interaction. These would form the basis for closely knit weblog communities. Yet the questions regarding how stable these small circles might be along a weblog's life span and how frequently those communities might evolve remain unanswered.

Weblogs, nicknamed as online diary, share many features of news sites. They both focus on current events, be it a social, political event or a technical problem recently raised. They are both updated frequently and have some established readership base. This raises the problem of the value of back issues. If we are going to study the community around a particular topic, how much historical data do we need to collect to ensure the accuracy of our community information.

To develop a better understanding of the problem, we used the publishing date and time information recorded on each blog entry and comment to get some preliminary idea of the average life span of a blog entry. We used the latest time a comment was made by somebody other than the author and the blog posting time to estimate the average life span of a blog entry. The life spans of entries vary significantly with most posts having a one day life span and a few having life spans as high as nearly two years. For instance, one entry in Eric Lipert's blog (http://blogs.msdn.com/ericlippert/rchive/2003/10/06/53150.aspx) originally posted in November, 2003 achieved some recent discussion around two years later. We discovered quite a few posts in Eric's weblog with more than 600 days' of life span. Table 2 give the descriptive statistics of entry life span for each weblog in the sample. Although varying enormously in terms of average life span, a consistent message coming through all those cases is that historical entries are not completely ignored by blog readers. This suggests that in analyzing weblog communities, we do have to include some historical data.

Table 2. Weblog entry life span

Unit: day	Mean	S.D	Range
MSN Search	31.4	50.1	210 (330)*
YSearchblog	60.3	86.5	343 (420)
MichKap	25.7	54.1	282 (330)
EricLippert	75.0	168.9	704 (760)
Micropersuasion	6.0	36.7	482 (550)
Schneier	7.8	9.3	47
buzzmachine	7.2	13.3	87 (110)
BobParsons	84.9	71.6	295(300)

* Weblog running days to October, 2005

5.4 Temporal Aspects

The concept of time graph and temporal community introduced in (Kumar et al. 2003) suggests certain bursty patterns along a weblog's life time. These may be generated by totally different groups of people or the same group of people. On the one hand, if bursts are generated by different groups, a natural conclusion would be that a weblog may be in different communities from time to time. In that case, it would be difficult to measure the stability of a community and predict any future interaction among different weblogs. On the other hand, if most bursts are generated by relatively stable groups of members, this suggests that communities around a weblogs are fairly stable and it is reasonable to use historical data to predict future trends.

We took a few weblogs in our sample with relatively long life time and extract the most active five comment authors along with all instances of their communications. The purpose was to see if there was clustering pattern along the time line, that is, comment authors tend to comment with in a short duration and may never come back. Figure 3 shows the monthly communication intensity distribution of the top five comment authors in MichKap, EricLippert and Micropersuasion weblogs. The size of the area is proportional to the number of communications in that month. We do see peaks from time to time which support findings in (Kumar et al. 2003). In Figure 3, different colors represent different authors. The numbers in the legend indicate the total number of communications made by that author. A consistent pattern is that majority of authors interact with the target weblog for a relatively long period of time.

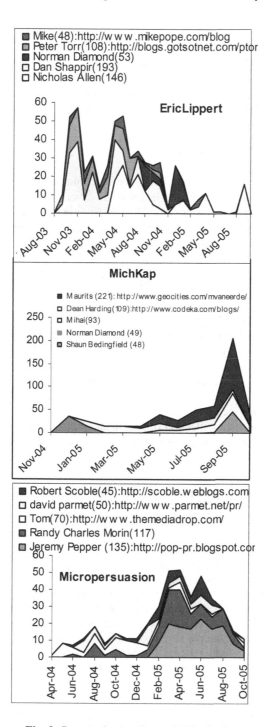

Fig. 3. Communication Strength Distribution

Except for a few cases, many authors maintain the commenting relationship for more than one year. However, some may be more active in the early stage, for instance, Dan Shappire in EricLippert Weblog. Others may be more active in late stage, for instance, Nicolas Allan in EricLippert Weblog. Both covered a period of more than one-and-a-half year. This suggests that the communities of readership for most weblogs in our sample are quite stable for a certain period of time.

6 Macro-scale Application

The above case study indicates the existence of community of webloggers and the types of link data that need to be collected to discover the weblog communities. To test those findings on a much larger scale, a web crawler was developed to collect link data from large collection of weblogs. Clustering is then applied on the data to identify the community structure.

The weblog crawler takes a weblog URL as seed and incrementally adds linked pages in the collection. Table 3 illustrates the main crawling algorithm. This weblog crawler can extract complete set of links from a weblog. This includes links on sidebar, links in blog entry and links in comment section. If any of those links points to another weblog, a complete link set from that weblog will be extracted as well. The crawling depth is controlled by the *maxDepth* variable and is currently set to 6 to reflect the "six degrees of separation" rule (Barabasi 2002). Internet was reported to have 19 degree of separation between any individual webpages (Barabasi 2002). Since our unit of analysis is the weblog and not the individual page, and each weblog represents a person who writes it, we think it is more appropriate to follow the six degrees of separation concept in our research.

The crawling result is a collection of relational records with two fields, the source weblog url and the target weblog url. Each record indicates a link from source to target, with a value of 1.

Table 3. Web Crawler Algorithm

1	Url = seed url;
2	$depth$ = 0;
3	**method** crawl (Url, $depth$)
4	**if** (depth < maxDepth)
5	**for** all hyper links $link$ in Url
6	**if** $link$ belongs to the same weblog
7	crawl ($link$, $depth$)
8	**else if** $link$ is a weblog post
9	find the home page of $link$ as $link.home$
10	add a record $Url.home$ and $link.home$
11	crawl(link.home, depth + 1)
12	**end if**
13	**end for**
14	**end if**
15	**end method**

We take Savas Parastadist's weblog (Savas.parastatidist.name) as seed in the experiment to run the web crawler. The key theme of Savas Parastadist's weblog is web services standards and products. The result contains around 3800 unique weblogs and over 33000 links. Multiple links between two weblogs are removed by summing up the number of links and use it as the link value between two weblogs. We then use Pajek (http://vlado.fmf.uni-lj.si/pub/networks/pajek/) to perform clustering on the collection. The clustering algorithm tries to discover clusters within a large graph so that each node in a cluster should have more communication with other nodes inside the cluster than with nodes outside the cluster.

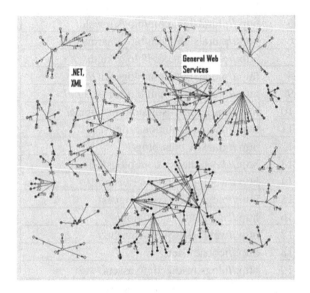

Fig. 4. Web Services blog communities

Figure 4 gives a visual display of the communities extracted from the data and the structure within each cluster. In total, 15 communities are identified from the data.

We inspected members in those communities. Table 4 give a list of members in the community that contains the original seed. The topics of those member weblogs include .NET, XML and general web services. Some communities are more focused on general web services while others focused on certain web services-related technologies such as XML and .NET. The result shows that it is possible to identify communities based on complete link data of weblogs.

However, we can collect more recent data to build communities based on clustering technique as well. From the result on individual comment author, not all comment authors are active throughout the life span of a weblog. Some may be more active in the early stage, while others may be more active in late stages. The clustering algorithm can be applied on feed data rather than on entire weblog pages (as what Google BlogSearch does). A sliding time window can be used to update the blogspace with new feeds and to remove obsolete data. However, we believe that there will not be a standard window size that can fit all sorts of welbogs. Different weblogs usually have very different average life spans.

Table 4. Community member list

1	http://savas.parastatidis.name
2	http://research.microsoft.com/news/msrnews/
3	http://pluralsight.com/blogs/dbox/
4	http://pluralsight.com/blogs/craig/
5	http://pluralsight.com/blogs/tewald/
6	http://pluralsight.com/blogs/aaron/ ***
7	http://pluralsight.com/blogs/keith/
8	http://pluralsight.com/blogs/fritz/
9	http://pluralsight.com/blogs/mgudgin/
10	http://msdn.microsoft.com/msdnmag/
11	http://unboxedsolutions.com/sean/
12	http://glazkov.com/blog/
13	http://devauthority.com/blogs/csteen *
14	http://weblogs.asp.net/ericjsmith/
15	http://blogs.msdn.com/smguest
16	http://samgentile.com/blog/
17	http://weblogs.asp.net/rhurlbut/
18	http://jcooney.net/
19	http://blogs.msdn.com/yassers
20	http://weblogs.asp.net/cweyer/
21	http://www.innoq.com/blog/st/
22	http://www.jonfancey.com/
23	http://codebetter.com/blogs/jeffrey.palermo
24	http://blog.whatfettle.com/
25	http://blogs.msdn.com/brada
26	http://blogs.msdn.com/mpowell
27	http://weblogs.asp.net/jgaylord/
28	http://blogs.msdn.com/robcaron **
29	http://weblogs.asp.net/despos/
30	http://www.theserverside.net
31	http://blogs.msdn.com/mfussell
32	http://weblogs.asp.net/mnissen/
33	http://blogs.msdn.com/trobbins
34	http://blogs.msdn.com/tomholl
35	http://weblogs.asp.net/wallym/
36	http://dotnetjunkies.com/WebLog/barblog

7 Conclusion

This research examined eight weblogs as special cases to study the link structure within weblogs. Two different types of links were examined: links embedded on blog entry and links created by comment authors. The result shows that most weblogs cited a wide range of other weblogs with approximate Zipf-like distributions. Many weblogs have large number of readers commenting on their writings. The distribution of commenting communication intensity also follows Zipf like curve. Majority of the readers left one or two comments on the average with a small number of readers left large number of comments. These Zipf like distributions observed with respect to entry links and comment authors suggest clustering patterns (communities) within the whole blogspace. We also examine the temporal features of weblogs. The average life span of a weblog entry is fairly long in most our sample cases. In addition, analysis of individual comment authors shows that in average, some active comment authors maintain a rather long relationship with a certain weblog. This suggests that historical data may be useful in understanding weblog communities. To test the above findings, we developed a program to collect complete link data from large number of interconnected weblogs and performed clustering analysis on it. Communities with common topics are successfully extracted from these link data.

References

Ada, E., Zhang, L.: Implicit Structure and the Dynamics of Blogspace. In: Workshop on the Weblogging Ecosystem. In: WWW2004, New York City (2004)

Adamic, A.L, Huberman, B.A.: Zipf's law and the Internet. Glottometrics 3, 143–250 (2002)

Barabasi, A.L., Jeong, H., Neda, Z., Ravasz E., Schubert A., Vicsek, T.: Evolution of the social network of scientific collaborations. arXiv:cond-mat/0104162 v1. 10 (April 2001)

Barabasi, A.L.: Linked: the new science of networks. Perseus Books Group (2002)

Judit, B.-l.: An ousider's view on "topic-oriented" blogging. In: WWW 2004, New York, USA (2004)

Ceglowski, M.: Www:identify-identify blogging tools based on url and content. Retrieved 2003 from http://search.cpan.org/ mceglows/WWW-Blog-Identify-0.06/Identify.pm

Downes, S.: Web logs at Harvard Law. The Technology source.(July/August 2003) Retrieved from http://ts.mivu.org/default.asp?show=article&id=2019

Flake, G.W., Lawrence, S., Giles, C.L.: Efficient identification of web communities. In: Proc. 6th ACM SIGKDD Intel. Conf. On Knowledge Discovery and Data Mining, pp. 150–160 (2000)

Granovetter, M.: The Strength of weak ties:a network theory revisited. Sociological Theory 1, 201–233 (1983)

Gruhl, D., Guha, R., Liben-Novell D., Tomkins A.: Information diffusion through blogspace. In: WWW2004, New York, USA (May 2004)

Kumar, R., Novak, J., Raghavan, P., Tomkins, A.: On the bursty evolution of blogspace. In: WWW2003, Budapest, Hungary (May 2003)

Kumar, R., Novak, J., Raghavan, P., Tomkins, A.: Structure and evolution of blogspace. Communications of the ACM 47(12) (2004)

Nanno, T., Fujiki, T., Suzuki, Y., Okumura, M.: Automatically collecting, mornitoring and mining Japanese Weblogs. In: WWW2004, New York City (May 2004)

Newman, M.E.J.: Scientific collaboration networks. I. Network construction and fundamental results. Physical Review 64, 016131

Rubel, S.: Finding Influential Blogs That Reach Your Key Audiences (October, 2004) Retrieved from http://www.micropersuasion.com/2004/10/finding_influen.html

Searls, D., Sifry, D.: Building with Blogs. Linux Journal, Issue 107 (March 2003)

Tedeschi, B.: Blogging while browsing, but not buying. The New York Times (July 4, 2005)

Wasserman, S., Faust, K.: Social Network Analysis. Cambridge University Press, Cambridge (1994)

Winer, D.: History of weblogs.(May 2002) Retrived from http://newhome.weblogs.com/historyOfWeblogs

Part IV

e-Learning

The Autotutor 3 Architecture

A Software Architecture for an Expandable, High-Availability ITS

Patrick Chipman, Andrew Olney, and Arthur C. Graesser

Institute for Intelligent Systems, University of Memphis, 365 Innovation Drive,
Memphis, TN, USA
pchipman@memphis.edu, aolney@memphis.edu, a-graesser@memphis.edu

Abstract. Providing high quality of service over the Internet to a variety of clients while simultaneously providing good pedagogy and extensibility for content creators and developers are key issues in the design of the computational architecture of an intelligent tutoring system (ITS). In this paper, we describe an ITS architecture that attempts to address both issues using a distributed hub-and-spoke metaphor similar to that of the DARPA Galaxy Communicator. This architecture is described in the context of the natural language ITS that uses it, AutoTutor 3.

Keywords: Intelligent tutoring systems, software architecture, Internet-based instruction.

1   Introduction

A great deal of advancement in the state of the art of intelligent tutoring systems (ITS) has occurred in the last several years. Primarily, these advancements have been focused on improving pedagogical strategies by incorporating established psychological research on human tutoring into tutoring systems (Graesser, Person, & Magliano, 1995; Aleven & Koedinger, 2002; VanLehn, Jones, & Chi, 1992); adding superior student knowledge modelling such as model-tracing (VanLehn et al., 2000); providing advanced authoring tools to facilitate the rapid use of the ITS in new domains of knowledge, or with different sets of learners with different levels of skills (Ainsworth & Grimshaw, 2002); or improving the interface by adding animated characters such as "talking heads," also known as animated pedagogical agents (Johnson, Rickel, & Lester, 2000), or natural language dialogue (Jordan, Rosé, & VanLehn, 2001).

However, behind all of these systems and their advancements must reside some form of computational architecture. In many cases, this architecture is monolithic, rarely discussed, and generally irrelevant. Intelligent tutoring systems that reside on modern desktop computers have vast resources available for their processing and a high user tolerance for failure, especially if the system is visually appealing, quick to respond, and otherwise meets the user's typical expectations of a "typical" application (Bouch & Sasse, 1999). In fact, the presence of an animated pedagogical agent can improve the subjective likeability of a system considerably (Moreno, Klettke, Nibbaragandla, Graesser, & TRG, 2002), which would further enhance the user's experience and allow him to overlook any flaws in the underlying software (Bouch & Sasse, 1999).

J. Filipe, J. Cordeiro, and V. Pedrosa (Eds.): WEBIST 2005/2006, LNBIP 1, pp. 323–332, 2007.
© Springer-Verlag Berlin Heidelberg 2007

However, for a web-based or Internet-based system, where the target platform's resources are often much lower than that of a modern desktop computer and much of the processing must be handled on a remote server for potentially hundreds or thousands of simultaneous users, architectures that provide consistent levels of availability and latency are mandatory if the system is to be adopted by users (Bhatti, Bouch, & Kuchinsky, 2000). Furthermore, such architectures must be able to handle the sorts of advancements in ITS technology that come at a rapid pace while simultaneously allowing developers and content creators to achieve domain and tutoring strategy independence. If all of these criteria are not met to some degree, it is probable that user acceptance, both with learners and content creators, will be low and will confine the ITS to laboratory use.

In this paper, we discuss the architecture of the third version of the venerable AutoTutor natural dialogue intelligent tutoring system. This architecture was designed specifically to balance the criteria of high availability and expandability, thereby offering a quality user experience while providing the extensibility necessary for the creation of more advanced ITSes in the future. Additionally, the architecture is sufficiently generic that other systems can be built around its principles; it is not solely restricted to use with our AutoTutor system.

2   What Is Autotutor?

A discussion of the architecture of AutoTutor 3 would not be complete without an explanation of the system itself. AutoTutor is a complex system that simulates a human or ideal tutor by holding a conversation with the learner in natural language (Graesser, Lu, et al., in press). AutoTutor presents a series of questions or problems that require approximately a paragraph of information to answer correctly. An example question in conceptual physics is "When a car without headrests on the seats is struck from behind, the passengers often suffer neck injuries. Why do passengers get neck injuries in this situation?" A complete answer to this question is approximately 3-7 sentences in length. AutoTutor assists the learner in the construction of an improved answer that draws out more of the learner's knowledge and that adaptively corrects problems with the answer. The dialogue between AutoTutor and the learner typically lasts 50-200 conversational turns for one question. Figure 1 shows an example of the AutoTutor 3 interface.

The AutoTutor system has undergone a variety of empirical tests to validate its pedagogical and conversational efficacy in both the domains of computer literacy (Graesser, Lu, et al., in press) and conceptual physics (Graesser, Jackson, et al., 2003). A "bystander Turing test" was performed to validate AutoTutor's conversational smoothness. In such an experiment, a subject is shown a section of tutorial dialogue randomly selected from real AutoTutor transcripts in which, half the time, the tutor move generated by AutoTutor has been replaced by a move generated by a human expert tutor. The subjects in this experiment, the bystanders, are asked to specify if the tutor move in question was generated by a human or a computer. The bystanders were wholly unable to make this distinction (Bautista, Person, & Graesser, 2002). Tests of pedagogical effectiveness have shown learning gains of 0.2 to 1.5 sigma

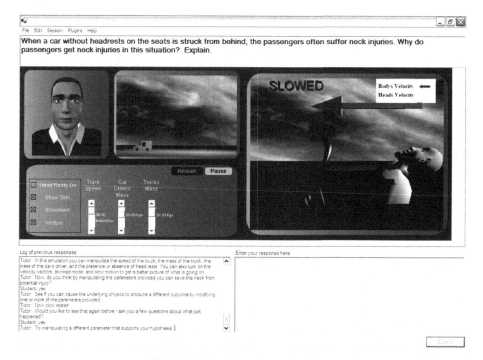

Fig. 1. The AutoTutor 3 user interface

(standard deviation units) with a mean of 0.8 sigma or around one letter grade of improvement. The performance varies based on the type of measure used and the content domain (Graesser, Jackson, et al., 2003). This is comparable to both the performance of unskilled human tutors, who produce learning gains of around 0.4 sigma, or half a letter grade of improvement (Cohen, Kulik, & Kulik, 1982), as well as to the performance of other intelligent tutoring systems without natural language dialogue, which produce learning gains of around 1.0 sigma (Corbett, 2001).

3 System Architecture

It has long been the desire of the Tutoring Research Group to offer AutoTutor to the widest audience possible, both in terms of learners and content creators, because of its impressive performance in empirical testing. As opposed to many intelligent tutoring systems, AutoTutor offers a natural language interface; this is posited to be critical for future ITS development (Jordan, Rosé, & VanLehn, 2001). However, this natural language interface requires a great deal of computational resources in both processing power and storage, making it difficult to deploy to desktop computers that are not state of the art. Furthermore, content creators offer up a great deal of intellectual property when creating the curriculum scripts that dictate the output of the system. It is unlikely these individuals will be willing to provide their content for local use by any number of learners. To solve both of these problems, it was decided to utilize a

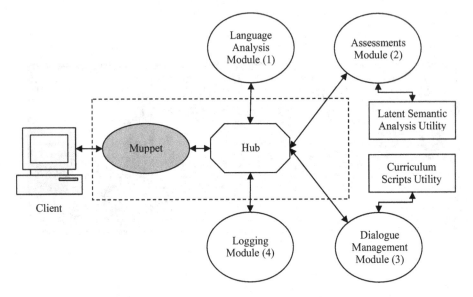

Fig. 2. An overview of the AutoTutor 3 Architecture

client-server architecture in which the AutoTutor 3 server resides at a fixed location and learners and content creators access its functionality remotely.

The system architecture is somewhat related to the DARPA Galaxy Communicator model, in which a variety of modules communicate, mediated by a central "hub" (Galaxy Communicator Documentation). In the AutoTutor 3 architecture, outlined in Figure 2, a central object known as the Hub (the octagon), hosted in the AutoTutor 3 server software, passes an object that contains the state of the system, the State Table (not shown), between a set of Modules (circles) that alter the state without having any specific knowledge of each other; the order of this process is specified by the Hub and, for the current AutoTutor 3 system, is expressed in the figure as a number after each Module's name. Each Module may access a number of Utilities (squares) that provide services through published interfaces. The State Table is sent to a variety of potential client types using one of many Multi-Protocol Personal Translators, or Muppets (shaded circle), that convert the State Table into a format that the client can understand. The objects contained within the dashed rectangle exist together in the main AutoTutor 3 server; all of the other objects are served through our custom-written generic object server, the Module Server, and can each exist on the same or different machines as load demands.

3.1 The .NET Framework and Remoting

The AutoTutor 3 system and its underlying architecture are implemented in a combination of C# and Visual Basic .NET, using the .NET Framework version 1.1 and the Common Language Runtime by Microsoft Corporation. The CLR provides a variety of advantages, not the least of which is the generic remote procedure call system known as .NET Remoting. This part of the Framework allows remote objects to be accessed as if they were inside the AutoTutor server process; short of a call into the Framework to "activate" the target object (whether it is a Module or a Utility), the object can be accessed identically across the network or on the local machine (Microsoft .NET Technology Overview). By using the Remoting system, it is possible for AutoTutor 3 Modules and Utilities to be split across multiple computers or multiple processes as required to "scale out" as load increases. The underlying complexities of accessing these remote objects are hidden behind the AT3Communicator class and the Remoting system.

Remoting provides a binary communication channel that, in our internal tests, allows the entire State Table for any turn to be conveyed using under 12 kilobytes of data, thereby reducing network transfer latency within the system and to clients. Our testing of the server under common experimental loads of around 30 simultaneous users reveals that the network latency of a system where the Modules and Utilities exist on separate machines is less than 1 ms, given a 100BaseT Ethernet interconnect.

3.2 State Table

In many ways, the State Table is the core of the AutoTutor 3 architecture. This extensible class contains the complete state of the system for any particular student interaction with the tutor. It normally survives for an entire problem and is discarded at the end of a problem. The State Table provides a logical separation of the data upon which the Modules work from the algorithms of the Modules themselves; in this way, it acts both as the storage space for the system's student model, as well as a sort of command object if one considers the architecture as an implementation of the chain-of-responsibility design pattern. Individual Modules store the results of their processing in the State Table. These results can then be read and further processed by other Modules, or simply ignored by other Modules if they are irrelevant to their processing. Because the state of the system is loosely coupled to the Modules that use it, it is relatively easy for new Modules to be added to the system to work on the data contained within the State Table.

The State Table is a class that is tied to a specific inheritance chain of interfaces. This ensures that Modules are themselves loosely coupled to the internal structure of the State Table; a Module created for an earlier implementation and older interface is guaranteed to work with newer versions of the State Table, because backward compatibility is mandated by the interface.

3.3 Hub

The Hub is the central manager of the AutoTutor architecture. This extremely simple class has only one function: to call each of the Modules of which it knows in the sequence required to produce a complete State Table. The AutoTutor server software handles loading the Module references into the Hub, which then makes the calls using Remoting. While it would seem necessary to rewrite the Hub whenever adding a new Module to the system, the current implementation of the Hub calls each of the Modules of which it knows in the sequence in which they were loaded; as this load sequence can be specified to the server in its configuration file, as long as dependencies in which Modules must be called more than once are avoided, the standard Hub implementation should be sufficient.

3.4 Modules and the AT3Communicator

Each Module in the system, as shown in Figure 2, represents a separate stage in the processing of a student move and the generation of an appropriate tutor turn. The internal mechanisms AutoTutor uses in each of those stages are covered in detail elsewhere (Olney, Louwerse, Mathews, Marineau, Mitchell, & Graesser, 2003; Mathews, Jackson, Olney, Chipman, & Graesser 2003; Graesser, Lu, et al. in press) and will not be detailed here. Each Module inherits from a master class called "AT3Communicator," which encapsulates the necessary public methods and implementations to link the Module to the system by taking messages and their associated State Tables from the Hub, acquiring references to the Utility objects, and handling thread synchronization should the Module be called by multiple users, and therefore multiple threads of processing, at once.

Because all of this functionality is encapsulated in this base class, those who wish to extend the capabilities of the AutoTutor system by adding a new Module or altering an existing one need only override a single virtual method called "Execute," which is analogous to a "Main" function in standard procedural programming. This overridden method is called by the base class and a copy of the State Table is passed in; the Module returns this copy with any necessary modifications. Utilities may be called by reading their references from a hash table, then calling methods on those references. The Remoting system, as previously mentioned, handles the resolution of those method calls.

While the AT3Communicator base class does handle thread synchronization with regards to the State Table itself and the Utility references, thread safety is not assured if the Module developer opts to add member variables to his Module's class. However, this problem can be readily avoided by using static variables in the Execute method and following standard programming practices that argue against the use of global variables; alternatively, the Module programmer can use the State Table to store the internal state of his module between calls. The current Dialogue Management Module uses this technique.

3.5 Utilities

The Utilities of the architecture are external objects called by Modules using Remoting. Unlike Modules, these objects have no fixed base class or interfaces, nor are they called by the Hub. Therefore, thread safety is not hidden from the developer. The complexities of Remoting are hidden from the Utility developer by the Module Server, however. In return, the developer of a Utility receives the flexibility to define his own interface and further gains the ability for his object's methods to be called directly from Modules, which can then share its functionality. In AutoTutor 3, we have chosen to use Utilities to encapsulate functionality used by multiple Modules, such as the Latent Semantic Analysis used to evaluate the similarity of strings (and thus the quality of student responses), or the Curriculum Scripts that dictate the pedagogical moves of the system and provide domain independence, as detailed by Mathews et al. (2003).

3.6 Muppets

Multi-Protocol Personal Translators ("Muppets") are the "glue" that connect clients to the system. They exist within the main AutoTutor server and translate the State Table into a format that a client can understand. Muppets allow the server to connect to clients in any programming language with any set of capabilities; smart clients written in a .NET language can connect to a Remoting Muppet, for instance, and have access to the entire State Table. A web browser could connect to a Web Server Muppet that turns the State Table into a web page with sufficient session management to keep track of each user connecting to the web site. Mobile phones could use an Instant Messaging Muppet that emulates an Instant Messaging service or chat room.

Muppets are perhaps the most complicated part of the system to develop, as they must deal with session management and network protocols; none of these low level details are hidden. To facilitate Muppet development and use of AutoTutor on multiple platforms, the architecture was developed with three Muppets: a .NET Remoting Muppet for smart clients, a text-based Muppet that uses simple TCP sockets, and a web-based Muppet that provides a simple World Wide Web interface.

3.7 Server Software

The AutoTutor 3 architecture uses only two pieces of server software: the AutoTutor Server, which handles Muppets and Hubs, and the Module Server, which is a generic server for offering .NET objects over Remoting. The AutoTutor Server is designed to bootstrap the entire system by using its configuration file to locate, instantiate, and initialize Muppets, Hubs, and all of the Modules and Utilities used by them. Each instance of an AutoTutor Server is capable of handling multiple Muppets and Hubs with the same or different sets of Modules and Utilities, which gives it the ability to support different "versions" of AutoTutor on a single machine that differ only in their interface to clients or in their internal processing steps.

The Module Server is not specific to this architecture. It is simply a generic server that can instantiate and offer objects or parts of objects, as defined by interfaces, through .NET Remoting. It is crucial to the proper operation of the architecture, but it can be used by any project in which Common Language Runtime objects need to be offered. Other distributed systems may readily make use of this server without implementing any part of the AutoTutor 3 architecture.

3.8 Client Software

Through the use of Muppets, specific client software is not required to use systems built on the AutoTutor 3 architecture. However, a smart client with support for plug-ins, an animated pedagogical agent, 3-D simulations, and client-side processing of data is available. Additionally, the Web Muppet provides a text-based interface on the World Wide Web.

4   Empirical Tests of Performance

The AutoTutor 3 system was completed approximately one year ago. It is a complete rewrite of the older AutoTutor 2 system (Graesser, VanLehn, Rosé, Jordan, & Harter, 2001). As such, empirical tests both of its ability to mimic this older system's abilities while adding new functionality and also of its architecture's raw performance are ongoing. Thus far, empirical tests look promising, with the AutoTutor 3 system matching the pedagogical performance of the AutoTutor 2 system and further enhancing it with the addition of 3-D simulations within the domain of conceptual physics.

With regards to the architecture's performance, internal profiling reveals that network latencies between components are less than 1 ms, though this is of course likely to increase if the components are further separated over a larger network. The Modules and Utilities of AutoTutor are CPU bound; their memory requirements are roughly constant, requiring only approximately another 100 kilobytes per simultaneous user atop a basic memory footprint of approximately 180 megabytes. Again, these values will vary based on the Modules used, but profiling shows that the architecture itself contributes very little to the memory or CPU footprint of the AutoTutor 3 processes.

Based on the average size of the State Tables in our internal stress testing using active users and distributed load generation with multiple computers, we estimate that any individual AutoTutor server instance can support at maximum approximately 800 simultaneous users, assuming all of the components of the system are located on a single server machine (a Pentium Xeon 1.4 gigahertz with 1 gigabyte of RAM in our tests) and the clients connect using 100BaseT Ethernet. Our testing of the system's architectural performance in the course of empirical testing of its pedagogy shows that it can readily support at least 30 simultaneous users with no detectable loss of responsiveness. A large study in which the system is used to support remote, naïve learners at other universities is in progress, but preliminary results have shown that a single AutoTutor 3 server is more than capable of providing advanced, natural language intelligent tutoring services to several hundred simultaneous users across the Internet while maintaining a high quality of service. Further empirical testing of the system's performance in the context of new experiments is currently in progress and should be completed by the end of 2005.

5   Future Directions

Beyond the need for further empirical performance testing, there is room for improvement in this architecture. At the moment, any form of load balancing or clustering must be handled manually by those hosting AutoTutor servers; monitoring application load and responding to it is a difficult and time-consuming task for system administrators. Future versions of this architecture, which will maintain backwards compatibility and provide these advantages to all existing code by leveraging the class inheritance system, will provide adaptive load balancing services through the strategic use of threading and dynamic load shedding. This will allow other computers to dynamically take over parts of the AutoTutor processing when the server is overloaded, or will allow a Muppet to transparently redirect a learner to a less crowded server providing the same content. Techniques such as the independent event queues and controllers of the SEDA architecture (Welsh, Culler, & Brewer, 2001) may be used to provide better quality of service under extremely heavy loads.

To make the AutoTutor system itself and not just its architecture more appealing to content creators, support for authoring tools that can manipulate the internal state of the Modules (such as the pedagogical strategies of the Dialogue Management Module) will be added, along with licensing support that can restrict use of tutoring systems based on this architecture, including AutoTutor, to those authorized to use the intellectual property contained within.

Acknowledgement

The Tutoring Research Group (TRG) is an interdisciplinary research team comprised of approximately 35 researchers from psychology, computer science, physics, and education (visit http://www.autotutor.org). The research on AutoTutor was supported by the National Science Foundation (SBR 9720314, REC 0106965, REC 0126265, ITR 0325428) and the DoD Multidisciplinary University Research Initiative (MURI) administered by ONR under grant N00014-00-1-0600. Any opinions, findings, and conclusions or recommendations expressed in this material are those of the authors and do not necessarily reflect the views of DoD, ONR, or NSF.

References

Ainsworth, S., Grimshaw, S.: Evaluating the Effectiveness and Efficiency of the REDEEM Intelligent Tutoring System Authoring Tool. Retrieved October 26, 2004 from the University of Nottingham, ESRC Centre for Research in Development, Instruction, and Training web site (2002) http://www.psychology.nottingham.ac.uk/staff/sea/techreport_69.pdf

Aleven, V., Koedinger, K.R.: An effective metacognitive strategy: Learning by doing and explaining with a computer-based Cognitive Tutor. Cognitive Science 26, 147–179 (2002)

Bautista, K., Person, N., Graesser, A.C.: Tutoring Research Group. In: Cerri, S.A., Gouardéres, G., Paraguaçu, F. (eds.) ITS 2002. LNCS, vol. 2363, pp. 821–830. Springer, Heidelberg (2002)

Bhatti, N., Bouch, A., Kuchinsky, A.: Integrating User-Perceived Quality into Web Server Design. In: Proceedings of the Ninth International World Wide Web Conference. May 2000. Amsterdam. Retrieved January 22, 2005 from http://www9.org/w9cdrom/92/92.html

Bouch, A., Sasse, M.A.: It ain't what you charge it's the way that you do it: A user perspective of network QoS and pricing. In: Proceedings of IM'99.IFIP, Boston (1999)

Cohen, P.A., Kulik, J.A., Kulik, C.C.: Educational outcomes of tutoring: A meta-analysis of findings. American Educational Research Journal 19, 237–248 (1982)

Corbett, A.T.: Cognitive computer tutors: Solving the two-sigma problem. In: Bauer, M., Gmytrasiewicz, P.J., Vassileva, J. (eds.) UM 2001. LNCS (LNAI), vol. 2109, pp. 137–147. Springer, Heidelberg (2001)

Galaxy Communicator Documentation. (n.d.) Retrieved December 17, 2004 from http://communicator.sourceforge.net/sites/MITRE/distributions/GalaxyCommunicator/docs/manual/index.html

Graesser, A.C., Jackson, G.T., Mathews, E.C., Mitchell, H.H., Olney, A., Ventura, M., et al.: Why/AutoTutor: A test of learning gains from a physics tutor with natural language dialogue. In: Proceedings of the 25th Annual Conference of the Cognitive Science Society pp. 1–6 Boston, MA: Cognitive Science Society (2003)

Graesser, A.C., Lu, S., Jackson, G.T., Mitchell, H., Ventura, M., Olney, A., Louwerse, M.M.: AutoTutor: A tutor with dialogue in natural language. Behavioral Research Methods, Instruments, and Computers (in press)

Graesser, A.C., Person, N.K., Magliano, J.P.: Collaborative dialogue patterns in naturalistic one-on-one tutoring. Applied Cognitive Psychology 9, 359–387 (1995)

Graesser, A.C., VanLehn, K., Rosé, C., Jordan, P., Harter, D.: Intelligent tutoring systems with conversational dialogue. AI Magazine 22, 39–51 (2001)

Johnson, W.L., Rickel, J.W., Lester, J.C.: Animated pedagogical agents: Face-to-face interaction in interactive learning environments. International Journal of Artificial Intelligence in Education 11, 47–78 (2000)

Jordan, P., Rosé, C., VanLehn, K.: Tools for authoring tutorial dialogue knowledge. In: Proceedings of AI in Education 2001 Conference, IOS Press, Amsterdam (2001)

Mathews, E.C., Jackson, G.T., Olney, A., Chipman, P., Graesser, A.C.: Achieving Domain Independence in AutoTutor. In: Callaos, N., Margenstern, M., Zhang, J., Castillo, O., Doberkat, E., (eds.) The Seventh World Multiconference on Systemics, Cybernetics, and Informatics Proceedings: Computer Science and Engineerings I, vol. 5, pp. 172–176. Orlando: IIIS (2003)

Microsoft. NET Technology Overview. (n.d.) Seattle, WA: Microsoft Corp. Retrieved October 11, 2004 from http://msdn.microsoft.com/netframework/technologyinfo/overview/default. aspx

Moreno, K.N., Klettke, B., Nibbaragandla, K., Graesser, A.C.: the Tutoring Research Group. Perceived characteristics and pedagogical efficacy of animated conversational agents. In: Cerri, S.A., Gouarderes, G., Paraguacu, F. (eds.) Intelligent Tutoring Systems, pp. 963–971. Springer, Berlin, Germany (2002)

Olney, A., Louwerse, M.M., Mathews, E.C., Marineau, J., Mitchell, H.H., Graesser, A.C.: Utterance classification in AutoTutor. In: Building Educational Applications using Natural Language Processing. Proceedings of the Human Language Technology - North American Chapter of the Association for Computational Linguistics Conference 2003 Workshop, pp. 1–8. Association for Computational Linguistics, Philadelphia (2003)

VanLehn, K., Freedman, R., Jordan, P., Murray, C., Osan, R., Ringenberg, M., Rosé, C., Schulze, K., Shelby, R., Treacy, D., Weinstein, A., Wintersgill, M.: Fading and Deepening: The Next Steps for Andes and Other Model-Tracing Tutors. In: Gauthier, G., VanLehn, K., Frasson, C. (eds.) ITS 2000. LNCS, vol. 1839, Springer, Heidelberg (2000)

VanLehn, K., Jones, R.M., Chi, M.T.H.: A model of the self-explanation effect. Journal of the Learning Sciences 2, 1–60 (1992)

Welsh, M., Culler, D., Brewer, E.: SEDA: An architecture for well-conditioned, scalable internet services. In: Proceedings of the Eighteenth Symposium on Operating Systems Principles (SOSP-18), pp. 230–243. ACM Press, New York (2001)

Redesigning Introductory Economics

Techno-Collaborative Learning

Maha Bali, Aziza El-Lozy, and Herb Thompson

The American University in Cairo, Cairo, Egypt
herbt@aucegypt.edu

Abstract. Does computer-mediation enhance student performance or student interest in the learning process? In this paper we present the somewhat tentative results of an experiment carried out in teaching/learning methodology and pedagogy. The goal of the experiment was to examine, compare and elicit results to identify the differences, if any, in learning outcomes between two classes. One class was taught using computer-mediated technologies in conjunction with "active" learning pedagogical principles; and the other class was taught by the same instructor with identical course syllabi and textbook, but using a more conventional approach of lectures and tests to achieve learning.

Keywords: Educational technology, tertiary education, computer mediation, pedagogy.

1 Introduction

As (Brahler et.al., 2000), argue, the combinatory effects of increased workloads, larger classes, changing learner needs and improved instructional technologies all have resulted in an increased demand for on-line teaching material. Consequently, the aim of this project was to focus on creating a learner-centred, formatively assessed, course that used Web-enabled technology. Introduction to Microeconomics, was chosen as the course to be redesigned because it has many sections and because it has a "broad institutional impact". In order to gather comparative data, another section of the same course was simultaneously offered by the same professor, utilising a more traditional "talking head", summatively assessed, approach.

We proceed in the following section with a literature overview of computer-mediated learning. This is followed by a description of the experiment and the methodologies used. Given the data gathered during the experiment, tentative results and conclusions are delineated.

2 Overview of Computer-Mediated Learning

Does computer-mediation enhance student performance or learning interests? In this paper we examine the relationship between computer-mediated technologies and student intellectual skills and abilities (Salomon, Perkins and Globerson, 1991). It has been argued, and the premise is accepted, that many students prefer the "talking head"

J. Filipe, J. Cordeiro, and V. Pedrosa (Eds.): WEBIST 2005/2006, LNBIP 1, pp. 333–342, 2007.

that enables them to sit and listen passively while information pertinent to examinations is organised for them. Other research shows that better retention, deeper thinking and higher motivation is initiated when students are actively involved in talking, writing and doing things relevant to their studies, both inside and out of class (Ahern and El-Hindi 2000: 385-396). Student evaluations exist for both types of educational practice (McKeachie 1997: 1219).

Implementing a change from the traditional classroom to one of collaborative, computer-mediated learning is not simple, either in organisation and structure, or in the process of carrying it out. The instructor is no longer the fount of wisdom or the only purveyor of interpretation. Even the hours of the class become manipulable by students given the ability to log on to discussion forums at any hour of the day and virtually, submit assignments, read announcements gather supplementary reading and ask or respond to questions (Fuller, et.al. 2000). In any case, even with the aforementioned technological advances, poor pedagogical models emphasising the passive absorption of "authoritative" information is being passed onto students, thereby wasting the immense potential of the Internet (Crook 1997; Kirkpatrick and McLaughlan 2000). Clearly, the challenge is to weave the technologies into the learning process so that they become part of the process rather than an adjunct to it.

Computer mediated technologies have and will continue to have major repercussions on the organisation and process of teaching and learning. For those of us encapsulated in this process, pedagogical approaches have come under more scrutiny. Giving the student the chance to participate more actively, interactively and collaboratively with both peer groups and instructors is not only possible but more easily achieved (Bailey and Cotlar 1994: 184-193; Ellsworth 1994; Ragoondden and Bordeleau 2000).

3 Description and Methodologies of the Experiment

Two parallel sections of the course ("traditional" and "innovative"), taught by the same professor, covering the same textual material, was offered in the same semester. See Table 1 below.

The traditional section involved lectures only (although students were encouraged to ask questions), using power-point slides in-class. The course syllabus and discussion forum was placed online utilising WebCT and a textbook was used for the required reading. Assessment was based on two hard-copy pop quizzes (10% each), a midterm exam (20%), two short reading assignments with students required to provide a summary analysis in the web-based discussion forum (15% each) class participation (20%) and a final exam (20%). In addition, a "learning styles" questionnaire (discussed below) was placed in WebCT online.

The innovative section involved very little lecturing by the instructor, but was facilitated mainly as student-centred, with open class participation and interaction. The students took turns giving short lectures on the textbook material using power-point slides in class. All course material, other than the same hard copy text used in the other class, was provided online and online discussion was overtly encouraged. Assessment in this section included 10 weekly online quizzes (1% each), class and electronic online participation (20%), a group collaborative project that was uploaded and assessed on WebCT for all students to see (30%), a learning journal that was shared with the rest of the class upon completion (15%) and the same final exam given to the other class (25%). Here too, a "learning styles" questionnaire was placed in WebCT online. Classes were primarily "open forums" with learning activities, peer instruction, group assignments and individual participation. All of the students in this class had a personal computer which was used for most of the class assignments and activities. Students were encouraged to use the computer as the search tool for questions and gathering of information. "Instruction" in this class was primarily one of coordination and facilitation with assistance provided as required when computer searching, peer instruction or collaborative assistance amongst the students was insufficient.

The usefulness and reasoning behind the group projects and learning journal is discussed further to stress the pedagogy involved.

3.1 Collaborative Group Projects

Utilisation of the Internet to assist in collaborative learning at a sophisticated level has been discussed in the literature for at least a decade (Crook 1997; Edwards and Clear 2001; Light, et.al. 1997; McAteer, et.al. 1997; Sosabowski, et.al. 1998). Team (collaborative) learning emphasises a high level of active involvement and a great deal of self-management by students. The challenges include determination of effective team member role behaviours and skill, dealing with 'free riders', and evaluation of individual performance within the group (Aiken 1991; Alie, R., Beam, H. and Carey, T. 1998; Boyatiz 1994; Malinger 1998; Ramsey and Couch 1994). It was emphasised from the beginning that the students were going to have to resolve all "management" problems themselves as the instructor was not going to "referee" squabbles or disagreements. Secondly, to handle the 'free rider' problem, one-third of the project grade was based on peer evaluation of their colleagues in the group (Cheng and Warren 2000). Grades were given by each student to the others in the group anonymously, and these marks were averaged by the instructor. The caveat by McCuddy and Pirie that: "students generally receive little guidance as to how to assess peers but are simply told to provide an evaluation for each team member", was taken seriously and given credence. It is recognised that "peer assessment is a challenge to experienced individuals and can be a daunting task for the uninitiated" [2004: 154]. Therefore, detailed guidance was given.

Group projects are problematic, to say the least. Some students do not wish to study/work with others as they feel that they are held back by the group, or forced to coordinate their efforts with others who may have very different study habits, initiative or ideas as to what is a "successful project". These students will insist that group work is time consuming with little benefit and in no way provides an enhancement of their learning. Computer-mediated communication may become a problem when members of the group log on at very different times or indeed, may not log on at all during times considered crucial for others in the group ("Is anyone going to respond to the point I made yesterday about sharing responsibility for the write-up..."). The point is that the technology is not living up to its promise NOW! (Harasim 1993: 119-130; Ragoondden and Bordeleau 2000) In fact, Repman and Logan (1996) argue convincingly that the benefits of group oriented pedagogy works primarily at a social and affective level rather than enhancing learning. One reason for this, also identified in the literature, is that collaboration does not work well within introductory courses, which attract a variegated group of students both in terms of backgrounds and interests. Rather collaboration appears to be more strongly correlated to learning in professional and graduate courses where homogeneity of background and interest is more closely aligned (Muffoletto 1997). However, in this class, small groups appeared to work reasonably well.

3.2 Learning Journals

What distinguished a learning journal in this course is the necessity to relate the theory and models of the classroom to lived experience. The intention is to both learn from the process of doing it, i.e., reflecting on lived experience in terms of information gained from the course, and to learn from the results, i.e., the application of classroom theory and models to actions, discussions, reading material or experiences that are encountered outside the classroom. The journal provides an intellectual platform for reflection on what is being learned as well as its usefulness. It counteracts "spoonfeeding" which are the hallmark of lecture notes and handouts. Instead, a personal approach to learning is emphasised allowing the learner to incorporate the material in their own terms of understanding.

The specific instruction provided to the student is as follows: You will complete a journal/diary of approximately 250 words per week, over a ten week period (2500 words total. You will keep a record as to what you have learned that is relevant to your studies and life, questions that have been raised in your mind, identification of issues that you never thought about before. This is not to be a diary about what we did in class. It is to be a reflective journal relating the material covered in class to the rest of your life's activities, such as conversations, experiences, economic activities in which you were specifically engaged, or articles in newspapers read based on the material covered in class. How do the theory and models learned in this course connect to your lived experiences outside class.

4 Available Data to Assess Impact on Students

4.1 Learning Styles Questionnaire

There may be as many different learning styles in a classroom as there are people, which should directly impact on the way teaching is organised. Research, experimentation and results of work by Richard M. Felder and Barbara A. Solomon in this area is made available. They have developed a questionnaire to delineate amongst four dichotomous pairs of learning styles. The four pairs are: 1) Active and Reflective Learners; 2) Sensory-based and Intuitive Learners; Visual and Verbal Learners; and 4) Sequential or Global Learners. Examination of their efforts at URL http://www.ncsu.edu/felder-public/ is recommended. This exercise was included in the project at hand. Of course there are numerous "ifs" and "buts" in the results of their work, but the questionnaire is a most practical and useful tool to get a mental image of the groups being taught. The results are more anecdotal, than analytical, but may provide room for consideration.

Results from questionnaire: Students in the Innovative section were all "active" learners, slightly sensory rather than intuitive, primarily visual, and all sequential learners.

Students in the Traditional section were half active and half reflective; slightly more sensory than the innovative section, similar in visual orientation to the innovative section and were split fairly evenly but slightly more global in approach.

Table 1. Summary and Comparison of Teaching/Learning Approaches in each Section

Characteristic	Traditional Section	Innovative Section
Population	20 (mostly 1st and 2nd year)	16 (mostly 1st and 2nd year)
Textbook	N. Gregory Mankiw, Principles of Economics Chapters 1-17	
Material Online	Syllabus, topic notes, glossary, ppt slides, learning styles questionnaire, required and additional reading, assignments, calendar, bonus questions, discussion forum.	Syllabus, topic notes, glossary, ppt. slides, learning styles questionnaire, study guide, chapter links to relevant internet material, links to classical scholars in economics, calendar, bonus questions, discussion forum and quizzes. Student group projects and learning journals were uploaded for viewing by the entire class.
Lecture	Lectures by instructor with .ppt slides. Students were encouraged to ask questions before and during lectures.	Lectures by students using .ppt slides. Student centred, open class participation and interaction encouraged (e.g., peer instruction, group activities collaboration and sharing of computer searches to solve problems or discuss issues)
Class Environment	One computer, projector and screen for professor	Class projector and screen for use by all. Each student supplied with a personal computer. Software (Timbuctu) allowed any of the computers to use projection screen.
Assignments	2 readings and summary analysis uploaded on WebCT discussion forum	Group project; Learning journal uploaded on WebCT
Quizzes	2 paper-based pop quizzes, with normal assessment of correct answers.	10 online quizzes – one per week. Following quiz, peers discuss answers. Credit given simply for taking quiz
Direct Assessment	2 pop quizzes – 20% Class participation – 20% Midterm – 20% 2 paper-based readings and summary analysis – 20% Final Exam – 20%	10 online quizzes – 10% Class/Web participation – 20% Class project – 30% Learning Journal – 15% Final Exam – 25%
Indirect Assessment	Pre- and Post-course tests, Student evaluations, a Small Group Instructional Diagnosis, Learning Styles questionnaire, WebCT tracking student activities	

The instructor is seen as completely reflective and much more intuitive than either of the sections, but equally visual and verbal in approach, while only slightly more global than sequential.

Description of Categories

ACTIVE – retain and understand best by doing, applying or explaining.

REFLECTIVE – prefer to think about problems quietly to begin with before acting.

SENSORY – prefer the facts and a "positivist" approach; good at memorisation and lab work.

INTUITIVE – look for possibilities and relationships and exceptions; comfortable with abstraction and seeks innovation.

VISUAL – prefer pictures, diagrams, flow charts, time lines, films and demonstrations

VERBAL – prefer written and/or spoken explanation.
GLOBAL – prefer the "big" picture, connections, interrelations and move almost randomly to solution.
SEQUENTIAL – prefer linear step by step approach to solution

4.2 Pre- and Post-Course Test Results

The pre-course test was taken from the Third edition of William B Walstad and Ken Rebeck 2001 *Test of Economic Literacy*, New York: National Council on Economic Education which is used to measure achievement of American high school students in economics. A norming sample was provided showing the aggregate statistics for a sample of 7,243 American students who had taken an economics course. The numbers below are representative of the number of correct answers out of 40 questions. Both sections did better than the norming sample, and had much lower standard deviations. This suggests, that on the average, a number of students in this course had previous experience with Economics at the secondary level.

The post-course test was taken from the Third edition of Phillip Saunders 1991 *Test of Understanding in College Economics*, New York: Joint Council on Economic Education which serves as a measuring instrument in the teaching of introductory economics at the college level for comparative purposes. A norming sample was provided showing the aggregate statistics for a sample of 1,426 American students who had taken the college course in economics. The numbers below are representative of the number of correct answers out of 33 questions. The Innovative section scored similarly to the American sample, whereas the mean of the Traditional section was lower than both, albeit with a smaller standard deviation. See Table 2 below.

4.3 Comparative Assessment of Final Exam and Final Grades

Summary: The results for the final exam and the final grades were very similar for both sections. The final exam results were (Innovative section – 75%, Traditional section 74%) and the final grades were (Innovative section had a mean grade of 83.8% while the traditional section had a mean grade of 78.7%)

4.4 Comparisons of Student Course Evaluation

In Table 3 the innovative section shows, overall, a more positive attitude towards the course itself, but the only significant difference is with reference to the "reading materials". This is most likely the result of the variegated possibilities that the computer offered the students in the classroom as a "library" reference source and the facilitation provided to gain access to up-to-date information relevant to the material being studied in the text. Table 4, with reference to the instructor, shows similar results. Although the innovative section ranks more positively (with the exception of "explains concepts clearly") the differences are slight in every instance. See Tables 3 and 4 below.

Table 2. Pre-course and Post-course test results

Pre-test results	Mean	Standard deviation
Traditional section	27.2	5.3
Innovative section	30.3	2.5
American sample	24.7	7.9
Post-test results		
Traditional section	13.4	3.9
Innovative section	16.5	5.1
American sample	16.67	6.3

Table 3. Evaluation (Mean) of Course on a scale of 1-5 with 1 = Strongly Disagree; 5 = Strongly Agree

Question	Traditional section	Innovative section	Economics overall	School of Business
Reading materials are challenging and stimulate my thinking	3.80	4.43	3.94	3.78
Tests and assignments reflect the purpose and content of the course	4.30	4.29	4.18	4.03
Tests and assignments challenge me to do more than memorize	4.40	4.57	3.97	3.86
The number and frequency of tests and assignments are reasonable	4.10	4.43	4.17	4.00
The working load is appropriate for the number of credits	4.30	4.43	4.08	3.91
Overall, this is a useful course	4.40	4.57	4.18	3.99

Table 4. Evaluation (Mean) of the Instructor on a scale of 1-5 with 1 = Strongly Disagree; 5 = Strongly Agree

Question	Traditional section	Innovative section	Economics overall	School of Business
Inspires student interest in course	4.29	4.33	4.08	3.94
Organised and prepared for class	4.43	4.56	4.45	4.23
Explains concepts clearly	4.00	3.94	4.19	4.01
Emphasises conceptual understanding and critical thinking	4.29	4.41	4.15	3.99

4.5 Small Group Instructional Diagnosis

In this exercise, the Director of the Center for Learning and Teaching and the Instructional technologist spent 30 minutes in each of the classes interviewing the students as to their impressions of the course half way through the semester. Below is a summary of their responses to two questions.

What helps you learn in this course?

Traditional section

Power-point slides in conjunction with lectures but there were a couple in the class who "hated" computers.

Understanding is expected more than memorization.

People asking questions: so that the point is covered again and professor is prepared to go over questions again.

Innovative section

WebCT: permanent interaction; helps us to learn in an innovative way (discussing amongst ourselves materials that we may not comprehend).

No need to memorize – no mid-terms, so there is a need to understand when writing in the learning journal. We have to take much more responsibility for our own learning.

An interesting teaching style.

Discussions in class and feedback through the online discussion is more important the sitting and listening to lectures.

Students become the role players in the class, asking each other questions and using the board and projector ourselves to show our understanding to other students who may not understand.

Always being up to date with what is going on in class and outside class.

What improvements would you like and How would you suggest that they be made?

Traditional section

Go slower

Spend more time covering class material relevant to quizzes.

Provide more worksheets with practical problems.

Show relations between chapters.

More participation and discussion needed in class.

Don't depend so much on WebCT

Innovative section

Provide more variety of choice for the group projects.

The discussion forum needs more structure and more input from the professor.

Make all courses like this.

5   Summary/Conclusions

5.1   Pre, Post, Final Exams

Given the intervening variables and relatively small sample of students it does not seem appropriate to discuss questions of "significant" difference. However, practically, it can be noted that in all three exams (Pre-test, Post-test and Final exam) the mean and median results were higher for the innovative section.

5.2 Course Evaluation

The numerical results of the course evaluation, and qualitative observation by the instructional technologist indicated better student disposition towards the effect of technology on learning as well as student motivation. General disposition towards computer mediation was much stronger for the "innovative" section students than for the traditional section students (suggesting that it did enhance their learning process, etc). The innovative course consistently showed better results than either, the traditional course, and other courses in Economics, or all courses in the School of Business.

5.3 SGID

According to the SGID results the innovative section students were more comfortable with the speed of the course, the use of technology, and the material covered. The traditional section students were uncomfortable with the speed of instruction; felt their questions were not sufficiently answered and that the course was not sufficiently interactive. Qualitatively, the students in the innovative section seemed much more interested both in taking more economics courses and/or taking economics as a major; whereas the students in the traditional section showed much less enthusiasm for the material covered, or for economics as a discipline.

5.4 Caveat

There is insufficient quantitative and qualitative data to allow clear, undifferentiated judgements. Furthermore, an excessive number of intervening variables blurred both the accuracy and interpretation of results, which, among other things, is the analogue of Heisenberg's "principle of uncertainty", i.e., the biases, attitudes and behaviour of the facilitator.

No information was gathered with respect to gender, major and minor degree interest, or student backgrounds in economics in secondary school or university.

To conclude qualitatively, on one level the results indicate that the amount of work that goes into creating an activity-based alternative to the "talking head" and conventional testing approach may be unnecessary. However, at another level there was sufficient evidence to show that the learning process (and economics) was enjoyed much more by the students when engaged in an open, active, collaborative manner. The depth of learning which takes place remains to be determined in further research.

References

Ahern, T., El-Hindi, A.E.: Improving the instructional congruency of a computer-mediated small-group discussion: A case study in design and delivery. Journal of Research on Computing in Education 32(3), 385–596 (2000)

Aiken, G.: Self-directed learning in introductory management. Journal of Management Education 15, 295–312 (1991)

Alie, R., Beam, H., Carey, T.: The use of teams in an undergraduate management program. Journal of Management Education 22, 707–719 (1998)

Bailey, E., Cotlar, E.: Teaching via the Internet. Communication Education 43, 184–193 (1994)

Boyatiz, R.: Stimulating self-directed learning through the managerial assessment and development course. Journal of Management Education 18, 304–323 (1994)

Brahler, C.J., Peterson, N.S., Johnson, E.C.: Developing on-line material for higher education: an overview of current issues. Education Technology and Society 3(1), 42–54 (2000)

Cheng, W., Warren, M.: Making a Difference: using peers to assess individual students' contributions to a group project. Teaching in Higher Education 5(2), 243–255 (2000)

Crook, C.K.: Making hypertext lecture notes more interactive: undergraduate reactions. Journal of Computer-Assisted Learning 13, 236–244 (1997)

Edwards, M.A., Clear, F.: Supporting the Collaborative Learning of Practical Skills with Computer-Mediated Communications Technology. Educational Technology and Society, 4(1) [WWW page] (2001) http://ifets.ieee.org/periodical/vol_1_2001/edwards.html

Ellsworth, J,: Education on the Internet. Indiana: Sams Publishing (1994)

Fuller, Dorothy, Norby, Rena, F., Pearce, Kristi, Strand, Sharon.: Internet Teaching By Style: Profiling the On-line Professor. Educational Technology & Society, 3(2) [WWW page] (2000), http://ifets.ieee.org/periodical/vol_2_2000/pearce.html

Harasim, L.: Collaborating in cyberspace: Using computer conferences as a group learning environment. Interactive Learning Environments 3(2), 119–130 (1993)

Kirkpatrick, D., McLaughlan, R.: Flexible lifelong learning in professional education. Education Technology and Society 3(1), 24–31 (2000)

Light, P., Colbourn, C., Light, V.: Computer mediated tutorial support for conventional courses. Journal of Computer-Assisted Learning 13, 228–235 (1997)

Malinger, M.: Maintaining control in the classroom by giving up control. Journal of Management Education 22, 43–56 (1998)

McCuddy, M.K., Pirie, W.L: Using teams in the classroom: Meeting the challenge of evaluating student's work. In: Ottewill, R., Borredon, L., Falque, L., Macfarlane, B., Wall, A. (eds.) Educational Innovation in Economics and Business: Pedagogy, Technology and Innovation, vol. VIII, pp. 147–160. Kluwer Academic Publishers, Dordrecht (2004)

McAteer, E., Tolmie, A., Duffy, C., Corbett, J.: Computer-mediated communication as a learning resource. Journal of Computer-Assisted Learning 13, 219–227 (1997)

McKeachie, W.: Student ratings: the validity of use. American Psychologist 52, 1218–1225 (1997)

Muffoletto, R.: Reflections on Designing and Producing an Internet-Based Course. TechTrends 42(2), 50–53 (1997)

Ragoondden, Karen, Bordeleau, Pierre.: Collaborative Learning via the Internet. Educational Technology & Society, 3(3) (2000), [WWW page] http://ifets.ieee.org/periodical/vol_3_2000/d11.html

Ramsey, V., Couch, P.: Beyond self-directed learning: A partnership model of teaching learning. Journal of Management Education 18, 139–161 (1994)

Repman, J., Logan, S.: Interactions at a Distance: Possible Barriers and Collaborative Solutions. TechTrends, November/December, pp. 35–38 (1996)

Salomon, G., Perkins, D., Globerson, T.: Partners in Cognition: Extending Human Intelligence with Intelligent Technologies. Educational Researcher 20(3), 2–9 (1991)

Sosabowski, M.H., Herson, K., Lloyd, A.W.: Enhancing learning and teaching quality: integration of networked learning technologies into undergraduate modules. Active Learning 8, 20–25 (1998)

Teaching Database Analysis and Design in a Web-Based Constructivist Learning Environment

Thomas M. Connolly and Carolyn E. Begg

School of Computing, University of Paisley, High Street, Paisley, United Kingdon
thomas.connolly@paisley.ac.uk, carolyn.begg@paisley.ac.uk

Abstract. The study of database systems is typically core in undergraduate and postgraduate courses related to computer science and information systems. However, there are parts of this curriculum that learners find difficult, in particular, the abstract and complex domain of database analysis and design, an area that is critical to the development of modern information systems. This paper reflects on these difficulties and describes an approach for teaching database analysis and design online motivated by principles found in the constructivist epistemology, which helps to overcome these difficulties and provides the learner with the knowledge and higher-order skills necessary to understand and perform database analysis and design effectively as a professional practitioner. The paper presents some preliminary results of this work and reflects on the findings.

Keywords: Database analysis and design, online learning, reflective practitioner, constructivist learning environments, project-based learning.

1 Introduction

The database is now the underlying framework of the information system and has fundamentally changed the way many companies and individuals work. This is reflected within tertiary education where databases form a core area of study in undergraduate and postgraduate courses related to computer science and information systems, and typically at least an elective on other data-intensive courses. The core studies, typically, are based on the relational data model, SQL, data modeling, relational database analysis and design and, increasingly, object-relational concepts. This supports industry where the object-relational DBMS is the dominant data-processing software currently in use. The core relational theory is a mature and established area now in relation to other parts of the computing curriculum. However, there are parts of this curriculum that learners find difficult, in particular, database analysis and design.

Mohtashami and Scher (2000) note that pedagogical strategies for teaching database analysis and design traditionally follow a similar modality to that of other technical courses in computing science or information systems. A significant amount of technical knowledge must be imparted with the teacher becoming a 'sage on stage' and the learners passive listeners. This is the objectivist model of learning, which views learning as the passive transmission of knowledge from the teacher to the

J. Filipe, J. Cordeiro, and V. Pedrosa (Eds.): WEBIST 2005/2006, LNBIP 1, pp. 343–354, 2007.

learner, heavily criticized for stimulating surface learning and knowledge reproduction. In contrast, the central tenet of the constructivist view is that learning is an active process where new knowledge is constructed based on the learner's prior knowledge, the social context, and the problem to be solved. In this paper, we describe a teaching approach that we have used to teach database analysis and design online motivated by principles found in the constructivist epistemology to help provide the learner with the knowledge and higher-order skills necessary to understand and perform database analysis and design effectively as a professional practitioner.

In the following section, we outline the high-level pedagogical aims of our database modules and consider some of the difficulties that arise in achieving these aims. In the subsequent section, we examine related work on constructivism and constructivist learning environments. In Section 4, we discuss how we have applied constructivist principles to our teaching of a database module delivered fully online. In Section 5, we present some early findings from our approach followed by some conclusions.

2 Pedagogical Aims

The database modules in the School of Computing at the University of Paisley have the following general educational aims:

- Develop a sound understanding of the principles and underpinning theory related to the study of database systems.
- Assist the development of a business ethos in the student that emphasizes fitness for purpose as the guiding principle in the design, development, and assessment of database systems and their components.
- Enable the student to take a disciplined approach to problem definition, and to the specification, design, implementation, and maintenance of database systems.
- Develop critical, analytical, and problem-solving skills and the transferable skills to prepare the student for graduate employment.
- Assist the student to develop the skills required for both autonomous practice and team-working.
- Create awareness of the continuing development of database technologies and applications and the need for continued study, reflection, and development throughout a career as a database professional.

In themselves, these aims are not unusual and are typical for many undergraduate database modules. Our modules have a vocational orientation and we expect our graduates to become professional database practitioners typically in a multi-disciplinary environment. Previous approaches to educating database designers and, more generally, software designers model scientific and engineering methodologies, with their focus on process and repeatability. In general, this approach is based on a normative professional education curriculum, in which students first study basic science, then the relevant applied science, so that learning may be viewed as a progression to expertise through task analysis, strategy selection, try-out, and repetition (Armarego, 2002). While students tend to cope well using this approach with many of the theoretical and practical components of the core database curriculum, for example, understanding the properties of the relational data model, the basics of SQL, and using a relational DBMS, one area that tends to be problematic is the abstract and complex domain of database analysis and design (for the purposes of this paper, we use the term database analysis and design to encompass system definition, requirements collection and analysis, conceptual database design, logical database design, and physical database design). A comparable problem has been identified with object-oriented analysis and design, which is also highly abstract (Hadjerrouit, 1999), requirements engineering (Bubenko, 1995), and software design and testing (Budgen, 1995).

While databases have become so essential to organizations, some students become deceived by the simplicity of creating small databases using products such as Microsoft Access and believe they can create more complicated databases just as easily. Unfortunately, the resulting databases are hard to use, barely meet system requirements, and are difficult to redesign. In addition, students require skills to work in a project team, skills to apply appropriate fact-finding techniques to elicit requirements from the client (both 'soft', people-oriented skills), skills to conceptualize a design from a set of requirements ('soft', analytical and problem-solving skills), skills to map a conceptual model to a logical/physical design ('hard', technical skills), and skills to reflect and review intermediate designs, particularly where information complexity is present (a combination of 'soft' and 'hard' skills). These are different skills from learning SQL, knowing the components of an ER model, or being able to recite the properties of the relational model. Students often have considerable difficulty comprehending implementation-independent issues and analyzing problems were there is no single, simple, well-known, or correct solution. They have difficulty handling ambiguity and vagueness, which can arise during knowledge elicitation. They can also display an inability to translate classroom examples to other domains with analogous scenarios, betraying a lack of transferable analytical and problem-solving skills. These problems can lead to confusion, a lack of self-confidence, and a lack of motivation to continue.

Software engineering (and therein database analysis and design) has been described as a *wicked problem*, characterized by incomplete, contradictory and changing requirements, and solutions that are often difficult to recognize as such because of complex interdependencies (DeGrace and Hulet Stahl, 1998). According to Armarego (2002), there is an educational dilemma in teaching such problems in software engineering because:

- complexity is added rather than reduced with increased understanding of the problem;
- metacognitive strategies are fundamental to the process;
- a rich background of knowledge and intuition are needed for effective problem-solving;
- a breadth of experience is necessary so that similarities and differences with past strategies are used to deal with new situations.

Schön (1983) argues that the primary challenge for designers is how to make sense out of situations that are puzzling, troubling, and uncertain. According to Schön the following are some of the key problems in teaching design:

- It is learnable but not didactically or discursively teachable: it can be learned only in and through practical operations.
- It is a holistic skill and parts cannot be learned in isolation but by experiencing it in action.
- It depends upon the ability to recognize desirable and undesirable qualities of the discovered world. However, this recognition is not something that can be described to learners, instead it must be learned by doing.
- It is a creative process in which a designer comes to see and do things in new ways. Therefore, no prior description of it can take the place of learning by doing.

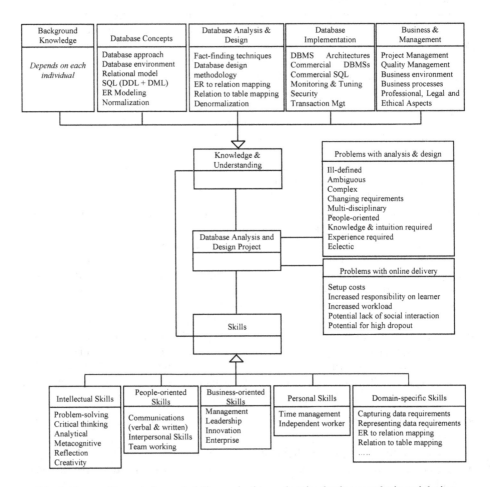

Fig. 1. Types of knowledge and skills required to undertake database analysis and design

As an additional complexity, to provide more flexible modes of study and capture new markets, tertiary education is providing more modules and courses in an online format, resulting in students who are geographical dispersed and have diverse backgrounds. While online learning has many advantages ("anytime, anywhere, anypace") there are also disadvantages such as increased setup costs, more responsibility is placed on the learner who has to be self-disciplined and motivated, increased workload on students and staff, non-involvement in the virtual community may lead to feelings of loneliness, low self-esteem, isolation, and low motivation to learn, which in turn can lead to low achievement and dropout, and dropout rates tend to be higher than in traditional face-to-face programs, often 10 to 20 percentage points higher (Connolly and Stansfield, 2006). To address these issues we require a different approach to traditional (face-to-face) teaching methods. Figure 1 provides a representation of the types of knowledge and skills required to undertake database analysis and design and the associated problems.

The above discussions suggest an alternative approach to teaching database analysis and design may overcome some of the above difficulties and in the next section we examine one such approach that we have found useful.

3 Previous Work

While traditional education has been guided by the paradigm of didactic instruction, which views the learner as passively receiving information, there is now an emphasis on *constructivism* as a philosophical, epistemological, and pedagogical approach to learning. Cognitive constructivism views learning as an active process in which learners construct new ideas or concepts based upon their current/past knowledge. The learner selects and transforms information, constructs hypotheses, and makes decisions, relying on a cognitive structure to do so. In addition, constructivism asserts that people learn more effectively when they are engaged in constructing personally meaningful artifacts. Social constructivism, seen as a variant of cognitive constructivism, emphasizes that human intelligence originates in our culture. Individual cognitive gain occurs first in interaction with other people and in the next phase within the individual (Forman and McPhail, 1993). These two models are not mutually exclusive but merely focus upon different aspects of the learning process.

According to Gance (2002) the main pedagogical components commonly associated with these models are:

- A cognitively engaged learner who actively seeks to explore his environment for new information.
- A pedagogy that often includes a hands-on, dialogic interaction with the learning environment (eg. designing a database is preferred to being told how to design a one).
- A pedagogy that often requires a learning context that creates a problem-solving situation that is realistic.
- An environment that typically includes a social component often interpreted as actual interaction with other learners and with mentors in the actual context of learning.

Dewey argued that knowing and doing are intimately connected and that learning occurs in the context of activity when an individual attempts to accomplish some meaningful goal and has to overcome difficulties in the process. Schön (1983) describes professionals as individuals who make this connection between knowing and doing through reflective practice, suggesting that professionals learn to think in action and learn to do so through their professional experiences. For Schön, practitioners (in our case, database designers) have their own particular knowledge codes fully embedded within their practices. They apply tacit knowledge-in-action, and when their problems do not yield to it, they *reflect-in-action*, using the languages specific to their practices. When they evaluate the event afterwards, they *reflect-on-action*, using the language of practice, not the language of science. In this way, professionals enhance their learning and add to their *repertoire* of experiences, from which they can draw in future problem situations. Schön believes that it is this ability to reflect both in, and on, action that identifies the effective practitioner from less effective professionals. For Schön the ideal site of education for reflective practice is the 'design studio' where, under the direction of a master practitioner serving as coach, the novice learns the vocabularies of the professional practice in the course of learning its 'operational moves'.

These arguments suggest that students can only learn about design by doing design, and rely less on overt lecturing and traditional teaching. This approach requires a shift in the roles of both students and teachers, with the student becoming an apprentice, exploring and learning about the problem in the presence of peers (who may know more or less about the topic at hand) and the teacher moving from being the 'knowledgeable other' towards becoming a facilitator, who manages the context and setting, and assists students in developing an understanding of the material at hand (Koehler and Mishra, 2005).

3.1 Constructivist Learning Environments

Many researchers have expressed their hope that constructivism will lead to better educational software and better learning (for example, Brown, Collins, & Duguid, 1989). They emphasize the need for open-ended exploratory authentic learning environments in which learners can develop personally meaningful and transferable knowledge and understanding. This has led to the development of guidelines and criteria for the development of a *constructivist learning environment* (CLE) - "a place where learners may work together and support each other as they use a variety of tools and information resources in their guided pursuit of learning goals and problem-solving activities" (Wilson, 1996, pp. 28).

According to Ben-Ari (2001) constructivist principles have been more influential in science and mathematics education than in computer science education. However, there are examples of the application of constructivism within computer science from the development of Logo – a programming language for schoolchildren (Papert, 1980), the teaching of programming (Pullen, 2001), computer graphics (Taxén, 2003), object-oriented design (Hadjerrouit, 1999), communication skills in computer science (Gruba and Søndergaard, 2001), to collaborative learning using the Web (Connolly, Stansfield, & McLellan, 2005).

Project-based learning (PBL) is a constructivist approach to learning knowledge and skills through a process structured around projects with complex and authentic tasks, objectives, questions, and problems. In PBL, the teacher (facilitator) is available for consultation and plays a significant role in modeling the metacognitive thinking associated with the problem-solving processes. These reflect a *cognitive apprenticeship* environment (Collins *et al.*, 1989) with *coaching* and *scaffolding* (e.g. offering hints, reminders, and feedback) provided to support the learner in developing metacognitive skills. As these skills develop, the scaffolding is gradually removed. The intention is to force learners to assume as much of the task on their own, as soon as possible. A further important element is *debriefing*, which provides the opportunity for learners to consolidate their experience and assess the value of the knowledge they have obtained in terms of its theoretical and practical application to situations that exist in reality.

4 Applying These Principles

We have developed a Web-based CLE using the above principles built around the cognitive apprenticeship model and project-based learning to teach some of the database modules in our undergraduate/postgraduate courses. A more complete discussion of the CLE can be found in Connolly and Begg (2006), however, in this paper we focus on the use of the online CLE for the Fundamentals of Database Systems (FDBS) module, a core module in the School's MSc Information Technology course, a conversion course for non-computing graduates. The students taking this module are reasonably experienced learners although not experienced in computing.

The FDBS module runs in a traditional face-to-face mode for full-time and part-time cohorts and since session 2001/2 in a fully online format for a part-time cohort. Since session 2002/3, we have used a CLE for the online cohort, which typically consists of 15-25 students, all from similar professional backgrounds. Scaffolding is provided through the teacher (facilitator) as well as through the creation of visualizations for a number of database concepts (eg. ER modeling, normalization, mapping an ER model to relations) and lower-level online units covering the relevant module material. When the students encounter problems they can drill down to the relevant material or use the higher-level visualizations. In the early stages, asynchronous online tutorials are run to discuss worked examples covering activities that groups would have to undertake as part of database analysis and design. It is important that students fully understand these examples and can apply the principles in the different contexts they will find themselves in.

The students self-select themselves into groups of size 3-4 and each group chooses a project that is of interest to all group members. These projects are generally from small businesses in the West of Scotland, which has the added advantage of benefiting these businesses and thereby the local economy. The facilitator provides background advice to ensure that a group does not take on a project that is too large or complex or alternatively too trivial. Students are encouraged to keep sufficiently detailed and formal records of their work and, in particular, the decisions made with supporting justifications. They are also encouraged to frequently reflect on these decisions and the processes that led to the decisions both as a group and as individuals. To support the notion of cognitive preference (Connolly, MacArthur, Stansfield, & McLellan, 2006), each group/individual is given scope to use whatever tools they feel most appropriate and most comfortable with. The FirstClass VLE is used for the online material as well as providing email facilities and discussions boards, both public (ie. available to the students and facilitators) and private (a student-only discussion area). Interestingly, while groups initially use these basic facilities, they also develop their own wikis and blogs, while using Skype/mobiles and instant messaging for more urgent communication. Groups use laptops and PDAs for recording meetings with the clients and the facilitator.

Support is provided by the facilitator as and when necessary but this is only in an advisory capacity: groups are not provided with solutions or partial solutions but are instead directed to where appropriate information can be found. This reinforces the principles of constructivism and emphasizes to the students that they are acting as professional database design consultants and have to act in this capacity. Debriefing is conducted at the end for all parties (facilitators, students, and clients) to reflect on the learning outcomes and to reflect on issues that had arisen in the performance of the projects. We discuss some of these issues in the next section.

5 Preliminary Results

This section presents some preliminary findings from using the project-based learning approach to teach database analysis and design in the FDBS module. A quantitative analysis of students' performance in the FDBS module is presented in Connolly et al. (2006). The paper compares the performance of 977 students divided into three groups, one of which used the constructivist project-based approach albeit through online delivery. The evidence supports our view that the constructivist approach can improve student learning. The results were not fully conclusive because the effect could have been entirely attributable to online delivery rather than the project-based approach and further quantitative research is required. However, the qualitative analysis of student and faculty feedback from the FDBS module that we undertook in parallel provides some interesting results to further support our view as we now discuss.

Finally, a qualitative analysis of student and faculty feedback provide further insight into this approach. Generally, student feedback was extremely positive, all students reporting that they had enjoyed the experience. They were able to compare this approach with the more traditional case study approach that they had encountered in their previous studies and had felt that the project-based approach with learning *in situ* had provided a better, more motivating, more engaging method to learn about database analysis and design. They also appreciated that this approach gave them relevant work experience that could help their employment prospects on completion of the course. The students were also very receptive to the concept of a reflective journal and, while it was sometimes difficult to find the time to maintain it, many reported that they had benefited from this approach and would keep a reflective journal for the remainder of their studies and into employment. On the negative side, most students reported that the workload was significantly higher than in other modules. They also found time-management was an issue, particularly as they had no real feeling at the outset for scope and complexity of the projects they had selected (many were led by their enthusiasm for working as a professional consultant). All were in agreement that the approach should be extended to other modules, but rather than having a project per module, they suggested that one assessment-based integrative project that extended over a number of modules would be an extremely powerful approach to teaching and learning.

Faculty were also enthusiastic of this approach and felt the students had learned more than with the case study approach, particularly in areas not traditionally covered in the database modules (use of fact-finding techniques, and people- and business-oriented skills). It was important that sufficient guidance was given during the project, particularly in the early stages when the groups were selecting projects (as noted above, student enthusiasm had to be tempered with realistic expectations). At the same time, as students were now working in an environment that had not been purpose-built for their effective learning, care had to be taken to ensure students were not overwhelmed with all the complexities that a real-world project can present, otherwise their initial enthusiasm quickly dissipated. The students needed guidance with both group and personal reflection initially until they found tools they were comfortable with (eg. wikis, blogs).

Typically each faculty member handled between 4-6 project groups compared to sometimes as many as 20 groups with the case study approach. Nevertheless, faculty found that their workload was significantly higher than with traditional approaches and that it was necessary to develop in-depth knowledge of each project to be able to support the students effectively. This gave rise to grave concerns over scalability and faculty felt that they could not have coped with any further project groups.

Faculty observed that students generally underestimated the time required to undertake the project and the facilitator needed to discuss the similarities and differences between case study assessments and project-based assessments. For example, some students underestimated the time spent securing a company's involvement in their project and establishing that relationship cannot always be rushed to fit a timescale that suits the students and meets the demands of faculty. It was also important for the facilitator to identify the gaps in the students' knowledge and skills and direct them to appropriate sources to enable them to undertake the project effectively. Failing to do this in a timely manner, led some students to lose confidence and meant they simplified and converted the project into a form of case study that they could cope with. However, this should and can be avoided with sufficient support from the facilitator to encourage students to accept the realities and complexities of PBL as a positive aspect of their work. It is the students' ability to cope with and manage the project that is being assessed and therefore it is necessary that they do not ignore or smooth over the problems of working with a real company.

While assessments based on case studies for database analysis and design usually present a simplified and contrived set of requirements that the students then analyse and solve, our PBL approach requires that the students must first capture the requirements for the new database. Capturing requirements require that students use fact-finding techniques that may be known in theory but not practised. Therefore, while case study assessments cover requirements analysis through to physical database design and possibly thereafter to implementation, PBL extends the coverage of the database system development lifecycle from the systems definition stage through to implementation. It is therefore clear that the skills required to undertake PBL differs to that of the case study approach.

As the success of the PBL approach is dependent on the support of industry, faculty emphasized that the facilitator must carefully guide students in their relationship with the company while ensuring that students achieve the specified learning outcomes. This sometimes required significant diplomacy from the facilitator when the academic objectives did not fully match the commercial objectives. It is important that faculty explain to companies at the outset what constitutes reasonable expectations for parameters such as project size, project complexity, and overall timescales. However, in most cases, both students and companies benefited from the relationship and this is why PBL has been well supported by companies over the last few years.

Occasionally, faculty encountered problems with group dynamics, for example, autonomous students tend to prefer to work individually, there can be lack of group cohesion, dominant group members, insecure group members, and free-riders (referred to in group dynamics research as 'diffusion of responsibility'). To highlight that these can occur in industry and need to be overcome, students were encouraged to tackle these problems as a group and only in extreme cases did faculty intervene to facilitate a solution acceptable to all.

There was agreement among faculty that the PBL approach was pedagogically sound for postgraduate courses and for third/fourth years of undergraduate courses, but were reluctant to use this approach in first or second year, on the grounds that students may not be sufficiently mature learners and may not have developed the necessary discipline and time-management skills required. Further, it was generally felt that rather than moving from being a 'sage on the stage' to a 'guide on the side', the facilitator had to be more of a 'fount of all knowledge' with project-based learning.

6 Conclusion

This paper has examined some of the issues surrounding the teaching of database analysis and design and has described a teaching approach motivated by principles found in the constructivist epistemology, based on the cognitive apprenticeship model and PBL. The approach used points toward learning about design by *doing* design, and relying less on overt lecturing and traditional teaching. Design is learned by becoming a practitioner, albeit for the duration of the module, not merely by learning about practice. In brief, students should engage in challenging problems that reflect real-world complexity. The problems should be authentic and ill-structured; that is, they should not have one predetermined, foregone solution but rather be open to multiple interpretations and multiple 'right answers'. Students should engage in actively working on solving problems in collaborative groups to reflect the social nature of learning.

This approach requires a shift in the roles of both students and faculty. The student becomes a cognitive apprentice, exploring and learning about the problem in the presence of peers. Faculty shifts from being the 'sage on the stage' to the 'guide on the side' (possibly, in the extreme, the 'fount of all knowledge'), becoming a facilitator who assists students in developing an understanding of the professional practice of database analysis and design.

The paper presents some preliminary results of this work that shows the approach can be used successfully. The preliminary qualitative findings show that students and faculty reacted extremely positively to the approach and found it more motivating and engaging than the more traditional case study approach. However, both students and faculty found the workload higher than with more traditional teaching methods and that scalability was an issue. Faculty also felt that this approach required mature learners and may not be entirely appropriate for first and second year undergraduates.

References

Armarego, J.: Advanced Software Design: A Case in Problem-Based Learning. In: Proceedings of the 15th Conference on Software Engineering Education and Training pp. 44–54, February 25–27, 2002, Covington, Kentucky, USA (2002)

Ben-Ari, M.: Constructivism in Computer Science Education. Journal of Computers in Mathematics and Science Teaching 20(1), 45–73 (2001)

Brown, J.S., Collins, A., Duguid, P.: Situated cognition and the culture of learning. Educational Researcher 18(1), 32–42 (1989)

Bubenko, J.: Challenges in Requirements Engineering. Keynote address. In: Second IEEE International Symposium on Requirements Engineering. York, England (1995)

Budgen, D.: Is teaching software design a 'wicked' problem too. In: Proceedings of the 8th SEI Conference on Software Engineering Education, pp. 239–254 New Orleans (La) (1995)

Collins, A., Brown, J.S., Newman, S.E.: Cognitive Apprenticeship: Teaching the Craft of reading, writing, and mathematics. In: Resnick, L. (ed.) Knowing, Learning, and Instruction: Essays in Honor of Robert Glaser, Lawrence Erlbaum, Hillsdale, NJ (1989)

Connolly, T.M., Begg, C.E.: A Constructivist-Based Approach to Teaching Database Analysis and Design. Journal of Information Systems Education (accepted for publication)

Connolly, T.M., Stansfield, M.H.: From eLearning to Games-based eLearning: Using Interactive Technologies in Teaching Information Systems. International Journal of Information Technology Management (submitted)

Connolly, T.M., MacArthur, E., Stansfield, M.H., McLellan, E.: A Quasi-Experimental Study of Three Online Learning Courses in Computing. Journal of Computers and Education (in print)

Connolly, T.M., Stansfield, M.H, McLellan, E.: An Online Games-Based Collaborative Learning Environment to Teach Database Analysis and Design. In: Proceedings of 4th IASTED International Conference on Web-Based Education. Grindelwald, Switzerland, February 2005 (2005)

DeGrace, P., Hulet Stahl, L.: Wicked Problems, Righteous Solutions: A Catalog of Modern Engineering Paradigms. Prentice Hall, Englewood Cliffs (1998)

Forman, E., McPhail, J.: Vygotskian perspectives on children's collaborative problem-solving activities. In: Forman, E.A., Minick, N., Addison, C. (eds.) Contexts for learning. Sociocultural dynamics in children's development, Oxford University Press, Oxford (1993)

Gance, S.: Are constructivism and computer-based learning environments incompatible? Journal of the Association for History and Computing 1 (2002)

Gruba, P., Søndergaard, H.: A constructivist approach to communication skills instruction in computer science. Computer Science Education 11(3), 203–219 (2001)

Hadjerrouit, S.: A Constructivist Approach to Object-Oriented Design and Programming. In: Proceedings of 4th Annual SIGCSE/SIGCUE Conference on Innovation and Technology in Computer Science Education (ITiCSE'99), pp. 171–174 (1999)

Koehler, M.J., Mishra, P.: Teachers Learning Technology by Design. Journal of Computing in Teacher Education 21(3) (2005)

Mohtashami, M., Scher, J.M.: Application of Bloom's Cognitive Domain Taxonomy to Database Design. In: Proceedings of ISECON (Information Systems Educators Conference) 2000. Philadelphia (2000)

Papert, S.: Mindstorms: children, computers and powerful ideas, Basic Books (1980)

Pullen, M.: The Network Workbench and Constructivism: Learning Protocols by Programming. Computer Science Education 11(3), 189–202 (2001)

Schön, D.A.: The Reflective Practitioner: How Professionals Think in Action. Basic Books: New York (1983)

Taxén, G.: Teaching Computer Graphics Constructively. In: Proceedings of International Conference on Computer Graphics and Interactive Techniques (pp. 1–4) San Diego, California (2003)

Wilson, B.: Constructivist learning environments: Case studies in instructional design. Educational Technology Publications, New Jersey (1996)

Is the Jury Still Out on "Blended Learning"?

Use of a Web-Based Collaborative Teaching Platform

Audrey Jennings[1], Alan Mullally[2], Catherine O'Connor[2], Dudley Dolan[2],
Adrian Parkinson[2], and James A. Redmond[2]

[1] MIS Department, Dublin Institute of Technology, Aungier Street, Dublin 2, Ireland
[2] Department of Computer Science, Trinity College, Dublin 2, Ireland
redmond@cs.tcd.ie

Abstract. Web-based collaborative platforms appear to show controversial potential for improving teaching and learning productivity and flexibility at Third Level. A pilot study was conducted at Trinity College Dublin (TCD) to explore pertinent operational, andragogical, support and social issues with a view to providing insights for the future. While a blended solution, i.e. a mixture of traditional and eLearning is often suggested, it appears that student support for it is not very high and proved disappointing in this study.

Keywords: Blended learning, Traditional learning, e-Learning, Web-based teaching, Collaborative platform, Distance learning, face to face learning.

1 Introduction

This research initiative focuses on the impact of online synchronous learning using a web-based collaborative platform with part-time, mature, evening Information Systems university students, in full-time employment. However there was some asynchronous learning in that the students could recall the saved lectures and replay them at a later date.

There is a dearth of research material in the area of web-based online synchronous delivery of learning in traditional universities *"Considering the massive adoption of e-learning, what is surprising and cause for concern, is that we know so little about the use of this medium to facilitate learning" (Gilbert, 2000)(Garrison, 2003).*

The Trinity College Dublin (TCD) project was funded under the European Union GENIUS (Generic E-Learning Environments for the new Pan-European Information and Communication Technologies Curricula) programme (Dolan, O'Connor, Mullally and Jennings, 2003) (Dolan, O'Connor, Mullally and Jennings, In press). The overall purpose of the project was to explore the real-life practical issues associated with applying a web-based collaborative platform embodying both synchronous and asynchronous dimensions. One of the goals was to assess the efficacy of the course presentation via web-based collaborative platform versus the traditional lecturing approach. A pilot study was carried out using the Web-based Collaboration platform, LearnLinc (parsecinfo, 2005) in TCD. It was envisaged that this would provide a basis for more substantial studies with these technologies in the future.

J. Filipe, J. Cordeiro, and V. Pedrosa (Eds.): WEBIST 2005/2006, LNBIP 1, pp. 355–366, 2007.

The purpose of this pilot study was to investigate practical and operational aspects and issues to do with using such a tool-set. A TCD staff member (DD) presented a course entitled "IT and the Enterprise" to a group of mature, evening attendance, computer-literate, undergraduate Information Systems students. Of this cohort of students more than 76% worked with computers greater than 30 hours per week.

2 Materials and Methods

The use of LearnLinc as a collaborative web-based platform was a requirement of the overall GENIUS project. LearnLinc provides two separate environments, the virtual "campus" and the virtual "classroom". The virtual campus is modeled on a physical college campus in that it provides administrative functions with registration of students for courses, course creation, class creation, adding of course materials and assigning lecturers to lectures. The virtual classroom provides an environment with whiteboard area, synchronized web browser, application sharing, text chat, hand raising, questions and answers, feedback, attendance list and an agenda for the class.

A participating student should be equipped with a computer conforming to at least the minimum specification as set out by LearnLinc and a network connection fast enough to support the LearnLinc server connection (Dolan, O'Connor, Mullally and Jennings, In press). Students were also required to have downloaded the client software. The students in a computer laboratory environment were issued with headsets (microphone and earphones) so that they could listen and speak to the lecturer without sound distortion and acoustic feedback from such a noisy environment. The individual student could communicate with the lecturer through text chat either privately, where only the lecturer sees it, or publicly where everyone in attendance sees the message. The student can also communicate by symbolically 'raising the hand' on the interface. The lecturer sees the indicator for the hand raise and can then give the floor to that student. A photograph of the student appears and he/she can speak to the lecturer and the class.

3 Pilot Study

Forty two Information Systems second year undergraduate students (average age was 29 years, about 75% male) of the Trinity College Dublin, Computer Science Department completed all three questionnaires in this pilot study. The students had full-time jobs and attended lectures in the evenings from 6 to 9 p.m. They were given a (sub)-course in "IT and the Enterprise" by a TCD lecturer (DD) using LearnLinc. This course, consisting of 4 weekly 2-hour evening slots, was part of a larger 22-week course. The whole 22-week course was examined conventionally, with one question devoted to the aspects of "IT and the Enterprise" covered in the web-based contribution. The students were distributed across various locations, at home, on campus (in computer laboratories) or at places of business. Three questionnaires were used in the TCD studies.

3.1 Questionnaire One

This questionnaire was presented on the first night of term to the students after the Lecturer had advised the students of the forthcoming teaching collaboration project. Questionnaire 1 was used to gather information about the availability of student computers with the required specification to partake in online lectures. Ideally students were to use either a computer in their workplace, in their home, or in a College computer laboratory, whichever location suited best. The main purpose of this questionnaire was to find out technical requirements and support information so that a support team, administrative issues and a computer laboratory could be made available for the students. Forty six students completed Questionnaire 1.

3.2 Questionnaires Two and Three

Questionnaires 2 and 3 were designed to capture the before and after mindset of the students. The questionnaires were in two parts, Section A and Section B. Section A had twenty seven quantitative questions (see Appendix) and Section B had ten qualitative questions. The twenty seven quantitative questions used a nine-point Likert scale varying from 1 (Strongly Disagree) to 9 (Strongly Agree). Forty nine students completed Questionnaire 2. Questionnaire 2 was used to assess the students' expectations of the upcoming online eLearning experience before the experiment started. It contained the core twenty seven questions and the ten qualitative questions. Forty nine students complete Questionnaire 2.

Questionnaire 3 was used to assess the students' opinions on the performance of the eLearning experience after the experiment finished. It contained the twenty seven core questions, the ten descriptive questions as in Questionnaire 2 and an additional twenty one questions focusing on the use of the facilities and functions of LearnLinc as used in the online lectures. These two questionnaires were used to assess the effectiveness of the use of Internet technology to create a virtual classroom to support or enhance the learning experience within the course 'IT and the Enterprise'. Forty two students completed Questionnaire 3.

4 Results

The results and conclusions below are a summary of the main quantitative findings (Jennings, 2005). The differences between the questionnaire question response means for the Performance (Post Experience) (Questionnaire 3) and the Expectations Pre Experience (Questionnaire 2) question response means are given in (Jennings, 2005) and the following Tables 1 - 4. The findings are discussed under four headings: Operations, Andragogical, Support and Social, four areas into which 26 of the 27 questions may be grouped. The following Tables give the Performance Means from Questionnaire 3 less the Expectation Means from Questionnaire 2 for each question (i.e. P - E (means)).

4.1 Operations

Table 1 indicates that the students found ease of access to computing facilities (Q1), found the technology easy to use (Q2), they also found access to a quiet space (Q3). They were happy with the ISP that they used (Q4), but had higher expectations of it. They were happy with the technical competence (Q5) and fast response time from support and they had a high level of confidence in the systems being used even though their expectations were higher than performance (Q6). Q7, which concerns disaster recovery, wasn't put to the test during the experiment, so perhaps that is why the score is low, 64% of the Performance Questionnaire respondents versus 94% of the Expectations Questionnaire respondents. The difference between the Performance mean minus the Expectation mean is –2, perhaps students' understanding of what was meant by disaster recovery was different. Q8 concerns the system response time and indicates that the performance exceeded expectation. Q9 concerns technical training and students seem disappointed with the level of training, 74% Performance versus 84% Expectations.   Disaster recovery (Q7) and training (Q9) account for the difference in the overall percentage of students' expectations, 92%, for the Agree-Strongly Agree scale 5 - 9, and the percentage of students' performance, 88%.

Table 1. Performance-Expectations Mean Response

Questions	Q1	Q2	Q3	Q4	Q5	Q6	Q7	Q8	Q9	Q10
Mean Response	7.4	7.8	7.6	7.6	7.4	7.2	5.3	6.2	5.8	6.9
S.D.	1.6	1.3	1.6	1.6	1.6	1.7	2.0	2	2.1	1.6
P-E (mean)	0.3	0.5	0.1	0	-0.3	-0.2	-2.0	0.2	-0.4	0.3

A student commented: "It was the first time that I used technology for education purposes so maybe that was the reason why I felt anxious and a bit unsure what to expect from the project. Also my class were the first to use the software so I expected LearnLinc to be troublesome and felt the class were the "guinea pigs" in trying to find bugs etc., in the program. Even though I had negative thoughts I was excited in using the software for the first time. It was something new and it was going to be a break from the traditional classroom lectures."

4.2 Andragogy

Andragogy deals with adult learners (Infed 2005).

Table 2 indicates that, in the main, the students did not find it, compared with Expectation (Questionnaire 2) to be a positive learning experience. Their commuting time was reduced (Q16), but the standard of presentation was not as high as expected (Q18), nor was the session as stimulating as expected (Q19). It was harder to concentrate (Q23), 73% down to 48%, and they participated less than in a face-to-face lecture (Q24), 67% down to 40%. There was no great difference in enriching the learning experience (Q25). The expectations in the use of technology improving

Table 2. Performance-Expectations Mean Response

Questions	Q13	Q16	Q18	Q19	Q20	Q22	Q23	Q24	Q25	Q27
Mean Response	7	6.3	6.4	5.9	4.4	5.2	4.6	4.2	5.8	5.2
S.D.	1.6	2.8	1.4	1.9	1.8	2	2	2	2.1	1.9
P-E(mean)	-0.3	-0.4	-1	-1.4	-0.8	-0.7	-1	-1.1	-0.6	-1

productivity (Q27) dropped from 82% to 60% after performance. When examining P – E (mean) figures they are all negative. Q18 - the standard of presentation – can be linked back to the removal of animation and colour images from the PowerPoint slides (to reduce the bandwidth load). Obviously the use of the synchronised Web Browser, Question & Answer facility didn't enhance the learning environment. Q19 – not more conducive to learning – can be related back to the newness of the virtual classroom environment and the short length of the experiment. Q23 – harder to concentrate – can be linked to the abuse of the text chat facility in the virtual classroom. Q24 – participated less than in face-to-face lecture – can be related back again to being comfortable with the environment and the newness of the technology. Q27 – improving productivity – the lecture was shorter, only an hour long, so perhaps students felt they had lost out, even though the lecturer was of the opinion that he covered material faster.

A student commented: *"It was obvious also that it is necessary to develop a degree of comfort with using the learning tool, and that this comfort must be acquired by both the lecturer and student. The first lecture was delivered at a speed which far exceeded what was usual, but by the final lecture the delivery was much more attuned to an appropriate pace for the particular learning environment."*

Another commented: *"I was surprised to observe that I didn't recall the content of the lectures as well as those which had been delivered in the traditional manner. I think my recall is partly tied up with visual cues received from the lecturer and in absence of more experience with remote learning this is difficult to assess. I also didn't take any notes to which I could refer later. This wasn't a conscious decision, as I came prepared for taking notes. I believe it was a consequence of engaging with this particular medium. At least temporarily, engaging in a cyber-space environment altered my behaviour."*

Veneema and Gardner (1996) have commented "....students might seem engaged but understand little because their response reflects more an attraction to the medium rather than an understanding....".

4.3 Support

As can be seen from the summary tables students were more negative about the actual support experience compared to their expectations. When analysed further, the students were happy with the training (Q9), response time of the system (Q8) and response time from support staff (Q10). The students were not so happy with the level

Table 3. Performance-Expectations Mean Response

Questions	Q8	Q9	Q10	Q11	Q21
Mean Response	6.2	5.8	6.9	6	5.5
Standard Deviation (S.D.)	2	2.1	1.6	2.4	2.1
Performance-Expectation(mean)	0.2	-0.4	0.3	-0.4	-1.1

of documentation to support training (Q21), expectations 90% down to performance of 69%. While the LearnLinc environment does not require a great deal of training, it does depend on the level of computer literacy and comfort with working with computers

A student comment commented on the support and the role of the ListServ email forum: *"This forum allowed students the opportunity to ask questions regarding their technical difficulties. It was apparent to me that a lot of the technical advice came from fellow students, thus promoting a sense of ownership and involvement by the students."*

Another student commented: *"The LearnLinc experiment fell very appropriately into our Information Systems and the Enterprise course because we could see first hand the approach, the planning and the implementation methods adopted by the Trinity LearnLinc management team to ensure the smooth installation of the process. The value of seeing our own team in action, understanding the planning, test issues and people's reluctance to change was a worthwhile experience, as someday it will be us implementing a similar concept within our own organizations."*

4.4 Social

The mean responses for all questions were negative relative to expectations. As can be seen the students felt that the technology reduced the interactive experience (Q12), but less than was expected, 61% down to 52%, just over half the participants. Some people changed their mind with regard to working on their own (Q14), and were comfortable with using the technology to communicate (Q15). They also felt that after using the technology they didn't need time to learn the environment that they thought initially they would, Q17, 69% down to 17%, which gives a very low average score.

Table 4. Performance-Expectations Mean Response

Questions	Q12	Q14	Q15	Q17
Mean Response	4.9	5.3	6.3	2.9
Standard Deviation (S.D.)	2.3	2	2.0	1.9
Performance-Expectation (mean)	-0.3	-0.1	-0.2	-2.5

One student commented negatively: *"I found the stifled silence of the computer labs distracting as I forced myself in vain to find a point of interest whilst I digested the information being fed to me. Personally I felt that I was not taking part in the chat area throughout each class. That said, I do not regret my participation in such an experiment, I found it to be of some value."*

Perhaps if the student had been in a position to benefit by accessing the lectures at home or at work, this isolated feeling would be eroded by that benefit (Hara and Kling, 1999).

Another student commented on the experience – *"Watching a match on television can't compare to "being there" in terms of experience, but it's warmer, you can watch replays and you don't have to leave your house. In some ways eLearning is the very same."*

Another student commented on the social impact: *"There are also social implications; the traditional evening course generates enormous pressure on families, while the mother or father attends a lecture for a few hours the other partner stays at home to look after the children. This can lead to marriage problems...."*

5 Blended Learning

Blended Learning can be defined as learning events that combine aspects of online and face-to-face instruction. It has been claimed that blended systems have been very effective (Spot+ 2004)).

A blend of traditional University teaching, pedagogies and strategies coupled with the use of emerging web-based collaboration platforms, both synchronous and asynchronous, would appear to offer significant potential for a blended eLearning solution at Institutional, Faculty and Student level.

This research describes the implementation of a blended learning environment, with the emphasis on implementing and evaluating the online experience that took place under the GENIUS project.

All course modules delivered in the degree course in Information Systems, up to now, were delivered in a traditional face-to-face lecture hall environment. This project involved a change to the delivery process for the part-time mature evening students. In effect the students would be participating in a blended learning approach. Where initially lectures would be delivered in a face-to-face environment, they would then partake in the series of online lectures and then revert to face-to-face delivery. It was hoped that the majority of students would partake in the course off campus in a learning environment was to be 'Same Time Different Place.'

Online students are more likely to feel isolated and require more support in that area. When students have a problem, its seriousness multiplies because they feel they are on their own, and it becomes much more frustrating (Hara and Kling). To enable a sense of community students should be encouraged to help each other, by using a facility like a Listserv or chat room. This also gives a feeling of belonging to a community.

The results of a question (Questionnaire 3 Section B Question 23) on Blended Learning is as follows in Table 5:

Table 5. Would you like to experience a blend of this type of learning and traditional learning in your future years at TCD? (Question after experiment)

Comment	%
If there is a good reason for it	2
Lecture time to be extended to cover material adequately	2
Only if technology/internet connection runs smoothly	6
Only in certain subjects	11
No, I prefer to attend college. Traditional method	13
Only to same extent. A few lectures a year. In moderation.	15
Yes, I would like to experience a blend of this type of learning and traditional learning in the future	51
	100

In answering this multi-part question, the respondents were restricted to choosing just one of the options. In evaluating the responses from this questionnaire, the results are not particularly supportive of blended learning. An interesting question in hindsight, but not asked at the time, was how much blending is desirable? In this study the eLearning component of the blended learning course comprised 18% of the total course.

A student commented: *"My final thoughts on the project and in using LearnLinc are very different from my initial thoughts. I would like to use it again but only as a supplement to the traditional classroom lectures."*

A smaller group preferred the traditional face-to-face environment and found face-to-face more conducive to learning. Marjanovic (1999) endorses the importance in having some face-to-face sessions before starting the online delivery sessions. This was found to play an important role in nurturing interaction and for students to understand the style of lecturing that the lecturer uses. It also helped to open up dialogue when moving to the online mode. This was one of the benefits of the blended learning approach.

Students expressed the view that they would not like to have online delivery all the time, but rather a blended solution of traditional and online. This is in line with what was found in the SPOT+ Survey of two thousand students in twelve European universities: "The 2,000 students surveyed in SPOT+ Project were interested in the use of ICT for information exchange, but expressed a stronger preference for traditional education methods" (SPOT+ 2004).

6   Conclusion

The key issues found under the four factors in this pilot study are as follows:

Operational
Students seemed disappointed with the level of training. The Performance was lower than Expectation for Q9.

Andragogical

The students didn't think the use of this internet technology improved productivity, Q27.

The main findings were that the session was not as stimulating as expected nor as conducive to learning as expected for these 10 categories. Students found it harder to concentrate and they felt that they participated less than in a face-to-face environment. They were also disappointed that the Internet technology did not improve productivity.

Support

Students would have liked better documentation to support technical training, Q21.

Social

Students felt that the technology reduced the interactive experience, Q12. Students felt that they didn't like the idea of working on their own away from fellow students, Q14. Students also felt that they didn't need as much time to learn the technology environment as they thought they would, Q17.

Other Issues

From a number of items of feedback, broadband is essential for good performance.

How much blending is desirable? 10:90; 20:80 or even higher? The students attend their course for four years, three nights per week. If one of these nights could be taken from home, it may give them appreciable relief.

What types of course are suitable? This question needs to explored further.

What learner situations are suitable e.g. distance learning, commuting, home problems, remediation? Blended learning is suitable for adults doing travel for business and those with domestic responsibilities. Some students in this pilot study attended from the UK, Seattle and South Africa for instance. It is also suitable for revision because the course lectures are saved and can be reprised later.

How best to overcome the deficiencies of the e- learning model, assuming that each one can ever be overcome?

Blended learning is not cheap. Considerable resources in terms of finance, time, staff (lecturing, support and training) were necessary to get this pilot study up and running.

What are the real advantages of the traditional face-to-face situation that we are overlooking?

Further Work Needed

Four sessions are probably too few to overcome the novelty effect for the students and also for the lecturers to move sufficiently further along the learning curve for this new medium. Longer courses and more courses are needed. Longer courses would allow more familiarity with the system and equipment for lecturers, support staff and students. More courses would also identify which courses and material were more suitable. The issue of further andragogical implications and their evaluation need to be addressed in the longer term. A full examination of the economic implications of this medium is needed.

It is obvious that some, but not all, of the issues which gave rise to problems in this study will diminish or disappear as Broadband and computer equipment continues to speed up.

However many other issues will not go away so easily. In particular, a lot of students preferred the traditional lecture over web-based presentation (Dolan, O'Connor, Mullally and Jennings, In press). The main advantage for students is reduced travelling time to lectures. However most of these students spend quite a large percentage of their time in front of computer screens at their work already and report that they see little advantage, other than reduced travel, in having the course material presented by screen. A blended approach, that is a mix of traditional lecturing with web-based presentation is probably what is needed with the blend, perhaps, being 90:10 in favour of traditional at present.

A better evaluation template for the process with the use of a control group is needed. A cross-over study with half the students getting traditional teaching for half the course while the other half get the web-based collaborative platform for that half, and vice-versa for the remainder of the course is needed in a more complete study. It is also necessary to measure the relative effectiveness of learning performance in both of these approaches.

The eLearning paradigm provides opportunities for the facilitation of individual differences. In future applications, this issue could also be addressed (Redmond and Parkinson, 2003) (Parkinson and Redmond, 2005). In terms of learning, not all personality and cognitive styles are amenable to this type of instructional medium.

This pilot study illustrates the difficulties of exploring virtual student/lecturer interactions in eLearning environments. One unexpected result is a much deeper appreciation of how much is involved in the "traditional" lecturing environment and how difficult it is to replicate it in a virtual classroom.

The term "blended" in blended learning seems to imply that both traditional and eLearning can be easily integrated. From these results it would appear the blending may have more of the characteristics of trying to blend oil and water.

The jury is not still out on blended learning. The answer from this pilot study is that blended learning needs considerable improvement before students will readily accept it, except in situations of necessity and in relatively small quantities.

Acknowledgements

We thank the Technical Support staff for their many strenuous efforts.

References

Dolan, D., O'Connor, C., Mullally, A., Jennings, A.: Experience in the use of synchronous eLearning in a traditional university for non-traditional learners. In: A. Méndez-Vilas, A., Mesa González), J.A., Badajoz, m., (eds.) Proceedings of Second International Conference on Multimedia and ICTs in Education Spain December 3-6, 2003 and in "Advances in Technology-based Education: Towards a Knowledge-based Society" Edited by A.Méndez-Vilas, J.A.Mesa González, J.Mesa González vol. II pp. 659–1335 84-96212-11-4 ISBN Published by: JUNTA DE EXTREMADURA, Consejería de Educación, Ciencia y Tecnología (Badajoz, Spain) (2003)

Dolan, D., O'Connor, C., Mullally, A., Jennings, A.: The implementation of on-line synchronous eLearning for non-traditional learners at traditional universities (In press)

Garrison, D.R., Henderson, T.: 2003 E-Learning in the 21st Century: A Framework for Research and Practice, Routledge Falmer (2003)

Gilbert, S.W.: A new vision worth working toward – connected education and collaborative change as referenced in Beyond Institutional Boundaries: reusable learning objects for multi-professional education (2000) available at http://www.tltgroup.org/gilbert/NewVwwt2000-2-14-00.htm

Hara, N., Kling, R.: Students frustrations with a web-based distance Education Course (1999) http://www.firstmonday.dk/issues/issue4-12/hara/

Infed 2005, http://www.infed.org/lifelonglearning/b-andra.htm

Jennings, A.: Implementing an Integrated Web-Based Synchronous eLearning Collaboration Platform at Tertiary Level for Part-Time Mature Evening Students TCD-CS-2005-67 University of Dublin, November 2005 (2005), http://www.cs.tcd.ie/publications/tech-reports/reports.05/TCD-CS-2005-67.pdf

Parkinson, A., Redmond, J.A.: The Accommodation of the Field-dependent Learner in Web Design. The Psychology of Education Review 29(1), 43–53 (2005)

parsec (2005), http://www.parsecinfo.nl/products/learnlinc.htm

Redmond, J.A., Walsh C., Parkinson, A.: Equilibriating Instructional Media for Cognitive Styles Inroads - SIGCSE Bulletin vol. 35(3), pp. 55–59 September 2003 ACM Press New York (2003) In: Finkel, D.(ed.) Proceedings of the 8th Annual Conference on Innovation and Technology in Computer Science Education (ITiCSE 2003) June 30 - July 2 Thessaloniki, Greece and also published in the online ACM Digital Library (2003), http://portal.acm.org

SPOT+ 2004. Students' perspective on technology in teaching and learning in European universitieshttp://www.spotplus.odl.org/downloads/Survey_report_final.pdf funded by the DG for Education and Culture of the European Commission http://www.spotplus.odl.org/

Veneema, S., Gardner, H.: Multimedia and Multiple Intelligences(1996), http://www.prospect.org/print/V7/29/veenema-s.html

Appendix

Questionnaire 3 A - Performance - Section A (Abridged somewhat).

1.	I found ease of access to computing facilities for this project.
2.	I found the internet technology to be easy to use.
3.	I was able to access a quiet space in which to use this technology at home/work/TCD.
4.	I found the internet service I used was able to support the use of this technology.
5.	I found a high degree of technical competence from college systems support staff.
6.	I had a high level of confidence in the systems I used
7.	I found that there was a provision for disaster recovery/fall-back position.

8.	I had excellent system's response time.
9.	I received excellent technical training.
10.	I had a fast response time from support staff to remedy problems
11.	I was in touch with my peers through the use of the e-mail support facility.
12.	I found the use of this technology reduced the interactive experience of the classroom.
13.	I found this learning experience to be positive
14.	I liked the idea of working on my own away from my fellow students
15.	I was comfortable communicating with others using this technology during live sessions.
16.	I found the use of this technology reduced my commuting time.
17.	I needed to find the time to learn the systems I used.
18.	I found a high standard of presentation of course material
19.	I found these sessions to be intellectually stimulating.
20.	I found this learning environment to be more conducive to learning than the traditional classroom.
21.	I had excellent documentation to support technical training.
22.	I found the use of this technology enhanced my ability to learn.
23.	I found that participating in the online sessions on my own allowed me to concentrate better.
24.	I participated in discussion more freely in the virtual classroom than in the traditional lecture theatre
25.	I found the use of this technology enriched my learning experience.
26.	I understand that the benefits derived by myself from the systems I use are being measured
27.	I found the use of this internet technology improved my productivity

A System for Automatic Evaluation of Programs for Correctness and Performance

Amit Kumar Mandal[1], Chittaranjan Mandal[1], and Chris Reade[2]

[1] School of Information Technology,
IIT Kharagpur, WB 721302, India
{amitm,chitta}@sit.iitkgp.ernet.in
[2] Kingston Business School, Kingston University
Chris.Reade@king.ac.uk

Abstract. This paper describes a model and implementation of a system for automatically testing, evaluating, grading and providing critical feedback for the submitted programming assignments. Complete automation of the evaluation process, with proper attention towards monitoring student's progress and performing a structured level analysis is addressed. The tool provides on-line support to both the evaluators and students with the level of granularity, flexibility and consistency that is difficult or impossible to achieve manually.

Keywords: Automatic Evaluation, XML Schema, Program Testing, Course Management System.

1 Introduction

The paper presents both the internal working and external interface of an automated tool that assists the evaluators/tutors by automatically evaluating, marking and providing critical feedback for the programming assignments submitted by the students. The tool helps the evaluator by reducing the manual work by a considerable amount. As a result the evaluator saves time that can be applied to other productive work, such as setting up intelligent and useful assignments for the students, spending more time with the students to clear misunderstandings and other problems.

The problem of automatic and semi-automatic evaluation has been highlighted several times in the past and a considerable amount of innovative work has been suggested to overcome the problem. In this paper we will be discussing the key approaches in the literature. Although our approach is currently limited to evaluating only C programs, the design and implementation of the system has been done in such a way that it takes over almost all of the burden from the shoulders of the students and the tutors. The tool can be controlled and used through the Internet. The evaluator and students can be in any part of the world and they can freely communicate through the system. Hence, the system helps in bringing alive the scenario of distant learning which is a crucial improvement for any large educational institute or university because they might have extension centers anywhere across the world. The same tutors can provide services to all the students in any such extension center.

J. Filipe, J. Cordeiro, and V. Pedrosa (Eds.): WEBIST 2005/2006, LNBIP 1, pp. 367–380, 2007.

2 Motivation

The scenario that motivated us to build such a system was the huge cohorts of students in almost all big educational institutions or universities across the world. In almost all the big engineering institutes or universities the intake of undergraduates is around 600 - 800 students. As a part of their curriculum, at the place of development of this tool, the students need to attend labs and courses and in every lab each student has to submit about 9-12 assignments and take up to three lab tests. That amounts to nearly 10000 submissions per semester. Even if the load is distributed among 20 evaluators, each evaluator is required to test almost 500 assignments. Without automation, the evaluators would be busy most of time in testing and grading work at the expense of time spent with the students and also on setting up useful assignments for them.

3 Related Work

A variety of noteworthy systems have been developed to address the problem of automatic and semiautomatic evaluation of programming assignments. Some of the early systems include TRY (Reek, 1989) and ASSYST (Jackson and M., 1997). Schemerobo (Saikkonen et al., 2001) is an automatic assessment system for programming exercises written in the Scheme programming language, and takes as input a solution to an exercise and checks for correctness of function by comparing return values against the model solution. The automatic evaluation systems that are being developed nowadays have a web interface, so that the system can be accessed universally through any platform. Such systems include GAME (Blumenstein et al., 2004), SUBMIT (Pisan et al., 2003) and (Juedes, 2003). Other systems such as (Baker et al., 1999), Pisan et al(2003) and Juedes(2003) developed a mechanism for providing a detailed and rapid feedback to the student. Systems like (Luck and Joy, 1999), (Benford et al., 1993) are integrated with a course maker system in order to manage the files and records in a better way.

Most of the early systems were dedicated to solve a particular problem. For example, some systems are concerned with the grading issue thus turning their attention from quality testing. Others are concerned with providing formative feedback and loosing their attention towards grading. We are concerned with addressing all aspects of evaluation whether it is testing, grading or feedback. The whole design and implementation of our system was focused toward bringing comfort to the evaluators as well as students, without being partial towards the quality of testing and grading being done. Our aim was to test the programs from all possible dimensions i.e. testing on random inputs, testing on user defined inputs, testing on execution time as well as space complexity, performing a perfect style assessment of the programs. Secondly, security was given much attention because, as the system was to be used by fresh under graduate students who do not have many programming skills, they might unknowingly cause harm to the system. Our third focus of attention was grading, which should not impose crude classification such as zero or full marks. Efforts have been made to make the grading process simulate the manual grading process as much as possible. Fourthly, the comments should not be confined to just a general list of errors that any student is likely to commit. All the comments should be specific to a particular assignment. As has been already mentioned, the system currently supports only the C language, so during implementation, the fifth and foremost focus was to make the model and design as general as possible so that the system could be easily upgraded to support other popular languages like C++, Java etc.

4   System Overview

4.1   Testing Approach

Black Box testing, Grey Box testing, and White Box testing are the choices available in literature to test a particular program. In Black Box testing, a particular submission is treated as a single entity and the overall output of the programs are tested. In Grey Box testing, component/function final output is tested. White box testing allows structure, programming logic as well as behavior to be evaluated. In an environment where the students are learning to program, testing only the conformance of the final output is not workable because conformance to an overall input/output requirement is particularly hard to achieve. Evaluations that relied on this would exclude constructive evaluation for a majority of students. Grey Box approaches involve exercising individual functions within the student's programs and are, unfortunately, language sensitive. Looking at the pitfalls of the above two strategies our decision was to choose the White Box approach, which is more general than the Black Box approach. White Box testing involves exercising the intermediate results generated by the functions, therefore, whether the program has been written in a particular way, following a particular algorithm and using certain data structures can be ascertained with greater probability.

4.2   High Level System Architecture

Fig.1 shows the High Level System Architecture diagram, the whole process of automatic evaluation begins with the evaluator's submission of the assignment descriptor, model solution of the problem stated in the assignment descriptor, testing procedure and an XML file. After the evaluator has finished the submission for a particular assignment, the system checks the validity of the XML file against an XML Schema. If the result of XML validation is negative, the system halts any further processing of the file and the errors are returned to the evaluator. The evaluator has to correct the errors and then resubmit the files. If the validation of the XML file against the XML Schema is positive, then the assignment description becomes available for students to download or view and subsequently submit their solutions.

These submissions are stored in a database. The system accepts the submissions only if they are submitted within the valid dates specified by the evaluator. The next criteria that should be passed for completion of submission is that proper file names are used, as specified by the evaluator in the assignment description. The above operations are performed by the File Verification module. After its operation is complete the next module which comes into the picture is the Makefile Prep/Compilation module with the task of preparing a makefile and then using this makefile to compile the code. This module generates feedback based on the result of the compilation. I.e. if there are any compilation errors, then the system rejects the submission and returns the compilation errors

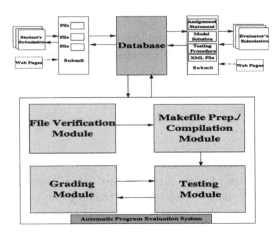

Fig. 1. High Level System Architecture

to the student. Thus the submission is complete only if the student is able to pass the operations of both file verification module and the compilation module. After the submissions are complete the next module executed is the testing module which includes both dynamic testing as well as static testing. The dynamic testing module accepts students' submissions as input, generates random numbers using the random number generator module[1](not shown in figure). It then uses the testing procedures provided by the evaluator to test a program on the randomly generated inputs. Sometimes it is not enough to test the program on randomly generated inputs (e.g. where the test fails for some boundary conditions). By using the randomly generated inputs we cannot be sure that the program undergoes specific boundary tests on which the test may fail.

To overcome this drawback, facilities have been provided by which the evaluator can specify his/her own test cases. The Evaluators have the freedom to specify the user defined inputs either directly in the XML file or he may also specify the user defined inputs in a text file (if the number of inputs is significant). This is an optional facility and the evaluator may or may not be using it based on the requirements of the assignment. If the results of testing the program on random input as well as user defined inputs are positive, then the next phase of testing that begins is the correctness of the program on execution time as well as space complexity. During this testing, the execution time and the space usage of the user program are compared against the execution time and the space usage of the model solutions submitted by the evaluator. During this testing, the execution time of the student program as well as the evaluator's program are determined for a large number of inputs. The execution time of the student's program and the evaluator's program are compared and analyzed to determine whether the execution time is acceptable or not. If the test for space and time complexity goes well then the next phase is the Static Analysis or the Style analysis. Static testing involves measuring some of the characteristics of the program such as, average number of characters per line, percentage of blank lines, percentage of comments included in the program, total

---

[1] This module generate the random numbers required for testing the programs.

program length, total number of conditional statements, total number of goto, continue and break statements, total number of looping statements, etc. All these characteristics are measured and compared with the model values specified by the evaluator in the XML file. Testing and Grading modules works hand in hand as testing and grading are done simultaneously. For example, after testing a program on random inputs as well as user defined inputs is over, the grading for that part is done at that moment, without waiting until all testing is complete. If at any point of time during testing, the programs are rejected or aborted, then the grading that has been done up to that point is discarded (but feedback is not discarded).

Security is a non-trivial concern in our system because automatic evaluation, almost invariably, involves executing potentially unsafe programs. This system is designed under the assumption that programs may be unsafe and executes programs within a 'sandbox' using regular system restrictions.

5   An Example

Let us start with an example that is very common for a data structures course, for example: the Mergesort Program. As the regular structure of a C program consists of a main function and a number of other functions performing different activities, we have decided to break down the Mergesort Program into two functions (1) Mergesort function - This function performs the sorting by recursively calling itself and the merge function. (2) Merge function - This function will accept two sorted arrays as input and then merge them into a third array which is also sorted. As a White Box testing strategy is followed, testing and awarding marks on correct output generated by the program will be of no use because this will not distinguish between different methods of sorting (Quick sort, Selection sort, Heap sort, Insertion sort etc.).

5.1   Our Approach

Our approach is to test the intermediate results that the function is generating, instead of a function final output or the program final output. This section explains one approach by which the mergesort program can be tested. Our aim is to test that the student has written the mergesort and the merge function correctly. Our strategy is to check each step in the mergesort program. Fig.2 explains the general working of the mergesort program. Our approach is to catch data at each step
(i.e. merge#1 to merge#7 of the example). This can be done by using an extra two dimensional array of size (n) * (n-1). The idea is to transfer the array contents to this two dimensional array at the end of the merge function.

After the execution of the student's program, a two dimensional array similar to Fig.3 will be created, this array can be compared with the two dimensional array that is formed by the model solution. If both the arrays are exactly the same then the student is awarded marks, but if the arrays are not similar, then the action initiated depends upon the action specified by the evaluator in the XML file. As has been mentioned previously, the array contents need to be transfered to the two dimensional array at the end of the merge function. This operation should be performed by the function as shown in Fig.4.

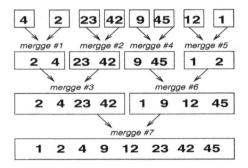

Fig. 2. Working Principle of Mergesort program

	0	1	2	3	4	5	6	7
0	2	4	23	42	9	45	12	1
1	2	4	23	42	9	45	12	1
2	2	4	23	42	9	45	12	1
3	2	4	23	42	9	45	12	1
4	2	4	23	42	9	45	1	12
5	2	4	23	42	1	9	12	45
6	1	2	4	9	12	23	42	45

Fig. 3. Two Dimensional Array

```
transfer(int *a, int size, int *b)
{int i;
 for (i=0;i<size;i++)
  *(b + depth*size +i) = *(a+i);
 depth = depth + 1;
}
```

Fig. 4. Auxiliary Transfer Function

5.2 Assignment Descriptor for the Mergesort Program

The assignment descriptor is one of the crucial submissions necessary for the success-ful completion of the whole auto-evaluation process. If the assignment descriptor is not setup up in a correct manner, it would be difficult for the student to understand the problem statement properly and most students will end up with a faulty submission. We have considered some of the general-purpose properties that an assignment descriptor should have: (1)Simple and easy to understand language should be used, so that it be-comes easy for the student to understand the problem statement; (2)Prototypes of the function to be submitted by the student must be specified clearly in the descriptor; (3) The necessary makefile and the auxiliary functions (for example, the transfer function shown in Fig.4) should be supplied as a part of the assignment descriptor to make it easier for the student to reach the submission stage.

5.3   Evaluator's Interaction

The Automatic Evaluation process cannot be accomplished without the valuable support of the evaluator. The evaluator needs to communicate a large number of inputs to the system. Since the number of inputs are large, providing a web interface is not a good idea to accept the values because it is cumbersome both for the evaluator to enter the values and for the system to accept and manage the data properly. Our idea is that, the evaluator will provide the inputs in a single XML file. In this XML file the evaluator is required to use predefined XML tags and attributes to specify the inputs. The XML is used to specify the following information: (1)Name of the files to be submitted by the students. (2)How to generate the test cases. (3)How to generate the makefile. (4)Marks distribution for each function to be tested (5)Necessary inputs to carry out static analysis of the program

Along with the XML file, the evaluator is also required to submit the model solution for the problem, Testing Procedure and the Assignment descriptor. The XML file is crucial because it controls the working of the system and if the XML file is wrong then the whole automatic evaluation process becomes unstable. Therefore it is necessary to ensure that the XML file is correct which can be done, to some extent, by validating the XML file against the XML Schema.[2] Fig.5 shows only a part of the main XML file that is submitted. This portion of the XML is used by the module that checks for proper file submissions. Fig.6 shows the part of the XML schema that is used to validate the part of the XML file as shown in Fig.5.

```
<source_files>
<file name="main_mergesort.c">
<text>File containing the main
                function</text>
</file><file name="merge.c">
<text>File containing the merge-
                function</text>
</file><file name="mergesort.c">
<text>File containing the merge-
            sort function</text>
</file></source_files>
```

Fig. 5. XML Spec. for checking file submission

5.4   Input Generation

The Automatic Program Evaluation System is a sophisticated tool, which evaluates the program using the following criteria:

- Correctness on dynamically generated random numbers
- Correctness on user defined inputs

---

[2] The purpose of the XML Schema is to define legal building blocks of an XML document. An XML Schema can be used to define the elements that can appear in a document, define attributes that can appear in a document, define data types of elements and attributes etc.

```
<xs:element name = "source_files">
 <xs:complexType><xs:sequence>
 <xs:element name="file" maxOccurs-
                     ="unbounded">
 <xs:complexType> <xs:sequence>
 <xs:element name="text" minOccurs
             ="0"> <xs:simpleType>
 <xs:restriction base="xs:string">
 <xs:minLength value="0"/>
 <xs:maxLength value="75"/>
 </xs:restriction></xs:simpleType>
 </xs:element></xs:sequence>
 <xs:attribute name="name" type=
                     "xs:string">
 </xs:attribute></xs:complexType>
 </xs:element>   </xs:sequence>
 </xs:complexType> </xs:element>
```

Fig. 6. XML Schema validating XML in Fig.5

- Correctness on time as well as space complexity
- Performs style assessment of the Programs
- Number of Looping statements
- Number of Conditional statement.

Initially the programs are tested on randomly generated inputs. For effective testing we cannot rely on fixed data because they are vulnerable to replay attacks. Evaluators have the option to write down their own routines in the testing procedures to generate inputs or, alternatively, the system provides some assistance in the generation of inputs. Currently the options are supported are as follows:

```
 random integers:
(array / single)
(un-sorted/sorted ascending/sorted descending)
(positive / negative / mixed)
random floats:
(array / single)
(un-sorted/sorted ascending/sorted descending)
(positive / negative / mixed)
strings:
(array / single)
(fixed length/variable length)
```

The evaluator can express his/her choice of the random numbers on which he/she wants the programming assignments to be tested in the XML file. Fig.7 shows the example of the XML statement that is used to generate input for the mergesort program.

```
<testing>
<generation iterations="100">
<input inputvar="a" vartype="array"
type="float" range="positive"min= "10"
max="5000"sequence="ascend">
<arraysize>50</arraysize></input>
</generation>
<user_specified source="included">
<input values="6,45,67,32,69,2,4">
</input>
<input values="5,89,39,95,79,7">
</input></user_specified></testing>
```

Fig. 7. XML Specification for Input Generation

The evaluator/tutor should specify the inputs in the *testing* element, the *generation* element is used to specify random inputs to be generated. This element has only one attribute named *iterations* and the *iterations* attribute can be used to specify the number of times the evaluator needs to test a program on random inputs. Any number of *input* elements can be placed between its starting and closing *generation* tag. The *input* element offers a lot of attributes to specify the type of random number to be generated. The *vartype* attribute of an *input* element is used to specify whether the randomly generated value should be an *array* or *single* value. The *min* and *max* attributes can be used to generate the inputs within a range. If the attribute is not mentioned explicitly in the XML then the system sets these attributes to the default values. The *type* attribute can be set to one of the three values *integer*, *float* or *string*. Another important attribute of *input* elements is the *range* attribute. This attribute is used to specify whether *positive, negative* or *mixed* (mixture of positive and negative) values is to be generated. The *inputvar* is the attribute that is used to name the variable to be generated. For example in Fig.7, the array which is generated randomly will be stored in *a*. Sometimes the evaluator may choose to generate the values in some order (ascending or descending) and this problem is resolved by the *sequence* attribute which can be set to any of the two values (*ascend* or *descend*). Every element that is specified between the tags of user_specified is used to supply user defined inputs to the program. The *user_specified* elements have only one attribute named *source* which can take one of the two values (*included* or *file*). If the attribute is set to *included* then the system looks for the user defined inputs in the XML itself, on the other hand if the attribute is set to *file*, then the system looks for the user defined inputs in a text file. Similar to the *generation* element, the *user_specified* element can have any number of *input* elements, but here the *input* element can have only one attribute named *values*. All the user defined inputs should be specified following the same sequence as followed for the generation of random inputs.

In Fig.7 an array(vartype="array") of size 50(<arraysize>50</arraysize>), containing ascending(sequence="ascend") positive(range="positive") float(type="float") values in the range of 10(min="10") and 5000(max="5000") is generated and supplied as input to the mergesort program. The above procedure is iterated 100(iterations="100") times. Fig.7 also shows that, two user defined inputs have been provided by the evaluator, these user defined inputs are supplied *as is* to the testing procedures.

5.5   Grading the Programs

The grading process is made as flexible and granular as possible. During testing of a program on user defined inputs, suppose the program is unsuccessful in satisfying the output of the model solution. At this moment the XML is parsed to determine the choice mentioned by the evaluator. The evaluator may have chosen to abort the test and award zero marks to the student or, alternatively, the evaluator/tutor may have chosen to move forward and test the program on other criteria. If the evaluator had decided to test the program on other criteria, then the tutor has the flexibility to either award full marks, zero marks or a fraction of the full marks meant for testing on random inputs and user defined inputs. Fig.8 shows the example XML for grading the Mergesort program.

```
<status marks="50" abort_on_fail="true">
<item value="0" factor="1"
fail="false"><text>Fine</text></item>
<item value="1"factor="0.6"
fail="false"><text>Improper</text>
</item> <item value="2" factor="0"
fail="true"><text>Wrong</text></item>
</status>
```

Fig. 8. XML Specification for Grading

Based on the result of the execution, some value is awarded to the program. For example, if the result of execution of the mergesort program is correct for both the user defined inputs as well as random inputs then the value awarded to the program is 0. If the result is incorrect for user defined inputs or random inputs, then the value awarded is 1. If the result of execution is incorrect for both the tests, then the value awarded is 2. Based on the value awarded, marking is done, i.e. if the value is 0 full marks are awarded for the test (factor = "1"), if the value is 1, then only 60% marks are awarded (factor="0.6") and if the value is 2 then no marks are awarded, the program is given *fail* status(fail="true") and the program execution is aborted(abort_on_fail="true").

5.6   Commenting on Programs

The system generates feedback comments, which are specific to a particular assignment. During testing the programs on random and user-defined inputs, if the test fails for some particular random input, then the comment would contain the specific information about the random input on which the test has failed. The student can run his/her program on the random input and find out what is wrong in the program. If the test fails for user defined inputs, then the system never returns the user-defined inputs because that may cause serious security flaws in the system. Instead, the system returns an error message mentioned by the tutor in the XML for that particular input.

5.7   Testing the Programs on Time and Space Complexity

Testing programs on their execution times and space complexity is an important idea because different algorithm often have different requirements of space and time during execution. For example, bubble sort is an in-place algorithm but inefficient, the merge-sort algorithm is efficient if extra space is used, the quick sort algorithm is an in-place algorithm and usually very efficient, the heap sort algorithm is an in-place algorithm and efficient. This section shows the analysis between two mergesort programs. One is submitted by the student and the other is submitted by the evaluator. These programs are different in the number of variables declared and the dynamic memory allocated during the execution of the programs. Fig.9 shows the execution time of the two mergesort programs.

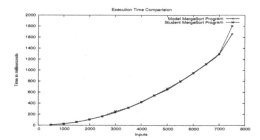

Fig. 9. Execution times of Mergesort program

As the execution time of the programs are nearly same, this suggests that we need to test the programs further. For a particular input the system executes the model program N times and determines the acceptable range of execution time for the student's program. For the same input the system then executes the student's program, determines the execution time and then checks whether it falls within the range determined after the execution of the evaluator's mergesort program. The above procedure will be iterated for a large number of inputs. After getting results for all the inputs, the system decides whether the program is acceptable or not. The same procedure is followed to test the programs on space usage. Fig.10 shows the space complexity of the above two programs i.e. the model mergesort program and the student's mergesort program. Fig.10 also shows the space requirement of another mergesort program where the student has not used the memory properly.

Here the space required shows the virtual memory resident set size which is equal to the stack size plus data size plus the size of the binary file being executed. It is evident from Fig.10 that if the student is using the memory properly, then the amount of memory required for the execution of the student's program will not vary drastically from the memory requirement of the Model Solution. When the student is not using the memory properly, for example when the student is not freeing the dynamically allocated memory, then the memory requirements of the program will increase drastically as compared to that of the model solution. These problematic programs get easily caught

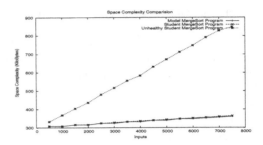

Fig. 10. Space Complexity of MergeSort programs

with the help of the same procedure as explained for testing the programs on execution times.

6   Security

From the outset of the implementation we have been concerned with making the system as secure as possible because we cannot rule out the possibility of a malicious program, that may intentionally or unintentionally cause damage to the system. Therefore, the system has been implemented under the assumption that the programs may be unsafe. The first aspect that has been taken into consideration is that, programs may intentionally or unintentionally have calls to delete arbitrary files. To override the above possibility, a separate login named as 'test' login has been created. During testing, the system uses Secure Shell (ssh) with RSA encryption-based authentication to execute necessary commands in this login. Necessary files are transferred to this login ('test' login) securely using the Secure Copy Protocol. As the test login do not have access to other directories, the programs executing in this login will not be able to delete them. To save the files that are present at the test login we have used the change file attributes on a Linux second extended file system. Only superusers have access to these attributes, and no user can modify them. After the file attributes are changed they cannot be deleted or renamed, no link can be created to this file and no data can be written to the file. Only a superuser or a process possessing the CAP_LINUX_IMMUTABLE capability can set or clear this attribute.

The next aspect under consideration is the problem of the presence of infinite loops in the student's program. In order to solve the problem of infinite loops, the system limits the resources available to the programs. Both the soft limit and the hard limit have to be specified in seconds. The soft limit is the value that the kernel enforces for the corresponding resource. The hard limit acts as a ceiling for the soft limit. After the soft limit is over the system sends a SIGXCPU signal to the process, if the process does not stop executing then the system sends SIGXCPU signal every second till the hard limit is reached, after the hard limit is reached the system sends a SIGKILL signal to the process. The *setrlimit* command has been used to limit both execution time and memory usage, same command can also be used to limit several other resources, such as data and stack segment sizes, number of processes per uid and also the execution time.

Care has been taken so that the student is not able to change the resources available to his/her program.

7 Conclusion

Our system has the potential to open up new horizons in the field of Automatic Evaluation of programming assignments by making the mechanism relatively simple to use. We have illustrated the flexibility of our system and explained the details of the automatic evaluation process with an example in a systematic way, ordering the phases serially as they occur in the practical environment. This covers: deciding the testing approach, designing the assignment descriptor, the teacher's interaction with the system, and testing programs. The tool pin-points each possible dimension for testing the programs i.e. testing the programs on random inputs, testing the programs on user defined inputs, testing the programs on time complexity, space usage and style assessment of the student's program. Students benefit because they know the status of their program before final submission is done. Evaluators benefit because they do not have to spending hours for grading the programs. But achieving peak evaluation benefits of our approach, requires further research and with more extensive use as well as studying the experience of the evaluators and students using the system. Currently we have built the system to work with a single programming language i.e. the 'C' language. This is done in the first instance to gain experience with the interactive nature of the system in a simple form. Implementation doors have been kept open, so that we can extend the system to test programming assignments in other popular languages such as C++, Java etc by making small changes in the code.

References

[Baker et al., 1999]   Baker, R.S., Boilen, M., Goodrich, M.T., Tamassia, R., Stibel, B.A.: Tester and visualizers for teaching data structures. In: Proceedings of the ACM 30th SIGCSE Tech. Symposium on Computer Science Education, pp. 261–265 (1999)

[Benford et al., 1993]   Benford, S.D., Burke, K.E., Foxley, E.: A system to teach programming in a quality controlled environment. The Software Quality Journal, 177–197 (1993)

[Blumenstein et al., 2004] Blumenstein, M., Green, S., Nguyen, A., Muthukkumarasamy, V.: An experimental analysis of game: A generic automated marking environment. ACM SIGCSE Bulletin 36(3), 67–71 (2004)

[Jackson and M., 1997]   Jackson, D., Usher, M.: Grading student programming using AS-SYST. In: Proceedings of 28th ACM SIGCSE Tech. Symposium on Computer Science Education, pp. 335–339 (1997)

[Juedes, 2003]   Juedes, D.W.: Experiences in web based grading. In: 33rd ASEE/IEEE Frontiers in Education Conference (2003)

[Luck and Joy, 1999]   Luck, M., Joy, M.: A secure online submission system. Software-Practice and Experience 29(8), 721–740 (1999)

[Pisan et al., 2003]   Pisan, Y., Richards, D., Sloane, A., Koncek, H., Mitchell, S.: Submit! a web-based system for automatic program critiquing. In: Proceedings of the fifth Australasian Computing Education Conference (ACE 2003), pp. 59–68 (2003)

[Reek, 1989]   Reek, K.A.: The try system or how to avoid testing students programs. In: Proceedings of SIGCSE, pp. 112–116 (1989)

[Saikkonen et al., 2001]   Saikkonen, R., Malmi, L., Korhonen, A.: Fully automatic assessment of programming exercises. In: Proceedings of the 6th annual conference on Innovation and Technology in Computer Science Education (ITiCSE), pp. 133–136 (2001)

Usability and Instructional Experience in a Web-Based Remote Internetworking Laboratory Environment

Shyamala Sivakumar[1] and William Robertson[2]

[1] Sobey School of Business, Saint Mary's University, Halifax, Canada
`ssivakumar@smu.ca`
[2] Internetworking Program, Faulty of Engineering, Dalhousie University, Canada
`bill.robertson@dal.ca`

Abstract. A web based remote Internetworking laboratory that delivers interactive laboratory experience to geographically remote graduate students is presented in this paper. The online Internetworking (INWK) laboratory learning environment employs remote interaction with networking equipment in both individual and group setting that correlates with the constructivist and collaborative pedagogical approaches. This paper discusses the pedagogical and technical factors that influence the usability of and instructional experience in the remote laboratory environment given the constraints of the special hardware and learning outcomes of the program. A survey instrument employing a 5 point scale has been devised to measure the usability and student instructional experience in the remote access INWK laboratory. These results demonstrate the success achieved in designing and implementing the remote access Internetworking laboratory.

Keywords: Remote internetworking laboratory, usability, student instructional experience.

1 Introduction

Online student learning is made possible by advancements in network infrastructure and development of voice/multimedia protocols for seamless transport of information. However, the developer of a web based remote access laboratory faces several challenges in designing an online learning environment that ensures strong effective interaction that best replaces the onsite face-to-face interaction taking place in labs. This is exacerbated in lab environments like those employed in Internetworking (INWK) and Information Systems (IS) courses which extensively use networking hardware and computer/simulation software tools. In addition to a clear understanding of the knowledge domain requirements, the challenge is in supporting good pedagogy and learning practices given technical constraints with regard to bandwidth, quality of service, real time interactions, and multiple users (Sivakumar et al., 2005).

Remote laboratories have been successfully used in electrical engineering education to interact with spectroscopy, measurements, control systems and simulation laboratories (Linge and Parsons, 2005) (Casini et al., 2003) (Zimmerli et al., 2003)

J. Filipe, J. Cordeiro, and V. Pedrosa (Eds.): WEBIST 2005/2006, LNBIP 1, pp. 381–391, 2007.
© Springer-Verlag Berlin Heidelberg 2007

(Llamas et al., 2001) (Karampiperis and Sampson, 2005). However, none of these works addressed the specific issues pertaining to pedagogy, facilitation, scalability, usability and instructional experience within a technical framework, other than mapping the instructional content to appropriate technologies. Although these experiences cannot be directly applied to INWK laboratory, the essential elements of improved learning spaces can be adapted to develop an online learning space that is scalable, accessible, interactive, and modular. An effective e-learning laboratory design framework must employ interactive laboratories, secure real-time student interaction and incorporate effective online lab learning strategies including appropriate pedagogy, facilitation and skill building techniques to impart knowledge and meet instructional outcomes. This paper contributes to existing e-laboratory education frameworks research by demonstrating the feasibility of designing usable e-laboratory systems for strong student instructional experience with remote equipment. In this paper we describe our experiences in designing web-based remote internetworking laboratory (RIL) that attempts to incorporate all the qualities of an effective onsite laboratory. This paper focuses on factors that affect the usability of the RIL. In addition we also consider factors that contribute to student's instructional experience. The paper is organized as follows: Section 2 discusses the design requirements for the remote internetworking laboratory. This section outlines the reengineering of the internetworking laboratory to enable students to interact online with the remote devices in the Halifax equipment room. Section 3 discusses the factors influencing the usability and student instructional experience in the RIL environment. Section 4 discusses a typical instructional scenario in the RIL. Sections 5 and 6 present the usability and student instructional measurements in the online RIL environment. Section 7 compares the results for the onsite versus the online scenarios. Section 8 presents conclusions.

2 Design Issues in the RIL

In our previous research (Sivakumar and Robertson, 2004) we have developed a remote Internetworking laboratory environment that supports text based synchronous student interaction. The Faculty of Engineering at Dalhousie University, Halifax, Canada has been offering a Master's degree program in Internetworking since 1997. The program also provides comprehensive "hands-on" laboratory experience in configuring, maintaining, troubleshooting and simulating computer networks. In the online context, the design and the implementation of an effective remote internetworking laboratory (RIL) environment is highly challenging on account of the special hardware, simulation and computing needs of the Internetworking courses. The internetworking laboratory equipment consists of personal computers (PC) and servers, networking devices including routers and switches from vendors including Cisco Systems and Nortel Networks, LAN/WAN network analyzers, and network simulation software OPNET. The networking equipment is placed on several racks with each rack having an identical set of routers, switches and hubs. The equipment consists of Ethernet, token ring, frame relay (FR) and asynchronous transfer mode (ATM) technologies. The laboratory has access to a DMS-100 telephone switch that provides ISDN and telephone connections.

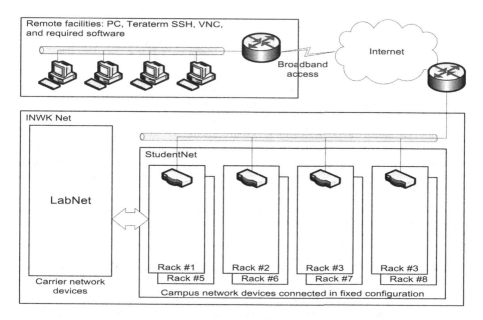

Fig. 1. RIL - Logical architecture

The onsite laboratory elements have been translated into the online RIL environment by allowing students at geographically remote sites to access and interact with internetworking hardware, simulators and software located at Halifax laboratory facility and is shown in Figure 1. The Internetworking laboratory network, INWKNet, consists of a number of enterprise and carrier-level internetworking devices such as routers and switches. The backbone network consists of special purpose devices that are commonly found in carrier networks and is configured in a fixed topology. The laboratory backbone is called the LabNet and resembles a miniature "Internet" that is always available to carry ATM, FR and Ethernet data traffic. The other internetworking devices are organized into a number of student racks, each containing an identical set of devices to be accessed by students and called the StudentNet. The StudentNet devices are used to build topologies similar to the topologies found in an enterprise network. The INWKNet mimics a typical network scenario where small enterprise LANs represented by the StudentNet are connected to a carrier's WAN represented by the LabNet. The remote Internetworking laboratory (RIL) is accessible by remote students through the Internet. The onsite internetworking laboratories have been redesigned and the equipment rewired in a manner that allows online students to construct different networks topologies without changing the physical wiring/cabling. The RIL is devised using de-facto networking standards, free software and commercial Internet browser. Real-time interaction and information transfer with the Halifax site are achieved independent of the technology available to the remote student. The RIL design and delivery mechanism are tailored to i) provide a constructivist pedagogical approach (Palloff and Pratt, 2003) ii) model a collaborative learning environment for group interaction (Hiltz et al., 2000) iii) match the characteristics of the delivery media to specific learning processes including the provision of unambiguous feedback and guidance iv) assign appropriate instructional roles and v) determine desirable student competency outcomes; all in a remote learning context. A 4-tier RIL role architecture consisting of faculty, facilitators at both the Halifax and remote sites and students, has been determined appropriate and adapted to maintain academic integrity, provide continuous assessment to track student performance, provide real-time interaction with equipment, and offer strong student instructional experience. The RIL is modeled as a remote synchronous, collaborative and directed learning environment as remote students interact simultaneously with Internetworking equipment under the active supervision and guidance of the remote site facilitator to achieve specific learning outcomes. The RIL limits individual access to laboratory resources only to authenticated students using an access control server. In this paper, our work supports the special requirements for, and is assessed for usability and student instructional experience in this online synchronous INWK laboratory framework.

3   Factors Influencing RIL Usability and Instructional Experience

The e-learning research framework proposed by Alavi and Leidner (Alavi and Leidner, 2001) urges study within the context of pedagogical strategies and learning processes. At the intersection of these strategies and processes are the methods of instructional delivery that can be viewed from student-centric, university-centric and technology-centric perspectives. E-learning system designers and universities use these metrics to guide the design, development/adoption and implementation of learnware, assessment of trade-offs, e-learning system infrastructure and to measure the usability of the system. Specifically, issues in the design of the pedagogical strategy that implements a student-centric learning process in a web based remote internetworking laboratory system must encourage student interaction by employing state-of-the-art networking equipment/simulators (Linge and Parsons, 2005) (Llamas et al., 2001), provide real-time response from equipment to engage students in active learning, ensure repeat student interaction, provide a collaborative learning environment for group interaction at a remote site, provide feedback and guidance when learning outcomes are not met and, track student performance to meet learning outcomes (Sivakumar et al., 2005).

The university-centric issues in implementing instructional delivery methods include curriculum quality, instructional pedagogy employed in the remote laboratory, technical infrastructure management for delivering learning material, scalability of laboratory infrastructure to handle increases in student enrolment, and continuous student assessment for grading purposes (Sivakumar et al., 2005)

From the technology-centric view point, the instructional delivery framework must use standard networking protocols and free software to connect the remote site to the central equipment facility, use secure interaction between the remote site and equipment facility, deliver laboratory notes, wiring information and diagrams to students at remote locations over the world wide web, and authenticate the student at the time of initial access to laboratory resources (Sivakumar and Robertson, 2004).

A detailed study of the above factors is given in (Sivakumar and Robertson, 2004) (Sivakumar et al., 2005). The design of the remote internetworking laboratory (RIL) is aimed at delivering an effective remote laboratory experience moderated by the laboratory facilitators.

4 RIL Instructional Scenario

In the RIL environment, students typically work in groups of 2-3 per group in the introductory and intermediate laboratory experiments. In advanced laboratory experiments, they still have to configure the networking equipment individually and then have to interact as a group with the equipment. It is essential that the remote site laboratory design makes use of active learning strategies in a collaborative environment (Palloff and Pratt, 2003) (Hiltz et al., 2000) (Jonassen et al., 1999) (Wenger, 1998). The activities in the remote laboratory are modeled to implement the nine instructional objectives as outlined by Gagne et al. (Gagne et al., 1992): 1) gain student attention, 2) inform students of the objective, 3) recall prior learning, 4) present stimuli, 5) provide learning guidance, 6) elicit performance, 7) provide feedback, 8) assess performance and 9) enhance retention. A typical remote online INWK laboratory exercise requires students to configure, analyze and troubleshoot the performance of the routing information protocol (RIP). Each group is assigned Internetworking devices in the StudentNet (see Figure 1) for configuration. The RIP experiment first requires each student learn to configure RIP on a router. Students capture and analyze the data packets using sniffers or protocol analyzers. The convergence of the RIP protocol is observed and analyzed by capturing routing protocol updates after intentionally generating a link failure event in the network. The typical work scenario in this environment is discussed in (Sivakumar and Robertson, 2004). All necessary wiring needed for this exercise is made in advance at the Halifax equipment facility. The wiring diagrams for laboratory equipment is available from the program website. In the following sections we measure the usability and student instructional experience in the RIL.

5 RIL Usability

The usability of an e-laboratory system is a function of system design and is determined by factors including ease of use, interactivity with the system, system accessibility, system reliability, availability of online help including lab handouts and wiring diagram information, support for multiple simultaneous interactions, system responsiveness, appropriateness of system response to student input, authenticity and state of art-ness of the networking laboratory environment, feedback from the lab instructor, and hands-on feeling. A survey questionnaire that has been developed based on these 12 issues is summarized in the Table 1.

Students were asked to respond on a five point scale of 1-5, from very poor, poor, satisfactory, good to very good, the usability of the online remote equipment laboratory. The survey was conducted as an anonymous post-course evaluation of the RIL environment design, organization and performance. Of a sample size of 83 students over

3 years (2004, 2005 and 2006), a total of 65 students took part voluntarily in the survey once. In determining the sample size the factors that played a major role are the student enrolment in these years. On average, the program intake consists of 28-30 students each year. Table 2 gives the cumulative percentages of students in these 3 years who rated the 12 different aspects of the online lab as very good, good or satisfactory. Table 3 gives the mean rating, the standard deviation and confidence measure for the 12 aspects of the remote laboratory. From Tables 2 and 3 it is seen that the students are highly satisfied with the technical design of the RIL environment as reflected by the cumulative (2004, 2005 and 2006) results for ease-of-use, response time, accessibility, reliability, system response characteristics, authenticity, and the "state-of-art"-ness of the equipment. Over 90% of the students rated these technical characteristics of the INWK networking equipment to be satisfactory, good or very good. 87% of students rated the state-of-art-ness of the networking environment to be satisfactory or good or very good. Also, the students are highly satisfied with the format of the online wiring information and laboratory handouts as over 90% of students rated these to be satisfactory or good or very good. The level of interactivity is generally considered a key indicator of quality [20]. Tables 2 and 3 indicate that, although 83% of students rated the interactivity with laboratory components to be satisfactory or good or very good, only 80% of students rated the level of "hands on" feeling experienced in lab sessions to be satisfactory or good or very good. Hence, the program needs to improve student interactivity with laboratory equipment and the "hands-on" feeling experienced by the student to improve the quality of interaction between the student and the equipment. Also, only 83% of students rated the feedback from the laboratory facilitator to be satisfactory or good or very good and this aspect showed the most variability. The program needs to better train the remote facilitator in providing timely and useful feedback to the student.

Table 1. Questionnaire used to measure the usability of the Remote Internetworking Laboratory

	On a scale of 1 to 5 rate: (1=Very poor, 2 = Poor, 3= Satisfactory, 4 = Good, 5= Very Good
UQ1	whether the INWK lab equipment was **easy to use**
UQ2	the level of **interaction** with lab components
UQ3	the **response time** of lab components
UQ4	Whether the switches, router and other networking gear could be **remotely accessed** on entering userID/password)
UQ5	the **reliability** of operation of switches, router and other networking gear
UQ6	the **appropriateness of the response** from switches, routers and other networking gear i.e., did the response from equipment help you better understand networking concepts and theories
UQ7	whether the **feedback from the lab instructor** was useful
UQ8	the **usefulness of lab handouts** and extra online information
UQ9	the **usefulness of the online wiring diagram information** (cabling between networking gear)
UQ10	the level of **"hands on" feeling** experienced when configuring/ troubleshooting networks with equipment in Internetworking labs
UQ11	the **authenticity of the networking environment** in the INWK lab (i.e., is the networking equipment used in the INWK labs similar to those in a real world networking environment)
UQ12	the **"state-of-the-art"-ness of lab components** / networking gear in the INWK lab (i.e., are the router/switches and other networking gear current)

Table 2. Usability: Percentage of student vs. ratings

Rating Years	Percentage of students who rated various aspects of the online labs as either very good (5), good (4) or satisfactory (3)											
	Q1	Q2	Q3	Q4	Q5	Q6	Q7	Q8	Q9	Q10	Q11	Q12
2004	78.6	80.0	100	86.7	86.7	92.3	66.7	86.7	86.7	53.3	80.0	80.0
2004 and 2005	90.4	81.1	90.4	92.5	90.6	98.1	78.9	90.6	90.6	77.4	90.6	86.8
2004, 2005 and 2006	89.1	83.1	90.6	93.9	92.3	96.9	82.8	90.8	92.3	80.0	89.2	87.7

Table 3. Usability: Cumulative Mean, Standard Deviation and Confidence measures (2004, 2005 and 2006 data set)

Rating	Q1	Q2	Q3	Q4	Q5	Q6	Q7	Q8	Q9	Q10	Q11	Q12
Mean	3.61	3.34	3.66	4.14	3.85	3.81	3.45	3.72	3.74	3.37	3.58	3.45
Std. Deviation	0.95	1.00	0.88	0.93	0.83	0.75	1.13	0.98	0.92	1.15	0.92	0.87
95% CI	0.23	0.24	0.21	0.23	0.21	0.18	0.28	0.24	0.22	0.28	0.22	0.21
90% CI	0.20	0.20	0.18	0.19	0.17	0.15	0.23	0.20	0.19	0.24	0.19	0.18

Note: CI - Confidence interval

6   Instructional Experience

As part of this study, students were asked to rate their instructional experience in the RIL. The student learning experience measures student perceptions regarding their level of confidence and the increase in the student's ability to configure, trouble shoot, monitor, design, implement, plan and manage a state-of-the-art networking environment. In addition, student's perception regarding their ability to understand and apply internetworking concepts and select appropriate technology was also measured. A student instructional experience survey questionnaire that has been developed based on these 10 issues is summarized in Table 4. Students were asked to respond on a five point scale of 1-5, from very poor, poor, satisfactory, good to very good, to rate the student instructional experience in the RIL. Of a sample size of 55

Table 4. Questionnaire used to measure the instructional experience in the RIL

	On a scale of 1 to 5 rate: (1=Very poor, 2 = Poor, 3= Satisfactory, 4 = Good, 5= Very Good) the extent to which the INWK laboratory learning experience has increased
IQ1	your overall level of confidence in working with INWK equipment
IQ2	your understanding of INWK theories, concepts and technologies
IQ3	your ability to configure equipment
IQ4	your ability to troubleshoot networks
IQ5	your ability to monitor networks
IQ6	your ability to design networks
IQ7	your ability to implement networks
IQ8	your ability to apply theoretical networking concepts
IQ9	your ability to select appropriate networking technologies
IQ10	your ability to plan and manage networks

Table 5. Student instructional experience: Percentage of student vs. ratings

	Percentage of students who rated various aspects of the online instructional experience as either very good (5), good (4) or satisfactory (3)									
Rating	IQ1	IQ2	IQ3	IQ4	IQ5	IQ6	IQ7	IQ8	IQ9	IQ10
Very Good	11.9	19.1	12.2	4.9	7.3	2.4	4.9	17.1	7.5	2.5
Very Good or Good	69.1	71.4	73.2	48.8	43.9	34.2	43.9	73.2	57.5	37.5
Very Good or Good or Satisfactory	95.2	90.4	97.6	87.8	87.8	85.3	87.8	95.1	92.5	90.0

Table 6. Student instructional experience: Mean, Standard Deviation and Confidence measures

Rating	IQ1	IQ2	IQ3	IQ4	IQ5	IQ6	IQ7	IQ8	IQ9	IQ10
Mean	3.76	3.81	3.83	3.39	3.37	3.20	3.32	3.85	3.58	3.30
Standard Deviation	0.73	0.86	0.67	0.83	0.86	0.78	0.88	0.76	0.75	0.69
95% CI	0.22	0.26	0.20	0.25	0.26	0.24	0.27	0.23	0.23	0.21
90% CI	0.18	0.22	0.17	0.21	0.22	0.20	0.22	0.20	0.19	0.18

Note: CI - Confidence interval

(37 students in 2005 and 18 students in 2006), a total of 42 students (30 in 2005 and 12 in 2006) took part voluntarily in the student instructional experience survey once. Table 5 gives the cumulative percentages of students in the two years who rated the 10 different aspects of the student instructional experience in the RIL as very good, good or satisfactory. Table 6 gives the mean rating, the standard deviation and confidence measure for these 10 student instructional experience issues. From Tables 5 and 6 it is seen that the students rated their instructional experience as highly satisfactory. From Table 5, it is seen that about 70% of the students found a good or very good increase in their level of confidence in working with Internetworking equipment. Also, over 90% of the students rated a satisfactory, good or very good increase in their understanding of concepts, ability to configure equipment, application of theoretical concepts, selection of appropriate technology, and plan and implement networks. Over 80% of the students rated a satisfactory, good or very good increase in their ability to trouble shoot, monitor, manage, and design networks.

7   Online vs. Onsite Labs

Onsite students were asked to respond on a five point scale of 1-5, from very poor, poor, satisfactory, good to very good, the following aspects of the onsite equipment laboratory: the physical access to equipment, suitability of the networking equipment, their experience using the lab and whether the lab helped them understand networking concepts better. Specific questions of the online survey were more detailed and refined than that of the onsite survey.

Table 7. Onsite issues and their correspondence to online usability measures

Onsite Survey		Online Survey	
Issue	Onsite Issue no.	Issues	Question no. (See Table 2, 5)
Physical access to equipment in laboratory	OQ1	"Hands on feeling"	UQ10
		Student interactivity with equipment	UQ2
Suitability of networking equipment	OQ2	Authenticity	UQ11
		State-of-art ness	UQ12
Experience using the lab	OQ3	Ease of use	UQ1
		Response time	UQ3
		Remote access to lab	UQ4
		Reliability	UQ5
Understand networking concepts	OQ4	Understand INWK theories, concepts and technologies	IQ2

Note: UQ: usability questionnaire. IQ: instructional experience questionnaire, OQ: onsite questionnaire

Table 8. Onsite vs. Online Surveys (2004, 2005, 2006): Mean, Standard Deviation and Confidence measures

Measure	Onsite				On line			
	OQ1	OQ2	OQ3	OQ4	UQ2, UQ10	UQ11, UQ12	UQ1, UQ3, UQ4, UQ5	IQ2
Mean	3.87	3.97	3.57	3.97	3.35	3.52	3.81	3.81
SD	0.86	0.98	1.22	1.07	1.08	0.89	0.92	0.86
CI – 95%	0.31	0.36	0.44	0.38	0.19	0.15	0.11	0.26

Note: CI – Confidence Interval

However, as shown in Table 7 the four onsite issues can be mapped to one or more corresponding online questions to enable comparison.

Table 8 lists the mean, standard deviation and confidence measures for the four onsite issues used to measure the design and implementation of the onsite laboratory and compares it with the corresponding figures for the online laboratory. From Table 8, it is seen that on average, onsite students are more satisfied with the physical accessibility to the equipment than their online counterparts. Similarly, students in the onsite program are more aware of the suitability of the networking equipment employed in the labs. The online students consistently rated the authenticity and the state-of-art ness of the networking environment lower than their onsite counterparts. Also, the onsite students were marginally more satisfied than the online students when asked whether the laboratory equipment helped them understand networking concepts better. However, the online students were more satisfied with their online laboratory experience than the onsite students and this may be attributed to the flexibility that the remote access provides to online students. For example, online students can access the laboratory at a time and from a place convenient to them and perform the labs at a suitable pace.

8   Conclusion

This paper describes an online remote internetworking laboratory (RIL) environment used to deliver remote laboratory experience by allowing students at geographically remote sites to access and utilize devices including routers, switches, LAN analyzers, and simulators located at Halifax. In the early stages, much of the development of the remote internetworking laboratory, has focused on understanding the system requirements and developing a viable test-bed to deliver the labs online by connecting students at remote sites to internetworking equipment at Halifax. The RIL system design ensures an accessible, reliable, easy-to-use and responsive remote laboratory environment that supports multiple simultaneous real-time interactions and effective information transfer between the remote site and the equipment at the Halifax equipment facility. The RIL uses effective student interaction with remote equipment and simulations that employ multimedia to create an engaging environment that enhances problem-solving skills. This is reflected by highly satisfactory ratings for the student instructional measures. Survey results used to measure the usability of the remote laboratory demonstrate the success achieved in designing and implementing the remote access Internetworking laboratory. Survey results also indicate that the online laboratory is perceived to be easier to use and more flexible than the onsite laboratory due to the formers remote access capability. However, the online laboratory is perceived to be less physically accessible and less interactive than the onsite laboratory. Based on the feedback from the faculty who have been involved both in the onsite and the online programs and the students' historical performance measures including grades, switching to the online remote laboratory format has not resulted in any degradation of the expected learning outcomes.

Future research will focus on evaluating how the facilitation process together with system use result in achieving the pedagogical goals of the program. System limitations include the fact that the current INWK laboratory can accommodate only 35 students maximum in a given time slot. The long-term goal of the program is to implement an asynchronous internetworking laboratory accessible from the student's home. Additional work is planned to address online facilitation and student instructional experience in the asynchronous environment.

References

Linge, N., Parsons, D.: Problem-Based Learning as an Effective Tool for Teaching Computer Network Design. the IEEE Transaction on Education 6 pages (2005) (to appear)

Casini, M., Prattichizzo, D., Vicino, A.: The Automatic Control Telelab: A user-friendly interface for distance learning. IEEE Trans. on Ed. 46(2), 252–257 (2003)

Zimmerli, S., Steinemann, M.A., Braun, T.: Educational environments: Resource management portal for laboratories using real devices on the Internet. ACM SIGCOMM Computer Communication Review 33(3), 145–151 (2003)

Llamas, M., Anido, L., Fernandez, M.J.: Simulators over the network. IEEE Trans. on Education 44(2), 24 (2001)

Karampiperis, P., Sampson, D.: Towards Next Generation Activity-Based Web-Based Educational Systems. In: Fifth IEEE Intl. Conf. on Advanced Learning Technologies, pp. 868–872 (2005)

Palloff, R.M., Pratt, K.: The virtual student: A profile and guide to working with online students. In: The Jossey-Bass higher and adult education series, John WileySons, West Sussex, England (2003)

Hiltz, S.R, Coppola, N., Rotter, N., Turoff, M., Benbunan-Fich, R.: Measuring the Importance of Collaborative Learning for the Effectiveness of ALN: A Multi-Measure, Multi-Method Approach. Journal of Asynchronous Learning Networks 4(2), 103–125 (2000)

Jonassen, D.H., Peck, K.L., Wilson, B.G.: Learning with technology: a constructivist perspective, Merrill, Upper Saddle River, NJ (1999)

Wenger, E.: Communities of Practice: learning, meaning, and identity. Cambridge University Press, Cambridge (1998)

Alavi, M., Leidner, D.E.: Research Commentary: Technology-Mediated Learning-A Call for greater Depth and Breadth of research. Info. Systems Research 12(1), 1–10 (2001)

Sivakumar, S.C., Robertson, W.: Development of an Effective Remote Interactive Laboratory for Online Internetworking Education. In: Proc. of 37th Hawaii Intl. Conf. on System Sciences, HICSS, 10pgs (2004)

Sivakumar, S.C., Robertson, W., Artimy, M., Aslam, N.: A Web-Based Remote Interactive Laboratory for Internetworking Education. IEEE Trans. On Education 48(4), 586–598 (2005)

Gagne, R., Briggs, L., Wager, W.: Principles of Instructional Design, 4th edn. HBJ College Publishers, Fort Worth, TX (1992)

Larkin-Hein, T., Budny, D.D.: Research on learning style: Applications in the physics and eng. classrooms. IEEE Trans. On Education 44(3), 276–281 (2001)

The VTIE Collaborative Writing Environment

Bart Busschots[1], Luke Raeside[1], John G. Keating[1], and Shelagh Waddington[2]

[1] Department of Computer Science
National University of Ireland, Maynooth
bart@cs.nuim.ie, lraeside@cs.nuim.ie, john.keating@nuim.ie
[2] Department of Geography
National University of Ireland, Maynooth
shelagh.waddington@nuim.ie

Abstract. This paper discusses the design of the VTIE Collaborative Writing Environment (CWE) and the functionality of the various components that make up this environment. The advantages of supporting collaborative writing are also discussed as well as different organizational schemes that can be used when structuring collaborative writing exercises. The paper also contains technical details on the implementation of the VTIE CWE.

Keywords: Collaboration, Collaborative Writing, Learning Environment.

1 Introduction

As broadband internet access becomes more wide-spread in schools more and more resources become available to teachers and students. Some great examples of such resources are the Telescopes in Education Project (telescopesineducation.com, 2005), Faulkes Telescope Project (faulkes-telescope.com, 2005) and Bug Scope (Thakkar et al., 2000). These projects allow students to do real science from their classroom with state of the art equipment, this was simply not possible in the past. The VTIE Portal was initially designed to provide teachers and students with the tools they need to get the most out of internet-based telescopes. As such some of the tools developed as part of the VTIE project are specifically targeted at Astronomy, however, other tools are much more general and are perfectly at home away from telescopes and astronomy. The VTIE CWE (Collaborative Writing Environment) described in this paper is one of these general tools.

A central aim of the VTIE project was to provide all the tools developed to schools in such a way as to make the tools as easy as possible to integrate into the school environment. It was considered important that schools not have to spend any money on software in order to be able to use the VTIE tools. This means that the VTIE tools themselves should be free but also that the tools cannot depend on any other software that is not free. The VTIE tools should also not be tied to any particular operating system so that all schools can participate. Finally, as schools do not tend to have dedicated computer technicians the VTIE tools should not require complicated installation in the schools. By creating all the VTIE tools in a web environment all these aims can be easily met. Hence, the entire VTIE portal is web-based and all schools need to take part

J. Filipe, J. Cordeiro, and V. Pedrosa (Eds.): WEBIST 2005/2006, LNBIP 1, pp. 392–401, 2007.

is an internet connection and the FireFox web browser (getfirefox.com, 2005) which is available on all major platforms (Windows, Mac, Linux and many Unixes).

The current VTIE CWE is the direct result of a rapid prototyping model including formative evaluations with students over a three-year period and a year of consultation with teachers from local primary and secondary level schools. Our initial prototype did not support collaborative writing but all our evaluations showed a need for the software to properly support group working and collaboration.

2 Collaboration

Collaboration is a very broad term, Erkens, *et al.* give the following definition; *"A collaborative learning situation may be defined as one in which two or more students work together to fulfil an assigned task within a particular domain of learning in order to achieve a joint goal"* (Erkens et al., 2005). Given this definition, it is possible that a wide variety of learning tasks can be envisaged as involving a degree of collaboration, ranging from those which are extremely practical, such as cultivating a garden and carrying out scientific experiments, to the group writing of a novel. The focus of the VTIE CWE is on the development and usage of collaboration both within the research process (in the form of the sharing of information gained) and in the production of a written report on the work.

Collaborative working can be seen as having a vital role in the development of students for their future lives as part of the knowledge society as *"Knowledge work is characterised by systematic knowledge advancement, sharing of expertise, and collaborative elaboration of knowledge products"* (Lakkala et al., 2005, p. 338). It has also been suggested that collaborative learning experiences can:

- Improve motivation some students find working with others encourages them to complete a task. This has been found to apply more to male students than females, for example a study by Hidi *et al* revealed that after receiving the same instructional programme, improvement in performance was improved more for male students than for female ones if the subsequent task involved collaboration with others (Hidi et al., 2002).
- Facilitate the construction of knowledge and the development of understanding, as the instant feedback from others encourages students to explore their current knowledge and exposes flaws or limitations and to review their ideas.
- Encourage the development of metacognition and reflection in thinking.
- Facilitate student-centred learning.

It is because of these wide ranging justifications for the use of collaboration in learning that Collaborative Learning Environments (CLEs) using ICT, including the present project, have been developed. The main areas of collaboration involve the sharing of resources/information between small groups of students and the production of a combined report on the project.

Writing is one area where *"co-operative work may be problematic as it was originally designed for individual learning"* (Klein et al., 1994). However, it has also been suggested that it is an area where collaboration is likely to improve the end product for many students and so various strategies have been explored to facilitate it. While there are, doubtless, a very wide range of possibilities for this, including e-mail exchanges and Wikipedia-type approaches, the present project, focussing on younger children was considered to require a more structured and less wide-ranging approach to collaboration, so that the students would feel more comfortable in participating.

It was decided that for each section of the report a draft should be produced which would then be revised based on comments from the other students in working on the report and rewritten to produce the final report. Zammuner identified three basic organizational approaches, some relating to pairs of collaborators, while others involved larger groups (Zammuner, 1995). Three basic variations were identified, as shown in Table 1:

Table 1. Organisational Approaches to Collaboration

Initial Draft	Revision	Final Version
Group/pair A	Group/pair B	Group/pair A
Group/pair A	Group/pair A	Group/pair A
Individual	Group/Pair	Individual *

The scheme adopted in our project is equivalent to the third organizational approach in Table 1. While there are arguments in favor of the adoption of all of the above strategies, Zammuner contrasted success in producing written work by students working individually, with those working in collaboration patterns 2 and 3, reporting that *"The most significant changes (usually improvements) in the quality of revision operations occurred when the revision was carried out cooperatively rather than individually"* (Zammuner, 1995, p. 122). He suggests that this was because the 'outsider' would provide immediate feedback, similar to that provided by another person in a conversation, unlike in the usual, solitary process of writing. As noted by Erkens, *et al.* (Erkens et al., 2005, p. 3), *"Collaborative writers need to test their hypotheses, justify their propositions and clarify their goals. This may lead to increased awareness of and more conscious control over the writing and learning process"*. It was, therefore, decided that this method of individual writing, followed by feed back from the rest of the group feeding back into revisions of the text would be adopted for the VTIE Collaborative Writing Environment.

Working successfully with CLEs can be extremely demanding on both students and teachers, particularly in relation to the need for students to develop the social skills and thinking skills necessary for collaboration simultaneously with the technical/ ICT skills. Many teachers express concerns that their role may become that of 'technician' if the CLE is technically demanding and the teacher is critical in determining the success or failure of the collaboration, as his/her role must be in *"organising the community's activities and establishing the underlying conditions of the learning environment, and building up appropriate infrastructures for collective effort"* (Lakkala et al., 2005, p. 338 - 339). This makes it essential that the environment produced be as simple to setup and use as possible and that the environment provide sufficient support and resources for the teacher and students. Ideally the technology would become transparent to the users and they would be free to concentrate entirely on the task at hand. This was one of the driving factors towards adopting a web based interface as this removed the need for complex software installation and allows users to transfer their existing knowledge and experience of using the internet to our environment.

3   The VTIE Collaborative Writing Environment

The VTIE CWE provides an interfaces to support both teachers and students throughout the writing process from project design right through to publication of the students' work. Our CWE can be considered to consist of three components:

1. The Project Design and management Interfaces
2. The VTIE ScrapBook
3. The Writing Interfaces

Our CWE is built around a model which has developed throughout our formative evaluations and our discussions with teachers and is in agreement with the research discussed in Section 2. Although our tools were designed around this process it should be noted that the environment does not force teachers or students to stick rigidly to this process, this makes the environment more flexible. The process starts with the teacher designing the structure of the projects that the students will complete. We envisage this design phase being completed in class with the teacher showing the students the evolving structure with a data projector and the students having an input into the design. The design of the project is represented in a graphical way and as as it is manipulated the visual representation changes. This same visual representation of the project is used throughout the rest of the process both in the teacher and student views. Once the structure is defined it is referred to as a Project Template and can be saved for re-use in the future. From this template the mentor can then create project instances and assign students to these instances. The teacher breaks the group/class into teams and assigns one team to each project instance. Within each project instance each section is assigned to a single student who then writes that section. The rest of the students in the team and the teacher can see the current state of each section and a messaging system is provided to allow them to provide advice and help as the student works from an initial draft towards a final version. This is consistent with Zammuner's third model shown in Table 1. It is envisaged that the students will use the internet to gather information for their project. The VTIE ScrapBook was developed to provide the students and the teacher with a means of gathering and sharing information and images they find on the web. Finally, when the teacher is happy with the project instance it is published to a digital library in both HTML and PDF format. This allows future students to use the work of past students as part of their research on a topic.

3.1   Project Design Interfaces

The project design interfaces allow the teacher to manage and control their projects and project templates and manage their students. They can create classes/groups, edit classes/groups, create templates, edit templates, create projects, view the progress of their students' work.

In order to protect the anonymity of students on the system we store no information about students at all, not even their names. All Students are referred to as 'Student 1', 'Student 2' etc within each class/group. The teacher can print off a table on which the students' real names can be written.

Projects are created with a direct manipulation interface. As the teacher clicks to add and edit sections a graphic representation of the template updates in real time to show the current design of the project template. A screenshot of a template being generated in this way is shown in Figure 1. Project Templates consist of global thoughts/notes and sections. Each section has a title, optional initial content and thoughts/notes for that section. When creating a project form a template the teacher is presented with a 4 step wizard. In the first step the mentor is asked to name the project, pick the class/group that will do the project and pick the amount of teams the class/group will be split into. The second step allows the teacher to name each team. By default the teams are named 'Team 1', 'Team 2' etc but it is envisaged that the teams could decide on their own names as a first group/team building activity. The third step allows the teacher to specify which students go into which team. Finally, the fourth step presents the teacher with a graphical representation of the template chosen but with extra features to allow the teacher to assign students to the different sections. At this point the teacher can edit the design of the project by adding sections, removing sections, editing sections and thoughts and editing the title. When the teacher is happy with the design and student allocations they can then click a button to generate the project instances, one for each team.

3.2   VTIE ScrapBook

The VTIE ScrapBook provides students and teachers with a personal portfolio. It has been implemented as a FireFox browser extension so that it is always available to the students and teachers while they are browsing the web as shown in Figure 2. At any stage they can drag and drop text, links or images onto a drop-zone to add them to their ScrapBook. The students and teachers can also create notes as they go and save those into their ScrapBook. Teachers can then make any of the information in their scrapbook available to students in one of their projects and students can share any of their information with the other students in one of the teams they belong to. All information stored in the VTIE ScrapBook is actually stored on the VTIE server rather than on the machine being used by the student/teacher at the time so as students move from one machine to another their portfolio will always be available to them.

The teacher can also see the contents of of all their students' portfolios and can delete any scraps they deem inappropriate for any reason. Each scrap also stores the URL from which it was saved so the teacher can see where the students got their information from.

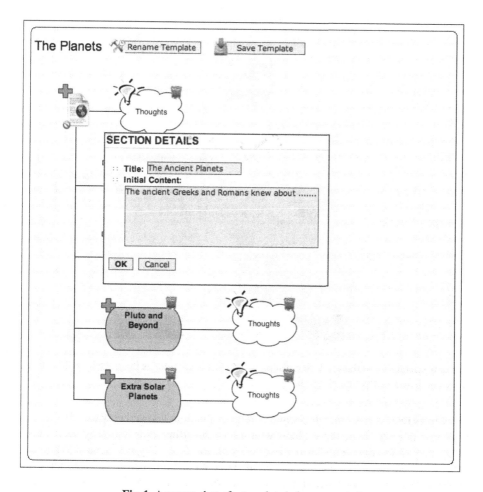

Fig. 1. A screen shot of a template being generated

The VTIE ScrapBook also interfaces directly with the Writing interface via JavaScript. This make it as easy as possible for students to incorporate the resources they find on the internet into their reports.

3.3   Writing Interfaces

When students or teachers view a project they are first presented with the graphical representation of the project. They can then view the content of any section by clicking on it which takes them to the writing view. In this view all the sections of the paper appear as tabs across the top and the contents of the current section appears in the main area of the page below the tabs.

When a student enters the writing view they can see the content of all the sections in the project but can only edit the sections they are assigned to. When editing a section the students are presented with a WYSIWYG (what you see is what you get) editor

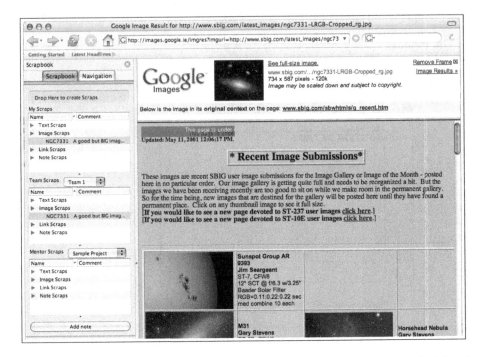

Fig. 2. A screen shot of the VTIE ScrapBook in use. The ScrapBook is the sidebar on the left and is always there when surfing the web.

that allows them to generate their content. Our evaluations showed very clearly that it is important not to provide the students with more formatting tools than they need, hence the WYSIWYG editor only provides them with the tools they really need. They can make text bold and italic and the can create bulleted and numbered lists and that is all the formatting they can do. In the writing view the students can also see all comments made by the other students in their team and their teacher on the current section. They can also add a new comment. Figure 3 shows a screenshot of a student using the writing interface.

Like a student a teacher can see the contents of all sections in their projects. The teacher can also see all the comments that have been made and can add additional comments to each section to help the student.

The writing view also provides access to a simple version control system for each section. There are always two backup version of each section, one the student controls and one the teacher controls. Both the teacher and the student can see both backup versions. The student's backup version is automatically updated each time the section is saved, then teacher's backup must be manually updated by the teacher. The student can choose to revert to their backup version at any time. The teacher's backup version should be updated by the teacher only when the teacher feels there has been progress. This mechanism ensures that if a student accidently makes a major mistake and looses good work in both the current and backup versions the teacher can still restore the section to the way it was the last time the teacher took a backup.

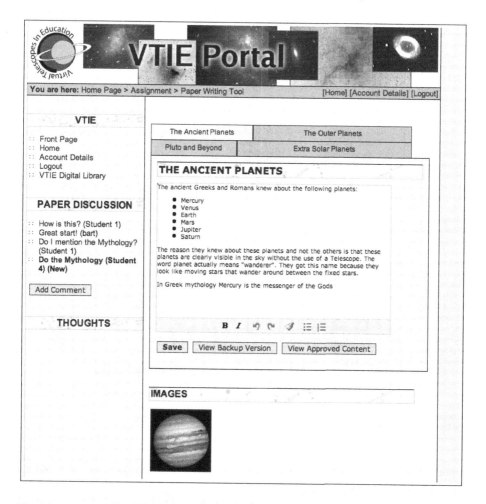

Fig. 3. A screen shot of the the Writing Interface in use by a student showing the WYSIWYG interface

4 Implementation

When the decision was made to implement our software as a web application a number of decisions were also taken on standards to develop to. Our web interfaces are all developed to comply with the following World Wide Web Consortium (W3C) standards; XHTML1.0 and CSS2.1. In order to prevent the need for so called CSS hacks to deal with the miss-implementation of the Box Model by browsers like MicroSoft's Internet Explorer, the decision was also taken to target the FireFox brower. As well as removing the need for messy CSS hacks this also has the added bonus that it allows us to implement some of our client-sode code as FireFox Browser Extensions like the VTIE ScrapBook. For the schools FireFox also has the added bonus that it is more secure and so less likely to bring viruses and trojans into the school's network. This is especially

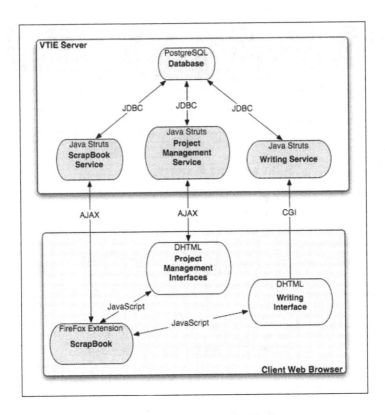

Fig. 4. The basic architecture of the VTIE CWE

important as many trojans today manifest themselves by displaying pop-up windows containing explicit advertisements for pornography.

The basic architecture of the VTIE CWE is shown in Figure 4. As you can see from this figure the code is distributed over the client and server side and utilizes many technologies.

The project management interfaces within the collaborative Writing Environment make extensive use of object-oriented JavaScript and DHTML. These interfaces communicate with the server via AJAX and make use XML to transfer the complex data involved between the client and the server.

On the server-side the decision was made to develop the code in Java. This decision was partly motivated by the number of Java packages available to help with the code and partly motivated by the skill-set of the VTIE team. The server-side code is implemented using Apache's Java Struts framework and is deployed with the Apache Tomcat Web Server.

As XML is used extensively within the VTIE system to store and transfer complex data types such as project templates and instances the initial prototypes of the VTIE Writing Environment used Apache's Xindice native XML database to store data but this technology is still very much underdevelopment and was found not to be up to the task yet. Instead the PostgreSQL relational database is used to store the data. Much of the data is still stored as XML but within a relational structure with meta-data stored separately to speed up searching of the database.

5 Conclusion

Based on Erkens' definition of Collaboration discussed in Section 2 the VTIE Collaborative Writing Environment supports collaboration in two ways. Our system supports collaborative writing by adopting a model in which a student creates an initial draft, all members of their sections all members of their team then comment on this draft and these comments feed into a cycle of revision resulting in the end product. According to the work of Zammuner this is one of the better approaches to collaborative writing. As well as supporting collaboration while writing the VTIE ScrapBook also supports collaboration while researching the topic the students will be reporting on by allowing them to easily share the relevant resources they find on the internet.

References

Erkens, G., Rogers, Y., Jaspers, J., Prangsma, M., Kanselaarm, G.: Coordination processes in computer supported collaborative writing. Computers in Human Behaviour 21(3), 463–486 (2005)

Hidi, S., Berndorff, D., Ainley, M.: Children's argument writing, interest and self-efficacy: an intervention study. Learning and Instruction 12, 429–446 (2002)

Klein, J.D., Erchul, J.A., Pridmore, D.R.: Effects of individual versus co-operative learning and type of reward on performance and continuing motivation. Contemporary Educational Psychology 19, 24–32 (1994)

Lakkala, M., Lallimo, J., Hakkarainen, K.: Teachers' pedagogical designs for technology-supported collective inquiry: a national case study. Computers & Education 45, 337–356 (2005)

Faulkes telescope project. Accessed June 3, 2005 (2005) Available online http://www.faulkes-telescope.com

The firefox web browser Accessed December 19, 2005 (2005) Available online http://www.getfirefox.com

Telescopes in education (Accessed June 3, 2005) (2005) Available online http://www.telescopesineducation.com

Thakkar, U., Carragher, B., Carroll, L., Conway, C., Grosser, B., Kisseberth, N., Potter, C. S., Robinson, S., Sinn-Hanlon, J., Stone, D., Weber, D.: Formative evaluation of bugscope: A sustainable world wide laboratory for k-12 Accessed 17 December, 2005 (2000) Available online at http://www.itg.uiuc.edu/publications/techreports/00-008/

Zammuner, V.L.: Individual and cooperative computer writing and revising: who gets the best results? Learning and Instruction 5, 101–124 (1995)

Participation in International Virtual Learning Communities

A Social Learning Perspective

Beverly Trayner[1], John D. Smith[2], and Marco Bettoni[3]

[1] Escola Superior de Ciências Empresariais, Setúbal, Portugal
btrayner@esce.ips.pt
[2] Learning Alliances and CPsquare, Portland, USA
john.smith@learningalliances.net
[3] Swiss Distance University of Applied Sciences, Brig, Switzerland
mbettoni@fernfachhochschule.cht

Abstract. A promise of new web-based technologies is that they provide learning opportunities for people distributed across the globe but who can participate across time and space in the same virtual learning community. How do they do it? In this paper we report on some of the experiences of a virtual learning community which has members from twenty-five countries across different time-zones and who communicate in English. Through a communities of practice perspective we focus on the social nature of learning and describe some of the challenges and design issues raised in this community as it explores and develops practices for learning in an international online environment. While our focus is on social practices, and on developing an identity of participation in relation to those practices, we also make some wishes for web-based technologies that would better support these practices in an international virtual learning community.

Keywords: International virtual learning communities, international online communities, identity of participation, communities of practice, social learning perspective, e-learning, technology wishes.

1 Introduction

Web-based technologies and increased access to the Internet promise learning solutions for anyone, at any time and in any place. As Paloff and Pratt, leading writers in the field of online learning communities, claim: "(t)he beauty of technology now is that software allows for the translation of material and allows all voices to be heard regardless of what one's native language might be." (2002: online seminar) They go on to attribute increased access to international learning communities as the result of advances in the use of technology: "Thanks to the software we're all using here, we're able to be a part of your (Brazilian) community and you a part of ours."

These are promising words in a challenging scenario for education, juggling competition for students, internationalization and e-learning. It represents a cozy view for training organizations competing for a share of the growing international learning

J. Filipe, J. Cordeiro, and V. Pedrosa (Eds.): WEBIST 2005/2006, LNBIP 1, pp. 402–413, 2007.

market as they increasingly turn to the idea of starting online communities of practice to share knowledge across cultures and borders.

However, our concern is that international online communities may be more problematic than Paloff and Pratt claim. What is referred to as an "international" learning community often refers to a course offered in English (Mason, 1998), possibly with translation of the materials and sold with some linguistic concessions to students or participants for whom English is not a first language. At the same time learning paradigms are moving away from the transmission of (easily translatable) content towards social constructivist views of negotiation of meaning and co-construction of content. If we are to take such a paradigm seriously, then how do we design for negotiating meaning with people who speak different first languages and who come from diverse social and cultural contexts?

Our principle aim in this paper is to report from a virtual learning community that has members from various work settings, professions and countries around the world with a view to sharing some of its practices. The authors are active members of this virtual learning community and have individually and collaboratively designed and presented a significant number of international courses and online workshops during the previous six years. For each of the practices we describe we also propose a wish for a web-based technology that could help support that practice.

Underlying our review and description of interaction practices are the words of Barab, Kling and Gray who emphasize that *"Building online communities in the service of learning is a major accomplishment about which we have much to learn"* (2004:4, italics in the original). We would add that paying attention to cross-national and cross-cultural dimensions in international online communities adds to the complexity, challenges and value in such an accomplishment.

2 A Theoretical Lens

Our social learning perspective has its roots in Bandura's social learning theory (1977) which emphasizes the importance of observing and modeling the behaviours of others. It draws on the notion of situated learning (Lave, 1988) where learning is a function of the activity, context and culture in which it occurs and where people move from the periphery of a community to the centre as they become more active and engaged in the practices of a community through a process of legitimate peripheral participation (Lave and Wenger, 1991).

In a communities of practice theory of learning the principle focus is that of social participation (Wenger, 1998:4) where participation means "being active participants in the *practices* of social communities and constructing *identities* in relation to these communities." (ibid. italics in the original). Participation, according to Wenger, is the process of taking part in a community of practice as well as the relations with others that reflect that process (ibid.:55). Participation includes but is not limited to collaboration; it involves all kinds of relations, cooperative and competitive, conflictual and harmonious, intimate and political (ibid.:56). Participation in this sense is not something that refers to specific activities with specific people; it is a constituent part of a person's identity. It is an accountability to a community and the meanings that are given through their participation in it (ibid.:57). Wenger refers to this identity that is constituted through participation as an *identity of participation*.

In this case our concern is with identities that arise from participation in the social practices of a community that spans different geographical locations and different first languages rather than with identities or practices that arise from particular national characteristics or traits. Therefore we have avoided traditional frameworks of viewing communication between people from different national cultures in terms of concepts such as high/low context cultures developed by Hall (1976) or cultural dimensions developed by Hofstede (1980). Rather, our premise has been that culture is in an ongoing process of negotiation of meaning and the development of an identity of participation in a third space, with the notion of a "third space" coming from writers of cultural and post-colonial studies such as Useem, Useem and Donoghue (1963) and Bhabha (1994).

Our primary focus with the *virtual* in a virtual learning community is to view it as a location for an ongoing transformation of practice and identity of participation in a process of doing things together; our secondary focus is on the technology that enables the virtual to happen. Our concern with the "*learning*" in e-learning is that in an environment that is mainly electronic, the social processes still need to enable learning or negotiation of meaning to happen.

In terms of terminology we have been casual in our use of the terms "online" and "virtual" learning communities as we use them interchangeably. Furthermore, "online" community implies that conversations only take place through an electronic environment, while some community conversations take place in telephone conferences and occasionally when some members manage to meet face-to-face. And finally, we have used "international" to refer to people participating across different linguistic and national boundaries in English, glossing over the overlaps and helpful use of the term "distributed" communities.

3   Context

Our main focus is on a virtual learning community, CPsquare[1], whose domain or topic is that of communities of practice. Conversations take place in Web Crossing[2], a community based discussion tool with a number of plug-ins developed over the years by some of its members. People come from more than 25 different countries and 15 different time-zones around the world and use English as the main language. In this community learning is not seen as transmission of content, and the question of translating materials is not an issue. Rather, its principle learning focus is that of sharing and supporting each others' professional practices in a process of dialogue, trust-building and mutual support. The professional practice of most members includes working in or with communities of practice in different contexts in different parts of the world.

Three years ago questions arose in the community about improving points of contact and communication in CPsquare between people living in different time-zones, from different national and cultural contexts and often with different first languages. In particular the writing of some international guidelines took place in 2003 as a response to some people feeling excluded from CPsquare events because of their geographical location, far from the United States. Meanwhile, some people were also asking the question: while CPsquare talks about international participation, how does,

---

[1] http://www.cpsquare.org
[2] http://www.webcrossing.com/Home/

or how should, that translate to practice? A discussion took place with the aim of producing some "emerging logistical, cultural and linguistic guidelines for facilitating, participating and collaborating in an online distributed community that includes people from different countries". The results of these discussions were published on the public community blog.[3]

In 2005 we decided to review the document written in 2003 to find out to what extent the guidelines were being used or had been helpful to people working in international communities. We collected data from three main sources. First we sent a short web based survey to all community members about the importance of these issues and the usefulness of the international guidelines to them in their communities. We also narrowed down the 60 original principles of the 2003 guidelines into seven key recommendations and invited members to contribute in the online discussion space with examples and stories of where these recommendations had been helpful (or not) in their practice. During this time we organized and recorded two telephone conferences to complement these discussions,

In response to a question about the importance of "issues such as different nationalities, languages, time zones, technology standards, etc." in the communities they worked with most closely, 95% of the thirty-nine responses to the web-based survey said that these issues were between "somewhat" and "very important."   As one community member said in response to an open-ended question "[They] *matter in some [communities] quite a bit, in others barely at all. It is totally context dependent."* However, we discovered in the survey that few people had actually read the guidelines or were even aware of their existence. This comment by one member reflects those of a number of others: *"I have only just read the CP2 guidelines and I think this document is an excellent starting point for a community. It lets them know of issues to consider."*

Interestingly, the discussions that came about in preparation for this paper stimulated more people to read the guidelines. A related finding was that over three quarters of the survey respondents considered that other community members, not the guidelines themselves, were the most helpful resources for improving their practices for supporting communities spanning different countries, cultures or languages. Such a finding reinforces the notion that role modeling of good practice is at least as important as providing guidelines.

Two of the authors of this paper were involved in producing the original guidelines. All three authors have similar and different types of experience of participating in international communities. One author lives and works in Portuguese speaking communities while her first language is English. The second author lives in the United States, coming from a family that is bilingual in Spanish and English. And the third author lives and works in Switzerland, his first languages being Italian and German. At many levels our practices and identity have shaped and are shaped by our immersion in different communities in different languages and in different social and cultural contexts.

---

[3] Internationalisation: guidelines and considerations, http://www.cpsquare.org/News/archives/000021.html

4 Examples of Practice

In our review of the International Guidelines written in 2003 we discussed that what may appear to be "little things" in the design, organization and facilitation of international virtual communities often represent practices that can have a high influence on someone's participation in a community. However, it is frequently these "little things" that are overlooked in the quest for creating communities around attractive content and the latest technology. What is more, with fewer visual cues and a slower response for repairing misunderstandings, the little things can become magnified to the extent that they can seriously affect a person's participation and the meaning they get from the community. We have selected seven of these "little things" from the original guidelines, highlighting some of the social practices that give meaning to participation in the community's learning processes. In summary they are:

1. Time for participation;
2. Use of user-friendly language;
3. A standard time unit for synchronous meetings;
4. Graceful ways of bringing people into conversations;
5. Articulation and reflection of cultural and learning expectations;
6. An "ecology of communication" modes and skills;
7. Modeling of good practice.

We discuss each of these practices, identifying some of the reasons why they have been important in CPsquare or in related workshops and learning environments designed or facilitated by CPsquare members. For each practice we make a wish for a web-based feature or tool that could be used to support it. Neither the practices nor the wishes are intended to be "solutions", they are reflections on practice. Moreover each practice and wish potentially brings a further challenge. Most of the wishes are already feasible as principles and features of new web-based technologies. However, they are not integrated in the Web Crossing platform. In common with many other virtual learning communities it would not be feasible or even desirable to be changing platforms to keep up with these new technologies. Rather, our wishes come in the context of being able to combine and integrate some of these new features into an existing system.

4.1 Time for Participation

Common to most people's experience in CPsquare is that participation in international communities requires taking more time: time for "talking", "listening" and negotiating meaning, and time for reflecting. Without taking the time to establish, maintain and reflect on the social practices of people whose first languages are different, and who come from different contexts, opportunities for negotiating meaning, and therefore learning, are lost.

However, Trayner's main finding in an inquiry into multilingual participation in an online workshop was that "Time, or lack of time, was a thread running through almost all reflections ... from both participants and ... organisers" (2003:417). It was also the main finding in a report on another international online workshop co-presented by White, Smith and Trayner, who wrote: "The overriding lesson for the workshop designers and facilitators was the excessive number of hours that it took to facilitate the workshop" (2004:17). They added that "(b)oth the multilingual nature of the workshop, the shifting elements of the group and the topic, and the expectations from sponsors and participants about the role of the facilitators led to an unsustainable work level" (ibid.).

A problem that arises in designing and allowing for more time to participate in social processes is that it often creates a tension in relation to host institutions, sponsors and participants who measure value in terms of amount of content covered rather than depth of learning and the negotiation of meaning. A further problem is that the time required of facilitators for working across languages and cultures can result in an unsustainable work level for facilitators but which is often invisible to participants and sponsors.

A technology wish for supporting "taking the time" would be a tool that helped make online interactions more visible. While web-based tools often count number of posts written, it is also helpful to know number of posts read. A personal tally that kept a record of the time an individual and groups spent in specific community spaces or activities could also be useful for managing and budgeting time, although there would be issues around transparency and who had access to this information. This would be particularly so if the information was to be used for assessment, evaluation or remuneration purposes. A more ambitious wish would be a way of measuring or making visible the practices involved in shaping and transforming an identity of participation in order that it could be recognized and valued by sponsors and participants.

4.2 Use of User-Friendly Language

It is common to hear people whose first language is English, say "We don't have a problem, we all just speak English." However, where many members are not using their first language, or indeed are using their third or fourth language, the choice of language, colloquialisms, abbreviations, jargon and culturally specific references can discourage participation. For example, to the American presenter welcoming people into a discussion of his work "a baby shower" seemed like an obvious reference to the discussion topic's parentage but it was mystifying to others. In another case, people doing doctoral research in Europe and Australia were puzzled and did not feel described by the label "grad students" in the call to a conversation by US participants. Specifically in terms of language, someone's use of "Let's move on" could have been easier to understand for people who spoke languages of Latin origin if the phrase had been "Let's continue".

In the international guidelines of 2003 we emphasized ways in which the English language can be "Latinized," making it more accessible to speakers of languages of Latin origin (p.10). However, it was pointed out that fine-tuning your sensitivities to the use of language and cultural references could be more helpful than a blanket rule of "Latinizing". It also looks as though those people in the community who have online friends with whom they can check their understanding or interpretations are more likely to continue participating in the face of potential misunderstandings than those who do not. This means that ensuring that the social processes and technological means are in place for checking meaning with fellow-participants could be as important as the choice and use of language.

In fact the tension between knowing and not-knowing what words mean is an opportunity to explore the shades of meaning and for the community to create new meanings and to develop and identities practices around those meanings. In an online event in this community three years ago someone referred to a Scottish slang word

"Glasweg". When asked to clarify the meaning he said it was "a Glaswegian usage" meaning that it was part of the dialect of Glasgow. A German participant understood his explanation to refer to a type of usage by a leading writer named "Glasgow", as if it were a Bandur-ian or Wenger-ian or Glasweg-ian usage. This misunderstanding led to the light-hearted creation of a fictitious character "Ian Glasweg" who, to this day, is a shared reference and mark of identity for some community members who participated in that event.

The ways in which new meanings are given to language and the jargon and colloquialisms that develop as a community matures can then appear incomprehensible to newcomers. This means that developing user-friendly language and managing the tensions and inventiveness of negotiating meanings in the third space is an ongoing enterprise that is not only limited to first and second speakers of English.

A technology wish for facilitating language would be an easy way for people to be able to create link titles over words, sentences or chunks of text. That way the author of a post could create a link title which showed up when a reader had their pointer hovering over the selected text giving synonyms, explanations or context. Similarly, software could automatically create links to explanatory entries to a resource like Wikipedia. However, such a wish would need to be modeled as a complementary language tool rather than as a substitute for playing with and creating new meanings.

4.3 A Standard Time Unit for Synchronous Meetings

Organizing collaboration in a group of people across many time zones and with widely-varying levels of experience can make an apparently simple thing like deciding when to meet, synchronously, a significant challenge. An example of a problem in CPsquare was that convenient meeting times for the majority of people in the group meant that a minority of members had to participate at five o'clock in the morning. Another problem was a difficulty expressing one's own local time in relation to others' so that people could effectively agree on a time to meet on a chat, phone conference or one-to-one telephone call. Merely arranging to meet at time in relation to "PST" or even "GMT" did not seem to be sufficient for people who do not know those abbreviations, nor did it help with the complex calculations necessary for working out the different local times of many people in different time-zones. Additional factors such as "daylight savings" and local holidays have turned a seemingly simple act of setting a meeting time into quite a complex one.

Using both a standard time reference such as GMT, and a time calculation tool such as The World Clock Meeting Planner[4] has proved to be one way of avoiding confusion. However, the issue of including more people at the cost of holding synchronous events at inconvenient times is one that a tool cannot help to solve: it still requires flexibility and social consideration. A technology wish would be a world clock meeting planner that is instantly customized with the name, location, time and public holidays of all community members when they join a community or register for an event. It would also be helpful to have easy access to member spaces which could contain RSS[5] calendar feeds, allowing members of a community to selectively share their calendars with each other.

---

[4] http://www.timeanddate.com/
[5] Real Simple Syndication

4.4   Graceful Ways of Bringing People into Conversations

Learning conversations develop their own momentum once people engage with a subject and with each other. However, many people need to overcome technical and social barriers to feel comfortable enough to fully engage in such a conversation. Most online courses or workshops provide instructions and manuals to help bring people into the online environment. However, even when they are read, manuals and instructions about how to operate the technology or how to interact in the platform are often misinterpreted. Comprehensive manuals and instructions can also be so detailed that they are overwhelming, especially if they are in someone's second language. What is more, strictly followed instruction manuals can discourage learning strategies such as exploration and invention.

More helpful than detailed instructions have been designs for incorporating social interaction and practice with technologies that help people into the conversation one-step-at-a-time. For example in an online facilitation workshop[6] for Portuguese participants we used a game at the beginning called "Just Three Words" where no posting could be more than three words and each posting followed on from the next. This simple game provided an opportunity for people to become familiar with the technology while also socializing in an informal and non-threatening way. A second example of graceful ways of including people was through the use of personal journals. People who were not confident of posting in the main forum (for language reasons, for example) could post their reflections and thoughts in personal journals. Those journals became places for reflecting aloud and developing a voice alongside or as an alternative to the conversations taking place in the main arena. The journals provided a bridge and a sheltered passage to the main forum. Finally a third example in the same workshop was that of bringing in new people to a community as guests. Building on the social bonds and group accomplishments that had accumulated over a 6-week period more senior practitioners were invited in as guest critics of a joint product that had been drafted by small groups during the workshop. Having a guest enter a space where a small group of participants played the role of hosts meant that people who had begun the process by feeling like "newcomers" now became "old hands" in the welcoming of new expertise into the community.

However, if it is difficult for a participant to navigate to the location where these activities are taking place, then the process is not such a graceful one. A technology wish would be a pop-up window or a personalized desktop where someone could find links to and navigate between those locations as soon as they entered the platform. A further wish would be an integrated desktop that included web conferencing, email, instant messaging, telephone conferencing and other media that allowed a participant or facilitator to easily select a technology for reaching out to people on the periphery of a conversation.

4.5   Articulation and Reflection of Cultural and Learning Expectations

Many people have stories of misinterpreted communication online when members were not familiar with someone else's expectations of collaboration or learning.

---

[6] Facilitação de projectos de aprendizagem em comunidades de prática: http://www.learningalliances.net/CoPs_ em_Portugal_2004/index_em_Portuguese.htm

These misinterpretations have been easily exaggerated in the absence of cues and feedback from the other person or fellow members.

Having a space within the online learning environment for members to keep personal learning journals has been a way of providing clues about people's changing perspectives of what is happening and about potential areas of miscommunication. For example in one workshop a participant wrote observations about the informal relationships between facilitator and participants compared to her own experiences in a Portuguese course. Another wrote her frustrations and anxieties about what looked like a "big confusion" rather than structured learning activities and uncertainty about what was expected of him. Some people followed a conversation in English but were able to reflect on the conversations in Portuguese. These examples provided opportunities for fellow members and facilitators to understand and use the reflections as a springboard for learning rather than an invisible reason for dropping out of the learning event. It has also been important to encourage people to articulate and reflect on their assumptions about each other. Importantly, a welcoming, encouraging style of communication from a facilitator who is curious and values discussing these issues is one that models openness and an attitude of "not knowing" in a way that helps surface people's assumptions about learning and expectations rather than taking one set of assumptions for granted.

However, despite good intentions of designing for this ongoing articulation and reflection of expectations, if other practices are not in place, then this is one that easily becomes side-tracked. For example, if a lot of time is spent becoming familiar with the technology or completing structured tasks, or if the language and cultural references make someone feel excluded, people rarely articulate and reflect aloud regardless of the facilitator's style or whether they have a personal learning journal.

A technology wish would be to have spaces for personal journals that are both easily accessible but which are sufficiently discrete so as not to overwhelm the online space. They would not be too complicated to set up, use, or administer (for example, in terms of controlling access). The journals would be private, open or shared with spaces for photographs, audio recordings or podcasts. It would also be helpful to be able to use RSS feeds in a journal so that it recorded entries from a blog kept outside the community space in a personal journal inside the community space.

4.6 An "Ecology of Communication[7]" Modes and Skills

While conversations in CPsquare began as asynchronous discussions with occasional telephone conferences, over the years the use of different modes for communicating and coming together has changed in number and complexity. For example, a member is invited to talk about a particular project she is working on and she begins with an online discussion that includes a paper or a set of slides and maybe some photographs. After two weeks of online discussion, a telephone conference is held with some members who continue or develop the discussion for an hour on the telephone. This telephone conversation is recorded and the audio file put in the online discussion space. Also, during the telephone conversation some members enter the Web Crossing chat room and take notes during the call. These notes are also posted to the online discussion space. Making sense of the discussion about a member's project through

---

[7] An expression coined by CPsquare member, Dr. Steve Eskow.

different modes is helpful in this cross-national and cross-linguistic setting for a number of reasons. It provides a range of modes for people to participate and facilitates access to people who have different types of linguistic competencies. Audio recordings and notes from telephone conversations are available for people to refer to and discuss even if they could not participate, for example because of a schedule conflict. Audio recordings also mean that conversations can be re-listened to if following or participating in the conversation was difficult the first time.

However, not only do different people have different access to different modes, but becoming competent in several or many modes can also be overwhelming. Telephone systems in different countries have different cost structures and different capabilities making it an easy option for some and an expensive one for others. Integrating synchronous conversations into a mainly asynchronous community conversation highlights the differences between countries even if it can bring members closer together. Moreover, adding different modes to the communication ecology is not an end in itself; this ecology includes layers of skills, practices and attitudes in the ongoing shaping and modeling of social practices.

A technology wish here is to make all of the resources of a community equally available and easy to integrate with each other. Currently, integrating several resources together requires considerable expertise on the part of facilitators and community leaders whereas it would be more helpful if these resources could be used selectively so that a facilitator did not feel that they had to use all the tools all the time and members would feel that they had a choice of tools for different events.

4.7 Modeling of Good Practice

Modeling good practice is integral to all the six practices we have discussed. Most people agreed that any set of guidelines and instructions were only as effective as the way in which they were put into practice by facilitators, leaders and co-members. They also reported that modeling an attitude of inquiry and reflection, or the use of user-friendly language, or graceful ways of bringing people into the conversation have been the basis of improved practice and learning in their communities. Hearing stories of success and how people overcame challenges in online communities that cross cultural or national boundaries is a key factor for learning and improving practice.

A technology wish that could help in noticing and reflecting on modeling would be to have ways to record and label representations of practice, such as an easy to use bookmark or "clippings" folder for recording, managing and referring to examples of practice. This would also include the possibility of making reflective notes about these clippings or bookmarks. There would be different ways to link, categorize and represent them to other members. The wish would also be for tools or standards that make it possible to share or compare clipping and bookmarks across platforms and systems, integrating disparate tools such as online discussions and telephone conferences.

5 Summary Conclusions

We began this paper by suggesting that participating in international virtual learning communities is more challenging than is sometimes acknowledged. This is particularly so when the philosophy for improved learning is that of developing recursive social practices for the negotiation of meaning-making or of developing an identity of participation, rather than merely developing better methods and technology functions for transmitting or sharing information. We highlighted seven social practices in a specific virtual learning community with a view to sharing a description, wish list and discussion of the ambiguities and complexities that each one currently and potentially presents in that community.

In the future we would like to reformulate both the content and the mode of presenting the guidelines in the community. The data and stories we collected about member's perspectives and experiences of international communication still need to be analyzed, reflected and written about in more detail in our cycle of action research. Further research also needs to be carried out into the identity of participation, not only in the context of one community but on how an identity of participation is negotiated in the context of membership in multiple communities that straddle different countries, time-zones and languages. Such research could possibly lead to a communities of practice framework for analyzing cultural, or third space, dimensions of online communication.

Acknowledgements

A heart-felt "thank you" to the people who participated in the online and telephone conversations and helped shape this paper, including Derek Chirnside, Joitske Hulsebosch, Ancella Livers, Barb McDonald, Susanne Nyrop, Ueli Scheuermeier, and Meena Wilson. In particular we used specific ideas from Nancy White and Steve Eskow. Thanks also to Sherry Spence who made comments and suggestions to an earlier draft. Thanks of course to Ian Glasweg who continues to help maintain a sense of humour in relation to international communities.

References

Bandura, A.: Social Learning Theory. General Learning Press, New York (1977)

Barab, S.A, Kling, R., Gray, J.H.: Designing for Virtual communities in the Service of Learning. Cambridge University Press, Cambridge (2004)

Bhabha, H.K.: The Location of Culture. Routledge, London, New York (1994)

Trayner et al.: CPsquare as a place for cultivating global literacies (2003) Retrieved October 1, 2005 from CPSquare Website: http://www.cpsquare.org/ News/archives/000021.html

Hall, E.T.: Beyond Culture. Random House, New York (1976)

Hofstede, G.: Culture's Consequences: international differences in work-related Vvlues. Sage, Newbury Park, CA (1980)

Lave, J.: Cognition in Practice. In: Mind, mathematics and culture in everyday life, Cambridge University Press, Cambridge (1988)

Lave, J., Wenger, E. (eds.): Situated Learning: legitimate peripheral participation. Cambridge University Press, Cambridge (1991)

Mason, R.: Globalising education: trends and applications. Routledge, London /New York (1998)

Pratt, R., Palloff, K.: Aquifolium Educational online seminar: Construindo Comunidades De Aprendizagem No Ciberespaço/Constructing Learning Communities in Cyberspace (2002)

Trayner, B.: The international café: a respectful critique. In: Wulf, V., et al. (eds.) Communities and Technologies, Kluwer Academic Publishers, Boston, MA (2003)

Trayner, B., White, N., Smith, J.: Workshop Report: facilitating learning projects in distributed communities of practice (2004)

Useem, J., Useem, R., Donoghue, J.: Men in the Middle of the Third Culture: The Roles of American and Non-Western People in Cross-Cultural Administration. Human Organization 22(3), 169–179 (1963)

Wenger, E.: Communities of Practice: Learning, Meaning and Identity. Cambridge University Press, Cambridge (1998)

New Electronic Multi-media Assessment System

Simon Chester[1], Giles Tewkesbury[1], David Sanders[1], and Peter Salter[2]

[1] Systems Engineering Research Group, University of Portsmouth, Anglesea Road,
Portsmouth, United Kingdom
`simon.chester@port.ac.uk`, `giles.tewkesbury@port.ac.uk`,
`david.sanders@port.ac.uk`
[2] Counterpoint MTC Ltd., Worthing, United Kingdom
`pete@counterpoint-mtc.co.uk`

Abstract. Assessment for learning is a new approach to assessment. Assessment for learning is the process of seeking and interpreting evidence for use by learners and their teachers to raise pupils' achievement. The key principle of Assessment for Learning is that pupils will improve most if they understand the aim of their learning, where they are in relation to this aim and how they can achieve the aim (or close the gap in their knowledge). Studies have shown that student achievement has been raised significantly where this method of assessment has been implemented. This paper examines existing electronic assessment systems and then describes the creation of a new multi-user system that assists teachers in the implementation of assessment for learning in the classroom.

Keywords: e-Learning, Assessment.

1 Introduction

In order to develop a new system for electronic assessment, an analysis of existing systems and modes of assessment was first researched. A literature search was conducted and five main methods of assessment were reviewed. Assessment for learning was identified as an assessment method that required new tools to aid teachers to implement this method in the classroom. A search for existing assessment systems was also conducted and three systems were identified. None of the systems reviewed allowed teachers within the school to share common information. Therefore, teachers' time was spent performing administrative tasks for their assessment systems rather than teaching.

The new system presented here aims to overcome the problem of entering and maintaining school-wide information by introducing software tools to share relevant information between teachers. The new system also aims to provide teachers and students with the functionality needed to implement assessment for learning. This new system was created by using a new centralised database system and a central administration web application. The results of this work are presented.

J. Filipe, J. Cordeiro, and V. Pedrosa (Eds.): WEBIST 2005/2006, LNBIP 1, pp. 414–420, 2007.

1.1 Modes of Assessment

There are five main types of assessment (Assessment Reform Group, 2002):

- Formative assessment
- Summative assessment
- Ipsative assessment
- Self-assessment
- Assessment for learning

Formative assessment is that which takes place on a regular basis involving both teacher and student in discussion about the students learning and work (Andrews, Jane as part of a review of: Torrance, H; Pryor, J, 2004). Feedback that is specific and diagnostic is given to individual students and the teacher will be concerned with moving students on as learners. This monitoring of students' progress provides teachers with an on-going record of their students' progress and also provides feedback on their own effectiveness in planning and teaching. Whilst formative assessment encourages teachers to listen to their students and identify the next steps required, it will not be effective unless the teacher is clear about what it is that they want to find out and what they are looking for (MacKrill, D, 2004).

Summative assessment is used to provide a summary of a student's progress at a given point in time measured against criteria, such as National Curriculum Levels (Wininger, Steven R, 2005). It will include records of the formative assessments made over time. A common form of summative assessment is, for example, an end of year report, and in music, an instrumental grade exam. Summative assessment is important but as Harlen *et al* commented "its prime purpose is not so much to influence teaching". MacKrill (2004) suggests that Teachers have been reluctant to adopt summative assessment because it has been closely associated with unpopular Government driven data collection initiatives.

Ipsative assessment informs students how they have performed and progressed, compared with their own previous performance or efforts (Harlen *et al* 1994). It is most effective when students themselves are involved in the process and promotes independent learning. However, it is often more successful when students and teachers have access to previous work. In subjects that are only timetabled once a week, like music and drama for instance, this is even more important but is difficult to implement because of the type of work being assessed, which is invariably practical in nature (MacKrill, D, 2004).

Self-assessment forms part of the process of formative assessment and can improve student motivation whilst providing the teacher with important information regarding a student's understanding and perception (Daniel R, 2001). Pratt & Stephens give self-assessment a priority in their publication "supporting the National Curriculum for music" (Pratt, G & Stephens, J., 1995).

In the late 1990's, a new approach to assessment began to be considered by Black and William (1998) who showed that where formative assessment was used to promote learning, student achievement was increased significantly. However, they noted that this would require changes in classroom practice.

There is a clear difference between assessment of learning and assessment for learning. Assessment of learning frequently includes both formative and summative assessment and involves assessing what students have learnt, often including marks or grades from tests and assignments (DfES, 2004). Assessment for learning has a different focus and is defined as "the process of seeking and interpreting evidence for use by learners and their teachers to decide where the learners are in their learning, where they need to go and how best to get there" (Assessment Reform Group, 2002).

Improving learning through assessment depends on five key factors:

- provision of effective feedback to students;
- active involvement of students in their own learning;
- adjusting teaching to take account of the results of assessment;
- recognition of the profound influence assessment has on the motivation and self-esteem of students, both of which are crucial influences on learning;
- need for students to be able to assess themselves and understand how to improve. (Assessment Reform Group, 1999)

Assessment for Learning is an area for development in schools that will require changes in teacher practice (MacKrill, D., 2004).

1.2   Existing Electronic Assessment Systems

The KAAN Keyboard And Audio Network System (KAAN) has been produced by the collaborating company. This system was created to assist teaching of music in the classroom.   From this, another system was then developed to accommodate the assessment of students' work in a wider variety of subjects.   The new system was marketed by the collaborating company under the brand name 'eSAAMS' (Electronic Student Assessment And data Management System).   The creation of these systems is described in Lassauniere (2003).

Student Information Management System (SIMS) is used by some schools in the UK. This product, produced by Capita Educations Services (Capita Education Services: SIMS, n.d.), provides functionality to store a wide range of administrative information (such as: students, classes, formal assessments, staff, etc). Typically, this software is primarily designed for school administrators. Although it may be used by Teachers, typically it is not used in the classroom.

AssessIT is an interactive software system, produced by Pearson Phoenix (n.d.), which tracks individual pupil attainment and group achievements. It supports teachers when monitoring and measuring progress and alerts them when pupils fall below targets.   The software places emphasis on implementing initiatives and promoting individual pupil attainment and group achievements.

1.3   Requirements of the New System

An electronic assessment system was made available by the collaborating company at the start of this work. However, it was designed for use by one teacher at a time on a single PC.   Although it was possible for the software to be installed on many computers, each instance of the software required its own separate database. This caused problems because these separate databases contained some information that was common to the whole school (not just a particular teacher) and there was no mechanism for synchronising changes to this information across the disparate databases. The research described aimed to create a new system for sharing information between teachers.

2 Description of the New System

The sharing of information involved setting-up a new central database. Figure 1 shows the central database on a server connected to a school's computer network. The database server was used as a single location for storing school-wide information. A number of database systems were evaluated including 'off-the-shelf' products and some open-source systems. Microsoft SQL Server 2000 was identified as the most suitable system because it provided close integration with the software language used. Initial systems analysis was conducted and key concepts were identified. These concepts were then used to create a new database structure which was implemented on the central database server.

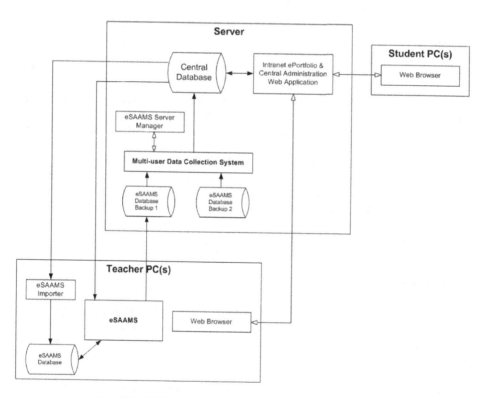

Fig. 1. Components of the new assessment system

In the new system, the eSAAMS software regularly performed a backup routine which made a copy of the database to a backup storage location on the server. This operation was performed by each instance of the assessment software to the same location on the network. The Multi-user Data Collection system was contained on the server. This new software component collected information from these distributed database backups across teachers PCs' and synchronised it with data in the new central database.

Finally, a new web-based application was created to allow students to view a portfolio of their work from any computer within a school's computer network. The web-application was located on the server. Students interacted with the web-application by using a web browser, as shown in Figure 1.

Much of the information in the central database was to be sourced from the distributed teacher databases. However, some information could not be gathered in this manner since there was no way of determining which distributed database was the authoritative source. Therefore, a new central administration system to allow teachers and school administrators to create and manage school-wide information centrally was created. This web-application was integrated with the Intranet ePortfolio system described previously in order to create a single user interface for administering Student information. These systems are shown in Figure 1 as the 'Intranet ePortfolio & Central Administration Web Application'.

The eSAAMS electronic assessment software allowed Teacher's to work in an 'offline' mode when disconnected from a network. It was therefore necessary to create a software application for copying centrally administered information from the central database system to the database for each electronic assessment system. This 'eSAAMS Importer' system is shown in Figure 1.

In order for the software applications to be able to communicate with the central database system, it was necessary to create software components that could be used to store and retrieve data from the database. Different models for data-access were evaluated and the application of an n-tier model was investigated using Microsoft Visual Studio 2003 and Microsoft Visual Studio 2005 (Microsoft Visual Studio, n.d.).

In particular, methods for automatically generating data-access code and database stored procedures were investigated. In particular, one code-generation tool was identified called 'My Generation' (My Generation Software, n.d.). This tool was designed to create templates for generating database stored procedures and code to access a database from visual studio.

3 Results

The electronic assessment system made available by the collaborating company at the start of this work has been installed and tested in over 100 schools. The software, known as eSAAMS (eSAAMS Software, n.d.), allowed Teachers to capture and record evidence of Student's work. This information was stored in a database on a Teacher's computer.

Code generation software was used to create templates that were then used to generate stored procedures and re-usable software components to access the central database. These components would normally have to be created manually. The use of code generation reduced the time needed to create the data access software used by the new software applications described here.

A new Multi-User Data Collection System was created that collected information from many single-user databases (one database per Teacher) and compiled this into the central database (school-wide information). This system was tested using a test to fail method and approved by the collaborating company.

An Intranet ePortfolio system for showing student report information was then produced. The system provided students with the ability to view a portfolio of their work. This allowed Students to view feedback from assessments of their work without increasing the workload for teachers. The provision of effective feedback to students is one of the key factors in implementing Assessment for Learning (Assessment Reform Group, 1999). This software helped Teachers to implement Assessment for Learning in the classroom. The information displayed to Students was sourced from the central database system. This system was tested and approved by Teachers in 22 schools.

A new central administration system to allow teachers and school administrators to create and manage school-wide information centrally was created. The system will be tested by the collaborating company using a 'test to fail' method.

Also, a software application for copying centrally administered information from the central database system to the database for each electronic assessment system has been created. The system will be tested by the collaborating company using a 'test to fail' method.

The completed system will be beta-tested in a two schools. At each beta testing site, the system will be used by at least two teachers and one school administrator. User interface experience information and usability information will be obtained through questionnaires issued to users and by direct observation. Also, information will be retrieved from error log files on the server and teachers' PC's.

4 Discussion and Conclusions

A new electronic assessment system was created and a number of its components were tested by the collaborating company and classroom teachers. This was the first intelligent multi-media assessment system to assist teachers implement assessment for learning practices in the classroom. Other systems, described previously, have tended to be administrative and designed for use by a school administrator.

Information in the central database was sourced from the backup databases by the new multi-user data collection software. The information in these databases was not synchronised so, inevitably, information could be duplicated. Since each teacher had equal administrative rights for the information contained within their database, the multi-user data collection software was unable to determine which database had the correct version of each entity. Therefore, information was processed on a 'first-in wins' basis. This was undesirable because there was no reliable way to determine which client database would be used to source school-wide information. In the future, new electronic assessment software to be used by teachers in the classroom will be created. Unlike the existing software, the information captured will be committed directly to the central database therefore avoiding unnecessary duplication of data described above.

References

Andrews, J., Torrance, H., Pryor, J.: Investigating Formative Assessment: Teaching, Learning and Assessment in the Classroom. Language Testing 21(3), 432–435 (2004)

Assessment Reform Group. Assessment for Learning: Beyond the black box. University of Cambridge, Cambridge (1999)

Assessment Reform Group. Assessment for Learning: 10 Principles. University of Cambridge, Cambridge(2002)

Black, P., William, D.: Inside the black box: Raising standards through classroom assessment. (1998) Retrieved December 1, 2005, from King's College London School of Education website http://www.kcl.ac.uk/depsta/education/publications/blackbox.html

Capita Education Services: SIMS (n.d.) (2005) Retrieved December 1, from Capita Education Services website http://home.capitaes.co.uk/sims/index.asp

Daniel, R.: Self-assessment in performance. British Journal of Music Education 18(3), 215–226 (2001)

DfES, Assessment for Learning: Guidance for Senior leaders.DfES, London (2004)

eSAAMS Software. (n.d.). Retrieved September 27, 2005, from the eSAAMS website: http://www.esaams.co.uk

Harlen, W., Gipps, C., Broadfoot, P., Nuttall, D.: Assessment and the improvement of education. In: Moon, B., Mayes, A.S. Teaching and Learning in the Secondary School. London: Routledge / The Open University (1994)

Lassauniere, A.: New Music Technology Systems and Methods to Assist Teachers. University of Portsmouth, Portsmouth (2003)

MacKrill, D.: MA Dissertation. University of Sussex (2004)

Microsoft Visual Studio. (n.d.). Retrieved September 27, 2005, from the Microsoft Developer Network website: http://msdn.microsoft.com/vstudio

MyGeneration Software. (n.d.). Retrieved September 27, 2005 from the MyGeneration software website http://www.mygenerationsoftware.com

Pearson Phoenix (n.d.). Retrieved 29th September 2005 from Pearson Phoenix web site http://www.pearsonphoenix.com

Pratt, G., Stephens, J.: Teaching Music in the National Curriculum. Heinemann, Oxford (1995)

Wininger, S.: Using Your Tests to Teach: Formative Summative Assessment. Teaching of Psychology 32(3), 164–166 (2005)

Author Index